D1431344

FRAGMENTARY
REPUBLICAN LATIN
VI

LCL 314

FRAGMENTARY REPUBLICAN LATIN

LIVIUS ANDRONICUS
NAEVIUS · CAECILIUS

EDITED AND TRANSLATED BY

ROBERT MALTBY

NIALL W. SLATER

HARVARD UNIVERSITY PRESS
CAMBRIDGE, MASSACHUSETTS
LONDON, ENGLAND
2022

First published 2022

LOEB CLASSICAL LIBRARY® is a registered trademark
of the President and Fellows of Harvard College

Library of Congress Control Number 2017940159
CIP data available from the Library of Congress

ISBN 978-0-674-99748-6

*Composed in ZephGreek and ZephText by
Technologies 'N Typography, Merrimac, Massachusetts.
Printed on acid-free paper and bound by
Maple Press, York, Pennsylvania*

CONTENTS

CONTENTS

CONTENTS

CONTENTS

CONTENTS

CONTENTS

A NOTE ON SPELLING
CONVENTIONS

This edition does not attempt to reproduce the original
archaic Latin spelling of the authors it contains, but aims
at consistency in following the modern (late to post-
Republican) spellings that will be familiar to most readers
and that are for the most part found in our transmitting
authors. Archaic poets of our period would have distin-
guished between the *ei* diphthong and long *i*, both of
which are represented by *i* in modern spelling; *seruos* and
quom would have been used in place of *servus* and *cum*.
The Greek letters υ ζ φ θ χ would have been transliterated
as *u*, *s* (or *ss*), *p* (or b), *t*, and *c* in place of the later *y*, *z*,
ph, *th* and *ch*. Finally, geminate consonants would have
been spelled as a single letter (e.g., *Aciles* for *Achilles*).
Some earlier editors are inconsistent in representing some
of these archaic spellings but not others. For the sake of
consistency in this volume, archaic spellings will for the
most part be avoided. There are three exceptions to this.
The first is where they are required by the meter, e.g.,
interead (Liv. Andron. *Trag.* F 16), *med* (Naev. *Com.* F 8,
to avoid hiatus). The second is where archaic spellings are
singled out for comment by our sources, e.g., *dusmus* (Liv.
Andron. *Trag.* F 21), *amploctor* (Liv. Andron. *Od.* F 16).
The third is where they are unanimously transmitted by

them, e.g., *-i* stem forms like *ocrim, ocris* [acc. pl.], and *ocri* [abl.] (Liv. Andron. *Trag.* F 23–26) and *advenientis* (Naev. *Trag.* F 38), or forms like *lubet* for *libet* (Liv. Andron. *Trag.* F 7) and *optumum* for *optimum* (Naev. *BP* F 24). It seems our sources were happy to transmit some archaic spellings, but not others. The Greek letter *v*, for example, is always transliterated as *y* (occasionally *i*), but never as *u*, in such words as Pylos (Liv. Andron. *Od.* F 7) or Clytaemestra (Liv. Andron. *Trag.* F 4). The overall policy, then, will be to follow the spelling of our transmitting texts for the fragments, which is mostly modern, except in cases where the meter requires another form.

GENERAL BIBLIOGRAPHY

1. EDITIONS AND COMMENTARIES CONTAINING FRAGMENTS OF THE POETS INCLUDED IN THIS VOLUME

1.1. Livius Andronicus

Baehrens, Aemilius, ed. *Fragmenta Poetarum Romanorum*. Leipzig, 1886.

Blänsdorf, Jürgen, ed. *Fragmenta poetarum Latinorum epicorum et lyricorum praeter Enni Annales et Ciceronis Germanicique Aratea, post W. Morel et K. Büchner editionem quartam auctam curavit.* Berlin / New York, 2011.

Bothe, Fredericus, H., ed. *Poetae scenici Latinorum. Collatis codd. Berolinensibus, Florentino, Friburgensi, Gothano, Guelpherbitanis, Helmstadiensibus, Monacensi, Palatino, Parisio, Ultrajectino, aliisque spectatae fidei libris. Volumen quartum: Fragmenta, Pars prior: Fragmenta tragicorum.* Halberstadt, 1823 [reissued Leipzig, 1834].

———, ed. *Poetae scenici Latinorum. Collatis codd. Berolinensibus, Florentino, Friburgensi, Gothano, Guelpherbitanis, Helmstadiensibus, Monacensi, Palatino, Parisio, Ultrajectino, aliisque spectatae fidei libris. Volumen quartum: Fragmenta, Pars posterior: Frag-*

menta comicorum. Halberstadt, 1824 [reissued Leipzig, 1834].

Carratello, Ugo, ed. *Livio Andronico.* Roma, 1979.

Courtney, Edward, ed. *The Fragmentary Latin Poets.* Oxford, 1993 [corr. repr. 2003].

Diehl, Ernst, ed. *Poetarum Romanorum veterum reliquiae selectae.* Kleine Texte für theologische und philologische Vorlesungen und Übungen, 69. Bonn, 1911 [repr. Berlin, 1967].

Duentzer, Henricus, ed. *L. Livii Andronici fragmenta collecta et inlustrata. Accedunt Homericorum carminum a veteribus poetis Latinis versibus expressorum reliquiae.* Berlin, 1835.

Ernout, Alfred, ed. *Recueil de textes latins archaïques.* Nouvelle edition. Paris, [2]1957 [[1]1916].

Flores, Enrico, ed. *Livi Andronici Odusia. Introduzione, edizione critica e versione italiana.* Forme materiali e ideologie del mondo antico 39. Napoli, 2011.

Klotz, Alfred, ed. *Scaenicorum Romanorum fragmenta. Volumen prius. Tragicorum fragmenta,* adiuvantibus Ottone Seel et Ludovico Voit. München, 1953.

Klussmann, Ernst, ed. *Livii Andronici, antiquissimi Romanorum poetae, dramatum reliquiae, pars prior (Livius Andronicus).* Gymnasialprogr. Rudolstadt, 1849.

Lenchantin de Gubernatis, Massimo, ed. *Livi Andronici fragmenta.* Torino, 1937.

Mariotti, Scevola. *Livio Andronico e la traduzione artistica.* Saggio critico ed edizione dei frammenti dell'*Odyssea.* Urbino, [2]1986 [Milano, [1]1952].

Morel, Willy, ed. *Fragmenta poetarum Latinorum epicorum et lyricorum praeter Ennium et Lucilium, post Aemilium Baehrens iterum ed.* Leipzig, [2]1927 [repr. Stuttgart, 1975].

Mueller, Lucian, ed. *Livii Andronici et Cn Naevi fabularum reliquiae.* Berlin, 1885.

Paladini, Mariantonietta, and Manuela Manzella. *Livio Andronico, Odissea: Commentario. Con un'avvertenza di Enrico Flores.* Forme materiali e ideologie del mondo antico 45. Napoli, 2014.

Ribbeck, Otto, ed. *Scaenicae Romanorum poesis fragmenta. Vol. I. Tragicorum Romanorum fragmenta.* Leipzig, [1]1852 / [2]1871 / [3]1897.

———, ed. *Scaenicae Romanorum poesis fragmenta. Vol. II. Comicorum Romanorum praeter Plautum et Terentium fragmenta.* Leipzig, [1]1855 / [2]1873 / [3]1898.

Schauer, Markus, ed. *Tragicorum Romanorum Fragmenta (TrRF). Volumen I. Livius Andronicus. Naevius. Tragici Minores. Fragmenta Adespota.* Göttingen, 2012.

Spaltenstein, François. *Commentaire des fragments dramatiques de Livius Andronicus.* Collection Latomus, Vol. 318. Bruxelles, 2008.

Traglia, Antonio, ed. *Poeti latini arcaici. Volume primo: Livio Andronico, Nevio, Ennio.* Classici Latini. Torino, 1986.

Viredaz, Antoine. *Fragmenta Saturnia heroica: introduction, traduction et commentaire des fragments de l'Odyssée latine de Livius Andronicus et de la Guerre punique de Cn. Naevius.* Schweizerische Beiträge zur Altertumswissenschaft 47. Basel, 2020.

Warmington, E. H., ed. and trans. *Remains of Old Latin.* 4 vols. Loeb Classical Library 294, 314, 329, 359. London, 1935–1940: Vol. 2, *Livius Andronicus, Naevius, Pacuvius and Accius.* London, 1936 [[2]1967, repr. 1988, etc.].

Wordsworth, John, ed. *Fragments and Specimens of Early Latin.* Oxford, 1874.

1.2. Cn. Naevius

Baehrens, Aemilius, ed. *Fragmenta Poetarum Romanorum*. Leipzig, 1886.

Barchiesi, Marino. *Nevio epico: Storia, interpretazione, edizione critica dei frammenti del primo epos latino*. Padova, 1962.

Blänsdorf, Jürgen, ed. *Fragmenta poetarum Latinorum epicorum et lyricorum praeter Enni Annales et Ciceronis Germanicique Aratea, post W. Morel et K. Büchner editionem quartam auctam curavit*. Berlin / New York, 2011.

Bothe, Fredericus, H., ed. *Poetae scenici Latinorum. Collatis codd. Berolinensibus, Florentino, Friburgensi, Gothano, Guelpherbitanis, Helmstadiensibus, Monacensi, Palatino, Parisio, Ultrajectino, aliisque spectatae fidei libris. Volumen quartum: Fragmenta, Pars prior: Fragmenta tragicorum*. Halberstadt, 1823 [reissued Leipzig, 1834].

—————, ed. *Poetae scenici Latinorum. Collatis codd. Berolinensibus, Florentino, Friburgensi, Gothano, Guelpherbitanis, Helmstadiensibus, Monacensi, Palatino, Parisio, Ultrajectino, aliisque spectatae fidei libris. Volumen quartum: Fragmenta, Pars posterior: Fragmenta comicorum*. Halberstadt, 1824 [reissued Leipzig, 1834].

Diehl, Ernst, ed. *Poetarum Romanorum veterum reliquiae selectae*. Kleine Texte für theologische und philologische Vorlesungen und Übungen, 69. Bonn, 1911 [repr. Berlin, 1967].

Ernout, Alfred, ed. *Recueil de textes latins archaïques*. Nouvelle edition. Paris, [2]1957 [[1]1916].

Flores, Enrico, ed. *Cn. Naevi Bellum Punicum: Introduzione, edizione critica e versione italiana*. Napoli, 2011.

————, ed. *Commentario a Cn. Naevi Bellum Punicum.* Forme materiali e ideologie del mondo antico 46. Napoli, 2014.

Klotz, Alfred, ed. *Scaenicorum Romanorum fragmenta. Volumen prius. Tragicorum fragmenta,* adiuvantibus Ottone Seel et Ludovico Voit. München, 1953.

Klussmann, Ernst. *Cn. Naevii poetae Romani vitam descripsit, carminum reliquias collegit, poesis rationem exposuit.* Jena, 1843.

Mariotti, Scevola. *Il Bellum Punicum e l'arte di Naevio. Saggio con edizione dei frammenti del Bellum Punicum.* Bologna, [3]2001 [Roma, [1]1955].

Marmorale, Enzo, ed. *Naevius Poeta. Introduzione bibliografica, testo dei frammenti e commento.* Firenze, [2]1950 [[1]1945, repr. 1953, 1967].

Mazzarino, Antonio, ed. *Naevi belli Poenici carminis fragmenta.* Messina, [2]1973 [[1]1966].

Morel, Willy, ed. *Fragmenta poetarum Latinorum epicorum et lyricorum praeter Ennium et Lucilium, post Aemilium Baehrens iterum ed.* Leipzig, [2]1927 [repr. Stuttgart, 1975].

Mueller, Lucian, ed. *Livii Andronici et Cn Naevi fabularum reliquiae.* Berlin, 1885.

Ribbeck, Otto, ed. *Scaenicae Romanorum poesis fragmenta. Vol. I. Tragicorum Romanorum fragmenta.* Leipzig, [1]1852 / [2]1871 / [3]1897.

————, ed. *Scaenicae Romanorum poesis fragmenta. Vol. II. Comicorum Romanorum praeter Plautum et Terentium fragmenta.* Leipzig, [1]1855 / [2]1873 / [3]1898.

Schauer, Markus, ed. *Tragicorum Romanorum Fragmenta (TrRF). Volumen I. Livius Andronicus. Naevius. Tragici Minores. Fragmenta Adespota.* Göttingen, 2012.

Spaltenstein, François. *Commentaire des fragments dra-

matiques de Naevius. Collection Latomus, Vol. 344. Bruxelles, 2014.

Strzelecki, W., ed. *Cn. Naevii belli Punici carminis quae supersunt.* Leipzig, [2]1964 [[1]1959].

Traglia, Antonio, ed. *Poeti latini arcaici. Volume primo, Livio Andronico, Nevio, Ennio.* Classici Latini. Torino, 1986.

Vahlen, Iohannes, ed. *Cn. Naevi De bello Punico reliquiae.* Leipzig, 1854.

Viredaz, Antoine, *Fragmenta Saturnia heroica: introduction, traduction et commentaire des fragments de l'Odyssée latine de Livius Andronicus et de la Guerre punique de Cn. Naevius.* Schweizerische Beiträge zur Altertumswissenschaft 47. Basel, 2020.

Warmington, E. H., ed. and trans. *Remains of Old Latin.* 4 vols. Loeb Classical Library 294, 314, 329, 359. London, 1935–1940: Vol. 2, *Livius Andronicus, Naevius, Pacuvius and Accius.* London, 1936 [[2]1967, repr. 1988, etc.].

Wordsworth, John, ed. *Fragments and Specimens of Early Latin.* Oxford, 1874.

1.3. Caecilius

Baehrens, Aemilius, ed. *Fragmenta Poetarum Romanorum.* Leipzig, 1886.

Bothe, Fredericus, H., ed. *Poetae scenici Latinorum. Collatis codd. Berolinensibus, Florentino, Friburgensi, Gothano, Guelpherbitanis, Helmstadiensibus, Monacensi, Palatino, Parisio Ultrajectino, aliisque spectatae fidei libris. Volumen quartum: Fragmenta, Pars posterior: Fragmenta comicorum.* Halberstadt, 1824 [reissued Leipzig, 1834].

Courtney, Edward, ed. *The Fragmentary Latin Poets*. Oxford, 1993 [corr. repr. 2003].

Diehl, Ernst, ed. *Poetarum Romanorum veterum reliquiae selectae*. Kleine Texte für theologische und philologische Vorlesungen und Übungen, 69. Bonn, 1911 [repr. Berlin, 1967].

Egger, A. E. ed. *Latini sermonis vetustioris reliquiae selectae*. Paris, 1843.

Ernout, Alfred, ed. *Receuil de textes latins archaïques*. Nouvelle edition. Paris, [2]1957 [[1]1916].

Estienne, Robert, and Henri Estienne, eds. *Fragmenta Poetarum Veterum Latinorum Quorum Opera Non Extant: Ennii, Accii, Lucilii, Laberii, Pacuvii, Afranii, Naevii, Caecilii, Aliorumque Multorum*. Geneva, 1564.

Guardì, Tommaso. *Cecilio Stazio: I frammenti*. Palermo, 1974.

Ribbeck, Otto, ed. *Scaenicae Romanorum poesis fragmenta. Vol. II. Comicorum Romanorum praeter Plautum et Terentium fragmenta*. Leipzig, [1]1855 / [2]1873 / [3]1898.

Schlüter, J., ed. *Caecilii Statii fabularum fragmenta comparatis graecorum comicorum reliquiis illustrata*. Andernach, 1884.

Spengel, L., ed. *Caii Caecilii Statii . . . Deperditarum Fabularum Fragmenta*. München, 1829.

Traina, Alfonso, ed. *Comoedia: Antologia della Palliata*. Ed. corretta e aggiornata. Padova, [3]1969.

Warmington, E. H., ed. and trans. *Remains of Old Latin*. 4 vols. Loeb Classical Library 294, 314, 329, 359. London, 1935–1940: Vol. 1, *Ennius. Caecilius*. London, 1935 [[2]1956, repr.].

Wase, Christopher, ed. *Animadversiones Nonianæ. Afranius Novius Pomponius Sollicitati. Cæcilius Item Le-*

viter Correctus. Turpilius Titinius Laberius Aliquoties Emaculati. Exercitatio II. Authore Christoph. Wase, Jur. Civ. in Univ. Oxon. Bed. Sup. England. Oxford, 1685.

Wordsworth, John, ed. *Fragments and Specimens of Early Latin.* Oxford, 1874.

2. EDITIONS OF
TRANSMITTING AUTHORS

2.1. Anonymus ad Cuimnanum (Anon. Cuim.)

Bischoff, Bernhard, and Bengt Löfstedt, eds. *Expositio Latinitatis.* Corpus Christianorum Series Latina 133D. Turnhout, 1992.

2.2. Apuleius (Apul.)

Helm, Rudolf, ed. *Apulei Platonici Madaurensis opera quae supersunt. Vol. II, Fasc. 1. Pro se de magia liber (apologia).* Editio stereotypa editionis alterius cum addendis. Leipzig, 1959 [[1]1912, [4]1963, [5]1972, repr.].

2.3. Flavius Sosipater Charisius (Charis.)

Barwick, Karl, ed. *Flavii Sosipatri Charisii artis grammaticae libri V.* Ed. C. B. Addenda et corrigenda collegit et adiecit F. Kühnert. Leipzig, 1964 [repr. Stuttgart / Leipzig, 1997].

Keil, Heinrich, ed. *Grammatici Latini. Vol. I. Flavii Sosipatri Charisii Artis grammaticae libri V, Diomedis Artis grammaticae libri III, ex Charisii arte grammatica excerpta.* Leipzig, 1857 [repr. Hildesheim, 1961].

2.4. M. Tullius Cicero (Cic.)

Clark, Albertus Curtis, ed. *M. Tulli Ciceronis orationes [I]. Pro Sex. Roscio, De imperio Cn. Pompei, Pro Cluentio, In Catilinam, Pro Murena, Pro Caelio. Recognovit brevique adnotatione critica instruxit.* Oxford, 1905.

Douglas, A. E., ed. *M. Tulli Ciceronis Brutus.* Oxford, 1966.

Giusta, Michelangelus, ed. *M. Tulli Ciceronis Tusculanae disputationes.* Torino, 1984.

Kumaniecki, Kazimierz F., ed. *M. Tulli Ciceronis scripta quae manserunt omnia. Fasc. 3. De oratore.* Leipzig, 1969.

Maslowski, Tadeusz, ed. *M. Tulli Ciceronis scripta quae manserunt omnia. Fasc. 23. Orationes in P. Vatinium Testem. Pro M. Caelio.* Stuttgart / Leipzig, 1995.

Plasberg, Otto, ed. *M. Tulli Ciceronis scripta quae manserunt omnia. Fasc. 45. De natura deorum.* Recognovit O. Plasberg. Iterum ed. appendicem adiecit W. Ax. Leipzig, 1933 [^{1}1917].

Powell, J. G. F., ed. *M. Tulli Ciceronis De re publica, De legibus, Cato maior de senectute, Laelius de amicitia. Recognovit brevique adnotatione critica instruxit.* Oxford, 2006.

Reynolds, L. D., ed. *M. Tulli Ciceronis De finibus bonorum et malorum libri quinque. Recognovit brevique adnotatione critica instruxit.* Oxford, 1998.

Shackleton Bailey, D. R., ed. *M. Tulli Ciceronis Epistulae ad Atticum.* 2 vols. Stuttgart, 1987.

———. *M. Tulli Ciceronis Epistulae ad familiares libri I–XVI.* Stuttgart, 1988.

Westman, Rolf, ed. *M. Tulli Ciceronis scripta quae manserunt omnia. Fasc. 5. Orator.* Leipzig, 1980.

2.5. Corpus Glossariorum Latinorum (Gloss.)

Goetz, G., ed. *Corpus Glossariorum Latinorum a Gustavo Loewe incohatum, auspiciis Societatis Litterarum Regiae Saxonicae, composuit, recensuit, edidit. Vol. V.* Leipzig, 1888 [repr. Amsterdam, 1965].

2.6. Diomedes (Diom.)

Keil, Heinrich, ed. *Grammatici Latini. Vol. I. Flavii Sosipatri Charisii Artis grammaticae libri V, Diomedis Artis grammaticae libri III, ex Charisii arte grammatica excerpta.* Leipzig, 1857 [repr. Hildesheim, 1961].

2.7. Aelius Donatus (Don.)

Keil, Heinrich, ed. *Grammatici Latini. Vol. IV. Probi Donati Servii qui feruntur de arte grammatica libri ex recensione Henrici Keilii; Notarum Laterculi ex recensione Theodori Mommseni.* Leipzig, 1864 [repr. Hildesheim, 1961].

Wessner, Paulus, ed. *Aeli Donati quod fertur Commentum Terenti, accedunt Eugraphi commentum et Scholia Bembina.* Vol. 1, Leipzig, 1902; Vol. 2, Leipzig, 1904.

2.8. Eusebius Caesariensis (Euseb.)

Mras, Karl, and Édouard des Places, eds. *Eusebius Caesariensis: Werke, Band 8: Die Praeparatio Evangelica.*

Teil 1: Einleitung. Die Bücher I bis X. Griechische Christliche Schriftsteller der ersten Jahrhunderte 43.1. Berlin, 1982 [repr. New York, 2012].

2.9. Sex. Pompeius Festus (Fest.) / Paulus (Paul. Fest.)

Lindsay, Wallace M., ed. *Sexti Pompei Festi De verborum significatu quae supersunt cum Pauli Epitome.* Leipzig, 1913 [repr. Hildesheim / New York, 1965].

2.10. M. Cornelius Fronto (Fronto)

van den Hout, Michael J. P., ed. *M. Cornelii Frontonis epistulae schedis tam editis quam ineditis Edmundi Hauleri usus iterum edidit.* Leipzig, 1988.

2.11. Aulus Gellius (Gell.)

Holford-Strevens, Leofranc, ed. *Auli Gelli Noctes Atticae. Recognovit brevique adnotatione critica instruxit.* 2 vols. Oxford, 2020a.

2.12. Eusebius Hieronymus (Hieron.)

Helm, Rudolf, ed. *Eusebius Caesariensis: Werke, Band 7: Die Chronik des Hieronymus / Hieronimi Chronicon.* Griechische Christliche Schriftsteller der ersten Jahrhunderte 47. Berlin, 1956 [repr. New York, 2012].

Hilberg, Isidorus, ed. *Sancti Eusebii Hieronymi Epistulae. Pars I: Epistulae I–LXX.* CSEL LIV: S. Eusebii Hieronymi opera I.I. Wien / Leipzig, 1910 [repr. New York / London, 1961, ed. altera suppl. aucta].

2.13. Q. Horatius Flaccus (Hor.)

Shackleton Bailey, D. R., ed. *Q. Horati Flacci opera*. Stuttgart, 1985.

2.14. Isidorus (Isid.)

Lindsay, Wallace M., ed. *Isidori Hispalensis Episcopi Etymologiarum sive originum libri XX. Recognovit brevique adnotatione critica instruxit*. 2 vols. Oxford, 1911.

2.15. Iulius Rufinianus (Iul. Ruf.)

Halm, Carolus, ed. *Rhetores Latini minores. Ex codicibus maximam partem primum adhibitis emendabat*. Leipzig, 1863.

2.16. T. Livius (Liv.)

Briscoe, John, ed. *Livius Ab urbe condita libri XXXI–XL. Tomus I: libri XXI–XXXV, Tomus II: libri XXVI–XL*. Stuttgart, 1991.

Conway, Robert, S., and Stephen K. Johnson, eds. *Titi Livi Ab urbe condita. Recognoverunt et adnotatione critica instruxerunt*. Vol. 4, Books 26–30. Oxford, 1935 [corr. repr. 1953].

Oakley, Stephen, P. *A Commentary on Livy Books VI–X. Volume II. Books VII–VIII*. Oxford, 1998.

2.17. Ambrosius Theodosius Macrobius (Macrob.)

Kaster, R. A., ed. *Ambrosii Theodosii Macrobii Saturnalia. Recognovit brevique adnotatione critica instruxit*. Oxford, 2011.

2.18. Nonius Marcellus (Non.)

Lindsay, Wallace M., ed. *Nonii Marcelli De compendiosa doctrina libros XX, Onionsianis copiis usus ed.* 3 vols. Leipzig, 1903 [repr. Hildesheim, 1964; includes page numbers according to edition of Mercerus].

2.19. Porphyrio (Porph.)

Meyer, Gulielmus, ed. *Pomponii Porphyrionis commentarii in Q. Horatium Flaccum. Recensuit.* Leipzig, 1874.

2.20. Priscianus (Prisc.)

Hertz, Martin, ed. *Grammatici Latini. Vol. II/III. Prisciani grammatici Caesariensis Institutionum grammaticarum libri XVIII.* Leipzig, 1855/59 [repr. Hildesheim, 1961].
Keil, Heinrich, ed. *Grammatici Latini. Vol. III. Prisciani grammatici Caesariensis De figuris numerorum, De metris Terentii, De praeexercitamentis rhetoricis libri, Institutio de nomine et pronomine et verbo, Partitiones duodecim versuum Aeneidos principalium. Accedit Prisciani qui dicitur liber de accentibus.* Leipzig, 1859 [repr. Hidesheim, 1961].

2.21. M. Fabius Quintilianus (Quint.)

Winterbottom, Michael, ed. *M. Fabi Quintiliani Institutionis oratoriae libri duodecim. Recognovit brevique adnotatione critica instruxit.* 2 vols. Oxford, 1970.

2.22. Rufinus (Rufin.)

Keil, Heinrich, ed. *Grammatici Latini. Vol. VI. Scriptores artis metricae. Marius Victorinus, Maximus Victori-*

nus, Caesius Bassus, Atilius Fortunatianus, Terentianus Maurus, Marius Plotius Sacerdos, Rufinus, Mallius Theodorus, Fragmenta et excerpta metrica. Leipzig, 1874 [repr. Hildesheim, 1961].

2.23. Scholia (Pseudacronis) in Horatium (Schol. ad Hor.)

Keller, Otto, ed. *Pseudacronis Scholia in Horatium vetustiora.* 2 vols. Leipzig, 1902/4.

2.24. Scholiastae Ciceronis (Schol. ad Cic.)

Stangl, Thomas, ed. *Ciceronis Orationum Scholiastae. Asconius. Scholia Bobiensia. Scholia Pseudasconii Sangallensia. Scholia Cluniacensia et recentiora Ambrosiana ac Vaticana. Scholia Lugdunensia. Volumen II: Commentarios continens.* Wien / Leipzig, 1912.

2.25. Scriptores Historiae Augustae (SHA)

Hohl, Ernst, Wolfgang Seyfarth, and Christa Samberger, eds. *Scriptores Historiae Augustae.* 2 vols. Leipzig, 1927.

2.26. Seneca minor (Sen.)

Reynolds, L. D., ed. *L. Annaei Senecae ad Lucilium Epistulae morales. Recognovit et adnotatione critica instruxit.* 2 vols. Oxford, 1965.

2.27. Servius and Servius Danielis (Serv. et Serv. Dan.)

Thilo, Georgius, ed. *Servii grammatici qui feruntur in Vergilii carmina commentarii. Vol. I. Aeneidos libro-*

rum I–V commentarii. Leipzig / Berlin, 1881 [repr. Leipzig / Berlin, 1923].

———. *Servii grammatici qui feruntur in Vergilii carmina commentarii. Vol. II. Aeneidos librorum VI–XII commentarii.* Leipzig / Berlin, 1884 [repr. Leipzig / Berlin, 1923].

———. *Servii grammatici qui feruntur in Vergilii carmina commentarii. Vol. III, Fasc. I. In Bucolica et Georgica commentarii.* Leipzig, 1887 [repr. Leipzig, 1927; Hildesheim, 1961].

2.28. C. Suetonius Tranquillus (Suet.)

Kaster, Robert A., ed. *C. Suetonius Tranquillus: De Grammaticis et Rhetoribus. Edited with a Translation, Introduction, and Commentary.* Oxford, 1995.

———, *C. Suetonii Tranquilli, De vita Caesarum libros VIII et De grammaticis et rhetoribus librum. Recognovit brevique adnotatione critica instruxit.* Oxford, 2016.

2.29. Quintus Aurelius Symmachus (Symm.)

Callu, Jean-Pierre, ed. *Symmaque: Lettres.* Collection des Universités de France. 4 vols. Paris, 1972–2002.

2.30. Terentianus Maurus (Ter. Maur.)

Keil, Heinrich, ed. *Grammatici Latini. Vol. VI. Scriptores artis metricae: Marius Victorinus, Maximus Victorinus, Caesius Bassus, Atilius Fortunatianus, Terentianus Maurus, Marius Plotius Sacerdos, Rufinus, Mallius Theodorus, Fragmenta et excerpta metrica.* Leipzig, 1874 [repr. Hildesheim, 1961].

2.31. P. Terentius Afer (Ter.)

Kauer, Robert, and Wallace M. Lindsay, eds. *P. Terenti Afri Comoediae. Recognoverunt brevique adnotatione critica instruxerunt Robert Kauer / Wallace M. Lindsay. Supplementa apparatus curavit Otto Skutsch*. Oxford, 1958.

2.32. Valerius Maximus (Val. Max.)

Briscoe, John, ed. *Valeri Maximi Factorum et dictorum memorabilium libri IX*. Stuttgart, 1998.

2.33. M. Terentius Varro (Varro)

De Melo, Wolfgang, ed. and trans. *Varro de Lingua Latina*. 2 vols. Oxford, 2019.

Flach, Dieter, ed. and trans. *Marcus Terentius Varro. Gespräche über die Landwirtschaft. Herausgegeben, übersetzt und erläutert*. 3 vols. Texte zur Forschung 65–67. Darmstadt, 1996–2002.

2.34. Vaticani Glossographi

Mai, Angelo, ed. *Classicorum auctorum e vaticanis codicibus editorum. 8: Thesaurus novus Latinitatis, sive lexicon vetus e membranis nunc primum erutum*. Roma, 1836.

3. SECONDARY LITERATURE: WORKS CITED

von Albrecht, Michael. "Zur *Tarentilla* des Naevius." *MH* 32 (1975): 230–39.

———. *A History of Roman Literature. From Livius An-*

dronicus to Boethius. With Special Regard to Its Influence on World Literature. Revised by Gareth Schmeling and by the author. 2 vols. Vol. 1 translated with the assistance of F. and K. Newman; Vol. 2 translated with the assistance of R. R. Caston and F. R. Schwartz. Mnemosyne Suppl. 165. Leiden / New York / Köln, 1997 [German original 1994].

————. *Roman Epic: An interpretative introduction.* Leiden / Boston / Köln, 1999.

Alfonsi, L. "Gli *Agrypnuntes* di Nevio." *Dioniso* 13 (1950): 184–89.

————. "Sul v. 265 Ribbeck di Cecilio Stazio." *Dioniso* 18 (1955): 3–6.

————. "Su un verso di Cecilio Stazio." *Dioniso* 40 (1966): 27–29.

————. "Una praetexta *Veii*?" *RFIC* 95 (1967): 165–68.

Allinson, Francis G. *Menander: Principal Fragments.* London, 1921.

Altheim, F. "Naevius und die Annalistik." In *Untersuchungen zur römischen Geschichte. I: Einzeluntersuchungen zur altitalischen Geschichte*, edited by D. Felber, 100–130. Frankfurt, 1961.

Antonelli Rinaldi, Maria R. "Intorno all'*Aegisthus* di Livio Andronico. Saggio di lettura dei frammenti." *Rivista di Cultura Classica e Medioevale* 24 (1982): 3–14.

Argenio, R. "I frammenti di Cecilio Stazio." *Rivista di Studi Classici* 13 (1965): 257–77.

Aricò, Giuseppe. "Sull'*Aegisthus* di Livio Andronico." In *Studi di Poesia Latina. Stud. coll. in on. A. Traglia*, 1:3–9. Roma, 1979.

————. "Sull'*Achilles* di Livio Andronico." In Φιλίας χάριν, *Stud. coll. in on. Eugenio Manni*, edited by

M. D. Fontane, M. T. Piraino, F. P. Rizzo, 1:129–41. Roma, 1980.

———, ed. *Atti del I seminario di studi sulla tragedia romana*. Palermo, 1987.

———. "La tragedia romana arcaica." *Lexis* 15 (1997): 59–78.

Arnott, W. Geoffrey. *Alexis: the Fragments: A Commentary*. Cambridge, 1996.

Austin, Colin. "From Cratinus to Menander." *Quaderni Urbinati di Cultura Classica* 63.3 (1999): 37–48.

Bader, B. "Three Notes on Naevian Comedies." *BICS* 18 (1971): 110–13.

Barchiesi, Alessandro. "Livio Andronico, Omero, e l'ironia dramatica (*Odyssea*, fr. 38 Mor. = 20 Mar.)." *RIFC* 113 (1985): 405–11.

———. "Figure dell' intertestualità nell'epica romana." *Lexis* 13 (1995): 49–67.

Barchiesi, Marino. "Personaggi neviani (Dite, Amulio)." *RFIC* 91 (1963): 302–22.

———. *La* Tarentilla *revisitata*. Pisa, 1978.

Barigazzi, Adelmo. "Note a Livio Andronico, Lucrezio, Cicerone." *Acme* 3 (1950): 425–33.

Barsby, John, ed. *Plautus: Bacchides*. Warminster, 1986.

———. *Terence: Eunuchus*. Cambridge, 1999.

Bartsch, Karl. *Der saturnische Vers und die altdeutsche Langzeile*. Leipzig, 1867.

Beare, W. "When Did Livius Andronicus Come to Rome?" *CQ* 34 (1940): 11–19.

———. "Naevius and the *Alimonium Remi et Romuli*." *CR* 63 (1949): 49.

———. *The Roman Stage. A Short History of Latin Drama in the Time of the Republic*. 3rd ed. London, 1964.

Bednarek, Bartlomiej. *The Myth of Lycurgus in Aeschylus, Naevius and Beyond*. Mnemosyne Suppl. 441. Leiden / Bonn, 2021.

Berchem, Maximilian, J. *De Gn. Naevii poetae vita et scriptis*. Münster, 1861.

Bergk, Theodor. Review of Köne 1840. *Zeitschrift für die Altertumswissenschaft* 9 (1842): 183–98.

———. *Kleine philologische Schriften von Theodor Bergk. Herausgegeben von Rudolf Peppmüller. I. Band. Zur römischen Literatur*. Halle a. S., 1884.

Bernardi Perini, Giorgio. "Sul fr. 32 Mor. del *Bellum Poenicum* di Nevio." In *Disiecti membra poetae*, edited by Vincenzo Tandoi, 3:3–11. Foggia, 1988.

———. "Livio Andronico, *Od*. fr. 3 Morel." In *Mnemosynum. Studi in onore di Alfredo Ghiselli*, 11–17. Edizioni e Saggi Universitari di Filologia Classica 42. Bologna, 1989.

Bernstein, Frank. "Der römische Sieg bei Clastidium und die zeitgeschichtliche Praetexta des Naevius." In Manuwald 2000, 157–73.

Bertini, F. "Naev. *Lycurg*. 33 Ribb., 35–6 Klotz, 10 Marmorale (ovvero: Un falso problema di tradizione manoscritta)." *ALGP* 9–10 (1972): 111–20.

Bettini, Maurizio. "*Odusia* 22 M." *GIF* ns. 5 (1974): 165–69.

———. "Vel Vibe di Veio e il re Amulio. A proposito di Naevio praet. 5 sg. Ribb.[2] e di bell. poen. 12 Mor." *MD* 6 (1981): 163–68.

Bickel, Ernst. "Die Skyrier des Euripides und der Achilles des Livius Andronicus." *RhM* 86 (1937): 1–22.

Biffi, N. "A proposito di Naev. fr. 53 R.[3] (= Marmorale 2 p. 214 sg.)." *GIF* 55 (2003): 235–44.

Biggs, Thomas. "*Primus Romanorum*: Origin Stories, Fictions of Primacy and the First Punic War." *CP* 112 (2017): 350–67.

———. *Poetics of the First Punic War*. Ann Arbor, 2020.

Blänsdorf, Jürgen. "Voraussetzungen und Entstehung der römischen Komödie." In Lefèvre 1978, 91–134.

———. "Livius Andronicus und die Anverwandlung des hellenistischen Dramas in Rom." In Manuwald 2000, 145–56.

Bleckmann, Bruno. "Regulus bei Naevius: zu fr. 50 und 51 Blänsdorf." *Philologus* 142 (1998): 61–70.

Borghini, Alberto. "Codice antropologico e narrazione letteraria: il comportamento del soldato valoroso (Naevio *Bellum Poenicum* fr. 42 M.)." *Lingua e Stile* 14 (1979): 165–76.

Borrelli, Isa. *L'Odyssia di Livio Andronico*. Roma, 1951.

Boscherini, S. "Norma e parola nelle commedie di Cecilio Stazio." *Studi italiani di filologia classica* 17.1 (1999): 99–115.

Boyle, Anthony, J., ed. *Roman Epic*. London / New York, 1993.

———. *An Introduction to Roman Tragedy*. London / New York, 2006.

Brakman, Cornelius. "Observationes ad tragicorum Romanorum fragmenta." *Mnemosyne* 2 (1935): 55–61.

Broccia, Giuseppe. *Ricerche su Livio Andronico epico*. Padova, 1974a.

———. "Livio Andronico *Odusia*, fr. 37 Mor. (= 46 Warm., 37 Lench., 24 Mar.)." *RIFC* 102 (1974b): 299–300.

———. "Postille a Livio Andronico epico, *Od*. Frr. 18 e 19 Mor." *Annali della Facoltà di Lettere e Filosofia dell'Università di Macerata* 8 (1975): 357–64.

Brown, Peter G. McC. "The Beginnings of Roman Com edy." In *The Oxford Handbook of Greek and Roman Comedy*, edited by Michael Fontaine and Adele Scafuro, 401–8. Oxford, 2014.

Brussich, Guerrino F. "La danza dei delfini in Euripide, nello pseudo-Arione e in Livio Andronico." *QUCC* 21 (1976): 53–56.

Büchner, Karl. "Livius Andronicus und die erste künstlerische Übersetzung der europäischen Kultur." *Symbolae Osloenses* 54 (1979): 37–70.

Buecheler, Franz. "Nävius' *bellum Punicum* bei den Grammatikern." *RhM* 40 (1885): 148–150 [repr. in Buecheler 1930, 61–63].

———. *Kleine Schriften*. 3 vols. Leipzig / Berlin, 1915 / 1927 / 1930 [repr. Osnabrück, 1965].

Camilloni, M. T. "Una ricostruzione della biografia di Cecilio Stazio." *Maia* 9 (1957): 115–43.

———. *Su le vestigia degli antichi padri*. Ancona, 1985.

Cancik, Hubert. "Die republikanische Tragödie." In Lefèvre 1978, 308–47.

Capelletto, Rita. "Livio Andronico, *Odyssea* fr. 31 Mor. (22 Mar.)." *RFIC* 112 (1984): 413–16.

Carratello, Ugo. *Livio Andronico*. Roma, 1979.

———. "Questioni nuove e antiche su Livio Andronico." *GIF* 38 (1986): 125–40.

Cavallo, Guglielmo, Paolo Fedeli, and Andreas Giardina, eds. *Lo spazio letterario di Roma antica. Volume V. Cronologia e bibliografia della letteratura latina*. Roma, 1991.

Cavazza, Albertina, and Anna R. Barrile. *Lexicon Livianum et Naevianum*. Hildesheim / New York, 1981.

Caviglia, Franco. "Livio Andronico, *Odyss. fr. 20 Mor.*" In

Disiecti membra poetae, edited by Vincenzo Tandoi, 1:3–12. Foggia, 1984.

Cazzaniga, Ignazio. "Sul frammento di Livio Andronico Nr. 30 Mor. (21 Mar.)." *RFIC* 94 (1966): 413–14.

Cervellera, Maria A. "Il senario tragico arcaico." *RCCM* 21/22 (1979/80): 21–43.

Chiarini, G. *Introduzione al Teatro Latino*. Milano, 2004.

Cichorius, Conrad. *Römische Studien: Historisches, Epigraphisches, Literaturgeschichtliches aus vier Jahrhunderten Roms*. Leipzig, 1922.

Cipriani, M. "Textkritische Bemerkungen zu zwei Fragmenten von Caecilius Statius im Terenz-Kommentar des Donat (34–35, 58–59 G.)." In , *Schrift – Text – Edition*, edited by C. Henke et al., 65–75. Tübingen, 2003.

———. "*Homo homini Deus*: la malinconica sentenziosità di Cecilio Stazio." In ΠΑΡΟΙΜΙΑΚΩΣ. *Il proverbio in Grecia e a Roma* 2, edited by Emanuele Lelli, 117–59. Philologia antiqua 3. Pisa / Roma, 2010.

Cole, Thomas. "The Saturnian Verse." *YCS* 21 (1969): 3–73.

Condorelli, Sebastiano. "*L'Achilles* di Livio Andronico." *Istituto d'Instruzione Superiore Gulli e Pennisi* (1986): 241–55.

Conte, Gian Biagio. *Latin Literature. A History*. Translated by Joseph B. Solodow. Revised by Don Fowler and Glenn W. Most. Oxford, 1994 [Italian original 1987].

Corbeill, Anthony. *Sexing the World: Grammatical Gender and Biological Sex in Ancient Rome*. Princeton / Oxford, 2015.

Costanza, S. "Tre frammenti di Nevio in Fulgentio." *Emerita* 24 (1956): 302–10.

Dahlmann, H. *Studien zu Varro "De poetis."* Akademie der Wissenschaften und der Literatur, Abhandlungen der geistes- und sozialwissenschaftlichen Klasse N. R. 10. Wiesbaden, 1962.

Dangel, Jacqueline, ed. *Accius, Œuvres (fragments)*. Paris, 1995.

D'Anna, Giovanni. "Contributo alla cronologia dei poeti latini arcaici." *RIL* 86 (1953): 211–32.

———. "Contributo alla cronologia dei poeti latini arcaici. III: Quando esordì Cn. Nevio?" *RIL* 88 (1955): 301–10.

———. "Una nuova proposta sull'argomento dei libri XVII–XVIII degli Annales di Ennio." *Athenaeum* 51 (1973): 355–76.

———. *Problemi di letteratura latina arcaica*. Roma, 1976.

De Durante, G. *Le fabulae praetextae*. Roma, 1966.

De Melo, Wolfgang, ed. and trans. *Plautus*. 5 vols. Loeb Classical Library 60, 61, 163, 260, 328. Cambridge, MA, 2011–13.

———. "Two Textual Problems in Book 7 of Varro's *De lingua Latina*." *CQ* 65 (2015): 397–401.

De Nonno, Mario. "Cecilio Stazio 34–35 R.[3] in Festo p. 118 L." In *Mousa: Scritti in onore di Giuseppe Morelli*, 233–48. Bologna, 1997.

———. "Rileggendo il *Bellum Poenicum* e l'arte di Nevio." *RFIC* 129 (2001): 335–52 [review of Mariotti [3]2001, listed in 1.2].

De Rosalia, Antonino. "Funzione comunicativa e funzione emotiva nel linguaggio dei tragici latini arcaici." *Dioniso* 54 (1983): 43–57.

———. "Aspetti linguistici del 'tradurre' nei tragici latini arcaici." In Aricò 1987, 7–27.

———. "Rassegna degli studi sulla tragedia latina arcaica (1965–1986)." *BStudLat* 19 (1989): 76–144.

Deufert, Marcus. *Textgeschichte und Rezeption der plautinischen Komödien im Altertum*. Berlin, 2002.

Di Salvo, Lucia. "Naevianae Danaes fragmenta." *Studi Noniani* 2 (1972): 61–66.

Duckworth, George, E. *The Nature of Roman Comedy. A Study in Popular Entertainment.* Princeton, 1952. *Second Edition. With a Foreword and Bibliographical Appendix by Richard Hunter.* Norman / Bristol, 1994.

Duentzer, Heinrich, "De Naevii Lycurgo et Ennii Iphigenia." *RhM* 5 (1837): 433–46.

Engelbrecht, August. *Studia Terentiana.* Wien, 1883 [repr. 2016].

Enk, P. J. "Roman Tragedy." *NPh* 41 (1957): 282–307.

Erasmi, Gabriele. *Studies on the Language of Livius Andronicus.* Ann Arbor, 1975.

————. "The Saturnian and Livius Andronicus." *Glotta* 57 (1979): 125–49.

Erasmo, Mario. *Roman Tragedy. Theater to Theatricality.* Austin, 2004.

Erskine, Andrew. "Trojan Horseplay in Rome." *Dialogos* 5 (1998): 131–38.

Faider, P. "Le poete comique Caecilius: sa vie et son œuvre." *Musée Belge* 12 (1908–9): 269–341.

Farrell, Joseph. "The Origins and Essence of Roman Epic." In *A Companion to Ancient Epic*, edited by John Miles Foley, 417–28. Malden, MA / Oxford, 2005.

Feeney, Denis C. *The Gods in Epic. Poets and Critics of the Classical Tradition.* Oxford, 1991.

————. *Beyond Greek. The Beginnings of Latin Literature.* Cambridge, MA, 2016.

Fleckeisen, Alfred. "Zu dem *Bellum Punicum* des Naevius." *Jahrbücher für classische Philologie* 83 (1861): 148.

————. "Zur lateinischen lautlehre in griechischen lehnwörtern." *Jahrbücher für classische Philologie* 93 (1866): 1–13.

Flores, Enrico. *Letteratura latina e ideologia del III–II a.C. Disegno storico-sociologico da Appio Claudio Cieco a Pacuvio.* Napoli, 1974.

———. "Il. fr. 4 Klotz ex inc. fab. di Livio Andronico e il ritorno da Troia di Agamennone." *Prometheus* 9 (1983): 243–46 [repr. in Flores 1998, 95–98].

———. *La Camena, l'epos e la storia. Studi sulla cultura latina arcaica.* Napoli, 1998.

Fraenkel, Eduard. *Plautinisches im Plautus.* Berlin, 1922; Engl. trans. *Plautine Elements in Plautus (Plautinisches im Plautus).* Translated by T. Drevikovsky and F. Muecke. Oxford / New York, 2007.

———. "Die Vorgeschichte des *uersus quadratus.*" *Hermes* 62 (1927): 357–70 [repr. in *Kleine Beiträge zur klassischen Philologie,* 2:11–24. Roma, 1964].

———. "Livius Andronicus." *RE Suppl.* 5 (1931): 598–607.

———. "Das Original der Cistellaria des Plautus." *Philologus* 87 (1932): 117–20.

———. "Naevius." *RE Suppl.* 6 (1935): 622–40.

Fränkel, Hermann. "Griechische Bildung in altrömischen Epen." *Hermes* 67 (1932): 303–11; 70 (1935): 59–61.

Frassinetti, Paolo. "Cecilio Stazio e Menandro." In *Studi di poesia latina in onore di Antonio Traglia,* 1:77–86. Storia e letteratura 146. Roma, 1979.

Funaioli, Hyginus, ed. *Grammaticae Romanae fragmenta.* Leipzig, 1907 [repr. Stuttgart, 1969].

Gaiser, Konrad. "Einige Menander-Fragmente in Verbindung mit Plautus und Terenz." *Wiener Studien* 79 (1966): 191–204.

————. "La commedia sul rilievo marmoreo di Napoli." *Rendiconti della Accademia di archeologia, lettere e belle arti, Napoli* 61 (1987–88): 167–90.

Gentili, Bruno. *Theatrical Performances in the Ancient World. Hellenistic and Early Roman Theatre.* London Studies in Classical Philology 2. Amsterdam / Uithoorn, 1979 [Italian original 1977; new edition 2006].

Gerick, Thomas. *Der versus quadratus bei Plautus und seine volkstümliche Tradition.* Tübingen, 1996.

Gildenhard, Ingo. "Buskins & SPQR: Roman Receptions of Greek Tragedy." In *Beyond the Fifth Century: Interactions with Greek Tragedy from the Fourth Century BCE to the Middle Ages*, edited by Ingo Gildenhard and Martin Revermann, 153–85. Berlin / New York, 2010.

Giovini, Marco. "Limare caput. Nonio, Livio Andronico e il più antico sintagma erotico della letteratura latina." In *Prolegomena Noniana*, edited by Ferrucio Bertini, 3:47–62. Genova, 2004.

Godel, Robert. "Virgile, Naevius et les Aborigènes." *Museum Helveticum* 35 (1978): 273–82.

Goldberg, Sander, M. "Saturnian Epic: Livius and Naevius." In Boyle 1993, 19–36.

————. *Epic in Republican Rome.* New York / Oxford, 1995.

————. "Early Republican Epic." In *A Companion to Ancient Epic*, edited by John Miles Foley, 429–39. Malden, MA / Oxford, 2005.

————. "Research Report: Reading Roman Tragedy." *IJCT* 13 (2007): 571–84.

Gordon, Arthur E. *Epigraphica I. On the first Appearance of the Cognomen in Latin Inscriptions of Freedmen.* University of California Publications in Classical Archaeology 1.4. Berkeley, 1935.

Grauert, W. H. "Prätexten des Nävius." *Philologus* 2 (1847): 115–30.

Grimal, Pierre. *Le siècle des Scipions. Rome et l'hellénisme au temps des guerres puniques.* 2ᵉ éd. refondue et augmentée, Paris, 1975.

———. *La littérature latine.* Paris, 1994.

Groton, Anne H. "Planting Trees for Antipho in Caecilius Statius' *Synephebi*." *Dionysus* 60 (1990): 58–63.

Gruen, Erich, S. *Studies in Greek Culture and Roman Policy.* Cincinnati Classical Studies. New Series. Vol. 7. Leiden / New York / Copenhagen / Köln, 1990 [paperback ed., Berkeley / London, 1996].

———. *Culture and National Identity in Republican Rome.* Cornell Studies in Classical Philology LII. Ithaca, NY, 1992.

Guardì, Tomasso. *Titinius e Atta. Frammenti. Introduzione, testo, traduzione e commento.* Milan, 1984.

———. "Un nuovo frammento di Cecilio Stazio." *Pan* 18–19 (2001): 263–64.

Hanses, Mathias. *The Life of Comedy after the Death of Plautus and Terence.* Ann Arbor, 2020.

Harrison, A. R. W. *The Law of Athens.* Oxford, 1968.

Havet, Ludovicus. *De saturnio Latinorum versu.* Paris, 1880.

Hermann, Gottfried. *Epitome doctrinae metricae.* Leipzig, 1852.

Hertz, Martin. "A. Gellius und Nonius Marcellus." *NJPhP / Jahrbücher für classische Philologie* 85 (1862): 779–99.

Hinds, Stephen. *Allusion and Intertext. Dynamics of Appropriation in Roman Poetry.* Cambridge, 1998.

Holford-Strevens, Leofranc. *Gelliana: A Textual Companion to the "Noctes Atticae" of Aulus Gellius.* Oxford, 2020b.

Horsfall, Nicholas. "The *Collegium Poetarum*." *BICS* 23 (1976): 79–95.

Hübner, Ulrich. "Zu Naevius' *Bellum Poenicum*." *Philologus* 116 (1972): 261–76.

Jacobson, H. "Trees in Caecilius Statius." *Mnemosyne* 30 (1977): 291.

Jannaconne, S. "Nuovi frammenti della poesia scenica latina." *Antiquitas* 1 (1946): 56–59.

Jensen, J. R. "Aulus Gellius als Literaturkritiker: Impressionist oder Systematiker?" *Classica et Mediaevalia* 48 (1997): 359–406.

Jocelyn, H. D. "The Poet Cn. Naevius, P. Cornelius Scipio and Q. Caecilius Metellus." *Antichthon* 3 (1969): 32–47.

———. "Caecilius, *Com.* 142–157." *Liverpool Classical Monthly* 10.1 (Jan. 1985): 10–11.

———. "Caecilius, *Com.* 150–152." *Liverpool Classical Monthly* 10.3 (Mar. 1985): 43.

Kearns, John. M. "Σεμνότης and Dialect Gloss in the *Odussia* of Livius Andronicus." *AJPh* 111 (1990): 40–52.

Keith, Alison. *Engendering Rome. Women in Latin Epic*. Cambridge, 2000.

Kenney, E. J., and W. V. Clausen, eds. *The Cambridge History of Classical Literature II. Latin Literature*. Cambridge, 1982.

Kessissoglu, Alexander. "Remarks to Livius Andronicus fr. 14 Mar., fr. 4 Mar." *Gymnasium* 81 (1974): 476–80.

Klimek-Winter, Rainer. *Andromedatragödien. Sophokles, Euripides, Livius Andronikos, Ennius, Accius. Text, Einleitung und Kommentar*. BzA 21. Stuttgart / Leipzig, 1993.

Klotz, Alfred. "Zu Naevius' *Bellum Poenicum*." *RhM* 87 (1938): 190–92.

GENERAL BIBLIOGRAPHY

Klussmann, Ernst. "Der Achilles des Ennius." *Neue Jahrbücher für Philologie und Pädagogik* 15 (1845): 325–28.

Knoche, U. Review of Morel (1927). *Gnomon* 4 (1928): 687–97.

Köne, J. K. *Über die Sprache der römischen Epiker.* Münster, 1840.

Korsch, Theodorus. *De versu Saturnio.* Moskva, 1868.

Kragelund, Patrick. "SO Debate: Historical Drama in Ancient Rome: Republican Flourishing and Imperial Decline?" *SO* 77 (2002): 5–105.

Kraggerud, Egil. "A Fragment of Naevius Reconsidered." *Glotta* 83 (2007): 95–97.

Kroll, W. "Der Tod des Naevius." *Hermes* 66 (1931): 469–72.

Kruschwitz, Peter. *Carmina Saturnia Epigraphica. Einleitung, Text und Kommentar zu den saturnischen Versinschriften.* Stuttgart, 2002a.

———. "Die antiken Quellen zum Saturnischen Vers." *Mnemosyne* 55 (2002b): 465–98.

———. "Zum Text von Livius Andronicus, *Odusia* frg. 1." *Philologus* 152 (2008): 154–55.

———. "*Ruminari* Rehashed. On Livius Andronicus, *Aegisthus* frg. IV R.2." *MD* 63 (2009): 157–64.

Kunz, Franz. "Die älteste römische Epik in ihrem Verhältnisse zu Homer. *Siebenter Jahresbericht des k.k. Staats-Gymnasiums in Untermelding bei Wien*, 3–26. Untermelding, 1890.

Ladewig, Theodor. "Analecta scenica." *Schulprogramm Neustrelitz* (1848): 1–40 [repr. in *Schriften zum römischen Drama republikanischer Zeit*, edited by by Ursula Gärtner and Ekkehard Stärk, 199–248. BzA 61. München / Leipzig, 2001].

Lallier, Roger. "Note sur la tragédie de Livius Andronicus intitule *Equos Troianus*." In *Mélanges Graux. Recueil de travaux d'érudition classique dédié à la mémoire de Charles Graux*, 103–9. Paris, 1884.

Lanowski, Jerzy. "Histoire des fragments des tragédies de Livius Andronicus." *Eos* 51 (1961): 65–77.

Lascu, N. "Intorno ai nomi degli schiavi nel teatro antico." *Dioniso* 43 (1969): 97–106.

Lattanzi, Luca. "Il Lucurgus di Nevio." *Aevum Antiquum* 7 (1994): 191–265.

La Ville de Mirmont, Henri de. *Études sur l'ancienne poésie latine*. Paris, 1903.

Lebek, W. D. "Livius Andronicus und Naevius. Wie konnten sie von ihrer dramatischen Dichtung leben?" In Manuwald 2000, 61–86.

Lefèvre, Eckard, ed. *Das römische Drama*. Darmstadt, 1978.

———. "Aitiologisch-politische Implikationen in Naevius' *Danae*." In Manuwald 2000, 175–82.

Lehmann, Aude. "La place de Naevius dans les écrits philologiques de Varron." *Ktema* 17 (1992): 263–72.

———. *Varron critique littéraire. Regard sur les poètes latins archaïques*. Collection Latomus Vol. 262. Bruxelles, 2002.

Lenchantin de Gubernatis, Massimo. "Appunti sull'ellenismo nella poesia arcaica latina." *ATT* 63 (1913): 389/91–456/68.

Lennartz, Klaus. *Non verba sed vim. Kritisch-exegetische Untersuchungen zu den Fragmenten archaischer römischer Tragiker*. BzA 54. Stuttgart / Leipzig, 1994.

Leo, Friedrich. *Der Saturnische Vers*. Göttingen, 1905.

———. *Plautinische Forschungen zur Kritik und Ge-*

schichte der Komödie. Berlin, [2]1912 [repr. Darmstadt, 1966].

―――. *Geschichte der römischen Literatur. Erster Band. Die archaische Literatur.* Berlin, 1913 [repr. Berlin, 1958; Darmstadt, 1967; Göttingen, 1999].

Lindsay, Wallace M. *Early Latin Verse.* Oxford, 1922.

Livan, Gabriele. *Appunti sulla lingua e lo stile di Cecilio Stazio.* Bologna, 2005.

Livingston, Ivy. *A Linguistic Commentary on Livius Andronicus.* New York / London, 2004.

Lo-Cascio, Santi. "L'influenza ellenica nell'origine della poesia latina." *RFIC* 20 (1892): 41–124.

Luck, Georg. "Naevius and Virgil." *Illinois Classical Studies* 8 (1983): 267–75.

Luppino, A. "Ancora sul contrasto fra Nevio e I Metelli." *GIF* 24 (1972): 96–101.

MacDowell, D. M. *The Law in Classical Athens.* Ithaca, NY, 1978.

Mandolfo, C. "La lingua di Nevio comico." *Sileno* 30 (2004): 143–62.

Manuwald, Gesine, ed. *Identität und Alterität in der frührömischen Tragödie.* Identitäten und Alteritäten, Bd. 3, Altertumswiss. Reihe, Bd. 1. Würzburg, 2000.

―――. *Fabulae praetextae. Spuren einer literarischen Gattung der Römer.* München, 2001.

―――. "Römische Tragödien und Praetexten republikanischer Zeit: 1964–2002." *Lustrum* 43 (2001 [2004]): 93–101.

―――. "Poetry, Latin: Overview: Archaic through Republic." *Oxford Bibliographies Online Classics* 2010, updated 2021.

―――. *Roman Republican Theatre.* Cambridge, 2011.

————. "Editing Roman (Republican) Tragedy: Challenges and Possible Solutions." In *Brill's Companion to Roman Tragedy*, edited by George W. M. Harrison, 3–23. Leiden / Boston, 2015.

Marconi, Giampietro. "Sull'attribuzione a Levio di quattro versi dell'*Ino*." *RCCM* 5 (1963): 131–45.

————. "La cronologia di Livio Andronico." *Academia Nazionale dei Lincei. Memorie: Classe di scienze morale, storia e filosofia.* Ser. 8.12 (1966): 125–213.

Mariotti, Scevola. *Livio Andronico e la traduzione artistica. Saggio critico ed edizione dei frammenti dell'Odyssea.* Urbino, ²1986 [Milano, ¹1952].

————. "Una similitudine omerica nel Lycurgus di Nevio." In *Poesia latina in frammenti. Miscellanea filologica*, edited by G. Puccioni, 29–34. Pubblicazioni dell'Istituto di filologia classica dell'Università di Genova 39. Genova, 1974.

Marzullo, A. *Dalla satira al teatro popolare latino: Ricerche varie.* Milano, 1973.

Mattingly, Harold B. "The Date of Livius Andronicus." *CQ* n.s. 7 (1957): 158–63.

————. "Naevius and the Metelli." *Historia* 9 (1960): 414–39.

————. Review of Marconi 1966. *Gnomon* 43 (1971): 680–87.

Maurach, Gregor. "Lieben Mädchen Männer? Zu Naevius fr. 36 Ribbeck (*Corollaria*)." In *Skenika: Beiträge zum antiken Theater und seiner Rezeption. Festschrift zum 65. Geburtstag von H. D. Blume*, edited by S. Gödde, 151. Darmstadt, 2000.

GENERAL BIBLIOGRAPHY

Mazzarino, Antonio. "Appunti sul *bellum Poenicum* di Naevio." *Helikon* 5 (1965): 157–58; 6 (1966): 639–44.

———. "I Feaci nell'*Odusia* di Livio Andronico." *Helikon* 18–19 (1978–79): 387–90.

Meini, Linda. "Né fiore né feccia." *Lexis* 22 (2004): 415–17.

Mengoni, Ettore. "Livio Andronico *Odusia* fr. 32 Büch. (= 38 Warm., 29 Lench., 19 Mar.). L'originale omerico, la forma linguistica." *Annali della Fac. di Let. e Filos. dell' Univ. di Macerata* 17 (1984): 337–49.

Merula, Paulus, ed. *Q. Enni, poetae cum primis censendi annalium libb. XIIX quae apud varios auctores superant fragmenta conlecta composita inlustrata.* Leiden, 1595.

Mesk, J. "Die römische Gründungssage und Naevius." *WS* 36 (1914): 1–35.

Mette, Hans Joachim. "Die römische Tragödie und die Neufunde zur griechischen Tragödie (insbesondere für die Jahre 1945–1964)." *Lustrum* 9 (1964): 5–200.

Molinelli, Marco. "Allitterazione e hapax legomena in Nevio. Nota a Com. 57 e 76 R." *AFML* 16 (1983): 213–20.

———. "Per l'interpretazione dell'aggettivo *citrosus*. Nota a Nevio, *Bellum Punicum*, fr. 10 Morel (22 Strzelecki; 19 Büchner)." *Göttinger Forum für Altertumswissenschaft* 7 (2004): 87–111.

———. "Lingua e stile in Nevio: il caso di *exanimabiliter* (Nevio, Com. 35 R³)." *Orpheus* 27 (2006): 92–100.

———. "*Prospica* e *despica*: due probabili sostantivi: per l'interpretazione di Nevio, Com. 25 R³." *Maia* 60 (2008): 201–13.

———. "Pantaleo Pisatilis: Nevio, Com. 131 R³." *Maia* 62 (2010): 236–39.

Monacelli, Lidia. "La tradizione e il testo a proposito di Cecilio Stazio." *Schol(i)a* 7 (2005): 39–79.

Monaco, G. "L'epistola nel teatro antico." *Dioniso* 39 (1965): 334–51.

Monda, Salvatore. "Le citazioni di Cecilio Stazio nella *Pro Caelio* di Cicerone." *Giornale italiano di filologia* 50.1 (1998): 23–29.

Morelli, Giuseppe. "La *gratulatio* di Amulio nel *Bellum Poenicum* di Nevio." *Studi Urbinati* 39 (1965): 130–55.

———. "Il modello greco della Danae di Nevio." In *Poesia latina in frammenti. Miscellanea filologica*, edited by G. Puccioni, 85–101. Pubblicazioni dell'Istituto di filologia classica dell'Università di Genova 39. Genova, 1974.

———. "Naev. *Bell. Poen.* 18 Mariotti (26 Strzelecki)." In *Mnemosynum. Studi in onore di Alfredo Ghiselli*, 445–50. Bologna, 1989.

Mueller, C. O., ed. *Sexti Pompei Festi De verborum significatione quae supersunt, cum Pauli epitome, emendata et annotata.* Leipzig, [1]1839 / [2]1880.

Negri, A. "Il *Plocium* di Menandro e di Cecilio." *Dioniso* 60 (1990): 54–57.

Negro, Innocenzo. *Studio su Cecilio Stazio*. Firenze, 1919.

Neumann, Günter. "Menanders ΑΝΔΡΟΓΥΝΟΣ." *Hermes* 81 (1953): 491–96.

Oniga, Renato. "*Importunae undae*. Livio Andronico *Od.* fr. 18 Büchner." *QUCC* n.s. 55 (1997): 43–47.

Ooms, Cornelia Willemina. *Studies on the Language of Caecilius Statius*. PhD diss., University of Minnesota, 1977.

Oppermann, Hans. "Zur Entwicklung der Fabula Palliata." *Hermes* 74 (1939): 113–29.

Paponi, Silvia. *Per una nuova edizione di Naevio comico*. Pisa, 2005.

———. "La funzione del prologo in Nevio." *Aevum Antiquum* 84 (2010): 145–60.

Paratore, Ettore. "Ancora su Naevio, *Bellum Poenicum*, fr. 23 Morel." In *Forschungen zur römischen Literatur. Festschrift zum 60. Geburtstag von Karl Büchner*, edited by Walter Wimmel, 224–43. Wiesbaden, 1970.

Parroni, Piergiorgio. "Nota a Liv. Andr. 18 Blänsdorf." In *Amicitiae Templa Serena. Studi in onore di Giuseppe Aricò*, edited by Luigi Castagna and Chiara Riboldi, 2:1213–19. Milano, 2008.

Pascal, Carlo. "Un poeta comico milanese nell'antica Roma." In Pascal Carlo, *Feste e poesie antiche*, 151–82. Milano, 1926.

Pasoli, Elio. "Sul frammento 21 Morel del *Bellum Poenicum* di Nevio." In *Poesia latina in frammenti. Miscellanea filologica*, edited by G. Puccioni, 67–83. Pubblicazioni dell'Istituto di filologia classica dell'Università di Genova 39. Genova, 1974.

Pasquali, Giorgio. *Preistoria della poesia romana*, con un saggio introduttivo di S. Timpanaro. Firenze, [2]1981 [Firenze, [1]1936].

Perna, Rafaelle. *Livio Andronico. Poeta di Puglia*. Bari, 1987.

Perutelli, Alessandro. "Note a Cecilio Stazio." In Alessandro Perutelli, *Frustula poetarum: Contributi ai poeti latini in frammenti*, 11–30. Bologna, 2002.

———. "Liv. Andr. *Odusia* 1." *Philologus* 149 (2005): 162–63.

Pighi, Giovanni, B. "Su alcuni frammenti della *Odissia Vetus*." *Euphrosyne* n.s. 8 (1977): 149–60.

Pisani, Vittore. *Testi latini arcaici e volgari, con commento glottologico*. Torino, ³1975 [¹1950, ²1960].

Pociña, Andrés. "El comediógrafo Cecilio Estacio." *Estudios clásicos* 25 (1981–83): 63–78.

Questa, Cesare. "Tentativo di interpretazione metrica di Cecilio Stazio vv. 142–157 R (*Plocium*)." In *Poesia latina in frammenti. Miscellanea filologica*, edited by G. Puccioni, 132–77. Pubblicazioni dell'Istituto di filologia classica dell'Università di Genova 39. Genova, 1974.

Reggiani, Renato. "Sulla morte di Cecilio Stazio. Una messa a punto del problema." *Prometheus* 3 (1977): 69–74.

Ribbeck, Otto. *Die römische Tragödie im Zeitalter der Republik*. Leipzig, 1875 [repr. with introduction by W.-H. Friedrich. Hildesheim, 1986].

Richlin, Amy. *Slave Theater in the Roman Republic: Plautus and Popular Comedy*. Cambridge, 2017.

Riedweg, Christoph. "Menander in Rom: Beobachtungen zu Caecilius Statius Plocium fr. I (136–53 Guardì)." In *Intertextualität in der griechisch-römischen Komödie*, edited by Niall W. Slater and Bernhard Zimmermann, 133–59. Drama 2. Stuttgart, 1993.

Ritschl, Friedrich Wilhelm. *Parerga zu Plautus und Terenz. Vol. 1*. Berlin, 1845.

———. *Opuscula Philologica. Vol. II*. Leipzig, 1868.

———. *Opuscula Philologica. Vol. III, ad litteras Latinas spectantia*. Leipzig, 1877 [repr. 2018].

Robson, D. O. "The Nationality of the Poet Caecilius Statius." *AJP* 59 (1938): 301–8.

Rocca, Rosanna. "Caecilius Statius Mimicus?" *Maia* 29–30 (1977–78): 107–11.

Ronconi, Alessandro. *Interpreti latini di Omero*. Torino, 1973.

Rossi, S. "Navius, Naevius et Novius." *GIF* 18 (1965): 334–36.

Rostagni, Augusto. "Equos Trioanus sive de vetere Romanorum fabula ex hellenisticis expressa." *RIFC* 44 (1916): 379–97 [repr. in Augusto Rostagni, *Scritti minori*. Vol. 2.2, *Romana*, 3–22. Torino, 1956].

Rowell, Henry, T. "The Original Form of Naevius' *Bellum Punicum*." *AJPh* 68 (1947): 21–26.

———. "The 'Campanian' Origin of C. Naevius and Its Literary Attestation." *Memoirs of the American Academy in Rome* 19 (1949): 15–33.

———. "The Scholium on Naevius in *Parisinus Latinus* 7930." *AJPh* 78 (1957): 1–22.

Rychlewska, Ludovika, ed. *Turpilii fragmenta*. Leipzig, 1971.

———. "Caecilius Statius, poeta vetus novusque." *Eos* 78 (1990): 297–314.

Sabbadini, Salvatore. *Nevio*. Udine, 1935.

Sanford, Eva Matthews. "The Tragedies of Livius Andronicus." *CJ* 18 (1922/23): 274–85.

Scafuro, Adele C. *The Forensic Stage: Settling Disputes in Graeco-Roman New Comedy*. Cambridge, 1997.

Scarsi, Mariangela. "Naev. *B.P.* fr. 23 Mo., Strz. in due lemmi di Nonio." *Studi Noniani* 12 (1987): 189–202.

Schaaf, L. "Die Todesjahre des Naevius und des Plautus in der antiken Überlieferung." *RhM* 122 (1979): 24–33.

Schierl, Petra. *Die Tragödien des Pacuvius*. Texte und Komentare 28. Berlin / New York, 2006.

Schwarte, K.-H. "Naevius, Ennius und der Beginn des Ersten Punischen Krieges." *Historia* 21 (1972): 206–23.

Sciarrino, Enrica. "The Introduction of Epic in Rome: Cultural Thefts and Social Contests." *Arethusa* 39 (2006): 449–69.

Seele, Astrid. "Vergnügliches Übersetzen." *Der Altsprachliche Unterricht* 35 (1992): 21–33.

Segal, Erich. *Roman Laughter: The Comedy of Plautus.* Harvard Studies in Comparative Literature 29. Cambridge, MA, [1]1968; New York, [2]1987.

Serrao, Gregorio. "Nevio *Bellum Poenicum* fr. 23 Mo." *Helikon* 5 (1965): 514–31.

Sheets, George, A. "The Dialect Gloss, Hellenistic Poetics and Livius Andronicus." *AJPh* 102 (1981): 58–78.

Skutsch, Otto. "Two Notes on Naevius." *CR* n.s. 1 (1951): 146–47.

———. "Caecilius 142–45." *Liverpool Classical Monthly* 10.1 (Jan. 1985): 9.

Spengel, Andreas. "Zu den Fragmenten der lateinischen Tragiker." *Blätter für das bayerische Gymnasialwesen* 38 (1899): 385–416.

Strzelecki, W. *De Naeviano Belli Punici carmine quaestiones selectae.* Kraków, 1935

———. "Miscellanea Naeviana." *Eos* 49 (1957–58): 65–70.

Suerbaum, Werner. *Untersuchungen zur Selbstdarstellung älterer römischer Dichter. Livius Andronicus, Naevius, Ennius.* Spudasmata 19. Hildesheim, 1968.

———. "Zum Umfang der Bücher in der archaischen lateinischen Dichtung: Naevius, Ennius, Lukrez und Livius Andronicus auf Papyrus-Rollen." *ZPE* 92 (1992): 153–73.

———. "Religiöse Identitäts- und Alteritätsangebote im *Equos Troianus* und im *Lycurgus* des Naevius." In Manuwald 2000a, 185–98.

———. "Naevius comicus. Der Komödiendichter Naevius in der neueren Forschung." In *Dramatische Wäldchen: Festschrift für Eckard Lefèvre zum 65. Geburts-*

tag, edited by Ekkehard Stärk and Gregor Vogt-Spira, 301–20. Hildesheim, 2000b.

―――, ed. *Handbuch der lateinischen Literatur der Antike. Erster Band. Die archaische Literatur. Von den Anfängen bis Sullas Tod. Die vorliterarische Periode und die Zeit von 240–78 v. Chr. (HLL 1).* HbdA VIII.I. München, 2002.

Suess, W. "Zur Cistellaria des Plautus." *RhM* 84 (1935): 97–141.

Tandoi, V. "Donato e la Lupus di Nevio." In *Poesia latina in frammenti. Miscellanea filologica*, edited by G. Puccioni, 263–73. Pubblicazioni dell'Istituto di filologia classica dell'Università di Genova 39. Genova, 1974.

―――. "Sul frammento neviano di Vibe (*Praet.* 5 sg. Klotz) in rapporto con Fabio Pittore." *Studi urbinati* 49 (1975): 61–71.

Täubler, Eugen. "Naeviana." *Hermes* 57 (1922): 156–60.

Terzaghi, Nicola. "Studi sull'antica poesia latina. Due tragedie di Livio Andronico, 1 *Equos Troianus*, 2 *Aegisthus*." *ATT* 60 (1925): 660–74 [repr. in Nicola Terzaghi, *Studia Graeca et Latina (1901–1956)*, 685–700. Torino, 1963].

Teuffel, Wilhelm Sigmund. *Caecilius Statius, Pacuvius, Attius, Afranius als Probe einer Bearbeitung der Römischen Litteraturgeschichte.* Tübingen, 1858.

Thomas, E., and G. M. Lee. "Notes de Lecture." *Latomus* 24.4 (1965): 951–55.

Timpanaro, Sebastiano. "Note a Livio Andronico, Ennio, Varrone, Virgilio." *Annali della Scuola Normale Superiore di Pisa* 18 (1949): 186–204.

―――. *Contributi di filologia e di storia della lingua Latina.* Roma, 1978.

Tolkiehn, Johannes. "Zu Livius Andronicus." *JKPh* 153 (1896): 861–62.

Tovar, A. "Altlatein und Romanisch: *sarrare* nicht *sardare*." *Glotta* 46 (1968): 267–74.

Traina, Alfonso. "Sulla *Odyssia* di Livio Andronico." *Paideia* 8 (1953a): 185–92.

———. "Naevianum. (Trag. 29 Ribb[3])." *Latinitas* 2 (1953b): 131–36.

———. "*pervellit pedem* (Naev. Com. 78 Ribb.[3])." In *Miscellanea Critica* 2, 343–47. Leipzig, 1965.

———. *Vortit barbare. Le traduzioni poetiche da Livio Andronico a Cicerone, Seconda edizione riveduta e aggiornata.* Roma, 1974 [[1]1970].

———. "Dal Morel al Büchner. In margine alla nuova edizione dei *Fragmenta Poetarum Latinorum*." *RFIC* 113 (1985): 96–119.

Ussani, Vincento, Jr. "Livio Andronico *Odys*. fr. 16 M." *Maia* 9 (1957): 144–53.

Verrusio, Maria. *Livio Andronico e la sua traduzione dell' Odissea omerica.* Napoli, 1942 [repr. Roma, 1977].

Warnecke, "Zur *Agitatoria* des Naevius." *RhM* 79 (1939): 411.

Waszink, Jan Hendrik. "Camena." *C&M* 17 (1956): 139–48.

———. "Tradition and Personal Achievement in Early Latin Literature." *Mnemosyne* 13 (1960): 16–33.

———. "Zum Anfangsstadium der römischen Literatur." *ANRW* I 2 (1972): 869–927.

Webster, T. B. L. *Studies in Menander.* Manchester, 1950.

———. Review of "Menander Vol. II. Reliquiae apud veteres scriptores servatae by A. Koerte." *JHS* 75 (1955): 159–60.

GENERAL BIBLIOGRAPHY

Welsh, Jarrett, T. "Accius, Porcius Licinus, and the Beginning of Latin Literature." *JRS* 101 (2011): 31–50.

Williams, Gordon W. *Tradition and Originality in Roman Poetry*. Oxford, 1968.

Wimmel, Walter. "Vergil und das Atlantenfragment des Naevius." *Wiener Studien* 83 (1970): 84–100.

Wright, John. *Dancing in Chains. The Stylistic Unity of the Comoedia Palliata*. Papers and Monographs of the American Academy in Rome XXV. Roma, 1974.

Zander, Carl, ed. *Versus saturnii, tertiis curis collegit et recensuit et examinavit*. Lund / Leipzig, 1918.

Zehnacker, H., and J.-Cl. Fredouille. *Littérature latine*. Paris, 1993.

Zetzel, James E. G. *Critics, Compilers, and Commentators. An Introduction to Roman Philology, 200 BCE–800 CE*. Oxford, 2018.

Zicàri, M. "Schedae sex." *Philologus* 102 (1958): 154–57.

LIVIUS ANDRONICUS

INTRODUCTION

LIFE

Livius Andronicus was, according to Roman literary tradition, a half-Greek (T 12) from Tarentum in Southern Italy (T 2) who came to Rome and served as a tutor in the family of M. Livius Salinator (T 2, 16). There were two Roman aristocrats of this name. The elder of these (henceforth Salinator [1]) was born around 274 BC and is recorded as being president of a priestly college (*magister Xvir. sac. fac.*) at the time of the *Ludi saeculares* in 236 BC. His son, M. Livius M. f. Salinator (henceforth Salinator [2]), was born around 254 BC, became consul in 219 and 207 BC, defeated Hasdrubal, Hannibal's brother, at a battle near Sena on the river Metaurus in 207 BC, and subsequently became dictator. There was a conflict between Rome and Tarentum in 272 BC, and Andronicus, then perhaps around the age of twenty, could have been taken to Rome on that occasion. The father of Salinator [1] could have acquired the well-educated Andronicus shortly after 272 BC to serve as tutor for his son. Salinator [1] probably kept Andronicus in his service after his father's death and entrusted him with the education of his own son Salinator [2]. When Salinator [2] had completed the early stage of his education around the age of fourteen, in around 240 BC, his tutor Andronicus was probably freed by Salinator [1] in recognition of his services to the family. This was the year in which Andronicus is said to have produced his first drama on stage in Rome (T 2, 3, 4, 13).

The next datable event in Andronicus' long life takes place in the year 207 BC, when he must have been around eighty years old. In May or early June 207, in the build-up to the battle of June 23 on the Metaurus, Andronicus was commissioned by the pontiffs to compose a new hymn in honor of Juno Regina (Juno the Queen). This hymn was part of an expiatory ceremony in reaction to portents that had followed the news of Hasdrubal's crossing the Alps to invade Italy from Spain. It was to be sung by a chorus of twenty-seven virgins in a procession across the city. When they were rehearsing in the temple of Jupiter Stator, lightning struck the temple of Juno Regina on the Aventine. Immediately, the decemvirs, including Salinator [2], who subsequently defeated Hasdrubal, took over the organization of the event and put on an elaborate procession in Greek style with the virgins singing their hymn in procession to Juno Regina's temple. Andronicus' connections with the influential Livii Salinatores would have eased his designation as the poet to compose this important public hymn. Festus (T 14) tells us that, as a reward for the success of this hymn, a college of writers and dramatists was established in his honor, which was allowed to meet and make offerings in the temple of Minerva on the Aventine.[1]

It is Cicero (T 2, 3, 4), based on his reading of ancient registers of dramatic performances (*antiqui commentarii*,

---

[1] For this college and its relation to the *collegium poetarum* mentioned by Val. Max. 3.7.11, see Horsfall 1976.

T 2), compiled by the *aediles*,[2] and on the evidence of his friend Atticus in his *liber annalis*, who informs us that Andronicus was the first to produce drama on the stage at Rome in 240 BC.[3] The same information with the same consuls' names is reported by Gellius (T 13). Cassiodorus (T 20) gives different consuls' names and indicates that Andronicus produced a tragedy and a comedy for the first time not in 240 BC but in 239 BC. Cassiodorus could be confusing the year with that of Ennius' birth, mentioned in the same context in his likely sources, such as Cicero (cf. T 2). The date of 240 BC for Andronicus' first play is accepted by most ancient and modern scholars.[4] However, Cicero also reports (T 2) that the poet and scholar Accius (170–86 BC) favored a later date.[5] Accius claimed that Andronicus was captured from Tarentum in 209 BC, when

---

[2] Minor public officials who were in charge of putting on the games.

[3] Dahlmann (1962, 584) argues that Varro's lost *On Poets* (*De poetis*) was Atticus' (and Cicero's) source for the date 240 BC.

[4] See D'Anna 1953; Douglas 1966, 3–4; Suerbaum 1968, 1ff., 297ff.; Waszink 1972, 873–74; Grimal 1975, 251–52; Verrusio 1977, 9ff.; Gruen 1990, 80ff.; Zehnacker and Fredouille 1993, 18–20; Grimal 1994, 67, 73, 527n1; Dangel 1995, 382, 388; Goldberg 1995, 5, 28–29; Kaster 1995, 49; Lehmann 2002, 57–89; Manuwald 2011, 188–89; Feeney 2016, 65–66; Viredaz 2020, 25–27.

[5] On Accius and his influence on Varro, see Dangel 1995, 26 and n. 49, 29 and n. 54, 48 and n. 100, 49 and n. 101, 51 and n. 106. In this case Varro in his *De poetis* deliberately rejected the conclusions of his master on the date of Livius Andronicus' first dramatic production. See Lehmann 2002, 60.

that town was taken by the Romans, and produced his first play in 197 BC at the games put on by M. Livius Salinator in that year. These were the *Ludi Iuventatis* that Salinator [2] had vowed to establish after the Roman victory over Hasdrubal at the battle of Sena in 207 BC.[6] This later chronology, originating with Accius, may have been followed by some ancient scholars such as Suetonius, since his lost *Lives of Poets* influenced Jerome's chronology (see Kaster 1995, 49), which puts Andronicus' *floruit* at 188/7 BC (T 16).[7] Cicero (T 2) rejects Accius' chronology on the grounds that it would make him younger than Plautus and Naevius, whereas the Roman tradition regarded Andronicus as the founder of Latin literature. Accius' relative dating of Homer and Hesiod was thought by later scholars to be unreliable (Gell. *NA* 3.11.4–5), and his dating of Andronicus may have been no better. Indeed, on this late chronology it would have been difficult for Andronicus to have become so established a literary figure in Rome as to have been commissioned, a mere two years after his arrival there, to compose the nationally important hymn to Juno Regina. It is quite possible that Andronicus did come from Tarentum, where Roman influence had been an important feature since the end of the Pyrrhic War in 272 BC, but some argue he could not have been captured as a slave before the defeat of Tarentum in 209 BC.[8] It is of

[6] Livy 36.36.5 dates Salinator's dedication of the temple of Iuventas to 191 BC.

[7] The two main modern defenders of Accius' chronology are Mattingly 1957 and 1971, and Marconi 1966.

[8] On the relations between Rome and Tarentum at this period, see Marconi 1966, 130–32.

course possible that Andronicus could have been working as a slave tutor to an aristocratic family in Tarentum at the time of his capture in 272 BC. It is clear that Andronicus was familiar with Greek literature. Suetonius (T 12) describes him, along with Ennius, as a *semigraecus* ("half-Greek"), who earned his living by interpreting Greek literature and giving readings of his own works in Latin.

Whichever chronology is accepted, and that suggested by Cicero seems preferable, the ancient tradition is unanimous in making Livius Andronicus the initiator of Latin literature. He is described as the first to introduce drama by Cicero (T 2, 3, 4), Gellius (T 13), and Evanthius (T 17), the first to introduce comedy by Scholia to Horace (T 6e) and Diomedes (T 18), and the first to introduce tragedy and comedy by Donatus (T 15), Cassiodorus (T 20), and *Glossaria Latina* (T 21).

NAME

In our earliest sources, Cicero, Horace, Livy, and Suetonius, the poet is known simply as Livius (T 1–6a, 7–9, 10, 12). This is probably, in accordance with the naming practice for freedmen, the *gentilicium* of the patron who freed him, M. Livius Salinator. The *cognomen* Andronicus, probably his original Greek name, occurs first in Quintilian (T 11), but its use by Festus (T 14) suggests it goes back to Festus' Augustan source, Verrius Flaccus.[9] In later commentators and grammarians, the simple Livius

---

[9] However, *cognomina* for freedmen are not preserved on inscriptions until 100 BC (see Gordon 1935). So Livius may not have used his original Greek name in this way.

remains the norm (in Gellius, Charisius, Nonius, Porphyrio, Festus, Priscian, Servius Danielis, and Isidore), but occasional instances of Livius Andronicus are found, so in Gellius (*Od.* F 1), Porphyrio (T 6b), Scholia to Horace (T 6e), Diomedes (T 18), Terentianus Maurus (*Trag.* F 32), Priscian (*Od.* F 2, 28, 30; Ps.-Andr. *Od.* F 1), Servius Danielis (T 19). The *praenomen* L. (Lucius) is given by Gellius (T 13) and Cassiodorus (T 20), whereas the *praenomen* T. (Titus) in Jerome (T 16) must be due to confusion with the more famous historian, Titus Livius (Livy).

WORKS

Andronicus' surviving fragments include tragedy, comedy, and epic (a translation/adaptation into Latin of Homer's *Odyssey*). He is also credited with the composition of a hymn to Juno for use in a public procession, of which nothing is extant (T 8, 9, 14). We have no clear evidence for the relative dating of these works. However, if the traditional dates for his first dramatic works (240 BC) and for the hymn to Juno (207 BC) are correct, they must have come at the beginning and the end, respectively, of his very long career. It is generally assumed without any firm evidence that the *Odyssia* came toward the end of his career. However, this translation/adaptation could have been a long process, and early parts of it, perhaps used in his capacity as a teacher of literature, could have led to his being commissioned to put on drama at the Roman Games of 240 BC.[10]

We know the titles of eight tragedies: *Achilles*, *Ae-*

[10] See Viredaz 2020, 27–28, 43.

gisthus, *Aias Mastigophorus*, *Andromeda*, *Danae*, *Equus Troianus*, *Hermiona*, and *Tereus*. Varro knew of a tragedy involving Teucer (*Trag. Inc.* t 1). Two verses of a tragedy named *Antiopa* are attributed by Nonius (p. 170.12–14 M. = 250 L.) to Andronicus, but most editors would now place them in a play of that name by Pacuvius, where they make perfect sense.[11] A hymn to Diana in a tragedy named *Ino* (*Trag.* F 32) is probably spurious, since it is written in a form of hexameter not used in the Latin of Andronicus' time. In tragedy, Andronicus' most frequent subject is the Trojan War (so in *Achilles*, *Aegisthus*, *Aias Mastigophorus*, *Equus Troianus*, *Hermiona*). As we see from Naevius' *Bellum Punicum*, the Romans linked the fall of Troy with the foundation of their own state by descendants of the Trojan fugitives, including Aeneas. A nation recently victorious in the First Punic War over the Carthaginians was also deeply concerned with questions of how the victors should behave toward their defeated enemies. Themes of fairness and piety figure prominently in the surviving fragments. In *Aegisthus*, for example, *Trag.* F 9 discusses the fair distribution of booty among the victors after the fall of Troy. In the same play, Agamemnon's piety (*Trag.* F 7) and concern for the feelings of the defeated Cassandra (*Trag.* F 6) are contrasted with Aegisthus' autocratic behavior (*Trag.* F 2). In *Aias Mastigophorus*, the hero is struck by the unfairness of the fact that the praise he won for his courage so quickly fades away (*Trag.* F 11). Since the fragments of Andronicus' tragedies are so few and so restricted in their content, it is impossible to tell what their Greek model was. Tragic titles of the same name are found

[11] See Schierl 2006, 107–8; Manuwald 2011, 190n14.

in Sophocles (*Aiax, Hermiona, Tereus*) and in Euripides (*Andromeda, Danae*), while *Aegisthus* deals with the same subject matter as Aeschylus' *Agamemnon*. Lost Alexandrian models for some plays (e.g., *Aegisthus, Aiax*) cannot be ruled out. It is also possible that Andronicus' originality extended to developing tragedies of his own construction based on Greek epic material on the Trojan War (e.g., *Achilles, Equus Troianus*). This is an area of literature in which his own *Odyssia* shows he was well versed. All the tragic titles surviving from Andronicus were taken up by later, or, in the case of Naevius, near-contemporary, Republican dramatists. We do not know whether Naevius' *Equus Troianus* and *Danae* came before or after Andronicus' plays of the same name. Ennius later produced an *Achilles, Aiax*, and *Andromeda*; Pacuvius a *Hermiona*; and Accius an *Achilles, Aegisthus, Andromeda*, and *Tereus*. How far these writers were influenced by Andronicus' plays as well as by their Greek models is difficult to establish given the fragmentary state of the surviving evidence.

Three titles of comedies from Livius Andronicus are known to us from Festus. Two of these, *Gladiolus* (*Com.* F 1) and *Ludius* (*Com.* F 2), are certain, whereas a third, † *Virgo* † (*Com.* F 4), is probably corrupt. Our sources attribute to him the role of initiator of Greek-based New Comedy in Rome (T 15, 18, 20, 21). On the evidence of the number of surviving fragments, it seems clear that his main interest lay with tragedy (thirty-one fragments) rather than comedy (six fragments). In this he may be contrasted with Naevius, who in drama has a preponderance of comic fragments. Andronicus' comic titles are in

Latin, but Greek equivalents for two of them were used by Greek comic poets: *Gladiolus* by Philemon and Diphilus, and *Ludius* by Antiphanes and Magnes (for full references to these Greek plays, see the introductions to *Com.* F 1 and 2). Andronicus' comic fragments are distinguished in style and content from their tragic counterparts. Mention of fleas, bugs, and lice in *Com.* F 1, and the use of the colloquial term of abuse "blockhead" in *Com.* F 5, are characteristic of comedy. At least two of the fragments, *Com.* F 1 and *Com.* F 6, seem to involve the comic braggart warrior figure.

We are told that Andronicus not only wrote plays but also acted in his own compositions (T 7: Livy; T 10: Valerius Maximus; T 17: Evanthius). Livy (T 7; followed by Valerius Maximus, T 10) further tells us he had a stand-in for the sung sections of his plays in order to save his voice, and from his time actors merely accompanied the sung meters with gestures and used their voice only in the spoken dialogue sections.[12] Most of Andronicus' dramatic works, both comedy and tragedy, are written in Greek-based meters, the iambic senarius and the trochaic septenarius, which remained current in the Roman theater till well into the first century BC. A passage from the *Equus Troianus* quoted by Nonius (*Trag.* F 14) in a mixture of trochaic and cretic meters probably belongs to a sung monody. Although the publicly performed hymn for Juno (T 8, 9, 14) has left no trace, Suerbaum (2002, 99) suggests

---

[12] The bibliography on this controversial statement by Livy (at 7.2.8) is long. For a summary of the question, see Oakley 1998, 40.

11

that the remark in Servius Danielis (T 19) about Andronicus telling of Africans triumphing over Romans may have come from this hymn.

Perhaps Andronicus' most famous work is his adaptation into Latin Saturnians of Homer's *Odyssey*. Suerbaum (2002) argues that this translation was much abbreviated and did not attempt to reproduce Homer's work in full. However, Viredaz (2020, 37) questions this thesis and argues for a more extensive work. The range of the quotations remaining[13] and their closeness in wording to Homer's original would argue that the work was in fact longer than Suerbaum suggests and need not have been restricted to a single roll. Andronicus did not know of the twenty-four-book division introduced after his time by the Alexandrian scholar Aristarchus at the beginning of the second century BC (see Courtney 1993, 46). In some cases, differences between Homer's text and Andronicus' translation may be accounted for by the fact that the text available to Andronicus may have differed from modern versions. So in *Od.* F 24 the mention of Circe in Andronicus is not present in our Greek. However, where our version of Homer says δώματα καλά ("beautiful house"), the indirect tradition reveals a variant reading δώματα Κίρκης ("Circe's house"), which is probably what Andronicus read. Similarly, in *Od.* F 25 Andronicus read and translated αἶψ' ("quickly") in his Greek, whereas we have ἄψ ("again"). Such textual problems may occasionally obscure the general faithfulness of Andronicus' version to the Greek.

[13] Taken from twelve of the twenty-four books of Homer's *Odyssey* (see Goldberg 1995, 46).

It is uncertain what title Andronicus gave to his adaptation of Homer's *Odyssey*. On the evidence of Gellius in *Od.* F 1 and 10, where the title is given in Greek, it is likely that Andronicus used the transliterated title *ODVS-SEIA*.[14] It has been conventional since Knoche (1928) to restore an assumed authentic old Latin spelling *Odusia*, on the basis that *y* for Greek *u* and double consonants were not introduced into Latin spelling until after Andronicus' time. This, however, may be a piece of false archaism. Despite using the Latinized *Ulixes* for Odysseus in his translation, Andronicus may have wished to keep the title as close as possible to the Greek original, as was frequently his practice in the case of the tragedies. None of our ancient sources mention the title *Odusia*, and, even within their own texts, they are inconsistent in their naming of the work. To some extent we may be at the mercy of the textual tradition, and the varied forms attested may all derive from Andronicus' transliteration. The Greek form is used only by Gellius (*Od.* F 1 and 10). The most common form in other authors is *Odyssia* (16 – Cicero, Gellius, Festus, Nonius, Charisius, Servius Danielis, with Festus and Charisius also referring to the *Odyssia vetus*), followed by *Odissia* (4 – Festus, Priscian) and *Odyssea* (2 – Festus, Diomedes). In line with the policy of this edition of using the classical Latin orthography of our source texts instead of attempting to restore the archaic orthography of Andronicus, the work will be referred to as *Odyssia* throughout.

The style of Andronicus' *Odyssia* was grander than that of his tragedies, preserving words and forms that were

[14] So Feeney 2016, 62–63 and nn. 101, 104.

already archaic in his time.[15] The aim is to distance its language from that of everyday speech[16] and to convey to his Roman audience the impression that the text of Homer would have had upon Greek speakers of Andronicus' day. Such features include the first declension genitive singular ending in -*as* (*Od.* F 11, 20, 22), the nominative singular *carnis* for *caro* (*Od.* F 30), the perfect form *gavisi* (*Od.* F 23), and items of lexicon such as *inseco* (*Od.* F 1). Andronicus' adaptation is often reasonably close to Homer in wording, though the proper names are Romanized, e.g., *Ulixes* for *Odysseus* (*Od.* F 15), *Saturnus* for *Cronos* (*Od.* F 2, 13), *Camena* for *Musa* (*Od.* F 1), *Morta* for *moira* (*Od.* F 10), and *Moneta* for *Mnemosyne* (*Od.* F 22). Other concessions were also made to the culture of his Roman audience.[17] In *Od.* F 12, for example, the use of *Graecia* ("Greece") for the land to which Homer's heroes returned from Troy is a Roman term that would not have been available to Homer or his Achaeans. In *Od.* F 9 Andronicus adapts Nestor's reference in Homer to Patroclus as "the peer of gods in council," replacing it with a phrase closer to the language and sentiment of Latin *elogia*, "the greatest hero . . . by far the first of men." Greek metaphors unfamiliar to the Roman ear are toned down. So in *Od.* F 3 the common Homeric idiom "the barrier of your teeth" is too distinctively Greek to be translated literally and is simply replaced by "mouth." Similarly, in *Od.* F 15

[15] See Feeney 2016, 78.

[16] Lehmann 2002, 80.

[17] Goldberg 1995, 67–72; Feeney 2016, 58–59; Viredaz 2020, 32.

Andronicus renders the metaphor expressing fear "Odysseus' knees and heart loosened" with a more acceptably Latin idiom, "the heart of Ulysses went cold with fear." Homer's heart is retained but the unfamiliar loosening knees are dropped. In some cases items familiar to a Roman audience, but alien to the original Greek context, are added to the narrative. So in *Od*. F 17 Nausicaa goes home from a washing expedition with her companions in a *carpentum*, a two-wheeled cart used by the Roman aristocracy, rather than in the four-wheeled cart described by Homer (*Od*. 6.69, 232), which would have been more practical for carrying washing. Andronicus adds an item that could not have been in his Greek text with the aim of endowing the conveyance of the king's daughter with a specifically Roman epic dignity. Although faithful on the whole to the wording of his original, Andronicus' work was intended to serve as a poetic adaptation rather than as a literal translation of Homer's epic.

The native Saturnian meter into which it is translated is problematic, and the license allowed in its scansion is not fully understood.[18] There is some evidence that it was used before Andronicus' time in Latin oracular responses, hymns, epitaphs and incantations.[19] It would perhaps have conveyed an impression of ancient Roman stateliness, which would have commended it to the author, who in his

[18] See Bartsch 1867; Korsch 1868; Leo 1905; Cole 1969; Erasmi 1979; Kruschwitz 2002b; Viredaz 2020, 86–90.

[19] Goldberg 1995, 47; Lehmann 2002, 24–25. For its use in popular nonliterary contexts, see Fraenkel 1927; Gerick 1996; and Kruschwitz 2002a.

dramatic works was perfectly capable of adapting Greek meters to the Latin language. Saturnians have a break, or caesura, mid-line, and one of the mannerisms developed to bridge this break was the use of phrases beginning *filius / filia* ("son / daughter") immediately after the caesura in apposition to a name in the first part of the line, e.g., *Od*. F 13, *sancta puer Saturni filia regina* ("the holy child of Saturn, his royal daughter"). Although perhaps introduced initially to avoid Greek patronymics such as Κρονίδη ("daughter of Cronos"), which had no equivalent in Latin, they seem to have become a standard means of adding dignity to the narrative, even where the Greek has no patronymic (so in *Od*. F 13, 14, 20, 22).[20] As well as adding such genealogical phrases, Andronicus could sometimes omit material. Epithets present in Homer such as "fair-faced" of Nausicaa in *Od*. F 16 and "who works from afar" of Apollo in *Od*. F 20 are omitted in Andronicus' translation. The reason could simply be the shorter length of the Saturnian line compared with Homer's hexameter. In other cases omissions could have been motivated by artistic considerations. In *Od*. F 5, when Telemachus is speaking to the disguised Athena, Homer's more colloquial "come now tell me" is replaced in Andronicus simply by "you must tell me"; similarly, Laodamas' remarks about the destructive nature of the sea in *Od*. F 19 are prefaced in Homer by "for I say there is nothing worse," whereas Andronicus plunges straight in with "nothing wastes." In

[20] Goldberg 1995, 65–66; Viredaz 2020, 90. The same is true of the positioning of *prognatus* and *filius* in nonliterary Saturnians; see Kruschwitz 2002a, 31.

both cases, Homer's colloquial earnestness disappears, to be replaced by a greater feeling of epic dignity.[21]

The fragments of Pseudo-Andronicus, *Odyssia* are set out separately after Andronicus' work, as they are not now considered to have been written by him (see introduction to Pseudo-Andronicus, *Odyssia*). Priscian is the only source to quote these fragments. Unlike Andronicus' work, they are composed in hexameters and are sometimes supplied by Priscian with book numbers (Ps.-Andr. *Od.* F 1, 2). Book numbers for Homer's text were not introduced until after Andronicus' time, and hexameters were probably introduced to Latin by Ennius.[22] These fragments from Priscian, then, are assumed to be an anonymous composition from a date later than that of Ennius.

RECEPTION

Andronicus paved the way for the introduction of Greek-based drama and epic to Rome, as well as working in other genres, such as the hymn. As plays came to be performed more frequently at Roman festivals by the end of the third century BC, his successors followed his lead in the way in which Greek plays and meters came to be adapted for their new Roman environment. Andronicus' contemporaries much appreciated his work, and the conferring in 207 BC of a meeting place for writers and actors in the

---

[21] Goldberg 1995, 69.

[22] Isid. *Orig.* 1.39.6: *hexametros autem Latinos prius fecisse Ennius traditur* ["Ennius is said to have first composed Latin hexameters"].

temple of Minerva on the Aventine in recognition of his poetic achievements (T 14) must have endeared him to his fellow poets.

However, his work soon came to be felt as somewhat old-fashioned, and later writers were less respectful. Early evidence of this comes from the anonymous re-writing of his epic in hexameters, perhaps within a generation of his death. None of the linguistic and metrical characteristics of these hexameters demands a *terminus post quem* later than the end of the third century BC.[23] Cicero (T 2) refers to Andronicus' *Odyssia* as a work of Daedalus, that is, archaic and primitive, and judges his plays not to be worth a second reading. We hear from Horace, who finds the *Odyssia* harsh and old-fashioned, of his bitter experience of being taught this work as a school text (T 6a). Similarly, Livy (T 8) found the hymn to Juno Regina repellent and uncouth for a modern audience.

As with Naevius, it is this same archaic character of his language, which later literary writers found unacceptable, that made Andronicus a prime target for excerptors and grammatical commentators. Their quotations furnish us with our only knowledge of his text. Our best source for the tragedies is Nonius, who quotes twenty tragic fragments, all but one with titles. Next comes Festus/Paulus with ten quotations, none of which comes with a title. A single titleless quotation from Priscian completes the total of thirty-one fragments. The rare (six in all) comic fragments are transmitted (in the late second century AD) by Festus (5), two with titles, and (in the early fourth century AD) by Vopiscus (1). Excluding the hexameter fragments

[23] Viredaz 2020, 45–48.

quoted by Priscian and assigned now to a Pseudo-Livius Andronicus, Andronicus' thirty-three *Odyssia* fragments come, in order of frequency, from Priscian (11), Festus / Paulus (9), Nonius (5), Gellius (4), and one each from Charisius, Diomedes, Servius, and Isidore. How many of these later authors still had access to a full text is uncertain. Whatever the fate of his actual text in the generations that followed, the importance of Livius Andronicus rests firmly on his achievements as an innovator in introducing Greek-based literature to Rome.

THE ARRANGEMENT OF MATERIAL IN THIS EDITION

For Livius Andronicus, the tragedies, followed by the comedies, are presented in alphabetical order of the title, with individual fragments under each play being quoted in the chronological order of the source text. The *Odyssia* fragments (including those from Pseudo-Andronicus) are quoted in the order of the Homeric book from which they are thought to derive; in some cases this position has to be based on likelihood rather than certainty.

TESTIMONIA (T 1–21)

T 1 Cic. *Leg.* 2.39 [= T 3 Naevius]

illud quidem ‹video› [*suppl. Vahlen*]: quae solebant quon-
dam compleri severitate iucunda Livianis et Naevianis
modis, nunc ut eadem exsultent ‹et cavea› [*add. Ziegler*]
... [*lac. proposuit Ziegler*] cervices oculosque pariter cum
modorum flexionibus torqueant.

T 2 Cic. *Brut.* 71–73 [= *BP* t 1 Naevius; T 18 Ennius]

Odyssia Latina est sic tamquam opus aliquod Daedali et
Livianae fabulae non satis dignae quae iterum legantur.
[72] atqui hic Livius primus fabulam C. Claudio Caeci filio
et M. Tuditano consulibus docuit anno ipso ante quam
natus est Ennius, post Romam conditam autem quarto
decimo et quingentesimo, ut hic ait, quem nos sequimur;
est enim inter scriptores de numero annorum controver-
sia. Accius autem a Q. Maximo quintum consule captum

---

1 Cicero's friend Atticus, who, in his *liber annalis* following
the lead of Varro (*De poetis*), established the year 240 BC as
the correct date (see Dahlmann 1962, 584; Lehmann 2002,
58n7). 2 The poet and scholar Accius, in his *Didascalia*,
written at the end of the second century BC, knowing that Livius
Andronicus was from Tarentum, argued that he must have been

TESTIMONIA (T 1–21)

T 1 Cicero, *On the Laws*

I ‹observe› this,[1] that those places, which once used to be
filled with the sweet severity of the music of Livius and
Naevius [see T 2 n. 6], the same now exult, ‹and the audience›... now twist their necks and turn their eyes in time
with the modulations of [our modern] meters.

[1] This passage is spoken by Cicero in dialogue with his friend
Atticus and Cicero's brother Quintus.

T 2 Cicero, *Brutus*

The Latin *Odyssey* [of Livius Andronicus] is, as it were,
like some work of Daedalus, and the plays of Livius are
not worth a second reading. [72] Yet this Livius was the
first to bring a drama on stage in the consulship of Gaius
Claudius, son of Caecus, and Marcus Tuditanus [240 BC,
cf. T 3, 4, 13] in the very year before Ennius was born, in
the 514th year after the founding of Rome, as he says,
whom we follow;[1] for there is an argument among scholars
about the chronology. Accius,[2] however, wrote that Livius

captured when that town was taken by the Romans in 209 BC.
He wrongly assigned his first play to 197 BC. His error was corrected by Varro and Atticus (see Gruen 1990, 80–82; Welsh 2011).

21

Tarento scripsit Livium, annis XXX post quam eum fabulam docuisse et Atticus scribit et nos in antiquis commentariis invenimus, [73] docuisse autem fabulam annis post XI C. Cornelio Q. Minucio consulibus ludis Iuventatis, quos Salinator Senensi proelio voverat. in quo tantus error Acci fuit, ut his consulibus XL annos natus Ennius fuerit; quoi si aequalis fuerit Livius, minor fuit aliquanto is, qui primus fabulam dedit, quam ei, qui multas docuerant ante hos consules, et Plautus et Naevius.

T 3 Cic. *Tusc.* 1.3 [= T 29 Ennius]

doctrina Graecia nos et omni litterarum genere superabat; in quo erat facile vincere non repugnantes. nam cum apud Graecos antiquissimum e doctis genus sit poetarum, si quidem Homerus fuit et Hesiodus ante Romam conditam, Archilochus regnante Romulo, serius poeticam nos acce-

---

[1] Greek lyric poet, 720–676 BC.

was captured at Tarentum by Quintus Maximus in his fifth consulship [209 BC], thirty years after Livius had produced his [first] play, as Atticus writes and as I have found in ancient commentaries.[3] [73] [Accius goes on to say] that Livius produced his first play eleven years after [his capture] in the consulship of Gaius Cornelius and Quintus Minucius [197 BC] at the *Ludi Iuventatis* [*Youth Games*],[4] which Livius Salinator [see T 16 n. 2] had vowed at the battle of Sena.[5] In this Accius' error was so great that under these consuls Ennius was forty years old; if Livius were a contemporary of his, he who was the first to produce a play was somewhat younger than those who had produced many plays before these consuls, both Plautus and Naevius.[6]

[3] The *antiqui commentarii* ("ancient commentaries") are the registers in which the aediles (junior public officials) recorded the plays, authors, and years of production for drama produced at festivals (see D'Anna 1953).   [4] Originally a Roman cult, which at this time was being assimilated to the Greek cult of Hebe.   [5] M. Livius Salinator, a possible patron of Livius Andronicus, defeated the Carthaginian Hasdrubal near the town of Sena in Umbria in 207 BC.   [6] Naevius' plays date to between around 235 BC to 204 BC and those of Plautus to between around 205 to 184 BC.

T 3 Cicero, *Tusculan Disputations*

In learning and in every branch of literature Greece surpassed us: in this it was easy to defeat those who did not fight back. For while among the Greeks the oldest class of intellectuals was that of the poets, if, at any rate, Homer and Hesiod lived before the foundation of Rome and Archilochus[1] in the reign of Romulus, we were rather late to

23

pimus. annis fere CCCCCX post Romam conditam Livius
fabulam dedit C. Claudio, Caeci filio, M. Tuditano consu-
libus, anno ante natum Ennium, qui fuit maior natu quam
Plautus et Naevius. sero igitur a nostris poetae vel cogniti
vel recepti.

T 4 Cic. *Sen.* 50

vidi etiam senem Livium, qui, cum sex annis ante quam
ego natus sum fabulam docuisset Centone Tuditanoque
consulibus, usque ad adulescentiam meam processit ae-
tate.

T 5 Varro, *Ling.* 5.9

non enim videbatur consentaneum quaerere me in eo
verbo quod finxisset Ennius causam, neglegere quod ante
rex Latinus finxisset, cum poeticis multis verbis magis
delecter quam utar, antiquis magis utar quam delecter. an
non potius mea verba illa quae hereditate a Romulo rege
venerunt quam quae a poeta Livio relicta?

admit the art of poetry. About 510 years after the foundation of Rome Livius [Andronicus] produced a play in the consulship of Gaius Claudius, son of Caecus, and Marcus Tuditanus [240 BC, cf. T 2, 4, 13], in the year before the birth of Ennius. [Livius Andronicus] was older than Plautus and Naevius. Poets were thus recognized and welcomed late by our people.

T 4 Cicero, *On Old Age*[1]

I even saw Livius [Andronicus], when he was an old man, who, though he brought out a play in the consulship of Cento and Tuditanus [240 BC, cf. T 2, 3, 13], six years before I was born, yet continued to live until I was a young man.

[1] The dialogue *On Old Age*, dedicated to Cicero's friend Atticus, is set in the year 155 BC. The speaker of this passage is Marcus Porcius Cato, then aged eighty-four, in dialogue with P. Cornelius Scipio Africanus Minor (b. 185 BC, consul 148 and 146 BC) and Gaius Laelius (b. about 190 BC, consul 140 BC).

T 5 Varro, *On the Latin Language*

For it did not seem right for me to search for the source in the case of a word that Ennius had created and to neglect that which king Latinus had created before, since I derive more pleasure than use from many poetic words and derive more use than pleasure from ancient words. Are not those words mine which have come down to me by inheritance from King Romulus, rather than those which have been left behind by the poet Livius [Andronicus]?

T 6

a Hor. *Epist*. 2.1.60–75

60   hos ediscit et hos arto stipata theatro
      spectat Roma potens; habet hos numeratque poetas
      ad nostrum tempus Livi scriptoris ab aevo.
      interdum vulgus rectum videt, est ubi peccat.
      si veteres ita miratur laudatque poetas
65   ut nihil anteferat, nihil illis comparet, errat;
      si quaedam nimis antique, si pleraque dure
      dicere credit eos, ignave multa fatetur,
      et sapit et mecum facit et Iove iudicat aequo.
      non equidem insector delendaque carmina Livi
70   esse reor, memini quae plagosum mihi parvo
      Orbilium dictare; sed emendata videri
      pulchraque et exactis minimum distantia miror;
      inter quae verbum emicuit si forte decorum,
      si versus paulo concinnior unus et alter,
75   iniuste totum ducit venditque poema.

b Porph. ad Hor. *Epist*. 2.1.62

ab aevo Livi scriptoris usque ad nostrum tempus quaedam
recte, quaedam prave iudicat populus. Livium autem dicit
Andronicum, qui primus omnium Latinas fabulas scripsit.

T 6

a Horace, *Epistles*

[60] Mighty Rome learns these poets by heart and watches them when packed in her narrow theater; these she counts and reckons as poets from the age of the writer Livius [Andronicus] down to our own time. Sometimes the common people see the right thing, sometimes they make mistakes. If they admire and praise ancient poets, [65] so as to put nothing above them, to compare nothing with them, they are wrong. If they believe some things they say are too old-fashioned and most things are harsh, if they admit that many things are flat, then they have taste and agree with me and make their judgment with Jove's assent. For myself I do not pursue him and [70] think that the poems of Livius [Andronicus] should be destroyed; poems which I remember Orbilius,[1] fond of beating, dictated to me as a small boy; but that they should be considered finished and beautiful, little short of perfect, amazes me. If by chance among them some appropriate word should shine forth, if one or other of his verses are a little better turned, [75] it is unjust that this should carry and sell the whole poem.

[1] On Orbilius, a rather cantankerous teacher who practiced in Rome from 63 BC, see Suet. *Gram. et rhet.* 8.3–9.5.

b Porphyrio, *Commentary on Horace*

From the age of the writer Livius [Andronicus] up to our own time the people judge some things correctly and other things wrongly. He is talking about Livius Andronicus, who was the first of all [poets] to compose Latin plays.

c Porph. ad Hor. *Epist*. 2.1.69

non censeo, inquit, delendum Livium, et hoc illi honoris causa defero propter vetustatem. ex libris eius saevus, inquit, Orbilius quondam librarius magister mihi dictata praebebat.

d Porph. ad Hor. *Epist*. 2.1.71

non delendum Livium, sed indignor illum pro perfecto et emendato auctore laudari.

e Schol. ad Hor. *Epist*. 2.1.62

Livius antiquissimus poeta fuit Andronicus, qui primus comoedias scripsit.

T 7 Liv. 7.2.8–10

Livius post aliquot annis, qui ab saturis ausus est primus argumento fabulam serere, idem scilicet, id quod omnes tum erant, suorum carminum actor, [9] dicitur, cum saepius revocatus vocem obtudisset, venia petita puerum ad canendum ante tibicinem cum statuisset, canticum egisse

c Porphyrio, *Commentary on Horace*

I do not think, he [Horace] says, that Livius [Andronicus']
[poems] should be destroyed, and this I grant him because
of the honor due to his [Livius'] old age. The fierce Or-
bilius, he [Horace] says, the reading master, once pro-
vided me with dictations from his books.

d Porphyrio, *Commentary on Horace*

I [Horace] do not think, [he says], that Livius [Androni-
cus'] [poems] should be destroyed, but I am indignant that
he is praised as a perfect and polished author.

e Scholia to Horace, *Epistles*

Livius Andronicus was a very old poet, who was the first
to write comedies.

T 7 Livy, *History of Rome*

Livius [Andronicus], some years later, was the first to dare
[to turn] from medleys[1] [cf. T 10] and to compose a play
with a plot. Like everyone else in those days, he acted in
his own plays, [9] and it is said that, since he had made his
voice hoarse through frequent encores, he asked for a fa-
vor, and when he had placed a boy before the piper to sing,
[cf. T 10], he acted the part himself [cf. T 14, 17, 21] with

[1] Livy uses *saturae* ("medleys," the origin of our "satire") to
refer to musical medleys performed with gesture to the accom-
paniment of a flute player (cf. Liv. 7.2.7). According to Livy,
Livius Andronicus was the first to turn from these medleys to a
more structured drama with a plot. The first extant Roman "sat-
ire" in our sense comes from Ennius (*FRL* II, pp. 270–85).

aliquanto magis vigente motu, quia nihil vocis usus impediebat. [10] inde ad manum cantari histrionibus coeptum, diverbiaque tantum ipsorum voci relicta.

T 8 Liv. 27.37.7–13

decrevere item pontifices ut virgines ter novenae per urbem euntes carmen canerent. id cum in Iovis Statoris aede discerent conditum ab Livio poeta carmen, tacta de caelo aedes in Aventino Iunonis reginae . . . [13] tum septem et viginti virgines longam indutae vestem carmen in Iunonem reginam canentes ibant, illa tempestate forsitan laudabile rudibus ingeniis, nunc abhorrens et inconditum si referatur.

T 9 Liv. 31.12.10

carmen praeterea ab ter novenis virginibus cani per urbem iusserunt [decemviri] donumque Iunoni reginae ferri. ea ut fierent C. Aurelius consul ex decemvirorum responso curavit. carmen, sicut patrum memoria Livius, ita tum condidit P. Licinius Tegula.

a somewhat more vigorous movement, since he was not impeded by the use of his voice. [10] From that time actors began to use singers to accompany their gestures, leaving only the dialogue parts for their own voice.

T 8 Livy, *History of Rome*

Likewise the pontiffs[1] decreed that three times nine virgins should sing a hymn as they walked through the city.[2] While they were learning this hymn composed by the poet Livius [Andronicus] [cf. T 14] in the temple of Jupiter Stator, the temple of Juno the Queen on the Aventine hill was struck by lightning . . . [13] Then the twenty-seven virgins, wearing long cloaks, went forth singing the hymn in honor of Juno the Queen, [a song] which at that time perhaps seemed praiseworthy to untrained minds, but now, if repeated, would be repellent and uncouth.

[1] The chief priests of ancient Rome.   [2] The date was 207 BC.

T 9 Livy, *History of Rome*

Furthermore [the decemvirs][1] ordered that a hymn should be sung through the city by three times nine virgins and that a gift should be taken to Juno the Queen. Gaius Aurelius the consul [in 200 BC] saw to this in accordance with the response of the decemvirs. The hymn, which in the memory of our fathers Livius [Andronicus] had composed [cf. T 8], was in this instance written by P. Licinius Tegula.[2]

[1] A college of priests who interpreted the Sibylline Books and dispensed religious advice.   [2] Possibly the Licinius Imbrex mentioned by Gellius, *Attic Nights* 13.23.16, as a writer of comedies.

T 10 Val. Max. 2.4.4

paulatim deinde ludicra ars ad saturarum modos perrep-
sit, a quibus primus omnium poeta Livius ad fabularum
argumenta spectantium animos transtulit, isque sui operis
actor, cum saepius a populo revocatus vocem obtudisset,
adhibito pueri ac tibicinis concentu gesticulationem taci-
tus peregit.

T 11 Quint. *Inst.* 10.2.7

turpe etiam illud est, contentum esse id consequi, quod
imiteris. nam rursus quid erat futurum si nemo plus effe-
cisset eo quem sequebatur? nihil in poetis supra Livium
Andronicum, nihil in historiis supra pontificum annales
haberemus.

T 12 Suet. *Gram. et rhet.* 1.2 [= T 69 Ennius]

initium quoque eius mediocre extitit, siquidem antiquis-
simi doctorum, qui idem et poetae et semigraeci erant—
Livium et Ennium dico, quos utraque lingua domi foris-
que docuisse adnotatum est—nihil amplius quam Graecos
interpretabantur aut si quid ipsi Latine composuissent
praelegebant.

T 10 Valerius Maximus, *Memorable Doings and Sayings*

Then gradually the dramatic art crept toward the use of satiric meters, and from these [cf. T 7] Livius [Andronicus] was the first poet of all to direct the mind of his spectators toward the plots of plays. He [Livius Andronicus] acted in his own works, and since he had made his voice hoarse through being frequently called back by the people [for encores], by using the music of a boy and of a flute player, he performed in gestures without speaking [cf. T 7, 14, 17, 21].

T 11 Quintilian, *The Orator's Education*

This is a disgraceful thing, to be content simply to follow a model you imitate. For what would have happened if no one had achieved more than the one he was following? We would have nothing in poetry to surpass Livius Andronicus and nothing in history beyond the annals of the pontiffs [cf. T 8].

T 12 Suetonius, *Lives of Illustrious Men. Grammarians and Rhetoricians*

The beginning of this [literary study] was also modest, since the oldest of our teachers, who were both poets and half-Greeks—I am referring to Livius [Andronicus] and Ennius, whom it has been noted taught privately and publicly[1] in both languages [Latin and Greek]—did nothing more than interpret the Greeks and give readings of anything they had composed in Latin.

[1] More likely than "at home and abroad" (see Kaster 1995, 51–52 ad. loc.).

T 13 Gell. *NA* 17.21.42

pace cum Poenis facta, consulibus <C.> Claudio Cen-
thone, Appii Caeci filio, et M. Sempronio Tuditano primus
omnium L. Livius poeta fabulas docere Romae coepit post
Sophoclis et Euripidis mortem annis plus fere centum et
sexaginta, post Menandri annis circiter quinquaginta duo-
bus.

T 14 Fest., pp. 446.29–48.4 L.

itaque cum Livius Andronicus bello Punico secundo scrip-
sisset carmen, quod a virginibus est cantatum, quia pros-
perius respublica populi Romani geri coepta est, publice
adtributa est ei in Aventino aedis Minervae, in qua liceret
scribis histrionibusque consistere ac dona ponere; in ho-
norem Livi, quia is et scribebat fabulas et agebat.

T 15 Donat. *Exc. de com.* 5.4

comoediam apud Graecos dubium est quis primus inve-
nerit, apud Romanos certum: et comoediam et tragoe-
diam et togatam primus Livius Andronicus repperit.

T 13 Gellius, *Attic Nights*

When peace had been made with the Carthaginians and the consuls were Gaius Claudius Centho, son of Appius Caecus, and Marcus Sempronius Tuditanus [240 BC, cf. T 2, 3, 4], the poet Lucius[1] Livius [Andronicus] was the first of all to begin staging plays at Rome, more than about one hundred and sixty years after the death of Sophocles and Euripides [both in 406 BC] and about fifty-two years after the death of Menander [292/1 BC].

[1] This is the first mention of the *praenomen* Lucius, which is also given by Cassiodorus (T 20).

T 14 Festus

And so, when Livius Andronicus had written a hymn in the Second Punic War [cf. T 8], which was sung by virgins, because the Republic of the Roman people had started to be ruled more successfully, the temple of Minerva on the Aventine [hill] was publicly assigned to him, in which writers and actors could meet and place gifts. This was in honor of Livius [Andronicus], since he both wrote plays and acted in them [cf. T 7, 10, 17, 21].

T 15 Donatus, *Excerpts on Comedy*

It is uncertain who first invented comedy among the Greeks, among the Romans it is certain: Livius Andronicus was the first to discover comedy, tragedy, and *togata* [comedy in Roman dress].[1]

[1] Livius Andronicus is not otherwise attested as a writer of *togatae*.

T 16 Hieron. *Ab Abr.* 1829–30 [188/7 a.C.] (p. 137 Helm)

Titus Livius tragoediarum scriptor clarus habetur. qui ob ingenii meritum a Livio Salinatore, cuius liberos erudiebat, libertate donatus est.

T 17 Evanth. *De com.* 4.3

Latinae fabulae primo a Livio Andronico scriptae sunt, adeo cuncta re [*Schopen*: ad has res *codd.*] etiam tum recenti [*Schopen*: recentes *codd.*], ut idem poeta et actor suarum fabularum fuisset.

T 18 Diom., *GL* I, p. 489.6–8

ab his [Graecis] Romani fabulas transtulerunt, et constat apud illos [Romanos] primum Latino sermone comoediam Livium Andronicum scripsisse.

T 19 Serv. Dan. ad Verg. *Aen.* 4.37

"triumphis dives" . . . Livius autem Andronicus refert, eos [Afros] de Romanis saepius triumphasse suasque porticus Romanis spoliis adornasse; merito ergo "dives triumphis."

T 16 Jerome, on the year 188/7 BC

Titus[1] Livius [Andronicus] was considered a famous writer of tragedies. On account of his intellectual merit he was rewarded with his liberty by Livius Salinator,[2] whose children he [Livius Andronicus] was teaching.

[1] Jerome is mistaken in giving the *praenomen* Titus, which belonged rather to the more famous historical writer, Titus Livius (Livy). [2] Because Jerome assigns the *floruit* of Andronicus to a later date than that assigned by Cicero and others, the Salinator referred to here is probably M. Livius M. f. Salinator (i.e., Salinator [2]), born in 254 BC and consul in 219 and 207 BC. Andronicus had probably served as a tutor in his father's house, and it was probably this earlier Salinator [1] who freed him (see Introduction to Livius Andronicus: Life).

T 17 Evanthius, *On Comedy*

Latin plays were first written by Livius Andronicus. The whole idea at that time was so new that the same man was both writer and actor of his own plays [cf. T 7, 10, 14, 21].

T 18 Diomedes

The Romans took over plays from them [the Greeks], and it is agreed that among them [the Romans] Livius Andronicus was the first to write a comedy in the Latin language.

T 19 Servius Danielis, *Commentary on Virgil*

[Africa] "rich in triumphs" . . . Livius Andronicus reports that they [the Africans] often triumphed over the Romans and adorned their porticos with Roman spoils; rightly, then, [Virgil says] "rich in triumphs."

T 20 Cassiod. *Chron*. II, p. 609 Mommsen, 316 a.u.c. [239 a.C.]

C. Manlius et Q. Valerius. his conss. ludis Romanis primum tragoedia et comoedia a Lucio Livio ad scaenam data.

T 21 *Gloss.* 2.11 (*CGF* I, pp. 72–73 Kaibel = *GL* I, p. 128)

Romae tragoedias comoediasque primus egit idemque etiam composuit Livius Andronicus duplici toga infulatus.

T 20 Cassiodorus, *Chronicle*, on the year 239 BC

Gaius Manlius and Quintus Valerius: under these consuls [239 BC][1] a tragedy and a comedy were produced on stage at the Roman Games for the first time by Lucius[2] Livius [Andronicus].

[1] Cassiodorus dates Andronicus' first dramas to one year later than the traditional date of 240 BC (cf. T 2, 3, 4, 13). Perhaps he confuses 240 with 239 BC since that was the year (239 BC) in which Ennius was born (see T 2, where both Andronicus' first play in 240 BC and Ennius' birth in 239 BC are mentioned by Cicero).   [2] For the *praenomen* Lucius, cf. Gellius (T 13).

T 21 *Glossaria Latina*

Livius Andronicus was the first man to act in and also to compose tragedies and comedies at Rome [cf. T 7, 10, 14, 17], wrapped in a double toga.[1]

[1] Normally the double toga was worn in Rome by priests performing sacrificial duties. The insistence on the religious origins of Roman, like those of Greek, drama may go back to ancient critics such as Varro (see Marconi 1966, 139; Lehmann 2002, 78–79).

TRAGOEDIAE (F 1–32)

Nonius is our best, in fact our only, source for tragic fragments of Livius Andronicus from named plays. He always cites them in the form Livius *with the play title (in the ablative), e.g., F 1* Livius Achille *("Livius in the Achilles"). The first nineteen tragic fragments are quoted in this way from eight plays (Achilles, Aegisthus, Aias Mastigophorus, Andromeda, Danae, Equus Troianus, Hermiona, and* Tereus*). In F 5 it is clear that* Lucilius Aegistho *should be corrected to* Livius Aegistho*, since Lucilius is not known to have composed tragedies. The only case in which Nonius quotes a tragic fragment of Livius Andronicus without a title is Trag. Inc. F 30. Festus (and his epitomist Paul the Deacon) by contrast never give a play title and F 20–29, quoted by them, all belong to the Trag. Inc. group, along with the already mentioned Nonius F 30 and Priscian F 31. The latter wrongly ascribes a fragment*

ACHILLES (F 1)

We know of seven Greek tragedies of this name, produced by Aristarchus Tegeates (14 F 1a TrGF), Iophon (22 F 1a TrGF), Astydamas II (60 F 1f TrGF), Carcinus II (70 F 1d TrGF), Cleophon? (77 F 1[3] TrGF), Euaretus (85 T 1 TrGF), and Diogenes Sinopensis (88 F 1a TrGF). Of these,

TRAGEDIES (F 1–32)

in tragic meter to the Odyssia, *which should be in the
Saturnian meter. All the* Trag. Inc. *group (F 20–31) are
assigned to tragedies on account of their content. Their
meter (either iambic senarii or trochaic octonarii; see
Introduction to Livius Andronicus: Works) is shared
with the comic fragments but distinguishes them from the*
Odyssia *in Saturnians. It is mainly on metrical grounds
that the* Ino *quotation (F 32), in a rare form of hexameter
quoted by Terentianus Maurus, is thought to be spurious.*

*Bibl.: Mette 1964, 41–50; De Rosalia 1989, 77–87;
Manuwald 2001 [2004], 93–101; Goldberg 2007. Comm.:
Spaltenstein 2008, 17–180. Lit.: Sanford 1922/23; Enk
1957; Waszink 1972, 891–902; Aricò 1987; 1997; Bläns-
dorf 2000, 145–56; Erasmo 2004; Boyle 2006; Gildenhard
2010; Manuwald 2011, 133–40; 2015.*

ACHILLES (F 1)

*only one line by Carcinus II has been preserved. The piece
by Aristarchus was familiar to Plautus (named at* Poenu-
lus *1–2) and was used by Ennius as the basis of his own
play of that name (*Trag. F 1–8 FRL*). Accius produced two
tragedies on the theme, his* Achilles *(Trag. 1–3 R.$^{2-3}$) and,*

if it is indeed a different play, his Myrmidones *(Trag. 4–21 R.[2–3]). Nothing is known of the source of Accius' or Andronicus' plays.*

The speaker in this, the single preserved fragment, is possibly Achilles, perhaps addressing Ulysses, who represents Agamemnon in an embassy made to persuade Achil-

1 (1 R.[3]) Non., p. 365.37–38 M. = 581 L.

PRETIUM, poenae exitum. Livius Achille:

tr[7]   si malas imitabo, tum tu pretium pro noxa dabis

malas *codd., Ribbeck[3]*: malos *Ribbeck[1–2]*   tu *Non., p. 473: om. Non., p. 365*   dabis *Non., p. 473*: dabit *Non., p. 365*

Cf. Non., p. 473.18–20 M. = 759 L.

AEGISTHUS (F 2–9)

This play, like Seneca's Agamemnon, *may have been influenced by the famous* Agamemnon *of Aeschylus' Oresteian trilogy, possibly via an intermediary Alexandrian play of that name (see Spaltenstein 2008, 28). As Spaltenstein admits, given the lack of evidence for Alexandrian tragedy, this claim could be made for any tragedy of Livius Andronicus or Naevius and so is of limited use. Similar material is found in Hom.* Od. *3.193–98, 4.303–10, 4.529–37; Soph.* Electra *95–99; Eur.* Electra *8–13. On the story of the murder of Agamemnon on his return from Troy by Aegisthus and Clytemnestra, see Apollod.* Epit. *6.23, Hyg.* Fab. *87 (Aegisthus), 117 (Clytemnestra). On the same theme, Accius produced tragedies named* Aegisthus *(Trag.*

*les to rejoin the war (cf. Hom. Il. 9.307ff.). The threat could
be intended to be relayed by Ulysses to Agamemnon, who
may have accused Achilles of cowardly behavior.*

    *Lit.: Klussmann 1845, 325–26; Bickel 1937; Waszink
1972, 891; Aricò 1980; Condorelli 1986. Comm.: Spalten-
stein 2008, 17–27.*

1 Nonius

pretium ["price"], the outcome of a punishment, Livius in
Achilles:

> If I imitate evil women,[1] then you will pay the price
>   for your wrong.

[1] The exact significance of "evil women" is uncertain. Some
editors emend to read "evil men."

AEGISTHUS (F 2–9)

*22–29 R.[2–3]) and Clytemnestra (Trag. 30–41 R.[2–3]), and
Pacuvius wrote a play on the theme of the vengeance
of Orestes called Dulorestes (Trag. 113–60 R.[2–3]; Schierl
2006, 240–70). Spaltenstein (2008, 31) argues that Sene-
ca's Agamemnon could have been influenced by Livius'
play, with the wording of Sen. Ag. 421–22 being particu-
larly close to F 9. This fragment appears to be part of a
messenger speech announcing the fall of Troy (and pre-
sumably Agamemnon's return), and F 8 similarly comes
from a description of the voyage home. F 6 is spoken by
Agamemnon shortly after his arrival, asking that Cassan-
dra be well treated. In F 7 Agamemnon is described as
giving thanks to the gods for his safe arrival. F 4, prob-*

ably spoken by Cassandra, describes the scene at the feast where Agamemnon was to be murdered, and a description of the murder occurs in F 3. In F 2 Aegisthus demands that Electra be dragged from her refuge in the temple. Finally, in F 5, perhaps either Aegisthus or Clytemnestra in a monologue asks rhetorically whether they are satis-

2 (13–14 R.[3]) Non., pp. 23.19–26 M. = 34–35 L.

PROCACITAS a procando vel poscendo . . . Livius Aegistho:

ia^6 quin, quod parere ‹mihi› vos maiestas mea
        procat, toleratis temploque hanc deducitis?

   1 mihi *suppl. Ribbeck et al. ante* vos; *Lindsay post* vos

Cf. Sen. *Agam.* 997–1000.

3 (12 R.[3]) Non., p. 110.32–33 M. = 158 L.

FLIGI, adfligi. Livius Aegistho:

ia^6 ipsus se in terram saucius fligit cadens

   ipsus *Bothe*: ipse *codd.*

Cf. Sen. *Agam.* 901–3.

4 (10–11 R.[3]) Non., p. 127.32–35 M. = 185 L.

IUXTIM pro iuxta . . . Livius Aegistho:

ia^6 . . . in sedes conlocat se regias;
        Clytaemestra iuxtim, tertias natae occupant

Cf. Sen. *Agam.* 879.

fied with the sight of the murdered Agamemnon, although other contexts for this fragment are possible, as discussed by Spaltenstein (ad loc.).

Lit.: Terzaghi 1925; Waszink 1972, 891–92; Brussich 1976; Aricò 1979; Antonelli Rinaldi 1982; Kruschwitz 2009. Comm.: Spaltenstein 2008, 28–73.

2 Nonius

procacitas ["importunity"] is said from *proco* ["insist"] or *posco* ["demand"] . . . Livius in *Aegisthus*:

> but since my majesty insists you obey ‹me›,
> why do you not submit and lead this woman from the
>   temple?

3 Nonius

fligi ["to be dashed"; an ante-classical verb for classical] *affligi*. Livius in *Aegisthus*:

> he dashed himself to the ground, wounded and
>   falling

4 Nonius

iuxtim ["next to"; rare form] for *iuxta* [main classical form] . . . Livius in *Aegisthus*:

> . . . he places himself in the royal seat;
> Clytemnestra is next to him, and his daughters
>   occupy the third place

45

5 (7 R.^{3}) Non., p. 132.29–30 M. = 192 L.

LAETARE et LAETISCERE, laetificare. Livius Aegistho:

ia^6 iamne oculos specie laetavisti optabili?

Cf. Non., p. 386.28–29 = 617 L.

6 (8 R.^{3}) Non., p. 166.23–27 M. = 245 L.

RUMINARI [*Voss*: ruminare *codd.*] dictum in memoriam revocare . . . Livius Aegistho:

ia^6 nemo haece vostrum ruminetur mulieri

nemo haece vostrum *L. Mueller*: nemo haec voster *codd.*: nemo haec vostrorum *Onions*

Cf. Sen. *Agam.* 800–801.

7 (9 R.^{3}) Non., p. 176.12 M. = 259 L.

SOLLEMNITUS pro sollemniter. Livius [*edd.*: Lucilius *codd.*] Aegistho:

ia^6 sollemnitusque deo litat laudem lubens

deo litat laudem *Ribbeck$^{1-2}$*: deo dicat laudes *L. Mueller*: adeo ditali laudet *codd.*, *Ribbeck^3*

Cf. Sen. *Agam.* 802–7.

8 (5–6 R.^{3}) Non., pp. 335.26–30 M. = 528–29 L.

LUSTRARE est circumire . . . Livius Aegistho:

ia^6 tum autem lascivum Nerei simum pecus
           ludens ad cantum classem lustratur . . .

5 Nonius

laetare ["to gladden"] and *laetiscere*, [the same as] *laetificare*. Livius in *Aegisthus*:

> and now have you gladdened your eyes with a
> desirable sight?

6 Nonius

ruminari ["recall"] is said in the sense of "to bring back to memory" . . . Livius in *Aegisthus*:

> no one of you should recall these things to the
> woman

7 Nonius

sollemnitus ["solemnly"; ante-classical *hapax legomenon*] for *sollemniter* [classical form]. Livius in *Aegisthus*:

> and solemnly he willingly gives praise to the god

8 Nonius

lustrare ["encircle"; active form; Livius Andronicus uniquely uses the verb as a deponent] means "to go round" . . . Livius in *Aegisthus*:

> but then the playful snub-nosed herd of Nereus[1]
> sporting to the song encircled the fleet . . .

[1] An old sea god.

---

1 autem *Non.*, p. *158*: om. *Non.*, p. *335*   2 lustratur *codd.*: lustrat navium *Klussmann*: lustratur choro *Ribbeck*: classium lustrat rates *Buecheler* (*coll. Sen.* Agam. *455:* lustrat ratem)

Cf. Non., p. 158.34–35 M. = 233 L.; Sen. Agam. 449–55.

9 (2–4 R.[3]) Non., pp. 512.31–40 M. = 824–25 L.

AEQUITER, pro aeque . . . Livius Aegistho:

ia[6]
 . . . nam ut Pergama
accensa et praeda per participes aequiter
partita est . . .

1 Pergama *edd.*: pergam *codd.*

Cf. Plaut. *Pers.* 757; Sen. *Agam.* 421–22.

AIAS MASTIGOPHORUS (F 10–11)

Aias Mastigophorus *("Ajax Whip-Bearer") was probably
influenced by the Ajax of Sophocles, but could also have
been influenced by an Alexandrian intermediary. Trage-
dies involving Ajax are also attributed to Astydamas II (60
T 1, F 1a TrGF), Carcinus II (70 F 1a TrGF), and Theo-
dectas (72 F 1 TrGF). Similar material is found in Aeschy-
lus'* Thressai *(F 83–5 TrGF). In Latin, Ennius also com-
posed an Ajax (Trag. F 9–11 FRL), and both Pacuvius
(Trag. 21–42 R.*[2–3]*; Schierl 2006, 131–61) and Accius (Trag.*

10 (15 R.[3]) Non., p. 127.13–21 M. = 184 L.

IAMDIU pro olim . . . Livius Aiace:

ia[6]   mirum videtur, quod sit factum iam diu?

9 Nonius

aequiter ["fairly"; ante-classical form] for *aeque* [classical form] . . . Livius in *Aegisthus*:

> . . . for when Pergamum
> was burned, and the booty among the participants
> was shared fairly . . .

AIAS MASTIGOPHORUS (F 10–11)

145–63 R.$^{2-3}$) *composed tragedies entitled* Armorum Iudi-cium *that touched upon related subject matter. The Ajax story is also related by Ovid (*Met. 13.1–398*). The epithet "Whip-Bearer" was added to the manuscripts of Sopho-cles' play in the Alexandrian period. The two fragments preserved from Andronicus seem to deal with the theme of men in later years forgetting the great deeds of Ajax at Troy.*

Lit.: Mariotti 1952, 52–53; Waszink 1972, 893–94; Lennartz 1994, 95–99. Comm.: Spaltenstein 2008, 73–83.

10 Nonius

iamdiu ["long since now"] for *olim* ["a long time ago"] . . . Livius in *Aias*:

> does that seem wonderful because it was done long
> ago?

11 (16–17 R.[3]) Non., p. 207.32–34 M. = 306 L.

GELU neutri generis . . . [Titus *codd., secl.* Iunius] Livius
. . . Aiace Mastigophoro:

tr^7 . . . praestatur virtuti laus, set gelu multo ocius
vento tabescit

    1 set gelu *Lindsay*: gelu set *codd.*   2 vento *cod.*: venio
codd.

Cf. Soph. *Aiax* 1266–67.

ANDROMEDA (F 12)

*Andromeda was the daughter of Cepheus, king of the
Ethiopians, and his wife, Cassiepeia or Cassiope. Cassie-
peia offended the sea gods by claiming she was more beau-
tiful than the Nereids. Poseidon took vengeance by flood-
ing the land and sending a sea monster to ravage it.
Cepheus consulted an oracle and learned that the only
cure was to tie his daughter to a rock on the seashore and
offer her up to the monster. This he did, but eventually
Andromeda was rescued by Perseus. Accounts of the myth
are found in Apollod.* Bibl. *2.4.3 = 2.43–44; Hyg.* Fab. *64;
Eratosth.* Catast. *17 (p. 21 Olivieri); Hyg.* Astr. *2.9, 2.11;
Schol. (Bas.) Germ. 184, 192, 201; Ov.* Met. *4.663–764.*

12 (18 R.[3]) Non., p. 62.15–17 M. = 86 L.

CONFLUGES, loca in quae rivi diversi confluant. Livius
Andromeda:

tr^7 confluges ubi conventu campum totum inumigant

    conventu *Iunius in marg.*: conventum *codd.*

11 Nonius

gelu ["ice"] with neuter gender . . . Livius . . . in *Ajax Whip-Bearer*:

> . . . praise is offered for courage, but much quicker
>   than ice
> in the wind it melts away

ANDROMEDA (F 12)

Greek tragedies of this title are known from Sophocles
(F 126–36 TrGF), Euripides (F 114–56 TrGF), Lycophron
(100 F 1c TrGF), and Phrynichus II (212 F 1c TrGF).
Latin versions were produced by Ennius (Trag. F 34–41
FRL) and Accius (Trag. 100–18 R.$^{2–3}$). It is unclear from
our single fragment which Greek author Andronicus took
as his model, but the play of either Sophocles or Euripides
is his most likely source. The surviving fragment of An-
dronicus seems to refer to the flood caused by Poseidon. It
is more likely to come from a messenger speech (Spalten-
stein 2008, 83) than from a prologue (Duentzer 1835, 120).
  Lit.: Waszink 1972, 896; Klimek-Winter 1993, 330–33.
Comm.: Spaltenstein 2008, 83–88.

12 Nonius

confluges ["confluences"; *hapax legomenon*], places into
which different rivers flow together. Livius in *Andromeda*:

> where confluences by their coming together flood the
>   whole plain

DANAE (F 13)

*Danae, the daughter of Acrisius and Aganippe, was fated
to bear a child that would kill Acrisius. Fearing this, her
father locked her away in a stone building, but Jupiter,
turning himself into a shower of gold, gained access to her,
and from their union was born Perseus. Acrisius had the
mother and child enclosed in an ark and sent to sea. The
ark was eventually washed up on the island of Seriphos,
where Danae was married to the king Polydectes, who took
Perseus under his protection. Acrisius found them there,
but Perseus promised never to kill him. However, when
king Polydectes died, Perseus accidentally killed Acrisius
with a discus throw that hit him in the head at the king's
funeral games, and thus brought to pass the prophecy.*

13 (19 R.^{3}) Non., p. 473.26–27 M. = 759 L.

MINITAS, pro minitaris. Livius Danae:

tr^7 . . . etiam minitas? mitte ea quae tua sunt magis quam
mea

EQUUS TROIANUS (F 14)

Equus Troianus *("The Trojan Horse") is based on events
from the end of the Trojan War. When the Achaeans were
unable to take Troy after ten years of fighting, Epeus, at
the suggestion of Minerva, constructed a wooden horse,
which was filled with Greek warriors. Leaving this horse
behind as an offering to Minerva, they moved camp to the
island of Tenedos. The Trojans thought the Greeks had*

DANAE (F 13)

*Ancient accounts of the story are to be found in Apollod.
Bibl. 2.4.1 = 2.34–35; Hyg. Fab. 63; Serv. Aen. 7.372,
8.345. Tragedies of the same name were written by Sopho-
cles (F 165–70 TrGF), Euripides (F 316–30a TrGF), and,
in Latin, Naevius (F 2–12 TrRF, Trag. F 2–12 FRL). Aes-
chylus' satyr play Δικτυουλκοί (F 47–49 TrGF) treats
related material. The Greek source of Andronicus' one
surviving fragment is uncertain. The exact context of F 13
is unclear, but it could contain a reply by Acrisius to the
threats or complaints of Danae, implying that she rather
than he was responsible for her own sufferings.*

    *Lit.: Lo-Cascio 1892; Rostagni 1916; Waszink 1972,
895; Erskine 1998. Comm.: Spaltenstein 2008, 89–94.*

13 Nonius

minitas ["you threaten"; archaic active form] for *minitaris*
[classical deponent form]. Livius in *Danae*:

    . . . do you threaten me then? Forget those things
      which are your responsibility rather than mine

EQUUS TROIANUS (F 14)

*returned home and at the instigation of Priam led the horse
into the sanctuary of Minerva. Ignoring the warnings of
Cassandra that the horse contained enemy fighters, the
Trojans spent the night in games and feasting. The Greek
warriors burst out, killed the guards on the gates, and let
in their companions, who finally captured Troy (cf. Verg.
Aen. 2.57–198, 234–67; Hyg. Fab. 108). This material*

forms the basis for the Pseudo-Homeric cyclic epic Iliou-
persis *and for Sophocles' play,* Sinon *(F 542–4 TrGF).
In Latin, Naevius composed a tragedy of the same name
(F 13 TrRF, t 1,* Trag. *F 13 FRL). The source of Androni-
cus' play is uncertain. The context of F 14 could possibly
be an appeal to Apollo by Cassandra, asking for his aid in*

14 (20–22 R.³) Non., p. 475.10–12 M. = 762 L.

OPITULA. Livius Equo Troiano:

cr⁴

                       . . . da mihi
hasce opes quas peto, quas precor. porrige,
opitula . . .

2 porrige *Scaliger*: corrige *codd.*

HERMIONA (F 15)

*The story of Hermiona [ante-classical form for the classical
Hermione] is related by* Hyg. Fab. *123 (Neoptolemus).
Neoptolemus had already had a son, Amphialus, from the
captive Andromache, when he heard that his betrothed
Hermione had been given in marriage to Orestes, and he
traveled to Sparta to ask Menelaus to recover her for him.
Menelaus did so, but Orestes, taking offense at this, killed
Neoptolemus while he was sacrificing at Delphi and recov-
ered Hermione. Greek tragedies of this name are known
by Sophocles (F 202ff. TrGF), Philoclis I (24 F 2 TrGF),
Theodorus (134 F 1 TrGF), and, in Latin, by Pacuvius
(*Trag. *161–90 R.²⁻³; Schierl 2006, 280–311). Related mate-
rial is found in Euripides,* Andromache; Apollod. Epit.

persuading the Trojans that the horse contains enemy warriors. Grimal (1975, 270) thinks this could have been the first tragedy Livius Andronicus produced in Rome.

Lit.: *Lallier 1884; Tolkiehn 1896, 861; La Ville de Mirmont 1903, 105–7; Lenchantin de Gubernatis 1913, 407–8; Rostagni 1916; Terzaghi 1925, 662; Waszink 1972, 896; Erskine 1998. Comm.: Spaltenstein 2008, 94–102.*

14 Nonius

opitula[1] ["help"; active form here only for classical deponent]. Livius in *The Trojan Horse*:

> . . . give me
> the aid I seek and pray for. Hold it out,
> help . . .

[1] On the use of this form, see Livingston 2004, 58.

HERMIONA (F 15)

6.14; Ov. Her. *8 (Hermione to Orestes); and Hyg.* Fab. *123 (Neoptolemus). Neither Sophocles nor Pacuvius seems to mention Andromache, who appears to be the speaker of F 15, and her son; so Andronicus could have been inspired by Euripides'* Andromache, *although her son there is called Molossus. The name Anchialus (for which Nonius preserves the old spelling Ancialus, without aspirate) is close to Hyginus' Amphilaus and occurs only in Andronicus. For these reasons it is impossible to be certain about Andronicus' exact model.*

Lit.: *Ribbeck 1875, 31; Waszink 1972, 897. Comm.: Spaltenstein 2008, 103–7.*

15 (23 R.[3]) Non., p. 111.7–14 M. = 159 L.

FUAM, sim vel fiam . . . Livius Hermiona:

tr^7 obsecro te, Anciale, matri ne quid tuae advorsus fuas

anciale *codd.*: anchiale *edd. nonnulli*

TEREUS (F 16–19)

The Thracian Tereus, who was married to Pandion's daughter, Procne, wished to be married to her sister Philomela and went to Pandion in Athens to ask for her hand, saying that Procne was dead. Pandion sent Philomela to him under escort, but Tereus drowned her guards and raped her. He then sent her to king Lynceus. Lynceus' queen Laethusa knew both sisters and brought them together. The couple Lynceus and Laethusa appear only in Hyginus' version of the myth. Neither are named in Andronicus, but Laethusa is possibly the speaker of F 19. The sisters planned revenge on Tereus. Meanwhile, Tereus heard from a soothsayer that his son by Procne, Itys, would be killed by a relative's hand and so killed his innocent brother Dryas. Procne killed her son Itys and served him at a feast to Tereus before fleeing with her sister. Tereus pursued them, but the gods took pity on the sisters and turned Procne into a swallow, Philomela into a nightingale, and Tereus into a hawk. A play of this name is known to have been written in Greek by Sophocles (F 581–95 TrGF), and Philocles also wrote a tetralogy on the same subject matter called Pandion *(24 F 2–3 TrGF). In Latin there is a* Tereus *by Accius (Trag. 634–50 R.[2–3]), which may relate to a different version of the myth, and*

15 Nonius

fuam ["I be"; ante-classical form] for [classical] *sim* or *fiam*
. . . Livius in *Hermiona*:

> I beg you, Anchialus, be not in any way turned
>   against your mother

TEREUS (F 16–19)

*the story is told in Ov. Met. 6.412–874. The myth is re-
counted in Apollod. Bibl. 3.14.8 = 3.193–95 and in Hyg.
Fab. 45 (Philomela). There can be no certainty as to An-
dronicus' source. Similarly, the context of Andronicus'
fragments must remain conjectural. F 19 is probably spo-
ken by Laethusa as she visits Procne bringing Philomela;
F 17 is perhaps from a monologue by Procne, denying that
her sister could have consented to adultery and so con-
firming the guilt of Tereus alone; F 16 is probably spoken
by Procne, concerning the child Itys, as part of her prepa-
rations for his murder; F 18 is probably spoken by Tereus,
either to himself or in dialogue, after discovering that he
has eaten his son. Andronicus may follow an alternative
version of the myth from that of Sophocles and Accius and
could be closer to the version of Hyginus and perhaps be
inspired by an Alexandrian intermediary. This thesis rests
on the attribution of F 19 to Laethusa. The two-word frag-
ment is, however, capable of other interpretations, and its
attribution to Laethusa is not universally accepted (see
Spaltenstein 2008, 111–12). Accius' version is closer to
that found in Apollodorus and probably in Sophocles. In
this version Tereus raped Philomela while bringing her
back from Athens to visit her sister, and subsequently had*

her expelled from his kingdom. However, Philomela sent a robe as a gift to her sister on which she had embroidered an account of her wrongs. In revenge, Procne killed Itys, her son with Tereus, and had his flesh served as a meal to Tereus. The transformation of Procne, Philomela, and Tereus into birds remains in this version. In another alter-

16 (26–27 R.^{3}) Non., p. 153.22–29 M. = 225 L.

PERBITERE perire . . . Livius Tereo:

tr^7 ego puerum interead ancillae subdam lactantem
           meae,
ne fame perbitat.

    1 interead *Ribbeck*^{2}: interea *Ribbeck*^{3}, *codd.*   lactantem
vel laetantem *codd.*

17 (28–29 R.^{3}) Non., pp. 334.2–10 M. = 525–26 L.

LIMARE etiam dicitur coniungere . . . Livius Tereo:

tr^7 . . . credito,
cum illo soror mea voluntate numquam limavit caput

    2 illo soror *Mercier*: illos soli *codd.*

18 (25 R.^{3}) Non., p. 475.34–37 M. = 763 L.

PRAESTOLAT pro praestolatur . . . Livius Tereo:

tr^7 nimis pol inprudenter servus praestolaras . . .

native version (e.g., Verg. Ecl. 6.78–79), the roles of Procne and Philomela are reversed, with Philomela being Tereus' wife. Given the sparsity of the fragments from this play, nothing can be stated with certainty about Andronicus' possible sources.

Comm.: Spaltenstein 2008, 110–29.

16 Nonius

perbitere ["to perish"; ante-classical for] *perire* ["to perish"; classical] . . . Livius in *Tereus*:

> I meanwhile will put the suckling boy to the breast of
>   my maid,
> lest he perish of hunger

17 Nonius

limare ["to file"; in ante-classical Latin *limare caput cum* "to rub heads with" = "to embrace"[1]] can also mean "to join" . . . Livius in *Tereus*:

>   . . . believe me,
> my sister never willingly rubbed her head with his

[1] On this expression, see Giovini 2004.

18 Nonius

praestolat[1] ["he waits"; active form, ante- and post-classical] for *praestolatur* . . . Livius in *Tereus*:

> too unknowingly, by god, you had stood there waiting
>   as a slave . . .

[1] On the use of the active form of this verb for the classical deponent, see Livingston 2004, 61–66.

19 (24 R.³) Non., p. 515.24–34 M. = 829 L.

RARENTER . . . Livius Tereo:

ia⁶   rarenter venio . . .

> venio *edd. plerique*: venio *vel* venito *vel* vento *codd.*

TRAGICA INCERTA
(t 1; F 20–31)

*When ancient authors quote fragments of Andronicus
without reference to any particular work, a fragment in
dramatic meter, as opposed to the epic Saturnian meter,
could be either from a tragedy or from a comedy. The tone
and content of F 20 to F 31 suggest that they come from*

t 1 Varro, *Ling.* 7.3

nec mirum, cum . . . Teucer Livii post XV annos ab suis
qui sit ignoretur.

---

¹ The reference is perhaps to a play *Teucer* or *Telamo*, in
which Teucer was not recognized at home in Salamis when he
returned home after fifteen years' absence in Troy. In fact, the
Trojan War lasted ten years; so we could assume that Teucer
delayed his journey home through guilt (although this is not at-
tested in our sources). In most versions of the myth Teucer was
sent into exile by his father, Telamo, after his return home to
Salamis, since Telamo was angry with him for failing to bring
home the arms and body of his half-brother, Ajax, who had com-
mitted suicide at Troy. He was also accused of not protecting Ajax'
son Eurysaces, who perished in a storm at sea on the return from
Troy. After his exile, Teucer is supposed to have founded another

19 Nonius

rarenter ["rarely"; ante- and post-classical] . . . Livius in
Tereus:

rarely I come . . .

UNASSIGNED TRAGIC FRAGMENTS
(t 1; F 20–31)

*tragedy (see Introduction to Tragedies). Varro in t 1 dis-
cusses a character from tragedy, Teucer, but whether he
gave his name to the tragedy in which he appeared in
Andronicus is unknown.*
Comm.: Spaltenstein 2008, 130–69.

t 1 Varro, *On the Latin Language*

and it is not surprising when . . . Livius [Andronicus']
Teucer is unknown by his own family after fifteen years.[1]

Salamis in Crete, named after his native city. In Greek, tragedies
called *Teukros* (*Teucer*) are attested for Sophocles (F 576–79
TrGF), Ion (19 F 34–35 *TrGF*), Euaretos (F 85 *TrGF*), and
Nikomachos (127 F 10 *TrGF*). Ennius' tragedy *Telamo* (the only
known instance of this name as a play title) focuses on the conflict
between Teucer and his father, Telamo (*Trag*. F 117–24 *FRL*),
but does not mention exile in the extant fragments. The story of
his return and subsequent exile is the theme of Pacuvius' *Teucer*
(*Trag*. 313–46 R.[2-3]; Schierl 2006, 468–514). Similar material is
treated in Aeschylus' *Salaminae* (F 216–20 *TrGF*), Schol. ad Pind.
N. 4.76, Hor. *Carm*. 1.7.21–29, Verg. *Aen*. 1.619–26, and Vell. Pat.
1.1.1. The story of Teucer's failure to be recognized at home in
Salamis is not attested elsewhere.

20 (30 R.³) Paul. *Fest.*, p. 10.16–17 L.

ANCLARE haurire a Graeco descendit. Livius:

ia⁶   florem anculabant Liberi ex carchesiis

anculabant *Scaliger*: anclabant *codd.*

21 (39 R.³) Paul. *Fest.*, p. 59.3–4 L.

ia⁶/tr⁷ ?   . . . dusmo in loco

apud Livium significat dumosum locum. antiqui enim in-
terserebant s litteram, . . .

22 (38 R.³) Paul. *Fest.*, p. 157.9–12 L.

NEFRENDES arietes dixerunt, quod dentibus frendere non
possint. alii dicunt nefrendes infantes esse nondum fren-
dentes, id est frangentes. Livius:

ia⁶   quem ego nefrendem alui lacteam inmulgens opem

nefrendem *codd.*: non frendem *ut vid., Fest., p. 156*

Cf. Fest., p. 156.26–30 L.

20 Paul the Deacon, *Epitome of Festus*

anclare ["to drain"], "to imbibe" comes from the Greek [from ἀντλέω, "to drain"]. Livius:

> they drained the flower of wine from goblets[1]

[1] A description of a feast, perhaps from *Tereus* or *Hermiona*.

21 Paul the Deacon, *Epitome of Festus*

> . . . in a bushy place[1]

in Livius means a *dumosus* ["bushy"] place [with archaic *dusmus*, used adjectivally, for classical *dumus* n. / *dumosus* adj.], for the ancients inserted a letter *s*, . . .

[1] The meter and context of such a short fragment must remain uncertain. It is likely to be tragic given its quotation by Paul the Deacon along with other tragic fragments, but some critics assign it to Andronicus' *Odyssia* (e.g., Flores 2011, *Od.* F 30).

22 Paul the Deacon, *Epitome of Festus*

nefrendes[1] ["not biting"] they called rams, because they cannot crunch [*frendere*] things with their teeth. Others call *nefrendes* infants who were not yet biting, that is not breaking. Livius:

> whom I fed as a nonbiting child, suckling him with a
> supply of milk[2]

[1] On this form, see Livingston 2004, 67–68.
[2] There can be no certainty about the context. Possibly Procne is speaking of Itys in *Tereus* or Clytemnestra of Orestes in *Aegisthus*.

23 (31 R.³) Fest., p. 192.1–4 L.

OCREM antiqui, ut Ateius Philologus in libro Glosema-
torum refert, montem confragosum vocabant, ut aput
Livium:

ia⁶   . . . sed qui sunt hi, qui ascendunt altum ocrim?

24 (32–33 R.³) Fest., p. 192.1–5 L.

OCREM antiqui, ut Ateius Philologus in libro Glosema-
torum refert, montem confragosum vocabant, ut aput
Livium . . . :

?   . . . celsosque ocris
         arvaque putria et mare magnum . . .

25 (34 R.³) Fest., p. 192.1–6 L.

OCREM antiqui, ut Ateius Philologus in libro Glosema-
torum refert, montem confragosum vocabant, ut aput
Livium . . . :

ia⁶/tr⁷   . . . namque Taenari celsos ocris

---

[1] Taenarus is a cape on the south coast of the Peloponnese. It
had a famous temple of Neptune and was thought to have been
one of the entrances to the underworld. It is unclear which play
such a context would suit.

23 Festus

ocrem ["crag"; attested only in Andronicus] is what the ancients, as Ateius the Grammarian[1] relates in his book of glosses, call a rocky mountain, as in Livius:

> . . . but who are these men who are climbing the high
> crag?[2]

[1] L. Ateius Philologus, captured as a slave in Athens in 86 BC, became an important teacher of grammar and rhetoric in Rome in the decade 60–50 BC (see Suet. *Gram. et rhet.* 10 [with Kaster 1995, 138–39 ad loc.]; Funaioli 1907, 136–41). [2] Possibly a line from *Andromeda* in which Perseus sees men attempting to expose Andromeda on a rock (cf. Euripides, *Andromeda*, F 125 *TrGF*).

24 Festus

ocrem ["crag"; attested only in Andronicus] is what the ancients, as Ateius the Grammarian relates in his book of glosses, call a rocky mountain, as in Livius . . . :

> . . . the high crags,
> the crumbling earth, and the vast sea[1] . . .

[1] Meter and context are uncertain. Spaltenstein (2008, 148–49) argues for a description of a voyage, possibly in an anapestic *canticum* by a tragic chorus.

25 Festus

ocrem ["crag"; attested only in Andronicus] is what the ancients, as Ateius the Grammarian relates in his book of glosses, call a rocky mountain, as in Livius . . . :

> . . . for the high crags of Taenarus[1]

26 (35 R.^{3}) Fest., p. 192.1–7 L.

OCREM antiqui, ut Ateius Philologus in libro Glosematorum refert, montem confragosum vocabant, ut aput Livium . . . :

ia^6   haut ut quem Chiro in Pelio docuit ocri

27 (41 R.^{3}) Fest., p. 306.8–12 L.

QUINQUERTIUM vocabant antiqui quod [*L. Mueller*: quem *cod.*] Graeci πένταθλον . . . Livius quoque ipsos athletas sic nominat:

ia^6   quinquertiones praeco in medium provocat

provocat *Ribbeck*: vocat *cod.*

Cf. Paul. *Fest.*, p. 307.1–7 L.

28 (37 R.^{3}) Fest., p. 408.25–31 L.

STRUICES antiqui dicebant extructiones omnium rerum . . . Livius:

tr^7   quo Castalia per struices saxeas lapsu accidit

26 Festus

ocrem ["crag"; attested only in Andronicus] is what the ancients, as Ateius the Grammarian relates in his book of glosses, call a rocky mountain, as in Livius . . . :

> not like the man Chiron taught on Pelion's crag[1]

[1] Perhaps from a play *Achilles*, possibly spoken by Achilles' former tutor, Phoenix, comparing Achilles' present behavior unfavorably with his actions in the past when being taught by the centaur, Chiron.

27 Festus

quinquertium ["pentathlon"; ante-classical word] the ancients called what the Greeks [refer to] as πένταθλον ["pentathlon"] . . . Livius also calls the athletes themselves by this name [in a different form *quinquertio*]:

> the herald calls the pentathlon athletes into the
> middle[1]

[1] Possibly a reference to funeral games, a subject relevant to *Achilles* or *Ajax Whip-Bearer*.

28 Festus

struices ["heaps"; ante-classical for classical *strues*] the ancients called structures of all kinds . . . Livius:

> where the Castalian stream[1] falls in its descent over
> rocky heaps

[1] A spring at the foot of Mount Parnassus, associated in later Latin literature with the home of the Muses, but in earlier Greek literature and in Andronicus' time its main significance would have been its use as a place of purification for the nearby oracle at Delphi.

29 (vacat R.[3]) Fest., p. 412.13–21 L.

STIR‹PEM hominum in masculino gene›re antiqui ‹usur-
parunt› . . . Livius tr‹ahens de Graeco› ‹quo›rundam
Rom‹anorum nomina et ipsam› conditam Romam ‹testis
est. nam sic ait Li›vius [*locum restituit Lindsay*]:

ia[6]   o Strymon ‹unde nomen Romani trahunt,
ex› Graio stirpe exo‹rti›

versus restituit Lindsay

30 (36 R.[3]) Non., p. 197.28–30 M. = 290 L.

QUIS et generi feminino adtribui posse veterum auctoritas
voluit. Livius:

tr[7]   mulier, quisquis es, te volumus . . .

31 (40 R.[3]) Prisc., *GL* II, pp. 230.27–31.12

puer, pueri, cuius femininum PUERA dicebant antiquis-
simi . . . Livius in Odyssia [F 3] . . . idem alibi:

ia[6]   puerarum manibus confectum pulcherrime

---

[1] The reference seems to be to an offering of some kind.
Spaltenstein (2008, 168–69) suggests either a cloak offered by
Clytemnestra to Aegisthus in *Aegisthus* or a veil offered to Athena
by the women of Troy and pillaged by the Greeks in the *Equus
Troianus*.

29 Festus

stirps ["stock"] ⟨of men⟩, ancient writers ⟨used in the masculine gender⟩ . . . Livius, deriving ⟨the names of certain Romans and⟩ the foundation of Rome itself from Greek ⟨is witness to this. For Li⟩vius says this:

> O Strymon,[1] ⟨whence the Romans took their name,[2] risen from⟩ a Greek stock[3]

[1] A river in Northern Greece.   [2] The ancient name of the Tiber was said to be *Rumon* (Serv. ad Verg. *Aen*. 8.63 and 8.90), which the Romans could have derived from Strymon.

[3] The whole passage has had to be heavily supplemented by the editors of Festus, so that neither his introductory comments nor the wording of the fragment is certain. If indeed it did mention Romans, the fragment could have come from a *praetexta* rather than a tragedy, but no play of this type is explicitly attributed to Andronicus.

30 Nonius

The pronoun *quis* ["who"] the authority of ancient writers wished to attribute also to the feminine gender. Livius:

> woman, whoever you are, we want you . . .[1]

[1] There can be no certainty about the context of such a general remark.

31 Priscian

puer ["boy"], [genitive] *pueri*, the most ancient writers said *puera* ["girl"] for its feminine . . . Livius in the *Odyssia* [*Od.* F 3] . . . the same author elsewhere:

> most beautifully made by girls' hands[1]

TRAGICUM SPURIUM (F 32)

Ino

Tragedies of this name were composed by Sophocles (F 732 TrGF) and Euripides (F 398–423 TrGF). Similar material is dealt with in the Athamas *of Aeschylus (F 1–4a TrGF) and Accius (Trag. 185–95 R.²⁻³; see Ribbeck 1875, 526–28). In later Latin poetry it appears in Ovid (Fast. 6.499–508; Met. 4.481–542). The story of Io is related by Apollodorus (Bibl. 3.4.3 = 3.27–28) and Hyginus (Fab. 2 [Ino]). The mythology concerning Ino is long and complicated, but the part of the story behind the present fragment seems to be the following. Ino and her husband, Athamas, brought up her sister Semele's child, Dionysus (son of Jove). In revenge for this, Jove's wife, Juno, drove the couple mad. While in this state, Athamas hunted and killed his son,*

32 (29¹⁻⁴ R.³) Ter. Maur., *GL* VI, p. 383, 1931–38

1931   Livius ille vetus Graio cognomine suae
       inserit Inoni versus, puto, tale docimen:
       praemisso heroo subiungit namque miuron,
       hymnum quando chorus festo canit ore Triviae:

SPURIOUS TRAGIC FRAGMENT (F 32)

Ino

Learchus. Ino ran from him, carrying her son, Melicertes, and jumped into the sea. Mother and son were finally transformed into the deities Leucothea and Palaemon. The address by the chorus to Diana in this fragment is probably a preliminary to the hunt of the maddened Athamas.

The style of this fragment (with the direct address to the goddess, the anastrophe of et *in line 1936, and the compound* odorisequos *in 1938) and in particular the fact that it is written in a form of hexameters before Ennius make most commentators reject the idea that it was written by Andronicus. Suggestions for an alternative author, possibly Laevius (often confused with Livius), remain conjectural (see Marconi 1963; Spaltenstein 2008, 169–76).*

32 Terentianus Maurus

That old Livius, the one with the Greek surname [Andronicus], inserted into his *Ino*, I think, a verse specimen of this kind: for to a preceding heroic hexameter he adds a *miurus*,[1] as when the chorus sings in festive voice a hymn to Trivia:[2]

---

[1] A form of the hexameter in which the final spondee is replaced by an iambus, as in verse 1936.   [2] A cult name of Diana.

Chorus

1935   et iam purpureo suras include cothurno,
        balteus et revocet volucres in pectore sinus,
        pressaque iam gravida crepitent tibi terga pharetra:
        derige odorisequos ad certa cubilia canes.

Cf. Verg. *Ecl.* 7.32, *Aen.* 1.336–37; Mar. Vict., *GL* VI, pp. 67.31–68.8.

Chorus

and now enclose your calves in purple boots,   1935
and let a belt hold back to your breast the flying folds,
and now let your back thump with your heavy quiver:
drive your scent-following hounds toward the well-
    known lairs

FABULAE PALLIATAE (F 1–6)

All the comic fragments, apart from F 6 provided by the fourth-century historian Flavius Vopiscus (in SHA), come from Festus. In two cases, Gladiolus *and* Ludius, *Festus gives the title. In the case of a third play,* † Virgo †, *the title he gives is corrupt. Nowhere are we told specifically by our sources that these fragments come from comedies. They are written in the same Greek-based iambic and trochaic meters as tragedy. The fact that they come from*

GLADIOLUS (F 1)

Gladiolus *("The Dagger") is the diminutive of Latin gladius ("sword"). Comedies of similar title in Greek (Ἐγχειρίδιον, "The Dagger-") are known from Menander (Loeb,* Menander, *vol. I, pp. 357–77), Philemon (F 21 K.-A.), and Sophilus (F 4 K.-A.). Nothing is known of their content. A dagger could figure in the plot of any comedy. F 1 suggests*

COMEDIES (F 1–6)

adaptations of Greek New Comedies has to be inferred either from the titles of the plays or from the content of the fragments. For Livius Andronicus as the initiator of comedy at Rome, see T 15, 18, 20, 21, and cf. T 13, where the mention of Menander implies that he adapted Menandrian New Comedy for the Roman stage as so-called Comoediae Palliatae [*"Comedies in Greek Dress"*].
   Comm.: Spaltenstein 2008, 180–202.

GLADIOLUS (F 1)

perhaps a humorous response to a braggart warrior figure who has been enumerating the victims he has killed, as in the parasite's words to the soldier in Plautus' Miles Gloriosus *("The Braggart Soldier"). The speaker undermines his bravado by asking whether those killed were fleas, bugs, or lice. In Plautus'* Curculio *the same list of creatures is mentioned in a comparison with pimps.*

1 (1 R.³) Fest., p. 230.20–25 L.

PEDES autem pro pediculis . . . Livius in Gladiolo:

tr⁷   pulicesne an cimices an pedes? responde mihi.

Cf. Plaut. *Curc.* 499–500, *Mil.* 42–45.

LUDIUS (F 2)

The title Ludius *probably means "The Lydian." A number
of Greek-based comedies are named after the nationality
of a chief character (e.g., Menander's* Samia*; Naevius'*
Tarentilla*; Plautus'* Poenulus*; Terence's* Andria*), and we
know of a play called* Λυδός *("The Lydian") by Antiphanes
the elder (F 144 K.-A.) and* Λυδοί *("The Lydians") by
Magnes (F 3–4 K.-A.). Ludus is reported as a possible
comedy title for Naevius (F 80 FRL), but the exact title of*

2 (2 R.³) Fest., p. 444.7–12 L.

SCENAM . . . Cincius in libro qui est de verbis priscis dola-
bram ait esse pontificiam. Livius in Ludio:

ia⁶   corruit quasi ictus scena, haut multo secus

Cf. Fest., p. 422.32–34 L.

COMEDIES: LUDIUS

1 Festus

pedes [usually = "feet"] however is used for *pediculi* ["lice"] . . . Livius in *The Dagger*:

fleas, or bugs, or lice? Answer me.

Cf. Plautus, *Curculio*: "In my opinion the race of pimps is among men like flies, gnats, bugs, lice, and fleas"; *Miles Gloriosus* ["The Braggart Soldier"]: "I remember one hundred and fifty in Cilicia, one hundred in Scytholatronia, thirty Sardinians, sixty Macedonians, these are the men you killed in a single day."

LUDIUS (F 2)

this play is disputed. The use of the form Ludius *in Livius Andronicus for the Greek* Λυδός *is not a serious objection to this title, given the common uncertainty about the representation of Greek terminations in Latin in his time. Those who reject this interpretation would take* Ludius *to be a Latin title referring to a stage performer or a gamester rather than to a Lydian (so Ritschl 1877, 820; R.[2–3]; Warmington [2]1967, 21; Spaltenstein 2008, 186).*

2 Festus

scena ["ax"; archaic and rare] . . . Cincius[1] in his book on ancient words says it is a priest's ax.[2] Livius in *The Lydian*:

he fell to the ground as if struck by an ax, not much different from that

[1] A grammarian from the end of the first century BC (see Funaioli 1907, 371–82). [2] See *OLD scena*[2]: "a sacrificial ax," alternative form of *suvena*, derived from *seco*, "cut."

COMICA INCERTA (F 3–6)

3 (4–5 R.³) Fest., p. 10.25–11.1 L.

AFFATIM dictum a copia fatendi, sive abundanter. Livius:

*tr*⁷?   adfatim edi, bibi, lusi . . .

4 (3 R.³) Fest., p. 182.12–18 L.

NOBILEM antiqui pro noto ponebant, et quidem per g litteram ut . . . Livius [*vel* leuius] in † Virgo † [Virgine *Scaliger*: Virga *Duentzer*: Verpo *vel* Vargo *Ribbeck*]:

*tr*⁷   . . . ornamento incedunt gnobiles ignobiles

> ornamento incedunt *Scaliger*: ornamentu incendunt *codd.*
> gnobiles *Ribbeck*: nobili *cod.*: gnobilid *Bothe*

COMIC FRAGMENTS OF UNKNOWN
OR UNCERTAIN TITLE (F 3–6)

3 Festus

affatim ["abundantly"] said from a fullness of speaking, or plentifully. Livius:

> I ate, drank, and played[1] abundantly . . .

[1] The verb, *ludere*, usually refers to enjoying the company of women.

4 Festus

nobilis ["noble"] the ancients put for *notus* ["known"], and furthermore spelled it with a *g* [*gnobilis*] as . . . Livius[1] in † *Virgo* †[2]

> . . . both known and unknown go forth in finery

[1] One manuscript attributes the play to Laevius rather than Livius, a common confusion.   [2] Various forms have been suggested for the ungrammatical *Virgo* given as the title, such as *in Virgine* ("in *The Virgin*"), *in Virga* ("in *The Rod*," as an instrument of slave punishment), *in Verpo* ("in *The Circumcised Man*"), and *in Vargo* ("in *The Tramp*").

5 (6–7 R.³) Fest., pp. 512.30–14.1 L.

VACERRAM et Aelius et alii complures vocari aiunt stipitem
. . . Ateius vero Philologus . . . vecors et vesanus, teste
Livio, qui dicit:

*ia*⁷   . . . vecorde et malefica vacerra

> vecorde *Ribbeck*: vecors *Scaliger*: corde *codd.*   vacerra
> *L. Mueller*: vecordia *codd.*

6 (8 R.³) *SHA, Car.* 13.5

ipsi denique comici plerumque sic milites inducunt ut eos
faciant vetera dicta usurpare. nam

*ia*⁶   lepus tute es; pulpamentum quaeris . . .

Livii Andronici dictum est.

Cf. Ter. *Eun.* 426.

5 Festus

vacerra ["stump"] Aelius[1] and many others say means a wooden post . . . but Ateius the Grammarian [see *Trag.* F 23] . . . [says it means] mad and evil, on the evidence of Livius, who says:

. . . by a mad and evil blockhead[2]

[1] Aelius Stilo, a Stoic and the first important Roman grammarian, born in Lanuvium around 150 BC. He taught Varro and influenced Cicero and Festus' source Verrius Flaccus (see Funaioli 1907, 51–76; Suet. *Gram. et rhet.* 3.1 [with Kaster 1995, 68–80 ad loc.]).   [2] Andronicus seems to use *vacerra* ("stump of wood") in a metaphorical sense for a stupid person, like Lat. *caudex* ("block of wood," "blockhead") and Eng. "chump."

6 *Historia Augusta*

Finally, the comic poets themselves usually bring soldiers on stage in such a way that they make them use old sayings, for:

you are a hare yourself, and yet you search for game[1] . . .

is a saying of Livius Andronicus.[2]

[1] The Latin is *pulpamentum*, which refers to a small piece of meat used as an hors d'oeuvre. As a hare was itself a tasty delicacy, it should not be seeking for what is in itself.   [2] The line is also spoken by the soldier Thraso in Terence's *Eunuch* (Ter. *Eun.* 426). Terence must have known it had occurred earlier in Livius Andronicus or elsewhere since he makes the soldier's parasite, Gnatho, ask him (*Eun.* 428) whether the saying is his, as he believed it was an old one. Thraso replies: "It's mine" (*Eun.* 429). Vopiscus, like Terence's audience, knows the true origin of the phrase, which later became associated only with Terence.

ODYSSIA (F 1–33)

This work is a translation into the old Latin Saturnian meter of parts of Homer's Odyssey *and represents the first example of epic in Latin. We are not sure of its exact Latin title (see Introduction to Livius Andronicus: Works). Our ancient sources refer variously to* Odyssia, Odyssea, *and* Odissia. *Gellius twice gives the title in Greek (F 1, 12). Festus (F 24, 25, 32) uses the title* Odyssia vetus *to distinguish Livius' work in Saturnians from a later translation of parts of the* Odyssey *into hexameters (see Pseudo-Andronicus,* Odyssia *and Introduction to Livius Andronicus: Works). On the evidence of Gellius (F 1), which mentions Livius Andronicus' work being contained in a* liber *(i.e., a papyrus volume), which would contain around 1,500 Saturnians, Flores (1998, 81–83) estimates that the total number of lines in the Latin work would amount to only around two books as compared with Homer's original twenty-four, but this seems unlikely (for arguments in fa-*

1 (1 Bl.) Gell. *NA* 18.9.2–6

"insecenda" quid esset quaeri coeptum. tum ex his qui aderant alter litterator fuit, alter litteras sciens, id est alter docens, doctus alter. [3] hi duo inter sese dissentiebant. et grammaticus quidem contendebat <mendosum librum esse> [*suppl. Holford-Strevens*: "insequenda" scribendum

ODYSSIA (F 1–33)

vor of a more extensive adaptation by Andronicus, see Introduction to Livius Andronicus: Works). Although later taught to Horace as a school text (T 6a), the original purpose of Andronicus' epic selections was probably for oral recital, just as in the Greek world selections from Homer were performed in the theater.

Bibl.: Flores 2011, 49–66; Paladini and Manzella 2014, 201–19, 259–63. Comm.: Paladini and Manzella 2014; Viredaz 2020. Lit.: Fränkel 1932; Borrelli 1951; Mariotti 1952; Traina 1953a; Ussani 1957 (F 15); Cazzaniga 1966 (F 29); Ronconi 1973; Bettini 1974 (F 21); Broccia 1974a; 1974b; 1975 (F 17, 18); Kessissoglu 1974 (F 7, 21); Büchner 1979; Caviglia 1984 (F 19); A. Barchiesi 1985 (F 28); 1995; Bernardi Perini 1989 (F 3); Kearns 1990; Goldberg 1993; 1995, 46–51; von Albrecht 1997; Oniga 1997 (F 19); Flores 1998; Farrell 2005; Sciarrino 2006; Biggs 2020, 35–52.

1 Gellius, *Attic Nights*

A discussion began on what *insecenda* meant. Of those who were present at the time one was a dabbler in literature, and another was an expert in it, that is to say one was a teacher, the other learned. [3] These two disagreed with each other. And the grammar teacher maintained that ⟨the book was wrong⟩. "[In Cato, *De Ptolemaeo contra*

83

esse *suppl. Hertz*]: "'insequenda' enim scribi," inquit
[grammaticus] "<oportuit> [*suppl. Hertz*] [apud Cato-
nem], non 'insecenda,' quoniam † 'insequens' significat
***, traditumque † esse 'inseque,' quasi 'perge dicere' et
'insequere,' itaque ab Ennio scriptum his versibus 'insece
Musa manu Romanorum induperator / quod quisque in
bello gessit cum rege Philippo'" [Enn. 10 *Ann.* F 1 *FRL*].
[4] alter autem ille eruditior nihil mendosum sed recte
atque integre scriptum esse perseverabat et Velio Longo,
non homini indocto, fidem esse habendam, qui in com-
mentario quod fecisset de usu antiquae lectionis scripserit
non "inseque" apud Ennium legendum esse sed "insece"
. . . [5] ego arbitror et a M. Catone "insecenda" et a Q.
Ennio "insece" scriptum sine u littera. offendi enim in
bibliotheca Patrensi librum verendae vestustatis Livii
Andronici, qui inscriptus est Ὀδύσσεια, in quo erat ver-
sus primus cum hoc verbo sine u littera:

virum mihi, Camena, insece versutum

factus ex illo Homeri versu [*Od.* 1.1] . . . [6] illic igitur
aetatis et fidei magnae libro credo.

versutum *codd., def. Kruschwitz 2008; Viredaz 2020, 99–100*:
vorsutum *Korsch 1868, 39; Perutelli 2005, 162, al.*

Cf. Hom. *Od.* 1.1: Ἄνδρα μοι ἔννεπε, Μοῦσα, πολύτροπον . . .

Cf. Paul. *Fest.*, p. 99.10 L.

---

[1] Grammarian of the early second century AD (*GL* VII,
pp. 48–81).   [2] Whether Andronicus invents the calque *in-
sece* ("tell") on the Homeric ἔννεπε (so Goldberg 1995, 64–65;
Hinds 1998, 58–63; Feeney 2016, 53–56) or whether the verb
already existed in Latin in the sense "tell" (so Viredaz 2020, 97–
99), he must have been aware, as a Greek speaker, of the close

Thermum F 17 Malc.] *insequenda* ⟨ought⟩ to have been written," [the grammar teacher] said, "not *insecenda*, since *insequens* means ***, and *inseque* has come down to us as "proceed to say" and "press on," and thus was written by Ennius in the following lines: "proceed, Muse, to say what deeds of arms each Roman commander accomplished in the war with King Philip" [Enn. 10 *Ann.* F 1 *FRL*] [4] But the other more learned man insisted there was nothing wrong, but that it was written correctly and appropriately and that we ought to trust Velius Longus,[1] a man not without learning, who in the commentary he had prepared on the use of archaic terms wrote that not *inseque* should be read in Ennius but *insece* . . . [5] I think M. Cato wrote *insecenda* and Q. Ennius wrote *insece* without the letter *u*, for in the library at Patras I came upon a book of revered antiquity by Livius Andronicus, called Ὀδύσ-σεια ("*Odyssia*"), the first line of which has this verb without the letter *u*:

Tell me,[2] Camena,[3] of the wily man

translated from this line of Homer [*Od.* 1.1] . . . [6] On such a point, then, I trust a book of great age and reliability.

similarity between the two words.   [3] Andronicus replaces the Greek "Muse" by the Latin "Camena," a good example of his Romanizing practice with proper names. Andronicus probably invented this correspondence, perhaps influenced by the phonetic similarity between *Camena* and *carmen* ("song," "poem"). The *Camenae* were originally river goddesses, possibly connected, like the *Carmentae*, with divination (see further Waszink 1956; Flores 1998, 51–62; Feeney 2016, 54–55; Viredaz 2020, 96–97).

Cf. Hom. *Od.* 1.1: Tell me, Muse, of the man of many wiles . . .

2 (2 Bl.) Prisc., *GL* II, p. 305.5–10

omnia in -us desinentia . . . in -e faciunt vocativum . . .
excipitur unum, quod tam in -e quam in -i facit vocativum,
quamvis sit appellativum, "o filie" et "o fili." Livius Andronicus in Odissia:

> pater noster, Saturni filie . . .

Cf. Hom. *Od.* 1.45: ὦ πάτερ ἡμέτερε Κρονίδη . . . (= *Od.* 1.81,
24.473).

3 (3 Bl.) Prisc., *GL* II, pp. 230.27–31.10

"puer, pueri," cuius femininum PUERA dicebant antiquissimi . . . Livius in Odyssia:

> mea puera, quid verbi ex tuo ore supra fugit?

puera *codd. Prisc.*: puer *codd. Charis.*   supra *codd.
Prisc.*: supera *Fleckeisen*: supra fugit *vel* supra fuit *codd.
Prisc.*:   supra fugit *codd. Prisc.*: audio *codd. Charis.*

Cf. Hom. *Od.* 1.64: τέκνον ἐμόν, ποῖόν σε ἔπος φύγεν ἕρκος
ὀδόντων; (= *Od.* 5.22, 14.492, 23.70).

Cf. Charis., *GL* I, p. 84.5–7 = p. 106 B.: puer et in feminino sexu
antiqui dicebant . . . ut in Odyssia vetere . . . : "mea puer, quid
verbi ex tuo ore audio?"

2 Priscian

All nouns ending in -*us* . . . form their vocative in -*e* . . .
except for one, which forms its vocative both in -*e* and in
-*i*, although it is a noun [namely *filius*, "son," which has the
vocatives] *o filie*[1] and *o fili*. Livius Andronicus in the *Odyssia*:

> our father, son of Saturn[2] . . .

[1] On this form, see Livingston 2004, 5–6.　　[2] Minerva
(Gk. Athene) addresses her father, Jove, son of Saturn (Gk. Zeus,
son of Cronos), asking for the speedy return of Ulysses (Gk.
Odysseus) to Ithaca.

Cf. Hom. *Od.* 1.45: O father of us all, son of Cronos . . . (= *Od.*
1.81, 24.473).

3 Priscian

puer ["boy"] [has the genitive] *pueri*, whose feminine form
puera ["girl"] the most ancient authors used . . . Livius in
the *Odyssia*:

> my daughter, what word fled up from your mouth?[1]

[1] The opening words of Jove's (Zeus') reply to Minerva
(Athene). Charisius quotes a very similar version of this line: "My
daughter (*mea puer*), what word do I hear (*audio*) from your
mouth," with *mea puer* ("my daughter") for Priscian's *mea puera*
("my daughter") and *audio* ("I hear") for Priscian's *supra fugit*
("fled up from"). It is impossible to know whether Charisius' line
comes from the same context as Priscian's (and, if so, which of the
two is correct), or whether it comes from elsewhere in Androni-
cus' translation.

Cf. Hom. *Od.* 1.64: my child, what word escaped the barrier of
your teeth? (= *Od.* 5.22, 14.492, 23.70).

4 (6 Bl.) Non., p. 544.20–22 M. = 873 L.

POLYBRUM, quod Graeci χέρνιβα, nos trullium vocamus.
Livius:

> argenteo polybro, aureo eclutro

polybro *codd.*: polubro *Stephanus*   eclutro *Baehrens*
(*cf. Gk.* ἔκλουτρον, *Pollux 10.46*): eglutro *C.O Mueller*: et glutro
codd.

Cf. Hom. *Od.* 1.136–37: χέρνιβα δ' ἀμφίπολος προχόῳ ἐπ-
έχευε φέρουσα / καλῇ χρυσείῃ ὑπὲρ ἀργυρέοιο λέβητος
(= *Od.* 4.52–53, 7.172–73, 10.368–69, 17.91–92).

Cf. *Corp. GL* II, p. 476.52: χέρνιβον trulleum.

5 (7 Bl.) Non., p. 509.20–29 M. = 819 L.

DISERTIM dicere plane, palam . . . Livius:

> tuque mihi narrato omnia disertim

Cf. Hom. *Od.* 1.169: ἀλλ' ἄγε μοι τόδε εἰπὲ καὶ ἀτρεκέως
κατάλεξον (= *Od.* 1.206, 224; 4.486; 8.572; 11.170, 370, 457;
15.383; 16.137; 24.256, 287).

4 Nonius

polybrum ["basin"], which the Greeks call χέρνιβα, we call *trullium*[1] ["washbasin"]. Livius:

> in a silver basin and a golden jug[2]

[1] The normal classical form is *trulleum*, from *trulla* ("ladle").
[2] The context is probably that of Telemachus providing hospitality for Minerva (Athene) in the guise of Mentes in Ulysses' (Odysseus') palace in Ithaca. Similar phrases recur in the context of ritual hospitality in Homer elsewhere, so that the exact Homeric line to which Andronicus' translation corresponds must remain uncertain.

Cf. Hom. *Od*. 1.136–37: then a handmaid brought water for the hands / in a beautiful jug of gold and poured it over a silver basin (= *Od*. 4.52–53, 7.172–73, 10.368–69, 17.91–92).

5 Nonius

disertim ["clearly"] [means] to speak "plainly," "openly" . . . Livius:[1]

> and you must tell me all this plainly[2]

[1] For Nonius' failure to cite the work, *Odyssia*, see F 29 n. 2. The use of the Saturnian meter here suggests it comes from the epic.   [2] Telemachus puts questions to Minerva (Athene), who is disguised as Mentes. However, this Homeric line occurs frequently elsewhere, and so the context for Andronicus' translation cannot be determined with any certainty.

Cf. Hom. *Od*. 1.169: come now tell me this and declare it truly (= *Od*. 1.206, 224; 4.486; 8.572; 11.170, 370, 457; 15.383; 16.137; 24.256, 287).

FRL VI: LIVIUS ANDRONICUS

6 (8 Bl.) Paul. *Fest.*, p. 252.3–4 L.

PROCITUM, cum prima syllaba corripitur, significat petitum. Livius:

matrem ‹proci› procitum plurimi venerunt

‹proci› *suppl. Zander metri causa*   plurimi *codd.*:
ploirume *Flores, cf. CIL I² 9*

Cf. Hom. *Od.* 1.248: τόσσοι μητέρ' ἐμὴν μνῶνται . . . (= *Od.* 16.125).

7 (9 Bl.) Fest., p. 208.3–7 L.

OMMENTANS, ‹Livius› [*suppl. cod. unus*] in Odyssea, cum ait:

‹primum› in Pylum devenies, haut ibi ommentans

significat obmanens sed ea significatione qua saepe fieri dicitur; is enim est mantare.

‹primum› *suppl. Flores:* ‹aut› *suppl. Guenther*   Pylum *codd.*: Pulum *Flores (cf. F 14)*   devenies *vel* deveniens *codd.*: adveniens *Scaliger*   haut *Leo:* aut *codd.*   ibi *vel* ubi *codd.*

Cf. Hom. *Od.* 1.284–85: πρῶτα μὲν ἐς Πύλον ἐλθὲ καὶ εἴρεο Νέστορα δῖον, / κεῖθεν δὲ Σπάρτηνδε παρὰ ξανθὸν Μενέλαον; *Od.* 2.317: ἠὲ Πύλονδ' ἐλθών, ἢ αὐτοῦ τῷδ' ἐνί δήμῳ.

6 Paul the Deacon, *Epitome of Festus*

procitum ["for the sake of wooing"; supine of *proco,* which in classical Latin would have the first conjugation form *procatum*], when the first syllable is short, means "for the sake of asking for." Livius:

> very many ‹suitors› have come to woo my mother[1]

[1] Telemachus to Minerva (Athene), who is disguised as Mentes.

Cf. Hom. *Od.* 1.248: so many men woo my mother . . . (= *Od.* 16.125).

7 Festus

ommentans ["remaining"; *hapax legomenon*]. ‹Livius› in the *Odyssia,* when he says:

> ‹first› you will come to Pylos, but not remaining there[1]

he/it means *obmanens* ["staying"], but with the meaning that it is said to happen frequently, for that is the force of [the frequentative] *mantare* ["to stay on"].

[1] Minerva (Athene) in disguise advises Telemachus to go to Pylos to ask Nestor where his father is, and to go from there to Sparta to ask Menelaus. Earlier editors compared Hom. *Od.* 2.317, where Telemachus tells the suitors how he will bring about their death, either seeking aid from Pylos or remaining here at home. The fact that Andronicus' *ibi* means "there" and not "here" has persuaded many against this identification, but for arguments in its favor see Viredaz 2020, 105–7.

Cf. Hom. *Od.* 1.284–85: first go to Pylos and question noble Nestor, / and from there to Sparta, to fair-haired Menelaus; *Od.* 2.317: either going to Pylos or here in this land.

8 (16 Bl.) Isid. *Orig.* 19.4.9

STRUPPI vincula loro vel lino facta quibus remi ad scalmos alligantur. de quibus Livius:

>   tumque remos iussit religare struppis

>   tumque <is> *suppl. Flores*

Cf. Hom. *Od.* 2.422–26: Τηλέμαχος δ᾽ ἑτάροισιν ἐποτρύνας ἐκέλευσεν / ὅπλων ἅπτεσθαι· τοὶ δ᾽ ὀτρύνοντος ἄκουσαν. / ἱστὸν δ᾽ εἰλάτινον κοίλης ἔντοσθε μεσόδμης / στῆσαν ἀείραντες, κατὰ δὲ προτόνοισιν ἔδησαν / ἕλκον δ᾽ ἱστία λευκὰ ἐϋστρέπτοισι βοεῦσιν (= *Od.* 15.287–91); *Od.* 4.782: ἠρτύναντο δ᾽ ἐρετμὰ τροποῖς ἐν δερματίνοισι (= *Od.* 8.53); *Od.* 8.37: δησάμενοι δ᾽ εὖ πάντες ἐπὶ κληῖσιν ἐρετμά.

9 (10 Bl.) Gell. *NA* 6.7.11

"adprimum" autem longe primum L. Livius in Odyssia dicit in hoc versu:

>   ibidemque vir summus adprimus Patroclus

Cf. Hom. *Od.* 3.110: ἔνθα δὲ Πάτροκλος, θεόφιν μήστωρ ἀτάλαντος.

8 Isidore, *Origins*

struppi ["straps"; rare Latinized form of the Greek στρό-
φος, "twisted cord"] are the bindings made of leather or
linen with which oars are tied to the rowlocks. Livius [says]
of them:

> then he ordered them to bind the oars with straps[1]

[1] The context is Telemachus' departure from Ithaca on his
voyage to Pylos. The wording may also contain echoes of Alci-
nous' words to the Phaeacians from *Od.* 8.37 and 8.53.

Cf. Hom. *Od.* 2.422–26: And Telemachus called to his men / to
take hold of the tackle; and they heard his call. / The mast of fir
they raised and set in the hollow socket / and bound it fast with
the forestays; then hauled up the white sail with well-twisted
thongs of ox hide (= *Od.* 15.287–91); *Od.* 4.782: they fitted the
oars in the leather straps (= *Od.* 8.53); *Od.* 8.37: when you have
all bound the oars well to the benches.

9 Gellius, *Attic Nights*

adprimum ["the very first"], however, is used by L. Livius
in this verse in the *Odyssia* with the meaning *longe pri-
mum* ["by far the first"]:

> and there also [fell] the greatest hero, Patroclus, by
> far the first [of men][1]

[1] Nestor tells Telemachus of the Greek heroes who died in
Troy. Andronicus replaces the Greek hyperbolic "peer of gods"
with the phrase "first [of men]," which would be more acceptable
to a Roman audience.

Cf. Hom. *Od.* 3.110: and there also Patroclus the peer of gods in
council.

10 (23 Bl.) Gell. *NA* 3.16.11

Caesellius . . . Vindex in lectionibus suis antiquis "tria" inquit "nomina Parcarum sunt: Nona, Decuma, Morta," et versum hunc Livii, antiquissimi poetae, ponit ex Ὀδυσσείᾳ:

> quando dies adveniet quem profata Morta est

sed homo minime malus Caesellius "Mortam" quasi nomen [Parcae] accepit, cum accipere quasi moeram [μοῖραν] deberet.

Cf. Hom. *Od.* 3.237–38: . . . ὁππότε κεν δὴ / μοῖρ᾽ ὀλοὴ καθέλῃσι τανηλεγέος θανάτοιο; *Od.* 2.99–100: . . . εἰς ὅτέ κέν μιν / μοῖρ᾽ ὀλοὴ καθέλῃσι τανηλεγέος θανάτοιο (= *Od.* 19.144–45, 24.134–35); *Od.* 10.175: . . . πρὶν μόρσιμον ἦμαρ ἐπέλθῃ.

---

[1] An early second-century AD grammarian, whose work was often criticized by Gellius and his contemporaries. Excerpts from his work on orthography are to be found at *GL* VII, pp. 202–7.

[2] On this form, see Livingston 2004, 23–29. [3] In the first Homeric passage, Athene makes a general statement to Telemachus about the impossibility for the gods to save a man they love from death (with reference to Odysseus); in the second, Penelope addresses the suitors about the funeral cloth she is weaving against the death of Laertes. Paladini (2014, 55 ad loc.) argues that the first passage is more likely the source here as the Latin *quando*, if interpreted as "whenever" rather than "when," is closer in meaning to the Greek conjunction used in that pas-

10 Gellius, *Attic Nights*

Caesellius . . . Vindex[1] in his *Ancient Readings* says: "there
are three names for the *Parcae* [Fates]: Nona, Decima and
Morta,"[2] and he quotes this line of Livius, the most ancient
poet, from his *Odyssia*:

> whenever the day comes which Morta has foretold[3]

but Caesellius, though by no means a bad scholar, took
Morta as a personal name [of one of the *Parcae*], when he
should have taken it as something like [the Greek] *moera*
["fate"].

sage. Viredaz (2020, 140–42), following Broccia (1974a, 51–58),
prefers to connect the verse with Hom. *Od.* 10.175, where Ulysses
tells his companions that the time has not yet come for them to
die. This interpretation is based on the correspondence of *dies*
("day") with ἦμαρ, *adveniet* ("comes") with ἐπέλθῃ, and *Morta*
("fate") with μόρσιμον, but involves changing the Greek πρὶν
("before") to Latin *quando* ("whenever").

Cf. Hom. *Od.* 3.237–38: whenever / the cruel fate of pitiless
death will take him; *Od.* 2.99–100: against the time when / the
cruel fate of pitiless death will take him (= *Od.* 19.144–45,
24.134–35); *Od.* 10.175: before the day of fate comes upon us.

FRL VI: LIVIUS ANDRONICUS

11 (31 Bl.) Prisc., *GL* II, p. 198.6–10

[primae] declinationis femininorum genitivum etiam in
-as more Graeco solebant antiquissimi terminare . . . Li-
vius in Odyssia:

atque escas habeamus mentionem . . .

"esacas" pro "escae."

habeamus *Hermann*: habemus *codd.*

Cf. Hom. *Od.* 4.213: δόρπου δ' ἐξαῦτις μνησώμεθα . . . ; *Od.*
10.177: μνησόμεθα βρώμης . . . ; *Od.* 20.246: . . . μνησώμεθα
δαιτός.

12 (11 Bl.) Fest., p. 160.3–6 L.

NEQUINONT pro nequeunt, ut solinunt, ferinunt pro so-
lent et feriunt dicebant antiqui. Livius in Odissia:

partim errant, nequinont Graeciam redire

nequinont *Ursinus*: nequinunt *cod. Gloss. III Abol. NE 22*:
neque nunc *cod.*

Cf. Hom. *Od.* 4.495: πολλοὶ μὲν γὰρ τῶν γε δάμεν, πολλοὶ δὲ
λίποντο; *Od.* 4.558: . . . ὁ δ' οὐ δύναται ἥν πατρίδα γαῖαν
ἱκέσθαι.

11 Priscian

The most ancient writers used to end the genitive singular of feminine nouns of the [first] declension also in -*as* in the Greek manner . . . Livius in the *Odyssia*:

> and let us take thought for food[1] . . .

[ancient genitive] *escas* ["of food"] for [the classical form] *escae*.

[1] Menelaus interrupts his speech to Telemachus to take a break for food. Other contexts are possible, such as *Od*. 10.177, when Odysseus returns to his boat with meat for his men, or *Od*. 20.246, of the suitors eating at Odysseus' expense.

Cf. Hom. *Od*. 4.213 (variations at *Od*. 10.177, 20.246): and let us once more think of food . . .

12 Festus

The ancients said *nequinont*[1] ["they cannot"] for *nequeunt*, like *solinunt* ["they are accustomed"] and *ferinunt* ["they strike"] for *solent* and *feriunt*. Livius in the *Odyssia*:

> part of them wander, they are unable to return to
> Greece[2]

[1] On this and similar forms, see Livingston 2004, 13–16.

[2] Proteus tells Menelaus of the fate of the Greeks after the fall of Troy. Andronicus perhaps contaminates this passage with *Od*. 4.558, where Proteus tells of Odysseus' detention on the island of Calypso. Homer's Achaeans would not have referred to their homeland as Greece (see Introduction to Livius Andronicus: Works).

Cf. Hom. *Od*. 4.495: for many of them were slain and many were left behind; *Od*. 4.558: and he cannot come to his native land.

13 (12 Bl.) Prisc., *GL* II, pp. 231.13–32.3

"hic" et "haec puer" vetustissimi protulisse inveniuntur . . .
Livius in Odyssia:

>sancta puer Saturni filia regina

Saturni / filia regina *Hermann*   filia *codd.*: *secl. Fleckei-*
sen: maxima *Baehrens*

Cf. Hom. *Od.* 4.513: . . . σάωσε δὲ πότνια Ἥρη; *Il.* 5.721:
Ἥρη, πρέσβα θεά, θυγάτηρ μεγάλοιο Κρόνοιο (= *Il.* 8.383).

14 (13 Bl.) Prisc., *GL* II, p. 210.6–9

quod autem Ionis et Calypsonis et Didonis dicitur, osten-
dit hoc etiam Caesellius Vindex in *Stromateo* his verbis:
Calypsonem. ita declinantum est apud antiquos. Livius:

>apud nympham Atlantis filiam Calypsonem

nympham *codd.*: numpam *vel* nimpam *edd.*   Calyp-
sonem *codd.*: Calupsonem *vel* Calipsonem *edd.*

Cf. Hom. *Od.* 4.557: νύμφης ἐν μεγάροισι Καλυψοῦς . . .
(= *Od.* 5.14, 17.143); *Od.* 1.52: Ἄτλαντος θυγάτηρ . . . (= *Od.*
7.245).

13 Priscian

The most ancient writers are found to have used *puer* ["child"] in the masculine and in the feminine . . . Livius in the *Odyssia*:

> the holy child of Saturn,[1] his royal daughter[2]

[1] Hera (= Juno) is not addressed as daughter of Cronos (= Saturn) in the *Odyssey*, but only in the *Iliad* (Hom. *Il*. 5.721, 8.383).

[2] Proteus tells Menelaus how Juno saved his brother, Agamemnon, from drowning at sea.

Cf. Hom. *Od*. 4.513: . . . queenly Hera saved him; *Il*. 5.721: Hera, the honored goddess, daughter of great Cronos (= *Il*. 8.383).

14 Priscian

As to the fact that one says *Ionis, Calypsonis*, and *Didonis* [genitives] Caesellius Vindex [early second-century AD grammarian] also shows this in his *Miscellany* with these words: "*Calypsonem* [for classical acc. *Calypso*, as in Ov. *Pont*. 4.10.3]. So it was declined among the ancients. Livius:

> at the house of the nymph Calypso, daughter of
> Atlas"[1]

[1] Proteus tells Menelaus how Ulysses was detained in the palace of Calypso.

Cf. Hom. *Od*. 4.557: in the halls of the nymph Calypso . . . (= *Od*. 5.14, 17.143); *Od*. 1.52: daughter of Atlas . . . (= *Od*. 7.245).

15 (30 Bl.) Serv. Dan. ad Verg. *Aen*. 1.92

"extemplo Aeneae solvuntur frigore membra": Graeci φρικτὰ dicunt quae sunt timenda . . . Livius in Odyssia:

igitur demum Ulixi cor frixit prae pavore

Cf. Hom. *Od*. 5.297: καὶ τότ᾽ Ὀδυσσῆος λύτο γούνατα καὶ φίλον ἦτορ (= 5.406, 22.147 [*de Ulyxe*], 23.205 [*de Penelopa*]); *Od*. 23.215–16 (*de Penelopa*): αἰεὶ γάρ μοι θυμὸς ἐνὶ στήθεσσι φίλοισιν / ἐρρίγει.

Cf. Macr. *Sat*. 5.3.9 ad Verg. *Aen*. 1.92.

16 (14 Bl.) Diom., *GL* I, p. 384.7–9

vulgo dicimus "amplector," veteres inmutaverunt "amploctor" crebro dictitantes, ut Livius in Odyssea:

utrum genua amploctens virginem oraret

Cf. Hom. *Od*. 6.141–42: . . . ὁ δὲ μερμήριξεν Ὀδυσσεύς / ἢ γούνων λίσσοιτο λαβὼν εὐώπιδα κούρην.

15 Servius Danielis, *Commentary on Virgil*

The Greeks call φρικτὰ ["frozen"] things which are to be feared . . . Livius in the *Odyssia*:

> then indeed the heart of Ulysses went cold with fear[1]

[1] The line could describe Ulysses' (Odysseus') fear during a storm at sea, as in Hom. *Od.* 5.297, although other contexts are possible in Andronicus. The same phrase "knees grew loose, and the heart within him melted" is used of Odysseus' fear at seeing the suitors arming themselves at Hom. *Od.* 22.147 and of Penelope's emotion at recognizing Odysseus at Hom. *Od.* 23.205. The idea of cold associated with fear could have come from the description of Penelope's fear of the suitors at Hom. *Od.* 23.215–16 ("always the heart in my breast shuddered with fear"). The line *Od.* 5.297 is the model for Virgil's description of Aeneas' fear at sea in *Aen.* 1.92 (to which Servius Danielis' comment applies): "suddenly Aeneas' limbs grow weak with chill dread," where the idea of "cold" may have been taken from Andronicus.

Cf. Hom. *Od.* 5.297: then Odysseus' knees grew loose, and the heart within him melted.

16 Diomedes

We commonly say *amplector* ["I embrace"], but the ancients changed it, frequently saying *amploctor* [a form attested only in Andronicus], like Livius in the *Odyssia*:

> whether he should grasp the maiden's knees and beg her[1]

[1] The first meeting of Ulysses (Odysseus) with Nausicaa. Grasping the knees was a Greek gesture of supplication.

Cf. Hom. *Od.* 6.141–42: . . . and Odysseus pondered / whether he should clasp her knees and pray to the fair-faced maiden.

17 (15 Bl.) Charis., *GL* I, p. 197.15–17 = p. 256 B.

DONICUM pro donec; ita Livius . . . :

> ibi manens sedeto donicum videbis
> me carpento vehentem domum venisse ⟨parentis⟩

2 vehentem domum *Parhassius, Fabricius*: vehentem en domum *Buecheler*: vehentem in domum *Hermann*: vehementem domum *codd.* ⟨parentis⟩ *suppl. Ritschl*: ⟨patris⟩ *suppl. Wordsworth*

Cf. Hom. *Od.* 6.295–96: ἔνθα καθεζόμενος μεῖναι χρόνον, εἰς ὅ κεν ἡμεῖς / ἄστυδε ἔλθωμεν καὶ ἱκώμεθα δώματα πατρός.

18 (17 Bl.) Fest., p. 182.18–23 L.

NOEGEUM quidam amiculi genus praetextum purpura; quidam candidum ac perlucidum, quasi a nauco, quod putamen quorundam pomorum est tenuissimum non sine candore, ut Livius ait in Odyssia:

> simul ac lacrumas de ore noegeo detersit

id est candido.

lacrumas *cod.*: dacrumas *Lindsay (1893, 150, 317), Flores*: dacrimas *Hermann, C. O. Mueller coll. Paul. Fest., p. 60.5 L. (dacrimas pro lacrimas Livius saepe posuit)*

Cf. Hom. *Od.* 8.88: δάκρυ᾽ ὀμορξάμενος κεφαλῆς ἄπο φᾶρος ἔλεσκε.

17 Charisius

donicum ["until," an archaic form] for [classical] *donec*; so
Livius . . . :

> sit there and wait until you see
> that riding on a wagon[1] I have come home to <my
>   father's> house[2]

[1] On Andronicus' use of the Latin *carpentum* ["wagon"] to
lend dignity to Nausicaa's conveyance, see *Introduction to Livius
Andronicus: Works.*   [2] Nausicaa addresses Ulysses (Odys-
seus), telling him to wait for her at the palace of her father, Alci-
nous.

Cf. Hom. *Od.* 6.295–96: sit down there and wait for a while until
we / come to the town and reach the house of my father.

18 Festus

Some say *noegeum* [*hapax legomenon*] is a type of cloak
fringed with purple; some say that it is white and translu-
cent, as if from *naucum*, which is the very thin and whitish
peel of certain fruits, as Livius says in the *Odyssia*:

> as soon as he had wiped away the tears from his face
>   with his cloak[1]

a white one, that is.

[1] Ulysses (Odysseus) wipes away the tears caused by the min-
strel Demodocus' song of the Trojan War.

Cf. Hom. *Od.* 8.88: [Odysseus] would wipe away his tears and
draw the cloak from his head.

19 (18 Bl.) Fest., p. 482.7–14 L.

TOPPER significare ait Artorius cito, fortasse, celeriter, temere . . . cito: . . . sic in eodem [Livio: *Scaliger*]:

> namque nullum peius macerat humanum
> quamde mare saevum; vires cui sunt magnae
> topper <citae> confringent inportunae undae

1 humanum *cod.*: homonem *Ursinus*   2 vires *Augustinus*: vis (pl.) et *Lindsay*: viret *cod.*   3 <citae> *suppl. Flores*

Cf. Hom. *Od.* 8.138–39: οὐ γὰρ ἐγώ γέ τί φημι κακώτερον ἄλλο θαλάσσης / ἄνδρα γε συγχεῦαι, εἰ καὶ μάλα καρτερὸς εἴη.

20 (19 Bl.) Prisc., *GL* II, p. 198.6–15

[primae] declinationis femininorum genetivum etiam in -as more Graeco solebant antiquissimi terminare . . . Livius in Odyssia [*Od.* F 11, 22] . . . in eodem:

> Mercurius cumque eo filius Latonas

pro "Latonae."

<venit> Mercurius *suppl. Bartsch*

Cf. Hom. *Od.* 8.322–23: . . . ἦλθ' ἐριούνης / Ἑρμείας, ἦλθεν δὲ ἄναξ ἑκάεργος Ἀπόλλων; *Il.* 1.9, 16.849: Λητοῦς . . . υἱός.

19 Festus

Artorius[1] says that *topper*[2] [a word found only in archaic Latin] means quickly, perhaps, swiftly, rashly . . . quickly: . . . thus in the same author [Livius Andronicus]:

> for nothing wastes a man worse
> than a savage sea; the man whose strength is great,
> him the merciless ‹swift› waves will quickly break[3]

[1] A grammarian of the Augustan Age (see Funaioli 1907, 480–81).   [2] On this form, see Livingston 2004, 17–21.
[3] The words are spoken by Alcinous' son Laodamas, with reference to Ulysses (Odysseus) and his sufferings at sea.

Cf. Hom. *Od.* 8.138–39: for I say there is nothing worse than the sea / for confounding a man, however strong he may be.

20 Priscian

The most ancient writers used to end the genitive singular of feminine nouns of the [first] declension also in *-as* in the Greek manner . . . Livius in the *Odyssia* [*Od.* F 11, 22] . . . in the same:

> Mercury [came] and with him Latona's son [Apollo][1]

Latonas [old genitive singular] for *Latonae* [classical genitive singular].

[1] Alcinous' minstrel, Demodocus, sings of how a procession of gods visits Vulcan's (Hephaestus') house to see how he has ensnared the adulterous pair Venus and Mars (Aphrodite and Ares).

Cf. Hom. *Od.* 8.322–23: . . . there came the helper / Hermes and lord Apollo, who works from afar; *Il.* 1.9, 16.849: Leto's son.

105

21 (20 Bl.) Prisc., *GL* II, p. 469.12–18

"nexo" quoque "nexas" vel "nexis" . . . Virgilius [*Aen.* 5.279] tamen . . . "nexantem" . . . Livius vero in Odissia:

> nexebant multa inter se flexu nodorum dubio

nexebant *codd.*: nexabant *Diom., GL I, p. 369.20; Prisc., GL II, p. 538.12*

Cf. Hom. *Od.* 8.378–79: ὀρχείσθην δὴ ἔπειτα ποτὶ χθονὶ πουλυβοτείρῃ / ταρφέ᾿ ἀμειβομένω . . . ; Schol. V ad 8.379: [ταρφέ᾿ ἀμειβομένω] πυκνῶς πλέκοντες εἰς ἀλλήλους ἐναλλασσόμενοι.

Cf. Diom., *GL* I, p. 369.19–20; Prisc., *GL* II, p. 538.11–13.

22 (21 Bl.) Prisc., *GL* II, p. 198.6–12

[primae] declinationis femininorum genetivum etiam in -as more Graeco solebant antiquissimi terminare . . . Livius in Odyssia . . . :

> nam diva Monetas filia docuit

diva *vel* divina *codd.*: divam *vel* divae *Merula*   filia *Scaliger*: filiam *codd.*: filia me *Fruterius*: filia med *Flores, qui confert Hom. Od. 22.347 de Phemio*

Cf. Hom. *Od.* 8.480–81: . . . οὕνεκ᾿ ἄρα σφέας / οἴμας Μοῦσ᾿ ἐδίδαξε . . .

---

1 Used here by false association with the Latin *monere* ("to remind") as an equivalent of the Greek mother of the Muses, Mnemosyne, derived from the Greek μιμνήσκειν ("to bring to mind"). The name Moneta may in reality be of Etruscan origin and occurs usually as a cult title of Juno.   2 Ulysses (Odysseus) at a feast at the Phaeacian court, wishing to reward Demodocus, praises poets as pupils of the Muse.

21 Priscian

nexo ["I entwine"; rare and mainly ante-classical] also [has the second person forms] *nexas* [first conjugation] or *nexis* [third conjugation] . . . yet Virgil [in *Aen.* 5.279 has] . . . *nexantem* ["entwining"; first conjugation] . . . but Livius in the *Odyssia* [uses the third conjugation form]:

> they entwined each other in many a confusing twist
>   of knots[1]

[1] The line describes the dance of Alcinous' two sons Halius and Laodamas at the Phaecian court.

Cf. Hom. *Od.* 8.378–79: the two began to dance on the bounteous earth, / tossing the ball between them . . .

Fränkel (1932, 306–7), followed by Waszink (1960, 24n2), posits Andronicus' knowledge of Homeric scholia on these lines, namely Schol. V ad *Od.* 8.379 ["tossing the ball between them"]: "frequently entwining with each other in their exchanges." However, there is no other evidence of Andronicus' use of Homeric scholia, except possibly in *Od.* F 25 (see *Od.* F 25 n. 3), and the verbal similarities are perhaps not significant enough to warrant such a theory (see Viredaz 2020, 130).

22 Priscian

The most ancient writers used to end the genitive singular of feminine nouns of the [first] declension also in *-as* in the Greek manner . . . Livius in the *Odyssia* . . . :

> for the divine daughter of Moneta[1] [the Muse] is
>   accustomed to teach [them][2]

Cf. Hom. *Od.* 8.480–81: . . . for them / the Muse has taught the ways of song . . .

FRL VI: LIVIUS ANDRONICUS

23 (22 Bl.) Prisc., *GL* II, p. 482.9–14

vetustissimi . . . "gavisi" pro "gavisus sum" protulerunt . . .
Livius in Odissia:

⟨haec⟩ quoniam audivi, ⟨tum⟩ magis gavisi

⟨haec⟩ *suppl. Mariotti*   ⟨tum⟩ *suppl. Flores*   macis
(= magis) *Flores: paucis codd.*

Cf. Hom. *Od.* 9.413: ὣς ἄρ' ἔφαν ἀπιόντες, ἐμὸν δ' ἐγέλασσε
φίλον κῆρ; *Od.* 16.92: ἦ μάλα μευ καταδάπτετ' ἀκούοντος
φίλον ἦτορ.

24 (24 Bl.) Fest., p. 482.7–27 L.

TOPPER . . . in antiquissimis scriptis celeriter et mature. in
Odyssia vetere . . . :

topper citi ad aedis venimus Circae

circae *cod.*: circai *Wordsworth, edd.*

Cf. Hom. *Od.* 10.252: εὕρομεν ἐν βήσσῃσι τετυγμένα δώματα
καλά [Κίρκης Plutarch, Iohannes Doxopater]; *Od.* 10.210, 287,
308, 445; 12.9: δώματα Κίρκης.

---

1 On this form, see Livingston 2004, 17–21.   2 Festus
does not specifically mention the author, but "the old *Odyssia*"
can refer only to Livius Andronicus (see Introduction to Livius
Andronicus: Works, and the introduction to Pseudo-Andronicus,
Odyssia). For the two lines immediately following this quotation
in Festus, but now not thought to belong to the same context, see
Od. F 32.   3 Ulysses (Odysseus) reports to Alcinous Eury-
lochus' account of how, with twenty-two companions, he found
the palace of Circe in the woods.   4 The indirect tradition
of this Homeric line has "of Circe" for "beautifully built," and this
may have been the text Livius was adapting (see Introduction to
Livius Andronicus: Works).

108

23 Priscian

The most ancient writers . . . used *gavisi*[1] ["I rejoiced"] for [the classical perfect form] *gavisus sum* . . . Livius in the *Odyssia*:

> when I heard ⟨these words⟩, ⟨then⟩ I became more
> joyful[2]

[1] On this form, see Livingston 2004, 37–38.   [2] The passage is corrupt and incomplete as it stands in the manuscripts. The reading adopted here is that of Flores (2011, 26). In this form the line corresponds better to *Od.* 9.413 (first suggested by Leo), in which Odysseus recounts to Alcinous how he tricked the Cyclops into crying out that "Nobody" was attacking him. In the line in question, Ulysses (Odysseus) tells how, when he heard the words of the other Cyclopes, refusing to come to their comrade's aid, he became more joyful. The *Od.* 16.92 passage in which Odysseus, not yet recognized, tells Telemachus of his sadness when hearing of the suitors' crimes, fits better with the original manuscript reading *paucis gavisi* ("I took pleasure in little"), but this litotes does not correspond well to the strong "you break my heart" of the suggested model.

Cf. Hom. *Od.* 9.413: thus they spoke and went away and my dear heart laughed; *Od.* 16.92: for truly you break my heart as I hear your words.

24 Festus

topper[1] ["quickly"; ante-classical] . . . in the most ancient texts means "fast" and "soon." In the old *Odyssia*[2] . . . :

> quickly we came in haste to the house of Circe[3]

Cf. Hom. *Od.* 10.252: we found in the mountain glens a beautifully built palace.[4] For the phrase "the house of Circe," see Hom. *Od.* 10.210, 287, 308, 445; 12.9.

25 (25 Bl.) Fest., p. 482.7–25 L.

TOPPER . . . in antiquissimis scriptis celeriter et mature. in Odyssia vetere:

topper facit homines ut rusus fuerint

Cf. Hom. *Od.* 10.395: ἄνδρες δ' αἶψ' [ἄψ Aristarchus, *cf. Schol. H. ad loc.*] ἐγένοντο νεώτεροι ἢ πάρος ἦσαν.

facit *cod.*: facti *Goldberg 1995, 64n11*   homines *cod., def. Mariotti (1952, 99)*: homones *C. O. Mueller, cf. Od. F 19.1*   ut rusus *Lennartz*: utrius *cod.*: ut prius *Duentzer*   fuerint *cod.*: fuerunt *Buecheler*

26 (26 Bl.) Gell. *NA* 6.7.12

idem Livius [cf. *Od.* F 9] in Odyssia "praemodum" dicit quasi admodum:

. . . parcentes

inquit,

praemodum

quod significat supra modum, dictumque est quasi praeter modum.

Cf. Hom. *Od.* 12.321: . . . τῶν δὲ βοῶν ἀπεχώμεθα . . . ; *Od.* 12.328: . . . βοῶν ἀπέχοντο λιλαιόμενοι βίοτοιο.

---

[1] The quotation is too limited to be sure of its exact source, but it could come from Ulysses' warning to his crew to abstain from eating the cattle of Helios (*Od.* 12.321) or from the description of how they did at first abstain (*Od.* 12.328).

25 Festus

topper[1] ["quickly"; ante-classical] . . . in the most ancient texts means "fast" and "soon." In the old *Odyssia*:

> quickly she brought it about that they became men
> again[2]

Cf. Hom. *Od.* 10.395: and they became men again,[3] younger than they were before.

[1] On this form, see Livingston 2004, 17–21.   [2] Ulysses (Odysseus) tells Alcinous how Circe turned his men back from pigs into human form.   [3] Andronicus' text probably read "quickly" in the Greek, hence his use of the word *topper* ("quickly") in his adaptation. After Andronicus' time, the Greek was emended to "again" by the critic Aristarchus, an idea perhaps suggested in Andronicus' *rusus* ("again"), if that is the correct reading. It is possible that this alternative reading was known to Andronicus before Aristarchus' time through the Homeric scholia (see discussion on *Od.* F 21 n. 1).

26 Gellius, *Attic Nights*

The same Livius [cf. *Od.* F 9] in the *Odyssia* uses *praemodum* ["beyond measure"] like *admodum* ["very"]:

> . . . sparing

he says,

> beyond measure[1]

which means "above measure," and is said as if it were *praeter modum*, "beyond measure."

Cf. Hom. *Od.* 12.321: . . . let us spare the cattle . . . ; *Od.* 12.328: . . . they spared the cattle, for they wished to save their lives.

27 (32 Bl.) Non. p. 475.13–17 M. = 762 L.

FITE imperativo modo . . . Livius Odyssia:

. . . sic quoque fitum est

Cf. Hom. *Od.* 13.40: ἤδη γὰρ τετέλεσται ἅ μοι φίλος ἤθελε θυμός; *Od.* 5.302: τὰ δὲ δὴ νῦν πάντα τελεῖται (= *Od.* 2.176, 13.178, 18.271); *Od.* 8.510: τῇ περ δὴ καὶ ἔπειτα τελευτήσεσθαι ἔμελλεν.

28 (4 Bl.) Prisc., *GL* II, p. 301.17–22

i ante -us habentia, abiecta -us faciunt vocativum, ut "hic Virgilius, o Virgili" . . . haec tamen eadem etiam in e proferebant antiquissimi "o Virgilie" . . . dicentes. Livius Andronicus in Odissia:

neque tamen te oblitus sum, Laertie noster

"Laertius" enim pro "Laertes" dicebant.

tamen *cod.*: enim *codd.*

Cf. Hom. *Od.* 14.144: ἀλλά μ' Ὀδυσσῆος πόθος αἴνυται οἰχομένοιο; *Od.* 1.65: πῶς ἂν ἔπειτ' Ὀδυσῆος ἐγὼ θείοιο λαθοίμην;

---

[1] On these vocative forms, see Livingston 2004, 5–6.

[2] The line adapts a Homeric line from the speech of the swineherd Eumaeus to Odysseus, whom at this stage he does not yet recognize. A direct address, "Laertius' son," replaces the third-person mention of Odysseus in the Greek and thus heightens the pathos. Closer in wording to our passage is Hom. *Od.* 1.65, in a speech from Zeus to Athene (Jove to Minerva) directly following Livius Andronicus *Od.* F 3, but such a direct address to Laertius' son is found by some (Leo 1905, 41n5; Mariotti 1952, 49n2) to be out of place in the mouth of Jove, especially in a speech to his daughter (see further A. Barchiesi 1985). However,

27 Nonius

fite in the imperative mood [of *fio*, "happen"] . . . Livius in the *Odyssia* [*fitum est*: perfect of *fio*]:

. . . so also it has come about[1]

[1] The most likely model is *Od.* 13.40, Odysseus' parting words to Alcinous, who has sent him on his way with gifts of friendship. Other possibilities discussed by Manzella (Paladini and Manzella 2014, 160, 164–65) are *Od.* 5.302 (Odysseus' self-apostrophe in a storm at sea) and *Od.* 8.510 (in Demodocus the minstrel's song about the Trojan horse).

Cf. Hom. *Od.* 13.40: for now all that my heart wished has come about; *Od.* 5.302: now all this is being brought to pass (= *Od.* 2.176, 13.178, 18.271); *Od.* 8.510: just as in the end it was to be brought to pass.

28 Priscian

Nouns having an *-i* before the [nominative] *-us*, lose the *-us* and make their vocative as follows: [nominative] *hic Virgilius,* [vocative] *o Virgili* . . . but these same nouns the most ancient writers also declined in *-e*, . . . saying *o Virgilie.*[1] Livius Andronicus in the *Odyssia*:

but I have not forgotten you, our Laertius' son[2]

For they said "Laertius" for "Laertes."

this attribution to Jove is defended by Viredaz (2020, 100–102). First, he thinks, Andronicus could have wished to add to the pathos of Jove's speech by making Jove address Ulysses in his imagination. Such familiarity between men and gods, he argues, could be seen as characteristic of Roman tragedy and epic.

Cf. Hom. *Od.* 14.144: it is longing for Odysseus, who has gone away, that seizes me; *Od.* 1.65: How should I, then, forget godlike Odysseus?

29 (27 Bl.) Non., p. 368.26–30 M. = 586 L.

PVLLVM non album . . . [Titus *secl. L. Mueller*] Livius:

> vestis pulla porpurea ampla . . .

* *trib. Liv. Odissiae Hertz 1862*

Cf. Hom. *Od.* 19.225–26: χλαῖναν πορφυρέην οὔλην ἔχε δῖος Ὀδυσσεύς, / διλπῆν· . . .

30 (28 Bl.) Prisc., *GL* II, p. 208.18–21

vetustissimi . . . etiam nominativum "haec carnis" proferebant . . . Livius Andronicus in Odyssia:

> . . . carnis

ait,

> vinumque quod libabant anculabatur

carnis / . . . anculabatur *Havet 1880*: carnis . . . anclabatur *codd.* (cf. *Trag. F 20*)

Cf. Hom. *Od.* 23.304–5: οἵ ἔθεν εἵνεκα πολλὰ, βόας καὶ ἴφια μῆλα / ἔσφαζον, πολλὸς δὲ πίθων ἠφύσσετο οἶνος.

29 Nonius

pullum[1] ["dark"], not white . . . Livius:[2]

> a cloak dark, purple, large[3] . . .

[1] On this word, see Livingston 2004, 39.   [2] In F 27 and F 31 Nonius specifies the work *Odyssia*, but in F 5 and here he says only Livius [Andronicus]. The Saturnian line here is incomplete, but the details *purpurea* ("purple") and *ampla* ("large") in the Latin suggest the fragment is an adaptation of this particular passage from Homer's *Odyssey*.   [3] Ulysses (Odysseus), disguised as the Cretan beggar Aethon, describes to Penelope the cloak Ulysses was supposed to have worn on a visit to Aethon's home. In both Homer and Andronicus, the cloak described, being purple and large or double, is of high quality, as befits Ulysses.

Cf. Hom. *Od*. 19.225–26: a woolen cloak of purple did noble Odysseus wear / of double fold . . .

30 Priscian

The most ancient writers . . . also use *carnis* ["meat"] as a nominative [for classical Lat. *caro*] . . . : Livius Andronicus in the *Odyssia*:

> . . . the meat

he says,

> and the wine that they poured were consumed[1]

[1] Penelope relates to Ulysses (Odysseus) the greed of the suitors. The match between the Greek passage and the Latin adaptation is not close enough for a definite attribution to this context to be made.

Cf. Hom. *Od*. 23.304–5: because of her they slew many beasts, cattle and fat sheep, / and much wine was drawn from the jars.

31 (29 Bl.) Non., p. 493.16–17 M. = 791 L.

DEXTRABUS pro dexteris. Livius [*Bentinus, edd.*: Laberius *codd.*] in Odyssia:

> deque manibus dextrabus . . .

Cf. Hom. *Od.* 24.534: . . . ἐκ χειρῶν ἔπτατο τεύχεα.

DUBIA (F 32–33)

32 (34 Bl.) Fest., p. 482.7–27 L.

TOPPER . . . in antiquissimis scriptis celeriter et mature. in Odyssia vetere . . . :

> simul duona eorum portant ad navis,
> multa alia in isdem inserinuntur.

2 multa *Buecheler*: millia *cod.*

Cf. Hom. *Od.* 12.16–19: . . . οὐδ' ἄρα Κίρκην / ἐξ Ἀΐδεω ἐλθόντες ἐλήθομεν, ἀλλὰ μάλ' ὦκα / ἦλθ' ἐντυναμένη· ἅμα δ' ἀμφίπολοι φέρον αὐτῇ / σῖτον καὶ κρέα πολλὰ καὶ αἴθοπα οἶνον ἐρυθρόν.

---

1 On this form, see Livingston 2004, 1–21. 2 These two lines follow on immediately after *Odyssia* F 24 in Festus, but they are not now considered to be part of the same quotation. Havet (1880, 307) posits a lacuna in Festus after F 24 followed by a line of Naevius' *Punic War* (see Flores, Naevius, *Bellum Punicum*, fr. LV), illustrating a use of *topper*, and connected to the two lines quoted here. If the two lines do come from Andronicus' *Odyssia*,

31 Nonius

dextrabus[1] ["from their right hands"; fem. abl. pl., *hapax legomenon*] for [classical Lat.] *dexteris*, Livius in the *Odyssey*:

and from their right hands . . .[2]

[1] On this form, see Livingston 2004, 43–44.   [2] The fragment is too short and general for a definite attribution to be made. In the Homeric passage cited, Athene orders the Ithacans, supporters of the suitors, to cease from fighting, and their weapons fall from their hands.

Cf. Hom. *Od.* 24.534: . . . their weapons flew from their hands.

FRAGMENTS WHOSE CONNECTION WITH THE *ODYSSIA* IS IN DOUBT (F 32–33)

32 Festus

topper[1] ["quickly"; ante-classical form] . . . in the most ancient texts means "fast" and "soon." In the old *Odyssia*:

straightaway they carry their goods to the ships,
many other things are stowed inside them[2]

they perhaps refer to Hom. *Od.* 12.16–19, where Circe and her maids come with food and drink to Odysseus' ships, after the burial of Elpinor. However, an attribution to this context is far from certain (see Viredaz 2020, 213–16).

Cf. Hom. *Od.* 12.16–19: . . . but Circe / was not unaware that we had returned from Hades, but she quickly / got ready and came; and her servants brought with her / bread and much meat and sparkling red wine.

33 (5 Bl.) Paul. *Fest.*, p. 383.15–16 L.

SUREMIT sumpsit . . . :

> inque manum suremit hastam . . .

trib. Liv. Odissiae Buecheler = *trag. inc.* 235 *Rib-beck* manum *cod. Fest.*: manu *codd. Paul. Fest.*

Cf. Hom. *Od.* 21.433: ἀμφὶ δὲ χεῖρα φίλην βάλεν ἔγχεϊ . . .

Cf. Fest., p. 382.34–35 L.

PSEUDOANDRONICI ODYSSIA
(F 1–5)

Five fragments attributed to Andronicus by Priscian are capable of being scanned not as Saturnians but as hexameters and have long been associated with a post-Ennian rewriting of Andronicus' epic known as Pseudo-Andronici Odyssia, Odyssia nova, *or, in Courtney (1993, 45–46), as* Livius refictus. *For a history of the scholarly discussion of these lines going back to the nineteenth century, see Timpanaro 1949 (= Timpanaro 1978, 83–96); Viredaz*

33 Paul the Deacon, *Epitome of Festus*[1]

suremit ["he took up"; *hapax legomenon*, the same as] *sumpsit* ["he took up"; classical perf. of *sumo*]

he took up his spear into his hand[2] . . .

[1] This fragment comes without author's name or identification of the work in our source. It is attributed to Andronicus' *Odyssia* by Buecheler on the grounds of its contents. Although R.[2-3] includes it among the tragic *incerta* (235), he points out that its meter is closer to the Saturnian used by Andronicus in his epic.

[2] If F 33 belongs to the *Odyssia*, which is far from certain, a possible context would be Hom. *Od*. 21.433, where Telemachus takes up his spear at the beginning of the fight with the suitors. Andronicus' fragment is too general in tone for the identification with this Homeric context to be secure.

Cf. Hom. *Od*. 21.433: he took his spear in his grasp . . .

PSEUDO-ANDRONICUS, *ODYSSIA*
(F 1–5)

2020, 43–48. The use of the title Odyssia vetus *by Charisius F 3 and Festus F 24 and F 25, when referring to the original version, is perhaps intended to distinguish it from this later adaptation into hexameters (see Timpanaro 1978, 83). Whereas Livius' original was not divided into books, since the Greek* Odyssey *was not so divided until after his time (by Aristarchus in the first half of the second century BC; see Courtney 1993, 46), it seems from F 1 and F 2 that the later hexameter version was so divided.*

1 (37 Bl.) Prisc., *GL II*, p. 321.6–9

"haec daps, huius dapis," sed nominativus in usu frequenti non est, quem Livius Andronicus in I Odissiae ponit:

quae haec daps est? qui festus dies? . . .

Cf. Hom. *Od.* 1.225–26: τίς δαίς, τίς δὲ ὅμιλος ὅδ᾽ ἔπλετο; τίπτε δέ σε χρεώ; / εἰλαπίνη ἠὲ γάμος; . . .

2 (vacat Bl.) Prisc., *GL II*, p. 151.18–21

LINTER quoque, quod apud Graecos masculinum est, ὁ λουτήρ, apud nostros femininum est. Livius in VI <Odissiae> [*suppl. Courtney 1993, 46*]:

. . . iam in altum expulsa lintre . . .

Cf. Hom. *Od.* 6.170–72: χθιζὸς ἐεικοστῷ φύγον ἤματι οἴνοπα πόντον· / τόφρα δέ μ᾽ αἰεὶ κῦμ᾽ ἐφόρει κραιπναί τε θύελλαι / νήσου ἀπ᾽ Ὠγυγίης.

---

[1] The poem is not named in Priscian, and some have thought *Livius* referred to the historian, but no parallel to this can be found in Livy's Book 6. The mention by Priscian of Livius followed by a book number is reminiscent of the way in which this author quotes the Pseudo-Andronican *Odyssia* (see F 1). Courtney (1993, 46) identifies this fragment as coming possibly from

1 Priscian

[Nominative] *haec daps* ["this feast"], [genitive] *huius dapis*, but the nominative is not in frequent use, though Livius Andronicus uses it in Book 1[1] of his *Odyssia*:

What is this feast? What is this festive day? . . .[2]

[1] This and F 2 below are the only occasions on which the Latin *Odyssia* is quoted with a book number, implying they refer to the later hexameter reworking (see Mariotti [2]1986, 56, 83).

[2] Minerva (Athene), disguised as Mentes, questions Telemachus about the unruly feasting of the suitors.

Cf. Hom. *Od.* 1.225–26: What feast, what gathering is this? What need have you of it? / Is it a drinking party or a wedding?

2 Priscian

linter ["boat"] also, which with the Greeks is masculine, ὁ λουτήρ [the derivation of *linter* from the Greek λουτήρ is incorrect], with us is feminine [except at Tib. 2.5.34]. Livius in Book VI ⟨of the *Odyssia*⟩:[1]

. . . when the boat had already been pushed out into the deep . . .

that work (adding "of the *Odyssia*") and scans it as the middle of a hexameter. He would see in it a distant echo of Hom. *Od.* 6.170–72, where Ulysses (Odysseus) explains to Nausicaa how he arrived on her island.

Cf. Hom. *Od.* 6.170–72: Yesterday, on the twentieth day, I escaped from the wine-dark sea: / during all that time the waves and the swift winds were carrying me / from the island of Ogygia.

3 (38 Bl.) Prisc., *GL* II, p. 96.5–7

ut "super superus" sic "nuper nuperus" debet esse. Livius in Odyssea:

> inferus an superus tibi fert deus funera, Ulixes?

Cf. Hom. *Od.* 10.64: . . . τίς τοι κακός ἔχραε δαίμων;

4 (39 Bl.) Prisc., *GL* II, p. 419.12–15

"mando, mandis": eius praeteritum perfectum quidem alii "mandui," alii "mandidi" esse voluerunt, Livius tamen in Odissia:

> cum socios nostros mandisset impius Cyclops

cum *codd.*: quom *Merula*   Cyclops *vel* Ciclops *codd.*: Cuclops *Merula*

Cf. Hom. *Od.* 20.19–20: ἤματι τῷ ὅτε μοι μένος ἄσχετος ἤσθιε Κύκλωψ / ἰφθίμους ἑτάρους . . .

3 Priscian

Just as [the adverb] *super* ["above"] [has the adjective] *superus* [ante-classical form], so *nuper* must have *nuperus*. Livius in the *Odyssia*:

> is it a lower or an upper god that brings death to you,
> Ulysses?[1]

[1] Ulysses (Odysseus) tells Alcinous how Aeolus questioned him about his shipwreck.

Cf. Hom. *Od.* 10.64: . . . what cruel god has attacked you?

4 Priscian

mando, mandis ["devour"]: some indeed have wished its perfect to be *mandui* and others *mandidi* [neither of these forms is attested], but Livius in the *Odyssia* [has *mandi*, the regular classical form[1]]:

> when the wicked Cyclops had devoured our
> comrades[2]

[1] On this form, see Livingston 2004, 41.   [2] In preparation for taking revenge on the suitors, Ulysses (Odysseus) reminds himself that he has suffered worse when the Cyclops ate his comrades.

Cf. Hom. *Od.* 20.19–20: on the day when the Cyclops, irresistible in strength, devoured / my stalwart comrades . . .

5 (40 Bl.) Prisc., *GL* II, pp. 334.13–35.3

hic et haec "celer" vel "celeris" . . . Livius in Odissia:

at celer hasta volans perrumpit pectora ferro

Cf. Hom. *Od.* 22.91–93: . . . ἀλλ' ἄρα μιν φθῆ / Τηλέμαχος κατόπισθε βαλὼν χαλκήρεϊ δουρὶ / ὤμων μεσσηγύς, διὰ δὲ σρτήθεσφιν ἔλασσε; Verg. *Aen.* 9.410–13: . . . toto conixus corpore ferrum / conicit; hasta volans noctis diverberat umbras / et venit abversi in tergum Sulmonis ibique / frangitur ac fisso transit praecordia ligno.

5 Priscian

celer ["swift": this form of the fem. sing. is a *hapax lego-menon*] or *celeris* can be masculine and feminine nominative forms . . . Livius in the *Odyssia*:

> but the swift spear in its flight burst through his
> breast with iron tip[1]

[1] Possibly from a description of Telemachus' killing the suitor Amphinomus with a spear throw. Again, there can be no certainty about the exact Homeric context of Andronicus' fragment. This fragment (along with Enn. 11 *Ann.* F 4 *FRL*) may have influenced Virgil in *Aen.* 9.410–13: "Straining with all his body he threw his iron / weapon. The flying spear whistles through the shadows of the night, / and reaches the turned back of Sulmo, and there / snaps, and with its broken wood pierces his midriff," where *ferrum* ("iron weapon") and *hasta volans* ("flying spear") have verbal correspondences in F 5.

Cf. Hom. *Od.* 22.91–93: . . . but Telemachus was too quick for him, / striking him from behind with his bronze-tipped spear / between the shoulders and he drove it through his breast.

OPERA INCERTA (F 1–7)

1 Paul., *Fest*. p. 61.21–2 L.
DEMUM, quod significat post, apud Livium
  demus
legitur.

2 Paul. *Fest*., p. 85.1–2 L.
  gnarigavit
apud Livium significat narravit. gnarivisse narrasse.

UNIDENTIFIED WORKS (F 1–7)

Cited here is a collection of mostly single word fragments (cf. Warmington, ROL II, p. 596; Spaltenstein 2008, 203–6) attributed in the sources to Livius Andronicus. Their brevity precludes the identification of any particular work or genre. In some cases [F 3, 4] the exact form of the word in Andronicus' text is uncertain.

1 Paul the Deacon, *Epitome of Festus*

demum ["at length"], which means "afterward," is read as *demus*

at length

in Livius.

2 Paul the Deacon, *Epitome of Festus*

he told

gnarigavit [archaic form, "he told"] in Livius means *narravit* [classical form, "he told"]. [similarly archaic] *gnarivisse* ["to have told," is the same as classical] *narrasse* ["to have told"].

3 Fest., p. 256.4–5 L.

<profanum

quod non est sacrum>. Livi<us> . . .

<quod . . . sacrum> *suppletum ex epit. Pauli*

4 Fest., p. 380.32–36 L.

suregit

et

sortus

ant<iqui ponebant pro surrexit> et eius parti<cipio, quasi sit surrectus, qui>bus L. Liviu<s frequenter usus> est [*suppl. C. O. Mueller ex epit. Pauli*].

Cf. Paul. *Fest*., p. 381.6–7 L.: "suregit" et "sortus" pro surrexit, et quasi possit fieri surrectus, frequenter posuit Livius.

5 Fest., p. 384.29–35 L.

SOLLO Osce dicitur id quod nos totum vocamus . . . Livius

sollicuria

in omni re curiosa.

3 Festus

⟨profane[1]

profanum ["profane"], a thing which is not sacred⟩. Livi⟨us⟩ . . .

[1] *profanum* is the lemma; it is not certain which form of this word Livius used.

4 Festus

suregit ["he stood up"; archaic perfect of *surgo*]

he stood up

and *sortus* ["drawn by lot"; archaic past participle of *sortio*]

drawn by lot

the ancients ⟨put for *surrexit*⟩ ["he stood up"; classical perfect of *surgo*] and its participle, ⟨as if it were *surrectus*⟩. These forms L. Livius ⟨used frequently⟩.[1]

[1] The forms *suregit* and *sortus* are lemmata and, as in F 3, it is uncertain which forms of these words Livius used.

5 Festus

sollo in Oscan is what we call *totum* ["whole"] . . . Livius *sollicuria*

completely curious

curious about everything.

6 Serv. ad. Verg. *Aen.* 10.636

"nube cava" erit nominativus "haec nubes"; nam

   nubs

non dicimus, quod ait Livius Andronicus, qui primus edidit fabulam Latinam apud nos.

7 (35 Bl.) *Corp. Gloss.* II, p. 23.42

   aroscit

πλανᾶται ὡς Λίβιος.

6 Servius, *Commentary on Virgil*

nube cava ["in a hollow cloud"]; its nominative will be *haec nubes* ["this cloud"; fem.]; for [the nominative form] *nubs* ["cloud"]

cloud

we do not use, but Livius Andronicus uses it, who was the first to produce a Latin play among us.

7 *Glossaria Latina*

wanders

πλανᾶται ["wanders'], as Livius [says].

NAEVIUS

INTRODUCTION

LIFE

We have little direct evidence for the life of Naevius. Gellius (T 11) tells us, on the basis of Varro's lost work *De poetis* and of a statement (now lost) by Naevius himself in his epic *Bellum Punicum*, that Naevius completed his military service in the First Punic War (264–241 BC). Using this evidence, most scholars would now put his date of birth between 280 and 260 BC. In the same T 11 Gellius dates the start of his dramatic career to 235 BC, a mere five years after the first presentation of a play in Rome by Livius Andronicus. We can date Naevius' historical play *Clastidium* to in or after 222 BC, the date of the Roman victory there over the Gauls by M. Claudius Marcellus. On the basis of Cicero's statement in *Rep.* 4.10 that *veteribus displicuisse Romanis* ("the ancient Romans did not like") to see living men depicted on stage, a date shortly after the battle on the occasion of the triumph of Marcellus in Rome is usually ruled out. Most critics prefer a later date for the play's production, either in 208 BC at the funeral games of Marcellus or in 205 BC on the dedication by his son of the temple of Honor and Courage, which had been vowed by Marcellus at Clastidium. However, Cicero's statement is not categorical enough to exclude an earlier production date in 222 BC (see Goldberg 1995, 32–33). Cicero speaks of the *Bellum Punicum* as a work of Naevius' old age (*Bellum Punicum* t 2). Depending on the year of his birth, old age could mean any time from 230 BC onward, though a more probable date for its composition, which could have been spread over a number of years, is during the time of the Second Punic War (218–201 BC). In T 4 Cicero gives the date of Naevius' death as 204 BC, but tells us that Varro thought he lived longer. In fact, Jerome (T 13) dates his death to 201 BC. It is possible that this inconsistency arose from the fact that 204 BC was the date of the production of Naevius' last play and that he died a few years later (so Suerbaum 2002, 106).

An epitaph quoted by Gellius (T 7) and said by him to have been written by the poet himself may or may not be by the author (see introduction to the epitaph). Gellius describes the epigram as *plenum superbiae Campanae* ("full of Campanian arrogance"), which suggests that Naevius may have come from Campania, in Southern Italy, possibly from Capua (see Marmorale 1967, 17–18; Lehmann 2002, 93). Of course, this could be a general statement and does not prove his Campanian origins. In fact, the presence of *Naevii* in Rome before the time of the author is shown by the name *Porta Naeviana* in the Servian wall (mentioned by Varro, *Ling.* 5.163, and Liv. 2.11.8). The name has a Latin origin from *naevus* ("birthmark, mole"). However, a number of details in the *Bellum Punicum* could owe their presence to a Campanian origin or to a particular link with this area (Viredaz 2020, 50): *BP* t 15 on the origin of the name Prochyta, an island situated off Naples; *BP* t 9 the mention of the Cimmerian Sibyl, situated in Campania; *BP* F 44 mentions a Samnite object of some kind; *Lucetius*, the Oscan name for Jupiter, appears in *BP* F 27; finally in *Com.* F 50 and *BP* F 31, Naevius mentions by name an Oscan item of clothing, *supparum*. More tentatively, the suggestion has been made that his criticism of C. Claudius Pulcher in *BP* F 20, for arrogantly wearing down the legions, suggests that he may have fought under the leadership of this consul in the *legio Campana* (see Marmorale 1967, 27; Lehmann 2002, 96). If he were from Campania, Naevius would probably have enjoyed limited citizen rights, the so-called *civitas sine suffragio* ("citizenship without the vote") (Goldberg 1995, 32).

Unlike Livius Andronicus, who appears to have been a client of the Livii Salinatores, there is no clear evidence that Naevius was the client of any particular noble family. The fact that he wrote on the battle of Clastidium suggests he may have had some connection with the family of its victor, M. Claudius Marcellus (Suerbaum 2002, 110). Whether he was a client of this family, as Jocelyn (1969, 34) suggests, is uncertain, and Goldberg (1995, 33) sees no basis for interpreting the play as the fulfillment of a formal obligation of *clientela* ("clientship"). His other historical play, the *Romulus*, celebrated mythical as opposed to contemporary achievements, and his epic *Bellum Punicum*, which contained a mixture of mythical and historical elements, a distinction perhaps not recognized as clearly by the Romans as by modern historians, seems to have been based on his own experience and did not champion the deeds of any particular Roman family.

There are hints in Naevius' plays of less cordial relations with other members of the aristocracy. Gellius (T 9) reports some lines from a comedy by Naevius (*Com. Inc.* F 87), which many interpreted as referring to Scipio Africanus. The lines refer to a man who has often performed outstanding deeds of valor, but whom, in his youth, his father had carried off from his girlfriend's house wearing but one simple *pallium* (short Greek cloak). Scipio is known to have worn such a cloak in Sicily, where he adopted Greek dress and manners (Liv. 29.19.12). However, Naevius does not name Scipio, and such a cloak would also be appropriate for a comic *miles gloriosus* ("braggart warrior") figure, who could be the object of discussion in these lines (see Goldberg 1995, 37). In T 8 Gellius further reports that Naevius' invective against the *principes civitatis* ("the leading men of the city") landed him in prison, where he wrote two plays. This imprisonment is assumed by scholars to be mentioned later by Plautus (*Miles Gloriosus* 211–12), but the connection with Naevius is incapable of proof. According to Gellius (T 8) Naevius was subsequently released by the tribunes of the plebs after he had apologized for his arrogant words. One verse from Naevius which a scholion on Cicero (T 5) says the powerful family of the Caecilii Metelli found insulting is preserved, with a reply in Saturnians from the Metelli (*Varia* F 2). The quarrel is also mentioned by Caesius Bassus in the first century AD (T 6), who records the reply by the Metelli *dabunt malum Metelli Naevio poetae* ("The Metelli will cause trouble for Naevius the poet "), but not Naevius' original verse. The meter of Naevius' verse *fato Metelli Romae fiunt consules* ("By fate the Metelli become consuls at Rome") is more likely to be iambic than Saturnian (see Cole 1969, 19–20). Whether it comes from a dramatic performance or from a free-standing poem is uncertain. Cicero's parody in the *Verrine Orations* 1.29, *nam hoc Verrem dicere aiebant, te non fato, ut ceteros ex vestra familia, sed opera sua consulem factum* ("they used to tell how Verres used to say that you were elected consul not by fate, like the rest of your family, but through his influence"), would have been insulting to its target, Q. Caecilius Metellus Creticus (praetor 74 BC, pontifex 73 BC, consul 69 BC), with its contrast between *fato* ("by fate") and *opera* ("through influence"). However, it is not clear how Naevius' "by fate" on its own could be read pejoratively, but see Marmorale (1967, 81–82) and Viredaz (2020, 365) for possible ambiguities in the word, which can mean both "by fate" (*OLD fatum* 5) and "by misfortune" (*OLD fatum* 6). Finally, Jerome (T 13) in his chronicle of the year 201 BC mentions that pressure from the Metelli led to Naevius' exile to, and subsequent death in, Utica in North Africa. No other writer mentions this exile, and Utica was not under Roman domination until after this period. While a quarrel between Naevius and the Metelli probably existed, since there was no reason to invent it, the account of it has come down to us through the filter of late Republican politics and leaves us in doubt as to its exact nature (see Suerbaum 1968, 31–42; Gruen 1990, 96–106; Goldberg 1995, 33–35; Lehmann 2002, 98).

WORKS

Like Livius Andronicus, Naevius wrote comedies and tragedies adapting Greek models in Greek meters for the Roman stage. He also produced an epic, the *Bellum Punicum*, in the native Roman Saturnian meter. Whereas Andronicus' epic in this meter had been an adaptation of

Homer's *Odyssey*, Naevius was the first to produce an epic on a Roman historical subject, the First Punic War. His innovation in writing on Roman topics independent of Greek models is also shown in his inauguration of a new literary genre, the *fabula praetexta*, or drama on a Roman theme (see Manuwald 2001, 134–61). Fragments of two of these plays have come down to us. The first, the *Clastidium*, treats a contemporary topic, the Roman victory at Clastidium over the Gauls in 222 BC. The second, the *Romulus*, deals with a mythological subject on the foundation of Rome. Cicero (*BP* t 2) tells us that Naevius wrote the *Bellum Punicum* in his old age, and it could be that the move from Greek models to purely Roman themes was a feature of his later career.

Naevius is best known as a writer of comedy. He is referred to by Jerome (T 13) simply as *comicus* ("the comic poet"). Surviving comic titles (around 35) and comic verses (around 140) outnumber tragic titles (7) and verses (60). Terence (T 1) likens Naevius' freedom in adapting his Greek models in this genre to that of Plautus and Ennius and compares this approach favorably with the more literal translation technique of such writers as Luscius Lanuvinus. In the first century BC, Volcacius Sedigitus (T 10) awards Naevius third place as a comic writer, after Caecilius and Plautus. Of the 30 *fabulae palliatae* ("comedies in Greek dress"), whose titles are not conjectural, 12 have Greek titles (*Acontizomenos, Agrypnuntes, Colax, Glaucoma, Gymnasticus, Lampadio, Nagidio, Philemporos, Stalagmus, Stigmatias, Technicus,* and *Triphallus*); 16 have Latin titles (*Agitatoria, Apella, Ariolus, Carbonaria, Corollaria, Dementes, Dolus* [could also be Greek], *Figulus, Nautae, Paelex, Personata, Proiectus, Quadrigemini,*

Tarentilla, *Testicularia*, *Tunicularia*); 2 are hybrids, with a Greek initial element followed by a Latin adjectival ending (*Clamidaria*, *Diobolaria*). Two of these titles are used later by Plautus (*Colax* and *Carbonaria*), but so little remains of Naevius' plays that it is impossible to see Plautus' relation with them, if any. In his *Eunuchus*, Terence (*Colax* t 2) tells us there were two Latin plays called *Colax*, one by Naevius and the other an early play (*veterem fabulam*) by Plautus, but he says nothing of the relation between the two. *Colax* is also the title of a later mime by Laberius (*Mim.* 26 R.$^{2-3}$).

Naevius, like Plautus after him, may have increased the importance of the slave roles in comparison with his Greek originals, and three of his plays receive their titles from slave characters: *Stalagmus* (also a slave name at Plaut. *Captivi* 875), *Figulus*, and *Lampadio*. Plautus was later to name his plays *Epidicus* and *Pseudolus* after their leading slave characters. Standard comic features to be found in Naevius are exaggerated comic abuse (*Com.* F 88, 89); slave beatings (*Com.* F 102); the presence of braggart soldiers with their attendant flatterers (*Com.* F 21, 24, 86); parasites and food related themes (*Com.* F 15, 40, 43, 91, 93, 100, 103); slaves aiding young men in their affairs against their fathers' wishes (*Com.* F 75); rivals in love (*Com.* F 30); twins or quadruplets giving rise to confused identity (*Com.* F 1, 2, 55); and double plots with two sets of fathers and two sets of sons (*Com.* F 59, 64; cf. Plaut. *Menaechmi*).

Metatheater and breaking the dramatic illusion has an important role to play in Naevius' comedies. Some examples of this probably come from prologues, as is suggested by their meter, the iambic senarius. So *Com.* F 3,

Acontizomenos fabula est prime proba ("*Speared* is an especially good play") and *Com.* F 65, where a slave refers to himself winning applause *in theatro* ("in the theater"), are probably from prologues. Like Plautus and Terence after him, Naevius could use prologues to address the audience on matters not directly concerned with the dramatic action. Such addresses to the audience need not be restricted to prologues, as is shown by *Com.* F 11, probably spoken by a slave and referring to what the author had achieved *in scaena* ("on stage"). Finally, the words *haec demolite* ("clear these things away") in *Com.* F 32 possibly refer to clearing props or scenery from the stage, a meta-theatrical reference to actions that regularly took place in full view of the audience (see Beare 1964, 172; Spaltenstein 2014, 123).

Naevius anticipates Plautus in finding humor in the insertion of Roman allusions into the framework of a Greek-based comedy. Some of these perhaps occurred in prologues, as with the reference in *Com.* F 78 to the *Compitalia* (Roman feast of the crossroads) and the *Lares* (Roman household gods) and with the mention of a dictator in *Com.* F 81, a possible prologue reference to the opening of the games in which the play was performed by T. Manlius Torquatus, who was "dictator for organizing elections and games" in 208 BC. But such features could also occur in the body of a play, as with the discussion of food suitable for guests from Praeneste and Lanuvium in *Com.* F 15 or with the father's distinctly Roman appeal for his sons to devote themselves to *domos patres patriam* ("homes, fathers, and fatherland") in *Com.* F 63. Themes of freedom and social justice make frequent appearances in the comic fragments, mostly perhaps in the mouths of sententious slaves: examples include *Com.* F 6 on the superiority of freedom to riches; *Com.* F 65 and F 92 on the exercise of freedom of speech by slaves; *Com.* F 5 on the fair treatment of the defendants at law; and *Com.* F 53 on the fair distribution of suffering. The overall impression given by Naevius' comic fragments is of an author who is well attuned to the demands of his Roman audience and who, like Plautus, can adapt with confidence a foreign medium to suit Roman tastes and attitudes.

We have fragments from seven tragedies by Naevius: *Andromacha*, *Danae*, *Equus Troianus*, *Hector Proficiscens*, *Hesiona*, *Iphigenia*, and *Lycurgus*. The titles of five of these occur in earlier Greek drama: *Andromache* by Euripides and by Antiphon (55 F 1 *TrGF*); *Danae* by Sophocles (F 165–70 *TrGF*) and by Euripides (F 316–30a *TrGF*); *Hector Proficiscens* by Astydamas II (*Hektor*, 60 F 1h–2a *TrGF*); *Iphigenia* by Euripides (*Iphigenia in Aulis* and *Iphigenia in Tauris*), by Aeschylus (F 94 *TrGF*), by Sophocles (F 305–12 *TrGF*), and by Polyidus (*Iphigenia in Tauris*, 74 F 1–2 *TrGF*); *Lycurgus* by Aeschylus, as part of a trilogy (T 67 and F 123b *TrGF*), by Euripides (F 473–79 *TrGF*), and by Polyphasmon (*Lykurgia*, 7 F 1 *TrGF*). The *Equus Troianus* and *Hesiona* have no extant Greek predecessor. Naevius shares with Livius Andronicus the titles *Danae* and *Equus Troianus*. The relative chronology of these plays is uncertain, and either author could have used the other in addition to the Greek model. Ennius shares two titles with Naevius, *Andromacha* (Enn. *Trag.* F 23–33 *FRL*) and *Iphigenia* (Enn. *Trag.* F 82–88 *FRL*). Our fragments of these plays are not extensive enough to allow us to judge whether Ennius made any use of his Roman predecessor's work.

Naevius introduced new topics to Roman tragedy, often taken, like *Equus Troianus* and *Hesiona*, from the Trojan cycle. These topics allowed the discussion of different reactions to the betrayal of Troy. A supposed connection between some of the Trojans who fled from Troy and the early Romans may have added to the appeal of this topic. Another innovation by Naevius was the depiction on stage of gods and the confrontation between gods and men.[1] This is clearest in the *Lycurgus*: in *Trag.* F 26 Lycurgus seems to accuse Liber of injustice; in *Trag.* F 29 Liber accuses Lycurgus of inflexibility; in *Trag.* F 33 Liber warns Lycurgus not to set his anger against that of a god. In *Danae* Jupiter appears on stage and in *Trag.* F 11 gives an account of contemplating Danae in her dungeon. Jupiter's unscrupulous behavior toward Danae is shown to involve her in undeserved suffering and guilt (*Trag.* F 7, 8, 10). The *Lycurgus* emphasizes the dire consequences of opposition between gods and men. In the climax of the play, Liber burns down Lycurgus' palace. The play could well have had a topical significance at a time when Eastern cults were being introduced into Rome. Shortly after the time of Naevius, the Dionysiac cult became the target of the senate's repressive *senatus consultum de Bacchanalibus* in 186 BC, and doubts about this cult could have surfaced much earlier. Naevius' choice of Aeschylus' Lycurgus story as a model rather than Euripides' story of Pentheus in the *Bacchae* may have been dictated by the greater opportunity the Aeschylean *Lycurgus* gave to il-

---

[1] For Jupiter appearing on stage in Roman tragedy, see Mercury's comments at Plaut. *Amph.* 91–92, and for a list of deities who had appeared as tragic prologists, see Plaut. *Amph.* 41–44.

lustrating the conflict between gods and men. The Bacchants are depicted as exotic and dangerous (*Trag.* F 32, 40, 41), and Lycurgus is shown to be unscrupulous in tracking them down by fair means or foul (*Trag.* F 19, 20, 21, 22, 27, 37). In the end, however, it is the power of the god that ultimately triumphs (*Trag.* F 23, 24, 39).

A feature that connects Naevius' tragedies with his comedies is their concern for the commonplaces of popular philosophy. In *Danae Trag.* F 9 a character expresses the view that one should be rewarded according to one's own deserts. Some of these may have a particularly Roman feel to them, as when Hector in *Trag.* F 14 is pleased to receive praise from his father who was himself praised, or when Hesione in *Trag.* F 16 uses a Latin wordplay on *lingula* ("sword") and *lingua* ("tongue") when drawing a contrast between words and force as a means of getting one's way. From tragedies of uncertain title come the reflections that what is ill-gotten is ill-spent (*Trag. Inc.* F 47) and that mortals must bear many evils (*Trag. Inc.* F 51).

Naevius' great innovation in drama is to take the conventions and structures of Greek tragedy and to apply them in his *praetextae* to Roman historical (*Clastidium*) or mythological (*Romulus*) themes. Similarly, in his development of epic he moves away from Livius Andronicus' adaptation of Homer to invent a new type of epic, the *Bellum Punicum*, based on a combination of Roman themes both historical (the First Punic War) and mythological (the flight from Troy to Italy). To some extent this division is modern rather than Roman, since the Romans considered the flight from Troy a historical event, simply happening much earlier than the war with Carthage. Naevius' *Bellum Punicum*, like Livius Andronicus' *Odyssia*, was not divided into books by its author, but was composed as a single, undivided, poem. The division into seven books, based perhaps on length rather than subject matter, was carried out a generation later by C. Octavius Lampadio (*BP* t 6), who probably used Ennius' *Annales* as a template (Feeney 2016, 193). Reference to Lampadio's book numbers in our later sources nevertheless allows us to see the structure of the work as a whole and to fit unassigned fragments within the narrative framework which this provides. It is clear that the work begins with the historical narrative of Manius Valerius' expedition to Sicily in 263 BC (*BP* F 1). Manius Valerius was consul in that year and secured the surrender of several communities in Sicily, compelling Hieron II of Syracuse to make peace with the Romans. This Sicilian narrative is interrupted at some point by the mythological or ancient historical story of the flight of Aeneas and his followers from Troy to Italy. This technique of embedding a mythological/archaic episode within a near-contemporary historical narrative is clearly Alexandrian in its inspiration (see Lehmann 2002, 111). The mythological narrative begun in Book 1, continues until the beginning of Book 4, when we return to the historical account of the First Punic War. Apart from *BP* F 1 and F 4 (on Agrigentum), all surviving fragments of the first book are concerned with Aeneas' flight from Troy (see *BP* Book 1: Introduction).

The mythological narrative of the first three books may plausibly be reconstructed as follows: Book 1 contains the flight of Aeneas and his companions from Troy (*BP* F 2, 40); it continues with a description of the primitive tribes they met on their voyage (*BP* F 3) over the sea as far as Campania in Southern Italy, where Aeneas consults the Cimmerian Sibyl (*BP* t 9). This Sibyl gives instructions for the burial of Aeneas' relative Prochyta on an island of

Southern Italy, which is named from her (*BP* t 15). Aeneas continues on his route but is blown off course by a storm, which causes Venus to intervene on his behalf with Jupiter (*BP* t 16, F 24, 29). In Book 2 a council of the gods is called (presumably in response to Venus' plea) (*BP* F 8, F 9), and through their intervention Aeneas and his crew are brought safely to Carthage, where a meeting (probably with Dido) takes place (*BP* F 7). In Book 3 the Trojans arrive in Italy (*BP* t 3, 4, F 10), where Anchises observes favorable omens (*BP* F 11). Although this order of events seems the most probable, it is impossible from the fragments that remain to reconstruct the narrative exactly. In particular it is uncertain when the storm took place and whether the Trojans came first to Prochyta or to Carthage. The historical body of the work, which began in Book 1 (*BP* F 1) with Valerius' Sicilian expedition in 263 BC, continues in Book 4 with the Roman sacking of Malta in 257 BC (*BP* F 13). No fragments are assigned to Book 5. The fragments from Book 6 deal with events in the years 249 to 247 BC, including the cruel command of C. Claudius Pulcher, consul of 249 BC (*BP* F 20). The historical background to Book 7 is provided by the treaty of 241 BC with the Carthaginians (*BP* F 21), made by the consul Q. Lutatius Catulus, after a Roman naval victory off the Agates islands. An address to the Muses in an unplaced fragment (*BP* F 26) probably stood at the beginning of the work.

RECEPTION

Naevius was an important model for later generations of Roman dramatists and epic poets in that he took the work of Livius Andronicus one step further, by using Greek generic models to treat Roman historical and mythological content in his *fabulae praetextae* and *Bellum Punicum*. His inclusion within his *fabulae palliatae* of Roman material and concepts within the basically Greek framework influenced the later comedies of Plautus, Caecilius, and Terence. His *Bellum Punicum* was the first epic on a Roman theme and paved the way for Ennius' *Annales* and Virgil's *Aeneid*, both of which follow Naevius' lead in beginning the story of Rome with the fall of Troy. Cicero (*BP* t 1) mentions, without giving precise details, the frequent use made by Ennius in his *Annales* of Naevius' *Bellum Punicum*. Given the difference in meter between the two works (Ennius replaces the Roman Saturnian by the Greek-inspired hexameter verse), these borrowings are unlikely to consist of extensive verbal echoes, but perhaps refer to Ennius' use of similar mythological versions of the Aeneas legend and the foundation of Rome. For example, in *BP* t 11 Servius Danielis relates how Ennius shares with Naevius the genealogy of Romulus. Virgil's borrowings from Naevius (see Mariotti 1955, 42–47) were probably of the same kind, involving the adoption of particular narrative themes rather than the use of extensive verbal echoes. For example, in *BP* t 16 Macrobius explains how the storm at sea and Venus' appeal to Jupiter in *Aeneid* 1.81ff. were taken from Naevius' epic. The *Bellum Punicum* remained an important school text down at least to the time of Horace in the late Republic (*BP* t 5). The poem seems to have been a firm favorite with Augustus (see Barchiesi 1962, 50; Lehmann 2002, 116–17), to whom its nationalistic spirit and interest in ancient Roman religion and moral values may have commended it. As is shown by the re-edition of the *Bellum Punicum* by Lampadio, Naevius' work became an object of interest to grammarians, lexicographers, and commentators as early as a generation after his death. It is the concern of these scholars for the unusual and archaic aspects of Naevius' language that has preserved for us so many fragments of his work.

Listed below in chronological order is the number of such quotations from each scholar. The figure in parentheses after each author gives the number of quotations for which no play title (or book number in the case of the *Bellum Punicum*) is given.

Comedies in Greek dress: Cicero 2 (2), Varro 13 (4), Fronto 2 (2), Gellius 2 (1), Festus / Paulus 15 (12), Nonius 19 (4), Donatus 2 (1), Charisius 32 (0), Diomedes 6 (2), Sergius 1 (0), Fulgentius 3 (0), Macrobius 1 (0), Priscian 7 (0), Isidore 1 (0); Tragedies: Cicero 3 (2), Varro 2 (2), Gellius 1 (0), Festus / Paulus 4 (3), Nonius 35 (0), Servius 2 (1), Jerome 1 (1), Macrobius 1 (0), Priscian 1 (0), Isidore 3 (3); *Praetextae*: Varro 4 (0), Festus 1 (0); *Bellum Punicum*: Varro 2 (2), Caesius Bassus 2 (2), Gellius 1 (1), Festus 9 (9), Nonius 15 (2), Donatus 1 (1), Charisius 1 (0), Servius 2 (1), [Probus] on Verg. *Ecl.* 1 (0), Macrobius 3 (1), Priscian 8 (4), Isidore 2 (2).

Over half the *Bellum Punicum* fragments are given without book number (25 out of 47), probably because the authors in these cases are quoting Naevius' original undivided edition. In the case of tragedies and comedies, only around a quarter of citations are given without title (comedies: 28 out of 106; tragedies: 13 out of 54). Varro (8 out of 17) and Festus (25 out of 29) stand out as the authors least likely to give play titles or book numbers. Cicero, who quotes only comedies and tragedies, gives titles in only one of his five examples. Whereas Charisius is our best source for comedies, with 32 citations, all with titles, he never quotes tragedies and has only one quotation from the *Bellum Punicum*. Nonius is our best source for tragedies, providing 35 citations, all with titles, and he consistently gives titles for comedies (in 15 out of 19 cases) and book numbers for the *Bellum Punicum* (in 13 out of 15 cases). In this, Nonius must be reflecting the practice of his earlier sources. The predominance with post-Augustan generations of Plautus and Terence in comedy and of Virgil in epic means that no complete work of Naevius, nor of any other Republican dramatist or writer of epic, has come down to us.

THE ARRANGEMENT OF MATERIAL IN THIS EDITION

In the case of Naevius, the comedies followed by the tragedies and *praetextae* are presented in alphabetical order of title, with individual fragments under each play (or under *incerta*) being quoted in chronological order of the source text. The *Bellum Punicum* fragments are quoted in the order of the books in which they are said to appear by our sources; under each book (or under "unplaced fragments" for those for which no book is given), the unplaced fragments are quoted in chronological order of the transmitting texts.

TESTIMONIA (T 1–13)

T 1 Ter. *An*. 15–21 [= T 1 Ennius]

    id isti vituperant factum atque in eo disputant
    contaminari non decere fabulas.
    faciuntne intellegendo ut nil intellegant?
    qui quom hunc accusant, Naevium Plautum Ennium
    accusant quos hic noster auctores habet,
20   quorum aemulari exoptat neglegentiam
    potius quam istorum obscuram diligentiam.

T 2 Cic. *Rep*. 4.11 [= T 3 Caecilius]

sed Periclen . . . violari versibus et eos agi in scaena non plus decuit, quam si Plautus, inquit, noster voluisset aut Naevius Publio et Gnaeo Scipioni aut Caecilius Marco Catoni maledicere.

---

[1] Cicero puts these words in the mouth of P. Cornelius Scipio Aemilianus Africanus Minor (185–129 BC), consul 147 BC and 134 BC, censor 142 BC, famous general, statesman, and patron of literature.   [2] P. Cornelius Scipio Africanus (236–183 BC), consul 205 BC (cf. T 9), and Cn. Cornelius Scipio Calvus,

TESTIMONIA (T 1–13)

T 1 Terence, *The Woman of Andros*

His opponents abuse him [Terence] for doing this [adding material from a second Greek play to the adaptation of a first] and argue that plays should not be contaminated in this way. But by being clever do they not bring it about that they understand nothing? When they accuse him, they accuse Naevius, Plautus, and Ennius, whom our author takes as his models, [20] and whose carelessness he would prefer to emulate, rather than the obscure pedantry of his critics.

T 2 Cicero, *On the Republic*

But for Pericles . . . to be insulted in verse and for these verses to be recited on stage was no more proper, he said,[1] than for our own Plautus or Naevius to have wished to abuse P. and Cn. Scipio[2] or for Caecilius to have wished to abuse Marcus Cato.[3]

uncle of Publius, consul 222 BC, who fought against the Carthaginians in Spain in 218–211 BC.   [3] M. Porcius Cato, the Elder (234–149 BC), consul 195 BC, censor 184 BC, renowned for his simple life and strict morals.

T 3 Cic. *Leg.* 2.39 [= T 1 Livius Andronicus]

illud quidem <video> [*add. Vahlen*]: quae solebant quon-
dam compleri severitate iucunda Livianis et Naevianis
modis, nunc ut eadem exsultent <et cavea> [*add. Ziegler*]
. . . [*lacunam proposuit Ziegler*] cervices oculosque pariter
cum modorum flexionibus torqueant.

T 4 Cic. *Brut.* 60

illius autem aetatis [belli Punici secundi] qui sermo fuerit
ex Naevianis scriptis intellegi potest. his enim consulibus
[M. Cornelio Cethego et P. Sempronio Tuditano], ut in
veteribus commentariis scriptum est, Naevius est mor-
tuus; quamquam Varro noster diligentissimus investigator
antiquitatis putat in hoc erratum vitamque Naevi producit
longius.

T 5 Schol. Ps. Ascon. ad Cic. *Verr.* 1.29.16–21 (= *Var.* F 2)

dictum facete et contumeliose in Metellos antiquum Nae-
vii est:

ia⁶?   fato Metelli Romae fiunt consules.

cui tunc Metellus consul iratus versu responderat senario
hypercatalecto, qui et Saturnius dicitur: "dabunt malum
Metelli Naevio poetae."

Cf. Cic. *Verr.* 1.29 [*de Q.Caecilio Metello Cretico*].

---

[1] The fifth-century scholion, probably derived from Q. Asco-
nius Pedianus in the first century AD, refers to Cicero's raising a
laugh at the expense of Verres' ally Q. Caecilius Metellus Creti-
cus.   [2] Q. Caecilius Metellus, consul 206 BC.

T 3 Cicero, *On the Laws*

I ⟨observe⟩ this,[1] that those places which used to be filled with the sweet severity of the music of Livius [T 1 *FRL*] and Naevius, the same now exult, ⟨and the audience⟩ . . . now twist their necks and turn their eyes in time with the modulations of [our modern] meters.

[1] This passage is spoken by Cicero in dialogue with his friend Atticus and Cicero's brother Quintus.

T 4 Cicero, *Brutus*

What the language was like at that time[1] can be learned from the writings of Naevius. In the consulship of these two men,[2] as is written in the early records, Naevius died, although our friend Varro,[3] a most painstaking investigator of history, thinks that this is an error and makes the life of Naevius somewhat longer.

[1] The time of the Second Punic War, 218–201 BC.
[2] M. Cornelius Cethegus and P. Sempronius Tuditanus, consuls in 204 BC.   [3] Probably in his lost work *On Poets*.

T 5 Ps.-Asconius, Scholia to Cicero, *Verrine Orations* (= *Var.* F 2)

There is an old remark, witty and insulting,[1] made by Naevius against the Metelli:

By fate the Metelli become consuls at Rome.

To him the consul Metellus[2] had then angrily replied in verse in a hypercatalectic senarius, also known as a Saturnian: "The Metelli will cause trouble for Naevius the poet."

T 6 Caesius Bassus, *GL* VI, p. 266.4–9

sed ex omnibus istis, qui sunt asperrimi et ad demonstran-
dum minime accommodati, optimus est quem Metelli
proposuerunt de Naevio aliquotiens ab eo versu lacessiti
"malum dabunt Metelli Naevio poetae." hic enim satur-
nius constat ex hipponactei quadrati iambici posteriore
commate et phallico metro.

T 7 Gell. *NA* 1.24.1–2 (= *Var.* F 3)

trium poetarum inlustrium epigrammata, Cn. Naevii,
Plauti, M. Pacuvii, quae ipsi fecerunt et incidenda sepul-
cro suo reliquerunt, nobilitatis eorum gratia et venustatis
scribenda in his commentariis esse duxi. epigramma Naevi
plenum superbiae Campanae, quod testimonium iustum
esse potuisset, nisi ab ipso dictum esset:

inmortales mortales si foret fas flere,
flerent divae Camenae Naevium poetam.
itaque postquam est Orcho traditus thesauro,
obliti sunt Romae loquier lingua Latina.

T 6 Caesius Bassus

But from all these [Saturnian verses], which are very rough and least suited to [metrical] analysis, the best is the one the Metelli offered concerning Naevius when they had been threatened a number of times by him in verse: "The Metelli will cause trouble for Naevius the poet."[1] For this Saturnian consists of the last part of a hipponactean[2] iambic tetrameter and a phallic foot.

[1] Cf. T 5.   [2] A verse form, also known as a scazon, named Hipponactean from its inventor Hipponax, a mid-sixth-century BC writer of satirical verse.

T 7 Gellius, *Attic Nights* (= *Var.* F 3)

There are three epitaphs of three famous poets, Cn. Naevius, Plautus, and M. Pacuvius, which they composed themselves and left to be inscribed on their tomb. Because of their distinction and charm I have thought they should be written out in these notes. The epitaph of Naevius is full of Campanian pride; had it not been composed by himself, it could have provided a fair judgment:

> Were it right for immortals to weep for mortals,
> the divine Camenae would weep for the poet
>   Naevius.
> And so, after he was consigned to the treasury of
>   Orcus,[1]
> in Rome they forgot how to speak the Latin tongue.

[1] God of the underworld, like the Greek Pluto; he was considered rich in his abundance of corpses.

T 8 Gell. *NA* 3.3.15

sicuti de Naevio quoque accepimus fabulas eum in carcere duas scripsisse, Hariolum et Leontem, cum ob assiduam maledicentiam et probra in principes civitatis de Graecorum poetarum more dicta in vincula Romae a triumviris coniectus esset. unde post a tribunis plebis exemptus est, cum in his quas supra dixi fabulis delicta sua et petulentias dictorum quibus multos ante laeserat diluisset.

Cf. T 12.

T 9 Gell. *NA* 7.8.5–6 (= *Com. Inc.* 87)

nos satis habebimus, quod ex historia est, id dicere: Scipionem istum, verone an falso incertum, fama tamen cum esset adulescens haud sincera fuisse, et propemodum constitisse hosce versus a Cn. Naevio poeta in eum scriptos esse:

etiam qui res magnas manu saepe gessit gloriose,
cuius facta viva nunc vigent, qui apud gentes solus
    praestat,
eum suus pater cum pallio unod ab amica abduxit.

3 pallio unod *Ribbeck*[3] (*de hiatu cf. Com. F 8*): palliod unod *Ritschl, Buecheler*: pallio ⟨olim⟩ uno *Seyffert*: pallio uno *codd.* amica *codd. det., edd.*: amico *codd. plerique*

---

1 P. Cornelius Scipio Africanus (236–183 BC), hero of the Second Punic War (cf. T 2).   2 The passage seems to be humorous in content and light in tone. It does not contain serious criticism of Scipio. Its natural context would seem to be a comedy,

T 8 Gellius, *Attic Nights*

So too we are told about Naevius that he wrote two plays in prison, *Ariolus* ["*The Soothsayer*"] and *Leon*, when he had been thrown into chains at Rome by the triumvirs on account of his constant abuse and insults directed toward the leading men of the city in the manner of the Greek poets. From there he was afterward released by the tribunes of the people, when in the above-mentioned plays he had apologized for his offences and the impudence of his language with which he had previously harmed many.

T 9 Gellius, *Attic Nights* (= *Com. Inc.* 87)

I shall be satisfied with relating this, which is a matter of historical record. It is uncertain whether this is true or false, but the story goes that the famous Scipio,[1] when he was a young man, did not have an unblemished reputation, and it was almost generally agreed that these verses by the poet Cn. Naevius were directed at him:[2]

Even the man who often achieved great feats of arms
    in glorious fashion,
whose enduring deeds live on to this day, who alone
    stands out among all nations,
him did his father drag away from his mistress, clad
    in a single cloak.[3]

perhaps where a young man in love justifies his exploits by comparing them to those of the great Scipio in his youth.

[3] The reference to the single cloak probably suggests that he had not had time to dress properly. The reference to his cloak as a Greek *pallium* ties in with Livy's statement that Scipio preferred Greek over Roman dress (Liv. 29.19.11).

[6] his ego versibus credo adductum Valerium Antiatem [F 29 *FRHist*] adversus ceteros omnis scriptores de Scipionis moribus sensisse.

T 10 Gell. *NA* 15.24 [= T 4 Ennius; T 2 Caecilius]

Sedigitus in libro quem scripsit *De poetis*, quid de his sentiat qui comoedias fecerunt . . . his versibus suis [Volcacius Sedigitus, F 1 *FPL*[4], F 1 Funaioli] demonstrat:

Caecilio palmam Statio do comico.
Plautus secundus facile exsuperat ceteros.
dein Naevius, qui fervet, pretio in tertio est.

1 comico *codd.*: mimico *Gronovius*: comicam *Mariotti*
3 qui *codd.*: quom *Shackleton Bailey*

T 11 Gell. *NA* 17.21.44–45 (= *Bell. Pun.* t 5)

anno deinde post Romam conditam quingentesimo undevicesimo [235 BC] . . . [45] . . . Cn. Naevius poeta fabulas apud populum dedit, quem M. Varro in libro *De poetis* primo stipendia fecisse ait bello Poenico primo idque ipsum Naevium dicere in eo carmine quod de eodem bello scripsit. Porcius autem Licinus serius poeticam Romae coepisse dicit in his versibus [Courtney 1993, 83, F 1]: "Poenico bello secundo Musa pinnato gradu / intulit se bellicosam in Romuli gentem feram."

---

[1] A poet from the last quarter of the second century BC (see Courtney 1993, 82–92).

[6] I believe it was because of these verses that Valerius Antias[4] [25 F 29 *FRHist*] was led to hold an opinion opposed to that of all other writers concerning Scipio's morals.

[4] Roman historian of the first century BC.

T 10 Gellius, *Attic Nights*

Sedigitus,[1] in the book which he wrote *De poetis* ["*On Poets*"], shows what he thought about those who wrote comedies . . . in these verses of his [Volcacius Sedigitus, F 1 *FPL*[4], F 1 Funaioli]:

I give the first prize to Caecilius Statius, the comic
    actor.
Plautus as second easily defeats the rest;
Then Naevius, who is passionate, comes third.

[1] Volcacius Sedigitus, a literary historian of the late second century BC, who wrote a book *De poetis* ["*On Poets*"], from which this quotation comes (see Funaioli 1907, 82–83; Courtney 1993, 93–96).

T 11 Gellius, *Attic Nights* (= *Punic War* t 5)

In the five hundred and nineteenth year after the foundation of Rome [235 BC] . . . [45] . . . the poet Cn. Naevius put on plays before the people. M. Varro in the first book of *De poetis* ["*On Poets*"] says that Naevius did his military service in the First Punic War [264–241 BC] and that Naevius himself tells us this in the poem that he wrote on that same [Punic] war. But Porcius Licinus[1] says that the poetic art began later than this in Rome [Courtney 1993, 83, F 1]: "In the Second Punic War [218–201 BC] the Muse with winged flight / brought herself to the fierce and warlike race of Romulus."

T 12 Paul. *Fest.*, p. 32.15–16 L.

barbari dicebantur antiquitus omnes gentes, exceptis Graecis, unde Plautus Naevium poetam Latinum barbarum dixit.

Cf. Plaut. *Mil.* 209–12: ecce autem aedificat: columnam mento suffigit suo. / apage, non placet profecto mi illaec aedificatio; / nam os columnatum poetae esse indaudivi barbaro, / quoi bini custodes semper totis horis occubant.

T 13 Hieron. *Ab Abr.* 1816 [201 a.C.] (p. 135 Helm)

Naevius comicus Uticae moritur pulsus Roma factione nobilium ac praecipue Metelli.

T 12 Paul the Deacon, *Epitome of Festus*

In ancient times all nations were called barbarians, except
the Greeks. Hence Plautus[1] called the Latin poet Naevius
a barbarian.

[1] In *Miles Gloriosus* ("*The Braggart Soldier*," quoted oppo-
site) 209–12: "But look, he's building something: he's supporting
his chin with a pillar. Get away; I don't like that kind of building
at all. For I have heard that a barbarian poet [Naevius, a Roman
poet, hence a barbarian in a play set in Greece] has a pillared face,
a man whom two guards [his chains] always lie with at all hours."
The reference is probably to Naevius' imprisonment by the Me-
telli (cf. T 6, 8, 13; *Var.* F 2).

T 13 Jerome, on the year 201 BC

Naevius, the comic poet, died at Utica, driven from Rome
by a faction of the nobles and in particular of Metellus.[1]

[1] Probably Q. Caecilius Metellus, consul in 206 BC (cf. T 5).

FABULAE PALLIATAE (F 1–108)

*In drama Naevius seems to have produced more comedies
than tragedies, and five times more comic titles survive for
him than tragic titles. In his Greek-based plays he shares
with Plautus and Terence a certain freedom in adapting
his Greek models for the Roman stage (see T 1). He intro-
duces Roman elements into the framework of plays osten-
sibly set in Greece (Com. F 15, 63, 77, 81). Like Plautus
he increases the importance of the slave roles in compari-
son with his Greek originals, and in the case of* Lampadio
and Stalagmus *these characters give their names to the
play. Of the 78 fragments quoted below where a play title
is given, the majority are provided by Charisius. The*

ACONTIZOMENOS (F 1–3)

The Greek original of Naevius' Acontizomenos *("Speared")
is unknown. It could possibly be an adaptation of the*
Ἀκοντιζόμενος *("Speared") of Dionysius (F 1 K.-A.), but
only one fragment of that play survives, and its plot is
unknown. On the basis of the four remaining lines, the*

COMEDIES (F 1–108)

transmitting authors in decreasing order of their frequency of such fragments are: Charisius 32, Nonius 15, Varro 9, Priscian 6, Festus/Paulus 4, Diomedes 4, Fulgentius 3, and one each from Donatus, Gellius, Isidore, Macrobius, and Sergius. Of the 30 fragments quoted with no (or with uncertain) title (Com. Inc. F 79–108), the transmitting authors are Festus/Paulus 12, Varro 4, Nonius 4, Cicero 2, Fronto 2, Diomedes 2, Anonymous compiler 2, Gellius 1, Donatus 1. Charisius and Priscian always give titles; Varro and Nonius give the title more often than not; Festus/Paulus more often quotes without a title, whereas Cicero, Fronto, and Diomedes never give a title. See further Introduction to Naevius: Works.

ACONTIZOMENOS (F 1–3)

background to the plot can be partially reconstructed as follows: the son of an unknown man has killed with a spear by mistake the wrong member of a pair of twins that he or his father was in dispute with.

Comm.: Spaltenstein 2014, 13–22.

1 (2–3 R.[3]) Charis., *GL* I, p. 199.21–23 = p. 259 B.

FALSO Naevius in Acontizomeno:

ia[6]   huius autem gnatus dicitur geminum alterum
falso occidisse

2 (4 R.[3]) Charis., *GL* I, p. 207.17–19 = p. 268 B.

NOCTU . . . Naevius in Acontizomeno:

?   sublustri noctu interfecit

    sublustri *Ribbeck*[2]: sulpicii *codd.*

3 (1 R.[3]) Charis., *GL* I, p. 211.7–8 = p. 273 B.

PRIME Plautus, ‹item Naevius› [*add. Schoell*] in Aconti-
zomeno:

ia[6]   Acontizomenos fabula est prime proba

AGITATORIA (F 4–9)

*Agitatoria ("The Play of the Charioteer") is based on a
conflict between father and son resulting from the son's
passion for chariot racing. The theme had appeared in
Greek Old Comedy at Aristophanes,* Clouds *12–16, and*

4 (8 R.[3]) Charis., *GL* I, p. 197.9–12 = p. 256 B.

DEDITA OPERA declinari quidem ut nomen potest, sed
tamen vim adverbii retinet: Naevius in Agitatoria:

ia[8]   quasi dedita opera quae ego volo ea tu non vis, quae
ego nolo ea cupis

    quae ego nolo *edd.*: quod ego nolo *codd.*

1 Charisius

falso ["by mistake"], Naevius in *Speared*:

> and this man's son is said to have killed the other
> twin by mistake

2 Charisius

noctu ["by night"] . . . Naevius in *Speared*:

> he killed him in the gloom of night

3 Charisius

prime ["especially"] is used by Plautus [cf. *Mil.* 794, *Truc.*
454] and ‹also by Naevius› in *Speared*:

> *Speared* is an especially good play

AGITATORIA (F 4–9)

*chariot racing was also a feature of contemporary Roman
life (cf. Ennius, 1 Ann. F 43, ll. 79–81 FRL). Com. Inc.
F 101 may come from this play. Nothing is known of the
title and author of this play's Greek original.*
    Comm.: Spaltenstein 2014, 24–43. Lit.: Warnecke 1939.

4 Charisius

dedita opera ["attention having been given"] can indeed
be declined as a noun phrase, but still it retains the force
of an adverb ["on purpose"]: Naevius in *The Play of the
Charioteer*:

> as if on purpose you do not want the things I want
>   and the things I don't want you desire

5 (13 R.[3]) Charis., *GL* I, p. 208.5–6 = p. 269 B.

NIMIO pro nimis Naevius in Agitatoria:

tr[7]   . . . nimio arte colligor. cur re inquaesita colligor?

6 (9–10 R.[3]) Charis., *GL* I, p. 210.24–26 = p. 273 B.

PLURIS Naevius in Agitatoria:

ia[8]   semper pluris feci ego
          potioremque habui libertatem multo quam pecuniam

1 semper pluris feci ego *Warmington*: ego semper pluris feci *codd.*

7 (14 R.[3]) Charis., *GL* I, p. 220.19–20 = p. 285 B.

SECUS pro aliter Naevius in Agitatoria:

ia[6]   secus si umquam quicquam feci, carnificem cedo

8 (5(5[1])–7 R.[3]) Charis., *GL* I, p. 239.12–15 = p. 312 B.

TAX PAX Naevius in Agitatoria:

ia[6]   (A) age ne tibi
          med advorsari dicas, hunc unum diem
          de meo equos sinam esse. (B) tax pax. (A) postea
          currentes ego illos vendam, nisi tu viceris

2 med *Bergk*: me *codd.*   3 de meo equos *codd.*: de meod
equos *Ribbeck*[3] (*de hiatu cf. Cic. Orat. 152; Spaltenstein 2014,
415–16*): Demea, meos equos *Warmington*   sinam esse
Buecheler: sinam ego illos esse *codd.*

5 Charisius

nimio ["too much'] for [classical Latin] *nimis* Naevius in *The Play of the Charioteer*:

> . . . I am bound too tightly. Why am I bound with my case untried?

6 Charisius

pluris ["of greater value"] Naevius in *The Play of the Charioteer*:

> I have always placed a higher value
> on liberty and thought it preferable by far to money

7 Charisius

secus ["differently"] for *aliter* [classical alternative] Naevius in *The Play of the Charioteer*:

> if I have ever done anything differently from this,
> bring on the executioner

8 Charisius

tax pax ["agreed"] Naevius in *The Play of the Charioteer*:

> (A – father?) Come on, don't
> say I'm against you; for this one day
> I will let the horses eat at my expense. (B – son?)
>   Agreed! (A) Afterward,
> if you don't win, I'll sell them as racehorses.

9 (11–12 R.[3]) Charis., *GL* I, p. 239.16–18 = p. 312 B.

EHO idem [Naevius] in eadem [Agitatoria]:

ia[6]   (A) eho an vicimus?
 (B) vicistis. (A) volup ‹est›. quo modo? (B) dicam
   tibi.

2 est *add. Bothe*

AGRYPNUNTES (F 10–11)

The plot and Greek original of Agrypnuntes *("The Insom-niacs") are unknown, though Naevius seems to have kept its original Greek title, although we cannot exclude the possibility that he chose a Greek title different from that of his model. The two fragments preserved in Nonius are*

10 (16–17 R.[3]) Non., p. 65.5–7 M. = 90 L.

PROMICARE, extendere et porro iacere, unde emicare. Naevius Agrypnuntibus:

ia[8]   si quidem vis loqui,
   non perdocere multa longe promicando, oratio est

1 vis loqui *Bothe*: loqui vis *codd.*

11 (17 R.[3]) Non., p. 150.28–30 M. = 219 L.

PRAEMIATORES NOCTURNI, praedones. Naevius Agryp-nuntibus:

ia[8]   nam in scena vos nocturnos coepit praemiatores
       tollere

9 Charisius

eho ["aha"] the same author [Naevius] in the same play
[*The Play of the Charioteer*]:

> (A – father?) Aha, did we win?
> (B – son?) You won. (A) I'm pleased. How? (B) I'll
> tell you.

AGRYPNUNTES (F 10–11)

*unrelated. The second seems to be addressed to the audi-
ence, and the implication of the Latin* in scena [*"on stage"*]
*is that it refers to the author. The first belongs to the in-
trigue proper and satirizes a long-winded speaker.*
  Comm.: Spaltenstein 2014, 44–53. Lit.: Alfonsi 1950.

10 Nonius

promicare means *extendere* ["to extend"] and *porro iacere*
["to throw forth"], from the same root as *emicare* ["to
shoot forth"]. Naevius in *The Insomniacs*:

> if you just want to tell me,
> and not to deliver a long lecture by throwing forth
> words far and wide, you can speak

11 Nonius

Nocturnal *praemiatores* ["robbers"], plunderers. Naevius
in *The Insomniacs*:

> for on stage he began to eliminate you nocturnal
> robbers

APPELLA (F 12–13)

The plot and Greek original are unknown. Even the meaning of the title is disputed. For some (Berchem 1861; Paponi 2005; Spaltenstein 2014) Appella is to be taken as a diminutive of Apula meaning "The Girl from Apulia." This is the interpretation followed here. For plays with titles referring to the nationality, we may compare Menander's Samia, Alexis' Brettia (Arnott 1996, fr. 34), Plautus' Poenulus ("The Little Carthaginian"), Naevius' own Ludus (= Lydus) ("The Lydian," possibly a slave name) and

12 (19 R.³) Prisc., *GL* II, p. 203.13–18

indeclinabile in singulari numero "hoc cepe, huius cepe" . . . quod in plurali numero femininum est primae declinationis "hae cepae, harum ceparum," quamvis antiquissimi in -a quoque singulare feminino genere hoc recte protulisse inveniuntur. Naevius in Appella:

ia⁶   ut illum di perdant, qui primum holitor protulit
cepam

> 1 di perdant *C. F. W. Mueller*: differant *codd.*
> 1–2 protulit / cepam *C. F. W. Mueller*: cepam protulit *codd.*

13 (18 R.³) Prisc., *GL* II, p. 204.1–2

frequentior tamen usus "hoc cepe" protulit. Naevius in Appella:

ia⁶   cui cepe edendo oculus alter profluit

> edendo *codd.*: edundod *vel* edundo *edd.* (*de hiatu cf. Com. F 8*).

APPELLA (F 12–13)

Tarentilla ("The girl from Tarentum"), and Terence's Andria ("The Girl from Andros"). For others (Ribbeck 1852; followed by Warmington 1936; Marmorale 1953; Traglia 1986) the title means "The Circumcised," based on Gloss. Labb.: apella: λειπόδερμος ["without foreskin"] and on an ancient scholion on Horace, Satires 1.5.100: Iudaeus Apella: finxit nomen, quasi sine pelle . . . qui praeputium non habet ["The Jew Apella: he made up the name, as if without skin . . . who has no foreskin"].

Comm.: Spaltenstein 2014, 54–63.

12 Priscian

The word cepe ["onion"] is indeclinable in the singular hoc cepe, huius cepe . . .; in the plural it is a feminine of the first declension hae cepae, harum ceparum, although the most ancient writers are found to have used it correctly also ending in -a as a feminine singular. Naevius in The Girl from Apulia:

> may the gods confound that vegetable grower who
> first brought forth
> the onion

13 Priscian

Still it was more frequent practice to use the neuter singular hoc cepe ["this onion"]. Naevius in The Girl from Apulia:

> who from eating an onion has one eye streaming

ARIOLUS (t 1; F 14–15)

Although F 15 with its mention of Praeneste and Lanu-
vium suggests a provincial Italian background, "The
Soothsayer" is probably based on a Greek original. In
some manuscripts the title is spelled with aspirate Hario-
lus (which is the classical Latin form). The spelling without
aspirate, favored by Ribbeck, is perhaps intended to give
the title a colloquial flavor. Plays with titles associated
with beggar priests and soothsayers occur regularly in
Greek New Comedy, e.g., Philemon, Ἀγύρτης ("The Beg-
gar Priest"; F 2 K.-A.); Antiphanes, Μητραγύρτης ("The

t 1 Gell. *NA* 3.3.15

Cf. T 8.

14 (20 R.³) Fest., pp. 196.36–98.3 L.

OREAE freni, quod ori inseruntur . . . Naevius in Hariolo:

ia⁶   deprandi autem leoni si obdas oreas

    leoni si *edd.*: leonis *cod.*

15 (21–24 R.³) Macrob. *Sat.* 3.18.6

nux haec Abellana seu Praenestina . . . est et illud apud
Naevium in fabula Ariolo:

ia⁶   (A) quis heri apud te? (B) Praenestini et Lanvini
      hospites.
    (A) suopte utrosque decuit acceptos cibo;

ARIOLUS (t 1; F 14–15)

Priest of Cybele"; F 152–53 K.-A.) and Οἰωνιστής *("The Augur"; K.-A. II, p. 406); Alexis,* Μάντεις *("The Sooth-sayers"; F 150 K.-A., Arnott 1996, 440–44); Menander,* Μηναγύρτης *("The Priest of Mene"; F 556–69 K.-A.). There may be some truth in the tradition passed on by Gellius that Naevius was imprisoned as a result of criticizing certain members of the nobility, but whether he wrote this play and* Leon *as palinodes remains uncertain (see T 8).*

Comm.: Spaltenstein 2014, 64–76.

t 1 Gellius, *Attic Nights*

Cf. T 8.

14 Festus

oreae ["the bit"], bridles, because it is inserted into the *os* ["mouth"] . . . Naevius in *The Soothsayer*:

if you apply a bit to a starving lion

15 Macrobius, *Saturnalia*

This nut is the filbert or the Praenestine nut . . . and there is this reference in Naevius' play *The Soothsayer*:

(A) Who dined with you yesterday? (B) Guests from Praeneste and Lanuvium.
(A) Each of them should have been welcomed with their own food.

altris inanem volvulam madidam dari
altris nuces in proclivi profundier

1 Lanvini *Ribbeck*[2–3]: Lanuvini *codd.*   3 et 4 altris *Ribbeck*[2–3]: alteris *codd.*   3 volvulam *L. Mueller, Ribbeck*[2–3]: bulbam *codd.*   4 profundier *Scriverius*: profundere *codd.*

ASTIOLOGA

Cf. *Com. Inc.* F 101.

ASTROLOGA

Cf. *Com. Inc.* F 101.

CARBONARIA (F 16)

Plautus wrote a play of the same name, of which three fragments remain (see De Melo 2013, vol. 5, p. 438), and a charcoal burner is mentioned at Plautus, Casina *437. It seems best, in view of Plautine titles such as* Aulularia *("The Pot of Gold," literally, "The Play about Gold") and Naevius' own* Agitatoria *("The Play of the Charioteer"), to*

To one lot[1] [the Lanuvians] you should have given
   cleaned and boiled sow's womb,
and for the other lot[1] [the Praenestians] you should
   have poured an abundant shower of nuts.

[1] Ribbeck[2–3] introduces the forms *Lanvini* (1) for *Lanuvini*
("men from Lanuvium") and *altris* (3 and 4) for *alteris* ("to one
lot . . . for the other lot") since they are required by the meter.
He argues they were intended to represent provincial dialect
forms.

ASTIOLOGA

Cf. *Com. Inc.* F 101.

ASTROLOGA

Cf. *Com. Inc.* F 101.

CARBONARIA (F 16)

take the feminine adjective Carbonaria *as referring to a*
fabula Carbonaria *("The Charcoal Play") rather than to a*
female ("Charcoal Maid"), as in Warmington. Nothing is
known of the Greek original of Naevius' play. The sole
fragment compares a rich man with a poor man; cf. Mega-
dorus and Euclio in Plautus' Aulularia.
   Comm.: Spaltenstein 2014, 78–81.

16 (26 R.³) Prisc., *GL* II, p. 522.8–12

vetustissimi . . . "edo edis edit" dicebant correpta prima syllaba. Naevius in Carbonaria:

tr^7 tibi servi multi apud mensam astant; ille ipse astat,
         quando edit

CEMETRIA

Cf. *Com. Inc.* F 83.

CLAMIDARIA (F 17)

The chlamys, or Greek cloak, from which Clamidaria *("The Cloak Play") is named, as well as the phrase* a pueris abscessit, *which looks like a translation of the Greek* ἐξ ἐφήβων γίγνεσθαι *("to leave boyhood"; see Spaltenstein 2014, 84), suggests the play is translated from the Greek,*

17 (26¹ R.³) Serg., *GL* IV, p. 559.26–30

quaesitum est, num [admodum] pro valde usque dicamus, et in usu fuit, ut apud Sallustium [*Hist. Inc.* 18 M. = 68 R.] "admodum vanus" et apud Naevium in Clamidaria:

ia^8 neque admodum a pueris abscessit neque admodum
         adulescentulust

16 Priscian

The oldest writers . . . said *edo, edis, edit* ["eat"], with the first syllable short. Naevius in *The Charcoal Play*:

> you have many slaves to wait on you at table; he
> himself waits on himself when he eats

CEMETRIA

Cf. *Com. Inc.* F 83.

CLAMIDARIA (F 17)

but we have no more precise information about its Greek original. For the involvement of a cloak in the play, cf. the palla [*"cloak"*] *in Plautus'* Menaechmi *("The Two Menaechmuses").*

Comm.: Spaltenstein 2014, 82–84.

17 Sergius

It is asked whether we should still say [*admodum*] for *valde* ["very much"]; in fact, it was used in this way, as in Sallust [*Hist. Inc.* 18 M. = 68 R.] *admodum vanus* ["very vain"] and in Naevius in *The Cloak Play*:

> he has neither very much left his youth nor is he very
> much a young man

COLAX (t 2; F 18–21)

Terence (t 2) mentions a Colax *("The Flatterer") of Naevius
and a play of the same name by Plautus (for the four re-
maining fragments of which see De Melo 2013, vol. 5,
p. 440) and suggests both are based on Menander's* Κόλαξ
("The Flatterer"; fragments in Barsby 1999, 305–11; Loeb,
Menander, *vol. 2, pp. 162–203).* Com. Inc. *F 102 could
also belong to this play. Eupolis also wrote a play entitled*
Κόλακες *("The Flatterers"; F 156–90 K.-A.), but this does*

t 2 Ter. *Eun.* 23–26, 30–31

> exclamat furem non poetam fabulam
> dedisse et nil dedisse verborum tamen;
25 Colacem esse Naevi et Plauti veterem fabulam,
> parasiti personam inde ablatam et militis . . .

30 Colax Menandrist, in east parasitus colax
> et miles gloriosus.

18 (30–31 R.[3]) Non., p. 64.9–10 M. = 89 L.

PROLUBIUM . . . Naevius Colace:

tr[7]   et volo et vereor et facere in prolubio est . . .

COLAX (t 2; F 18–21)

*not appear to be related to the present piece. There was a later mime with this title by Laberius (*Mim. 26 R.[2–3]*). As in Menander and in Terence's* Eunuchus *("The Eunuch"), as well as in the* Miles Gloriosus *("The Braggart Soldier") of Plautus, the flattering parasite figure was probably coupled with a boastful soldier, who could have been a love rival of the young man of the piece.*

Comm.: Spaltenstein 2014, 86–102. Lit.: Molinelli 2006 (F 19).

t 2 Terence, *The Eunuch*

He shouted that a thief, not a poet, had made this play, but still he had not made fools of us. [25] There was *The Flatterer* of Naevius and an old play by Plautus, and the characters of the parasite and the soldier had been taken from them . . . [30] *The Flatterer* is a play of Menander and in it there is a flattering parasite and a braggart soldier.

18 Nonius

prolubium ["inclination"] . . . Naevius in *The Flatterer*:

I want to, and I am afraid, and it is my inclination to do it[1] . . .

[1] Probably spoken by a young man, balancing his desires against their social consequences.

19 (35 R.³) Non., pp. 376.12–13 M. = 598–99 L.

nonnulli veterum pro eo quod "protinus" est "protinam"
vel "protinis" converterunt . . . Naevius in Colace:

*ia*⁸   ubi vidi, exanimabiliter timidus pedibus protinam me
       dedi

20 (32–34 R.³) Non., pp. 462.31–63.2 M. = 741 L.

MULTARE cum sit condemnare, positum est augere, votis
compotem reddere. Naevius Colace:

*ia*⁶   et asseri
    laudes ago, cum votis me multat meis,
    quod praeterquam vellem audiebam hoc mihi eminus

    2 multat *Hermann*: multatis *codd.*   3 eminus *ed. 1469*:
ennius *codd.*

21 (27–29 R.³) Prisc., *GL* II, pp. 491.20–92.3

"polluceo, polluxi" . . . Naevius in Colace:

*ia*⁶   qui decimas partes? quantum mi alieni fuit
    polluxi tibi iam publicando epulo Herculis
    decimas

    1 mi *add. Hermann*   2 polluxi *Hermann*: polluxit
codd.   iam *Hermann*: a *codd.*

---

1 The flatterer is probably addressing the soldier, whom he
likens to Hercules. For the tithe (tenth) offered to Hercules cf.
Plautus, *Bacchides* ("*The Two Bacchises*") 665, *Stichus* 233; Cic-
ero, *De natura deorum* ("*On the Nature of the Gods*") 3.88, and
for the public feast offered to Hercules cf. Plautus, *Trinummus*
("*Three-Dollar Day*") 468ff.

19 Nonius

Some ancient writers changed what is *protinus* ["straight away"] into *protinam* or *protinis* . . . Naevius in *The Flatterer*:

> when I saw this, I took straight to my heels, half dead with fear[1]

[1] Perhaps spoken by a fearful youth.

20 Nonius

multare ["to punish"], although it means "to condemn," is put for "to enrich," "to grant one's wishes." Naevius in *The Flatterer*:

> and to this beam[1]
> I give praises, since it grants me my wishes,
> because beyond my desires I heard all this from a
> distance

[1] The speaker praises a beam or a doorpost that has provided him with a crack through which to listen.

21 Priscian

polluceo ["to offer"] [perfect tense] *polluxi* . . . Naevius in *The Flatterer*:

> what do you mean tithes? In so far as I have access to
> another's means,
> I have already offered up tithes to you by making
> public a feast for
> Hercules[1]

COMMOTRIA

Cf. *Com. Inc.* F 83.

COROLLARIA (F 22–33)

The Greek playwright Eubulos has a play named Στε-φανοπώλιδες ("The Garland Sellers"; F 97 K.-A.), which could have had a similar plot, but none of the surviving fragments corresponds with those of Naevius. As with Carbonaria, there is some ambiguity in the title Corollaria, *which could mean either "The Garland Play" (the translation adopted here) or, so Warmington, "The Garland Girl,"*

22 (48[1] R.[3]) Varro, *Ling.* 7.60

In Mercatore: "non tibi istuc magis dividiaest quam mihi hodie fuit" [Plaut. *Merc.* 619]. hoc eadem ⟨vi⟩ [*add. Goetz / Schoell*] est in Corollaria Naevius ⟨usus⟩ [*add. Spengel*]:

dividiae

dividia ab dividendo dicta, quod divisio distractio est doloris.

Cf. *Com.* F 33.

COMMOTRIA

Cf. *Com. Inc.* F 83.

COROLLARIA (F 22–33)

although the normal name for a female garland maker would be Coronaria. *The fragments suggest a rivalry, possibly between a soldier and a young man, for the young garland maker's affections. Any such match is opposed by her patron.* Com. Inc. *F 102 could also belong to this play.*

Comm.: Spaltenstein 2014, 105–28. Lit.: Costanza 1956 (F 33); Maurach 2000 (F 25).

22 Varro, *On the Latin Language*

In *The Merchant*: "This is no more of a torment [*dividiae est*] to you than it was to me today" [Plautus, *Mercator* 619]. Naevius ⟨used⟩ this word with the same ⟨meaning⟩ in *The Garland Play*:

torment[1]

dividia ["torment"] is derived from *dividere* ["to tear apart"] because tearing apart is a pulling asunder by pain.

[1] Varro does not say what form of the word Naevius used, but the dative singular *dividiae + esse*, meaning "to be a torment," is its normal context; cf. *Com.* F 33, a passage Varro may have in mind. The only exception is the nominative *dividia* at Acc. *Trag.* 152 R.[2–3]. The word is restricted to early comedy and tragedy.

23 (48² R.³) Charis., *GL* I, p. 196.1 = pp. 254–55 B.

CONFESTIM . . . Naevius . . . in Corollaria:

confestim

24 (39–40 R.³) Charis., *GL* I, p. 198.5 = p. 257 B.

DAPSILITER Naevius in Corollaria:

ia⁷?   . . . ultro meretur, quam ob rem ametur:
tr⁷?   ita dapsiliter suos amicos alit . . .

25 (36–38 R.³) Charis., *GL* I, p. 198.12 = p. 257 B.

EFFLICTIM Naevius in Corollaria:

ia⁶   nolo ego
hanc adeo efflictim amare; diu vivat volo
ut mihi prodesse possit

26 (43 R.³) Charis., *GL* I, p. 205.8 = p. 266 B.

MORDICUS . . . Naevius in Corollaria:

?   . . . utinam nasum abstulisset mordicus

---

[1] There is nothing in the Latin to indicate the gender of the subject, but such behavior in comedy is more typical of women (see Spaltenstein 2014, 120).

184

23 Charisius

confestim ["straight away"] . . . Naevius . . . in *The Garland Play*:

> straight away

24 Charisius

dapsiliter ["feastfully"; *hapax legomenon*]. Naevius in *The Garland Play*:

> . . . of his own accord he has earned the right to be
>   loved:
> so feastfully does he feed his friends[1] . . .

[1] Describing perhaps a soldier, the young man's rival, who feeds a circle of admirers as in Plautus, *Menaechmi* ["*The Two Menaechmuses*"] 98–99, or Terence, *Eunuchus* ["*The Eunuch*"] 1082.

25 Charisius

efflictim ["mortally"]. Naevius in *The Garland Play*:

> I do not want
> this girl to be so mortally in love; I want her to live a
>   long time
> so that she can be of service to me[1]

[1] Probably spoken of a dependent girl, the garland maker, by her patron.

26 Charisius

mordicus ["at a bite"] Naevius in *The Garland Play*:

> . . . I wish she[1] had taken his nose off at a bite

27 (45 R.[3]) Charis., *GL* I, p. 208.7 = pp. 269–70 B.

NIMIS . . . Naevius . . . in Corollaria:

tr^7? nimis homo formidulosust . . .

28 (44 R.[3]) Charis., *GL* I, p. 215.26 = p. 279 B.

QUIPPIAM Naevius in Corollaria:

? num quippiam? . . .

29 (48[3] R.[3]) Charis., *GL* I, p. 239.19 = p. 312 B.

TRIT. Naevius in Corollaria.

trit

significat autem, ut ait Plautus in quadam [Plaut. *Curc.* 295], crepitum polentarium, id est peditum.

30 (41–42 R.[3]) Charis., *GL* I, p. 240.22–24 = p. 313 B.

ATTATTATAT ATTATAE Naevius in Corollaria:

ia^8 (A) salve! (B) quid istud salve? attattattat attatae!
(A) rivalis salve! quid istud vero te advertisti tam cito?

1 salve! quid istud salve? *Mariotti 1952; Traglia 1986*: quid salve? *codd., Warmington*

---

[1] An expression of surprise. [2] The term *rivalis* usually refers to a rival in love. [3] The text has been altered slightly from that transmitted in Charisius for reasons of meter and interpretation.

27 Charisius

nimis ["too"] . . . Naevius . . . in *The Garland Play*:

the fellow is too fearful . . .

28 Charisius

quippiam ["anything"] Naevius in *The Garland Play*:

is there anything else?[1] . . .

[1] A variation on the common leave-taking formula *numquid vis*? ["is there anything you want?"]; cf. Plautus, *Truculentus* 432: *num quippiam aliud me vis*? ["do you want anything else from me?"].

29 Charisius

trit [onomatopoeic word representing the sound of a fart]. Naevius in *The Garland Play*:

pop

It means, as Plautus says in one of his plays [Plautus, *Curculio* 295: *exciam crepitum polentarium*, "I will drive out a barley-fed pop"], a barley-fed pop, that is a fart.

30 Charisius

attattatat attatae[1] ["ah, ah, ah"]. Naevius in *The Garland Play*:

(A – young man?) Good day! (B – soldier?) What's this good day? Ah, ah, ah!
(A – young man?) Good day, rival![2] Why did you turn around so quickly at that exclamation?[3]

31 (46–47 R.[3]) Charis., *GL* I, p. 240.25 = p. 314 B.

ST Naevius in Corollaria:

ia[6]   . . . st! tace!
    cave verbum faxis . . .

    1 st! tace! *Haupt*: setale *codd.*

32 (48 R.[3]) Diom., *GL* I, pp. 400.29–401.2

DEMOLIO . . . Naevius in Corollaria:

P   haec demolite . . .

33 (vacat R.[3]) Fulg. *Serm. ant.* 37

desiduo dicitur diuturno. unde et Varro [*errore pro* Nae-
vius, cf. *Com.* F 22] in Corollaria ait:

P   dividiae[1] mihi fuerunt tum desiduo afuisse te

    fuerunt *codd.*: fuerit *Spaltenstein*

    1 Cf. *Com.* F 22.

COSMETRIA

Cf. *Com. Inc.* F 83.

31 Charisius

st ["sh!"] Naevius in *The Garland Play*:

> . . . sh! be quiet!
> mind you don't say a word . . .

32 Diomedes

demolio ["clear away"] . . . Naevius in *The Garland Play*:

> clear these things away[1] . . .

[1] The reference here is not to "demolishing" a building, but to "clearing away." "These things" could refer to stage scenery, which was removed from the stage in full view of the audience (Beare 1964, 172). Spaltenstein (2014, 123), while seeing the removal of stage scenery as a possibility, does not exclude the idea, more likely in his view, that the objects referred to could simply be items linked to the intrigue.

33 Fulgentius

desiduo is said for *diuturno* ["for a long time"]. Hence Varro[1] too says in *The Garland Play*:

> it was a torment for me then that you were away for
> such a long time

[1] Fulgentius confuses the source for the quotation, Varro, with its author, Naevius.

COSMETRIA

Cf. *Com. Inc.* 83.

DEMENTES (F 34)

With only one fragment remaining, it is impossible to iden-
tify a Greek original for this play. Ribbeck and Warming-
ton compare the Μαινόμενος *("The Madman") of Diphilus*
(F 55 K.-A.), and Marmorale (1953) mentions a play of the
same name by Anaxandrides (t 51 K.-A.). A similarity of
title, however, can tell little about the content, and, in any

34 (49 R.[3]) Diom., *GL* I, p. 344.33

HABEO et habito dicimus, ut apud Naevium in Dementi-
bus:

℗ animae pauxillulum in me habet

habet *Ribbeck[1]*: habitat *codd.*

DEMETRIA

Cf. *Com. Inc.* F 83.

DEMETRIUS (F 35)

As only one word survives, we know little of Naevius' ver-
sion of this play. A play of the same name Δημήτριος
("Demetrius") or Φιλέταιρος *("Dear Friend") was pro-*
duced by Alexis (F 46–51 K.-A.; Arnott 1996, 155–72, fr.
46–51), and this play was adapted by Turpilius (Com.
14–36 R.[2–3]; Rychlewska 1971, fr. 15–38). In Turpilius'
play a young man falls out with his girlfriend, and sub-
sequently they make up. Plautus, Bacchides ("The Two

DEMENTES (F 34)

case, Naevius' plural ("The Madmen") suggests a different theme from the Greek singular titles ("The Madman"). The theme of simulated madness occurs in Plautus, Menaechmi *("The Two Menaechmuses") 832ff. and* Casina *621ff., and the present play could have been based on a similar intrigue.*

Comm.: *Spaltenstein 2014, 129–31.*

34 Diomedes

we say both *habeo* and *habito* [in the sense "dwell"] as in Naevius in *The Madmen*:

a tiny little breath of life dwells in me

DEMETRIA

Cf. *Com. Inc.* F 83.

DEMETRIUS (F 35)

Bacchises") 911–12: satin est si plura ex me audiet hodie mala, / quam audivit umquam Clinia ex Demetrio? [*"Isn't it enough if he is going to hear more bad things from me today than Clinia ever heard from Demetrius?"*] *could be an addition by Plautus to his Menandrian original in which he refers to a recent production of Naevius'* Demetrius *(so Barsby 1986, ad loc.). The name Demetrios in Alexis' play is unlikely to have referred to a historical*

35 (49[1] R.[3]) Varro, *Ling.* 7.107

apud Naevium . . . in Demetrio persibus[1] a perite, itaque
sub hoc glossema "callide" subscribunt:

persibus

[1] De significatione cf. Fest., p. 238.20–21 L.: PERSIBUS peracutum significare videtur.

Cf. *Com. Inc.* F 94.

DIOBOLARIA (F 36)

The play is of doubtful authenticity, as it is cited by Fulgentius only, whose evidence cannot always be trusted. The fragment does not appear in Ribbeck or Warmington, but is taken up, with some reservation, by Traglia (1986, 246) and Spaltenstein (2014, 135–36). Again, there is some uncertainty about the form and the meaning of the title. Traglia favors Diobolaria *("The Two-Obol Woman"), referring to a cheap prostitute who cannot charge more than this small sum. This is also the translation favored by the*

figure such as Demetrios of Phaleron or Demetrios Poly-
orcetes, but will simply have referred to a fictive young
man.

    Comm.: Spaltenstein 2014, 132–34.

35 Varro, *On the Latin Language*

In Naevius . . . in *Demetrius persibus* ["very clever"; a very
rare word restricted to early Latin comedy] from *perite*
["expertly"]; and so they write under this difficult word
callide ["cleverly"]:

    very clever[1]

[1] The word *persibus* occurs again in F 94. It is uncertain
whether both quotations refer to the same passage of the *Deme-*
trius. The word is a loan from Sabellic *sibus* + *per* intensive, cf.
Oscan *sipus* ["knowing"] and its Latin cognate *sapere* ["to know"]
(see De Melo 2019, 1032). It is uncertain whether the word is an
adjective or an adverb. It is interesting that Varro mentions it in
connection with the adverbs *perite* ["expertly"] and *callide* ["cle-
verly"].

DIOBOLARIA (F 36)

present edition. An obol is a low denomination of Greek
currency (one-third of a drachma). Support for this inter-
pretation comes from Varro (Ling. 7.64, with De Melo
2019, 975–76 ad loc.), who quotes Plautus, Cistellaria
("The Casket Comedy") 407, diobolares, schoenicolae,
miraculae ["*two-obol women, smelling of cheap scent,*
freakish"] *and explains* diobolares *as* a binis obolis ["*from*
two obols each"]. *Alternatively, Klussmann (1843) argues*
for a title Diabolaria *("The Play of the Slanderer") and*

193

compares two Greek plays with the title Διάβολος *("The Slanderer"), one by Nicostratus (F 9 K.-A.) and one by*

36 (vacat R.[3]) Fulg. *Serm. ant.* 43

miropolam dicunt qui unguenta vendunt . . . Naevius in Diobolaria ait:

tr[7]   miropola affatim
mi unguentum largitus est quo me venustarem . . .

DOLUS (F 37)

Dolus *("The Trick") is unlikely to be related to the tricky character Dolon, a Trojan killed by Odysseus and Diomedes in* Iliad *10, or to the play named* Δόλων *("Dolon")*

37 (49[2] R.[3]) Varro, *Ling.* 7.107

apud Naevium . . . in Dolo:

?   caperrata fronte

a caprae fronte

Cf. Paul. *Fest.*, p. 41.27–28 L.; Non., p. 8.25–26 M. = 13 L.

ERULARIA

Cf. *Com. Inc.* F 100.

Apollodorus of Carystos (F 6–7 K.-A.), about both of which we know nothing.
   Comm.: Spaltenstein 2014, 135–36. Lit.: Costanza 1956.

36 Fulgentius

They say *miropola* ["perfume seller"] of those who sell ointments . . . Naevius says in *The Two-Obol Woman*:

                         the perfume seller
   has provided me with an ample supply of ointment
      with which to beautify myself . . .

DOLUS (F 37)

(possibly a slave name) by Eubulus (F 29–31 K.-A.). It simply refers to a trick, which is often central to the action of a comedy, but little else can be known of its content.
   Comm.: Spaltenstein 2014, 137–38.

37 Varro, *On the Latin Language*

in Naevius . . . in *The Trick*:

   with a wrinkled forehead

derived from *caprae frons* ["a she-goat's forehead"][1]

   [1] This derivation is uncertain (see De Melo 2019, 1032), although it is repeated by Paul the Deacon, *Epitome of Festus*, and Nonius.

ERULARIA

Cf. *Com. Inc.* F 100.

FIGULUS (F 38)

Plays named after occupations are not uncommon in New Comedy, e.g., Plautus' Mercator ("The Merchant") and Naevius' Gymnasticus ("The Athlete") and Nautae ("The Sailors"). No other Latin play carries the name Figulus ("The Potter"), though in Greek one can compare Κοροπλάθος ("The Figurine Maker") of Antiphanes (F 125

38 (49³ R.³) Charis., *GL* I, p. 208.7 = pp. 269–70 B.

NIMIS. Naevius . . . in Figulo:

?   nimis avarus

FRETUM

Cf. *Com. Inc.* F 84.

GLAUCOMA (F 39)

A cataract of the eye is an old person's complaint, and the title Glaucoma ("The Cataract") may have to do with a central senex ("old man") figure. Physical defects were often made fun of in comedy, and Titinius'[1] Caecus ("The Blind Man"; see Ribbeck ³1898, 159–60) has a similar title in Latin, while Alexis' Ἀπεγλαυκωμένος ("The Cataract Sufferer") (F 16–18 K.-A.; Arnott 1996, 85) provides an exact equivalent. With only one line of Naevius' play sur-

FIGULUS (F 38)

K.-A.) *and* Ἐκπωματοποιός *("The Potter") of Alexis (F 67–69 K.-A.; Arnott 1996, 194). Being a potter (unlike being a merchant or an athlete) may have been a slave occupation, and the title could refer to a prominent slave character in the play.*
    Comm.: Spaltenstein 2014, 140–42.

38 Charisius
nimis ["too much"]. Naevius . . . in *The Potter*:

    too greedy

FRETUM

Cf. *Com. Inc.* F 84.

GLAUCOMA (F 39)

viving, it is impossible to tell what the role of the cataract (real or feigned) was or whether the play was an adaption of Alexis' original. Arnott (1996, 85) sees a link in the emphasis on food and shopping in the fragments of both plays.
    Comm.: Spaltenstein 2014, 144–48.

[1] Roman dramatist who wrote comedies on native Italian themes (*togatae*) in the first half of the second century BC. For his fragments, see Ribbeck [3]1898, 157–88, and Guardì 1984.

39 (50–51 R.[3]) Prisc., *GL* II, p. 524.2

"pungo, pupugi" vel "punxi" . . . Naevius in Glaucoma:

tr[7]   quod de opsonio stilo mihi in manum pupugit . . .

mihi *Klussmann*: mi *codd.*

GYMNASTICUS (F 40–47)

*Athletes and gym teachers were a source of humor among
Latin intellectuals, and the title* Gymnasticus *("The Ath-
lete") may refer to a boastful example of this freeborn type,
parallel in many ways to the figure of the boastful soldier.
Such a figure could provide a love rival for the young man
of the piece, and the parasite mentioned in F 43 could have
played the role of his flatterer. The title is Greek, but no*

40 (57 R.[3]) Non., p. 95.26–27 M. = 135 L.

DISPULVERARE est dissolvere. Naevius Gymnastico:

tr[7]   saxa silvas lapides montes dissicis dispulveras

41 (53–54 R.[3]) Non., pp. 136.4–7 M. = 197–98 L.

MUSTUM non solum vinum, verum novellum quidquid est,
recte dicitur. Naevius Gymnastico:

tr[7]   (A) . . . utrum est melius, uirginemne an viduam
                                        uxorem ducere?
         (B) virginem, si musta est.

utrum est *codd.*: dic utrum est *Ribbeck*[2–3]

Cf. Plaut. *Stich.* 118–19.

39 Priscian

pungo ["to prick"] [has the perfect form] *pupugi* or *punxi*
. . . Naevius in *The Cataract*:

> as to the fact that he pricked me in the hand with his
> stylus from the shopping . . .

GYMNASTICUS (F 40–47)

*Greek play of that name survives. The nearest parallels in
Latin are* Pugil *("The Boxer") of Caecilius (Com. 193–94
R.²⁻³, 183 Warmington, F 1 FRL) and* Pancratiastes *("The
All-round Champion") of Ennius (Com. F 2–4 FRL),
where the characters, by contrast, are likely to have been
of lower servile status.*
    *Comm.: Spaltenstein 2014, 149–71. Lit.: Molinelli 1983
(F 40); Biffi 2003 (F 41).*

40 Nonius

dispulverare ["to crush to dust"; *hapax legomenon*] means
dissolvere ["to dissolve"]. Naevius in *The Athlete*:

> rocks, woods, stones and mountains you scatter and
> crush to dust[1]

[1] Perhaps spoken by a flattering parasite to the athlete.

41 Nonius

mustum ["young"] is said correctly not only of wine, but of
whatever is new. Naevius in *The Athlete*:

> (A) . . . Which is better, to take a virgin or a widow
>   for your wife?
> (B) A virgin, if she is fresh.

42 (56 R.³) Non., p. 159.5–7 M. = 234 L.

PECUA et pecuda ita ut pecora veteres dixerunt. Naevius
Gymnastico:

tr   homines pecua beluasque . . .

43 (60 R.³) Non., p. 224.30–34 M. = 332 L.

SIMILE EST pro similis est; pro masculino positum neu-
trum . . . Naevius Gymnastico:

ia⁶   pol haut parasitorum aliorum simile est . . .

        haut *edd.*: aut *codd.*

44 (52 R.³) Non., pp. 279.43–80.1 M. = 430 L.

DESTITUI est desolari. destitui rursum statui. Naevius in
Gymnastico:

ia⁶   in alto navem destitui iubet ancoris

        destitui iubet ancoris *cod.*: iubet destitui ancoris *codd.*

45 (59 R.³) Non., pp. 392.15–32 M. = 628–29 L.

SPISSUM significat tardum . . . Naevius Gymnastico:

tr⁷?   at enim tu nimis spisse atque tarde incedis . . .

46 (55 R.³) Non., pp. 421.21–27 M. = 681–82 L.

CUPIDINEM cum feminino genere dicimus, cupiditatem
significamus . . . cum masculino deum ipsum . . . Naevius
Gymnastico:

ia⁸   edepol, Cupido, cum sis tam pauxillus, nimis multum
            vales

        cum sis tam pauxillus *Ribbeck²*: cum tam pauxillus sis *codd.*

42 Nonius

The ancients said *pecua* ["farm animals"] and *pecuda* [both ante-classical] for *pecora*. Naevius in *The Athlete*:

men, farm animals, and wild animals[1] . . .

[1] Possibly from the same context as F 41.

43 Nonius

simile est ["is like"] for *similis est*, neuter placed for masculine . . . Naevius in *The Athlete*:

by Pollux, he's nothing like other parasites . . .

44 Nonius

destitui ["to be deserted"] means *desolari* ["to be abandoned"], it also means *statui* ["to be halted"]. Naevius in *The Athlete*:

he ordered the ship to be held fast in the deep by anchors

45 Nonius

spissus ["stiff"; adv. *spisse*] means slow . . . Naevius in *The Athlete*:

but you walk too stiffly and slowly . . .

46 Nonius

When we use *cupido* in the feminine gender, we mean "desire" . . . when in the masculine, we mean the god [Cupid] himself . . . Naevius in *The Athlete*:

by Pollux, Cupid, although you are so small, you have too much power

47 (58 R.[3]) Non., p. 486.29–31 M. = 781 L.

HEREM pro heredem, Naevius Gymnastico:

tr[7]
                                        atque meis bonis
    omnibus ego te herem faciam . . .

LAMPADIO (F 48)

The play is probably named after its central slave charac-
ter. Lampadio is the name of a slave in Plautus' Cistellaria
("The Casket Comedy") and in an anonymous fragment of
comedy cited by Nonius, p. 187.12 M. = 275 L. It is un-

48 (60[1] R.[3]) Varro, *Ling.* 7.107

apud Naevium . . . in Lampadione PROTINAM, a protinus,
continuitatem significans:

    protinam

LEON

Cf. T 8.

NAGIDO (F 49)

Ribbeck[1] thinks this is an ethnic name referring to a person
(probably a slave character) originating in the town of
Nagido in Asia Minor. Slave names denoting ethnic origin
(e.g., Geta, Syrus), are common in comedy, but as a play
title the word could simply be an adjective denoting ethnic

47 Nonius

herem ["heir"; ante-classical acc.] for *heredem*, Naevius in *The Athlete*:

> and to all my goods
> I will make you heir . . .

LAMPADIO (F 48)

likely to be connected with plays named Λαμπάς ("The Torch") by Alexis (F 128 K.-A.; Arnott 1996, 356) and Antiphanes (F 135 K.-A.). We have no way of knowing anything about the plot of this play.
  Comm.: Spaltenstein 2014, 172–74.

48 Varro, *On the Latin Language*

in Naevius . . . in *Lampadio*, *protinam* ["forthwith"; early Latin verse only], from *protinus* ["straight away"; classical Latin form], denotes immediacy:

> forthwith

LEON

Cf. T 8.

NAGIDO (F 49)

origin rather than a proper name, cf. Plautus' Poenulus ("The Little Carthaginian") and Persa ("The Persian"). We have no way of knowing anything of the play's content.
  Comm.: Spaltenstein 2014, 177–78.

49 (60² R.³) Varro, *Ling*. 7.107

apud Naevium . . . in Nagidone CLUCIDATUS suavis, ta-
metsi a magistris accepimus mansuetum:

> clucidatus

clucidatus *Scaliger* (*cf. Paul.* Fest., *p. 48.13 L.*): glucidatus
Warmington (*cf. Paul.* Fest., *p. 87.24–25 L.*): caudacus *codd.*

NAUTAE (F 50)

*For plays named after professions in Naevius, see the dis-
cussion on F 38. Here the plural "The Sailors," may suggest
a group, like the fishermen in Plautus'* Rudens *["The
Rope"] or the captives in Plautus' play of that name,* Cap-

50 (60³ R.³) Fest., p. 406.8–16 L.

SUPPARUS . . . Naevius de <bello Puni>co [*BP* F 31]. et in
Nautis:

> supparus

Cf. Paul. *Fest*., p. 407.6–7 L.

NERVULARIA

Cf. *Com. Inc.* F 100.

49 Varro, *On the Latin Language*

in Naevius . . . in *Nagido*, *clucidatus*[1] ["sweet"; attested in literature only here] means *suavis* ["pleasant"], even though our teachers told us it meant tame:

sweet

[1] The form of the word in Naevius is uncertain. The forms *clucidatus* and *glucidatus* are attested once each in Paul the Deacon. The manuscripts here have *caudacus*. On the connection of *clucidatus* with the Greek γλυκύς ["sweet"], see De Melo 2019, 1033.

NAUTAE (F 50)

tivi. *The merchants involved in trading by sea are a frequent subject of comedy, and the play probably had a maritime theme. Otherwise, there is little to learn from the single word quotation in a garbled passage of Festus.*
   Comm.: Spaltenstein 2014, 179–80.

50 Festus

supparus ["woman's cloak"] . . . Naevius in <*The Punic War*> [*Bellum Punicum* F 31]. And in *The Sailors*:

woman's cloak

NERVULARIA

Cf. *Com. Inc.* F 100.

PAELEX (F 51)

*There are three plays named "The Concubine" in Greek:
two named Παλλακή, by Alexis (F 174 K.-A.; Arnott 1996,
512) and by Menander (F 280–85 K.-A.), and one called
Παλλακίς (with the same meaning) by Diphilus (F 58
K.-A.). There is no evidence about the plot of the present*

51 (66 R.^{3}) Non., p. 223.21–23 M. = 330 L.

SOCRUS et masculino genere veteres dici posse voluerunt.
Naevius Paelice [*Ribbeck*$^{2–3}$: pellico *codd.*: pellice *Bothe*]:

ia^6 desine socru tuo, fratri patrueli meo

 socru *Quicherat*: socro *Bothe*: socri *codd.*   patrueli *edd.*:
patrui *codd.*

PERSONATA (t 3)

The title Personata *("The Masked Play") could refer to the
fact that it was played by masked players (the interpreta-
tion discussed by Festus) or that it was about masks in the
sense that the intrigue involved a character disguised in
a mask. Disguise in general occurs in a number of new
comedies, e.g.,* Plautus, Miles Gloriosus *("The Braggart*

t 3 Fest. p. 238.12–20 L.

Personata fabula quaedam Naevi inscribitur, quam putant
quidam primum ‹actam› a personatis histrionibus. sed
cum post multos annos comoedi et tragoedi personis uti
coeperint, verisimilius est eam fabulam propter inopiam

PAELEX (F 51)

*play or the similarly named Greek plays, and since the
presence of a concubine is common to many new comic
plots, we cannot assume that Naevius' play is based on any
of these three Greek plays.*

Comm.: Spaltenstein 2014, 183–86.

51 Nonius

The ancients wanted *socrus* [usually "mother-in-law" in
classical Latin] to be able to be used also in the masculine
gender [to mean "father-in-law," usually *socer* in classical
Latin]. Naevius in *The Concubine*:

> cease [to speak ill] to your father-in-law, to my cousin

PERSONATA (t 3)

Soldier") *1175ff.*, *Persa* ("The Persian") *329ff.*, Pseudolus
751ff., Poenulus ("The Little Carthaginian") *576ff.*; Ter-
ence, Eunuchus ("The Eunuch") *370ff*. *It is possible that
both explanations retailed by Festus were invented by
later scholars who had no knowledge of the play.*

Comm.: Spaltenstein 2014, 187–89.

t 3 Festus

A certain play of Naevius is entitled *The Masked Play*,
which certain people think was the first ‹to be acted› by
masked players. But since it was many years after this that
comic and tragic actors began to use masks, it is more
likely that, because of a lack of comic actors, that play,

comoedorum actam novam per Atellanos, qui proprie
vocantur personati; quia ius est is non cogi in scena ponere
personam, quod ceteris histrionibus pati necesse est.

PHILEMPOROS (F 52)

*Like F 36, Philemporos ("The Merchant") is of doubtful
authenticity as it is cited by Fulgentius only. The fragment
does not appear in Ribbeck or Warmington, but is taken
up, with some reservation, by Traglia (1986, 246) and
Spaltenstein (2014, 190–91). Plays based on merchants
and traders, often with a maritime theme (cf. F 50), are
common in New Comedy. Epicrates (F 6 K.-A.), Philemon
(Plaut. Mercator 9), and Diphilus (F 31–36 K.-A.) all have
plays named* Ἐμπόρος *("The Merchant"), and in Latin
Plautus' Mercator (likewise, "The Merchant") is based on*

when first produced, was acted by Atellan players, who are properly called masked, because they have the right of not being forced to lay aside their masks on stage, which other actors are forced to submit to.[1]

[1] Festus' notice is inconsistent in that his "more likely" explanation also involves comic actors wearing masks, which he says did not take place till many years after the play was produced. His explanation perhaps contains a memory of the fact that, while most actors were forced to remove their masks at the end of the play, Atellan players were not compelled to do so and were called "masked players" for this reason. Atellan was a name of a native Italian farce originating in the Campanian city of Atella.

PHILEMPOROS (F 52)

Philemon's play. The line quoted by Fulgentius is close in content to Plautus, Casina *496–97, . . .* sculponeae, / quibus battuatur tibi os, senex nequissime [*"clogs with which to beat in your face, you worthless old man"*]. *Fulgentius, however, is wrong in his interpretation of* sculponeae, *which refer to the wooden clogs worn by slaves, rather than to boxing gloves. For footwear used as a weapon, cf. Gnatho's threat to Thraso in Terence's* Eunuchus *("The Eunuch") 1028: "I wish I could see your head softened up with a sandal" [*sandalio]*.*

Comm.: Spaltenstein 2014, 190–91.

52 (vacat R.³) Fulg. *Serm. ant.* 21

SCULPONEAS dici voluerunt cestus plumbo ligatos, unde Naevius in Philemporo comoedia ait:

ia⁶   sculponeis batuenda huic latera sunt probe

batuenda *L. Mueller*: battenda *codd.*   huic latera sunt *L. Mueller*: huic sunt latera *codd.*

PROIECTUS (F 53–54)

The plot of Proiectus *("Rejected") probably revolved around a boy who was exposed at birth or rejected by his family in some other way and was later reconciled. Many plays in New Comedy concerned characters who were exposed or rejected in this way, though these were mostly girls, and who fall into slavery or prostitution to be recognized later as freeborn and thus allowed to marry, e.g.,* Menander, Samia *("The Girl from Samos"),* Andria *("The Girl from Andros"—adapted into Latin by Terence),* Kolax *("The Flatterer"),* Plautus, Cistellaria *("The Casket Com-*

53 (67 R.³) Diom., *GL* I, p. 400.22

item PATIO. Naevius in Proiecto:

ia⁶?   . . . populus patitur, tu patias

52 Fulgentius

By *sculponeae* ["clogs"] they meant boxing gloves bound with lead; hence Naevius in his comedy *The Merchant* says:

> his sides should be well battered with clogs

PROIECTUS (F 53–54)

edy") and Curculio. *Caecilius also has a play entitled* Hypobolimaeus *in Greek or* Subditivos *in Latin ("The Changeling") in which a father sends one of his two sons off to live permanently in the country (Caec.* Com. *71–86* Warmington = F 1–8 FRL*), but there is no exact equivalent title extant in Greek comedy. The two surviving fragments occur together in Diomedes and illustrate the same grammatical point. However, they are unlikely to be from consecutive lines in the play, as they are printed in Warmington, but probably occurred some distance apart.*

Comm.: Spaltenstein 2014, 192–97.

53 Diomedes

similarly *patio* ["I suffer"; active form for classical *patior*]. Naevius in *Rejected*:

> . . . the people suffers, you must suffer

54 (68 R.[3]) Diom., *GL* I, p. 400.22–23

MORO item. Naevius in eodem:

ia[6]?   . . . (A) quid moras? (B) quia imperas

QUADRIGEMINI (F 55)

Plays based on twins, especially identical twins, would provide much opportunity for intrigue based on confused identity, as in Plautus' Menaechmi ("The Two Menaech-muses"), and Naevius must have already touched on this theme in Acontizomenos *("Speared": F 2). With* Quadri-gemini *("The Quadruplets"—referring possibly to two sets*

55 (69 R.[3]) Non., p. 153.20–21 M. = 225 L.

PARCUIT, pepercit. Naevius Quadrigeminis:

ia[6]   . . . suo labori nullus parcuit

    labori *vel* labori is *edd.*: laboris *codd.*

STALAGMUS (F 56)

The play, like Terence's Phormio, *is named after its central character, Stalagmus. This slave name occurs also in Plau-tus'* Captivi *("The Captives"). Little can be known of the play's content from the surviving fragment, which is prob-ably spoken by the scheming slave who claims to have*

54 Diomedes

moro ["I delay"; active form for classical *moror*] similarly.
Naevius in the same play [*Rejected*]:

> . . . (A) why are you delaying? (B) because you order
> me to

QUADRIGEMINI (F 55)

*of twins), the opportunities for farce would be multiplied.
There is no extant Greek comedy with this name, and the
single surviving fragment, which illustrates the early Latin
use of the perfect form* parcuit [*"spared"*], *offers little clue
as to the plot.*
    Comm.: Spaltenstein 2014, 200–212.

55 Nonius

parcuit ["spared"] [for classical] *pepercit*. Naevius in *The
Quadruplets*:

> . . . no one was sparing of his labor

STALAGMUS (F 56)

*another character in his power. There is a close parallel in
F 56 with the slave Pseudolus' words at Plautus,* Pseudolus
381: illic homo meus est, nisi omnes di me atque homines
deserunt [*"That man is mine, unless all the gods and men
desert me"*].
    Comm.: Spaltenstein 2014, 205–8.

56 (70 R.³) Donat. ad Ter. *Phorm*. 74

"memini reliqui me deo irato meo": mihi videtur ad hoc addidisse "meo" ne esset ἀμφίβολον cui diceret irato deo. Naevius in Stalagmo:

*ia*⁶   nisi deo meo propitio, meus homo est

    nisi *L. Mueller*: visam *Ribbeck*³: nisa *codd*.

STIGMATIAS (F 57)

The title Stigmatias *("The Branded Slave") comes from the Greek* στιγματίας. *The use of a Greek title implies it comes from a Greek play, but no Greek comedy of this name is known. The line quoted by Varro refers to an*

57 (71 R.³) Varro, *Ling*. 7.107

apud Naevium . . . in Stigmatia PRAEBIA a praebendo, ut sit tutus, quod sint remedia in collo pueris

    praebia

Cf. Fest., p. 276.12–13 L.

56 Donatus, *Commentary on Terence*

"I remember I left with my god angry with me": He [Terence] seems to me to have added *meo* ["my"] to this to avoid uncertainty about whom he should say the god was angry with. Naevius in *Stalagmus*:

> unless with the favor of my god the man is mine

STIGMATIAS (F 57)

amulet worn round the neck of children to keep off evil. Such an amulet could be the type of recognition token that enables lost children to be recognized in traditional comic plots.
Comm.: Spaltenstein 2014, 209–11.

57 Varro, *On the Latin Language*

In Naevius . . . in *The Branded Slave praebia*[1] ["amulets"; attested only here outside the grammarians] from *praebere*[2] ["to provide"], so that [a boy] may be safe, because they are remedies hung on boys' necks:

> amulets

[1] The form of the word in Naevius is uncertain.

[2] Varro's etymology from *praebere* is correct (see De Melo 2019, 1033). The verb could originally have meant something like "ward off" from *prohibere* (see *TLL* 10(2).391.14 and cf. Fest., p. 276.12–13 L.: *ea vocari ait* [Verrius Flaccus] *praebia quod mala prohibeant* ["Verrius Flaccus says they are called *praebia* because they *prohibeant*, 'ward off,' evil"]).

TARENTILLA (F 58–72)

Plays called Ταραντῖνοι *("The Men from Tarentum") in Greek are known to have been written by Alexis (F 222–27 K.-A.; Arnott 1996, 624) and the younger Cratinus (F 280–85 K.-A.), but the Greek adjective is masculine plural, and the plays make fun of Pythagorean philosophers. They are clearly not connected with Naevius' play, which concerns a girl from Tarentum. There are enough fragments remaining for a rough reconstruction of the plot. Two young men*

58 (93³ R.³) Varro, *Ling.* 7.107–8

apud Naevium . . . [108] in Tarentilla PELLUCIDUM [*Barchiesi*: praelucidum *C. O. Mueller*: pallucidum *Klussmann*: pacui dum *codd.*] a luce, illustre:

pellucidum

59 (86 R.³) Charis., *GL* I, p. 127.3–6 = p. 161 B.

DUUM . . . Naevius in Tarentilla:

tr^7 salvi et fortunati sitis duo duum nostrum patres!

60 (93¹ R.³) Charis., *GL* I, p. 196.1–6 = pp. 254–55 B.

CONFESTIM . . . Naevius in Tarentilla:

confestim

TARENTILLA (F 58–72)

are living abroad in Tarentum squandering their fathers'
wealth (F 64). Their fathers travel from Athens in search
of them (F 64), eventually find them (F 59, 70), and per-
suade them to mend their ways and return home (F 62,
63). "The Girl from Tarentum" is probably a courtesan
(F 72) on whom the young men spend their fathers' money.

Comm.: Spaltenstein 2014, 215–62. Lit.: Traina 1965
(F 72); von Albrecht 1975; M. Barchiesi 1978; Molinelli
1983 (F 72).

58 Varro, *On the Latin Language*

in Naevius . . . [108] in *The Girl from Tarentum* pel-
lucidum[1] ["very bright"] from *lux* [*lux, lucis*: "light"],
shining:

> very bright

[1] The form of the word in Naevius is uncertain.

59 Charisius

duum ["of two"] . . . Naevius in *The Girl from Tarentum*:

> hail and good luck to you, the two fathers of us two!

60 Charisius

confestim ["straight away"] . . . Naevius in *The Girl from*
Tarentum:

> straight away

61 (80 R.[3]) Charis., *GL* I, p. 198.1 = p. 257 B.

DEFRICATE Naevius in Tarentilla:

?   facete et defricate

62 (90–91 R.[3]) Charis., *GL* I, p. 208.7–10 = p. 269 B.

NIMIS Naevius in Tarentilla:

tr[8]   numquam quisquam amico amanti amica nimis fiet
        fidelis,
    nec nimis erit morigera et nota quisquam . . .

    2 morigera et nota *Zicàri 1958*: morigeret nota *codd.*: mori-
gera et † nota † *Warmington*: morigera et devota *Ribbeck*[3]

63 (92–93 R.[3]) Charis., *GL* I, p. 212.15–26 = p. 275 B.

PEREGRE cum abit quis dicimus in locum . . . PEREGRI
autem cum in loco est . . . Naevius in Tarentilla:

tr[7]   primum ad virtutem ut redeatis, abeatis ab ignavia,
    domos patres patriam ut colatis potius quam peregri
        probra.

    2 probra *Ribbeck*[1]: probro *codd.*

64 (83–84 R.[3]) Charis., *GL* I, pp. 212.27–13.2 = p. 275 B.

PEREGRE pro peregri Naevius in Tarentilla:

ia[6]   . . . ubi isti duo adulescentes habent
    qui hic ante parta patria peregre prodigunt?

61 Charisius

defricate ["elegantly"; *hapax legomenon*] Naevius in *The Girl from Tarentum*:

> wittily and elegantly

62 Charisius

nimis ["too"]. Naevius in *The Girl from Tarentum*:

> never will any girlfriend be too faithful to a loving
>   boyfriend,
> nor too compliant nor too sure[1] . . .

[1] Possibly a warning from a father to his son.

63 Charisius

We say *peregre* ["abroad"] when someone goes away to a place . . . but *peregri* ["abroad"] when they are in a place . . . Naevius in *The Girl from Tarentum*:

> first that you return to virtue and leave idleness,
> that you devote yourselves to your homes, fathers,
>   and fatherland, rather than to misdeeds abroad[1]

[1] An exhortation from one of the fathers to the sons.

64 Charisius

peregre ["abroad"] for *peregri* Naevius in *The Girl from Tarentum*:

> . . . where do those two young men live
> who squander here abroad the wealth once acquired
>   by their fathers?

65 (72–74 R.^{3}) Charis., *GL* I, p. 216.10–16 = p. 279 B.

QUANTI cum interrogamus nec emimus; QUANTO cum emptam rem quaerimus . . . Naevius in Tarentilla:

ia^6 quae ego in theatro hic meis probavi plausibus,
       ea non audere quemquam regem rumpere,
       quanto libertatem hanc hic superat servitus.

66 (88–89 R.^{3}) Charis., *GL* I, pp. 216.31–17.2 = p. 280 B.

RURSUS negant dici debere sed rursum, ut iterum. Maro tamen [Verg. *Aen.* 2.655] "rursus in arma feror." et tamen in bonis ‹libris› Naevii rursus inveni. nam is in Tarentilla:

tr^7 qua, pro! confidentia ausus verbum cum eo fuerim
       facere ‹rursus›?

1 ausus *Bothe*: rusus *Keil*: usus *codd.*
2 rursus *Warmington*: rusus *Ribbeck*$^{2–3}$: *om. codd.*

67 (85 R.^{3}) Charis., *GL* I, p. 220.24 = p. 285 B.

SERIO pro vere. Naevius in Tarentilla:

?   . . . vereor serio

65 Charisius

We say *quanti* ["how much"] when we ask the price but
do not buy, *quanto* ["how much"] when we ask the price
of something we have bought . . . Naevius in *The Girl from
Tarentum*:

> as for what I have proved here in the theatre with my
>   applause,
> ‹to think that› no aristocrat dare contradict it –
> by what a lot does slavery here surpass this freedom![1]

[1] The passage suggests that the slave playing his role in the
theater has greater freedom of speech than his aristocratic audi-
ence. On the theme of slave freedom, cf. *Com. Inc.* F 92.

66 Charisius

They say one should not use *rursus* ["again"] but rather
rursum like *iterum* ["again"]. However, Virgil [*Aen.* 2.655]
says "I run again [*rursus*] into battle." And indeed in good
‹manuscripts› of Naevius I have found *rursus*. For in *The
Girl from Tarentum* he says:

> what optimism, by god, made me bold enough to
>   speak
> with him ‹again›?[1]

[1] Probably spoken by a father in disgust at his son's behavior.

67 Charisius

serio ["seriously"] for "truly." Naevius in *The Girl from
Tarentum*:

> . . . I am truly afraid

68 (81 R.^{3}) Charis., *GL* I, p. 223.30 = p. 288 B.

UTRUBI Naevius in Tarentilla:

tr^7 . . . utrubi cenaturi estis, hicine an in triclinio?

69 (93^2 R.^{3}) Charis., *GL* I, p. 229.21–24 = p. 297 B.

ATQUE pro et . . . Naevius . . . in Tarentilla:

   atque

70 (87 R.^{3}) Charis., *GL* I, p. 239.23–24 = p. 312 B.

EI EI. Naevius in Tarentilla:

tr^7 ei ei! etiamne audent mecum una apparere? . . .

   etiamne *Keil*: etiam se *codd.*

71 (82 R.^{3}) Charis., *GL* I, p. 239.25–26 = p. 312 B.

ATATTATAE idem [Naevius] in eadem [in Tarentilla]:

tr^7 atattatae!
   cave cadas amabo!

   2 amabo *edd.*: ambo *codd.*

Cf. Plaut. *Most.* 324: (Callidamates, adulescens) duc me amabo.
(Delphium, meretrix) cave ne cadas, asta.

---

[1] Spoken perhaps by one drunken son, supporting the other,
or possibly his girlfriend, cf. Plautus, *Mostellaria* ["*The Ghost*"]
324, where the drunken young man Callidamates asks for support

68 Charisius

utrubi ["in which of two places?"] Naevius in *The Girl from Tarentum*:

> . . . in which of two paces will you dine, here or in the dining room[1]?

[1] Probably addressed by the girl or her servant to the two young men.

69 Charisius

atque ["and"] for *et* . . . Naevius . . . in *The Girl from Tarentum*:

> and

70 Charisius

ei ei ["alas"]. Naevius in *The Girl from Tarentum*:

> alas! Do they even dare to show themselves in my presence?[1] . . .

[1] Perhaps spoken by one of the fathers on seeing their drunken sons (see F 63).

71 Charisius

atattatae ["oh, ah"] the same author [Naevius] in the same play [*The Girl from Tarentum*]:

> oh, ah!
>
> Mind you don't fall, please![1]

from his girlfriend, Delphium: "*Cull.* Guide me, please. *Delph.* Mind you don't fall, stand up!"

72 (75–79 R.[3]) Isid. *Orig.* 1.26.2

Naevius [*edd. ex epit. Pauli*: Ennius *codd.*, *cf. Enn.* Com. Inc. *F* 5 FRL] de quadam impudica:

tr[7]   quasi pila
   in choro ludens datatim dat se et communem facit.
   alii adnutat, alii adnictat, alium amat, alium tenet.
   alibi manus est occupata, alii pervellit pedem;
5   anulum dat alii spectandum, a labris alium invocat,
   cum alio cantat, at tamen alii suo dat digito litteras.

1–2 pila / in choro *Bothe*: in choro pila *codd.*   2 se *Otto*: sese *codd.*   3 *ex epit. Paul.*: alium tenet, alii adnutat, alibi manus *codd. Isid.*   4 pervellit *codd.*: percellit *Scaliger*
   5 anulum dat alii *C. F. W. Mueller*: alii dat anulum *codd.*
   6 alii suo dat digito *Ribbeck*[1]: aliis dat digito *codd.*

Cf. Paul. *Fest.*, p. 26.14–15 L.: ADNICTAT . . . Naevius in Tarentilla: "alii adnutat, alii adnictat, alium amat, alium tenet."

TECHNICUS (F 73)

The meaning of the title Technicus *is not certain. It could refer to an expert of some kind (as in Quint.* Inst. *2.13.15), but it would be normal in a play's title to make plain what type of expert was referred to, e.g.,* Gymnasticus *("The Athlete": F 40–47). According to Ritschl (1868, 499) and R.*[2–3]*, it is more likely to refer to a charlatan, a person who*

72 Isidore, *Origins*

Naevius[1] of some shameless woman:

> as though she were playing
> at a ball in a circle, she gives herself to all by turn and
>   makes herself common property.
> To one she nods, at another she winks; one she hugs,
>   another she embraces.
> Elsewhere her hand is occupied; another man's foot
>   she jerks.
> She gives another her ring to look at; she invites   5
>   another blowing a kiss from her lips.
> With another she sings, but for another she draws
>   letters with her finger.

[1] The name is restored from Paul the Deacon's epitome; Isidore's text has Ennius (not Naevius), and many scholars now accept the fragment as Ennian (cf. Ennius, *Com. Inc.* F 5 *FRL*).

Cf. Paul the Deacon, *Epitome of Festus*: *adnictat* ["winks at"] . . . Naevius in *The Girl from Tarentum*: "To one she nods, at another she winks; one she hugs, another she embraces."

TECHNICUS (F 73)

invents stories, rather like Ariolus *("The Soothsayer": F 14–15). "The Charlatan" is the translation favored in the present edition. The Greek spelling suggests it derives from a Greek play, but no Greek comedy with this title is known.*
     Comm.: Spaltenstein 2014, 262–65.

73 (93[4] R.[3]) Varro, *Ling.* 7.107

apud Naevium . . . in Technico CONFICTANT a conficto
convenire [*codd.*: conficto a confingere *Ribbeck, Coroll.*,
p. xvii] dictum:

> confictant

> confictant *Turnebus, edd.*: conficiant *codd.*

TESTICULARIA (F 74)

Although the unusually frank title of Testicularia *("The
Testicle Play") is in Latin, there is no reason to suppose a
Greek original did not exist. We cannot establish the exact
role of testicles in the play from the single line fragment
that remains. Possibly there was a pun on* testis *("witness")*

74 (94 R.[3]) Prisc., *GL* II, p. 516.14–15

scindo, scidi; vetustissimi tamen etiam SCICIDI profere-
bant . . . Naevius in Testicularia:

tr[7]   immo quos scicidimus conscindam atque abiciam . . .

> scicidimus *codd.*: scicidi in ius *Ribbeck*[2–3]

TRIBACELUS

Cf. *Com. Inc.* F 104.

73 Varro, *On the Latin Language*

In Naevius . . . in *The Charlatan, confictant* ["they invent a story together"; the verb is found only here and once in Pacuvius, *Trag.* 337–39 R.[2–3] = F 255 Schierl] is said from *conficto convenire* ["to agree on a fabrication"]:

they invent a story together

TESTICULARIA (F 74)

and testis *("testicle") as at Plautus,* Cucrculio *31:* quod amas amato testibus praesentibus [*"love what you love with your* testes *present"*]. *In both Greece and Rome, adulterers could be castrated.*
   Comm.: Spaltenstein 2014, 266–70.

74 Priscian

scindo ["I cut"] [has the perfect form] *scidi*; but the ancients also had [the perfect form] *scicidi* . . . Naevius in *The Testicle Play*:

no, those we have cut off I will cut up and throw
   away . . .

TRIBACELUS

Cf. *Com. Inc.* F 104.

TRIPHALLUS (F 75)

The play's title Triphallus *(literally, "Triple Phallus" =
"with a big phallus") is an adjective applied, perhaps in
jest, to the fertility god Priapus at Priapeia 83.9, but pre-
sumably in this play refers to a man. His role in the play
may not have been central, and he has no part to play in
the surviving fragment, but it must have been striking
enough to lend it his name (cf. Com. Inc. F 104). The title*

75 (96–98 R.³) Gell. *NA* 2.19.4–6

aliter enim dictum esse "rescivi" aut "rescire" apud eos qui
diligenter locuti sunt nondum invenimus quam super is
rebus quae aut consulto consilio latuerint aut contra spem
opinionemve usu venerint . . . [6] Naevius in Triphallo ita
scripsit:

ia⁶   umquam si quicquam filium rescivero
        argentum amoris causa sumpse mutuum,
        extemplo illo te ducam ubi non despuas

1 umquam si *Carrio*: sicumquam *Bergk*: si umquam *codd.*
2 sumpse *Fruterius*: sumpsisse *codd.*

Cf. *Com. Inc.* F 104.

TRIPHALLUS (F 75)

*in Greek is given to Varro's Menippean Satire 562 (cf.
Non., p. 131.27 M. = 191 L.) on virility. A play of Aris-
tophanes named* Triphales *with the same meaning (K.-A.
III 2, p. 285) is concerned with Alcibiades and has no
connection with the present play; nevertheless, Naevius'
Greek title suggests a lost Greek original.*
    Comm.: Spaltenstein 2014, 272–77.

75 Gellius, *Attic Nights*

I have never yet found that *rescivi* ["I got to know"] or
rescire ["to get to know"] were used by those who were
careful in their diction otherwise than in connection with
those things which were concealed by express purpose or
happened contrary to hope and expectation . . . [6] Nae-
vius wrote as follows in *Triphallus*:

> if ever I discover that my son
> has borrowed any money for a love affair,
> I will immediately lead you to a place where you
>   cannot spit downward[1]

[1] The place alluded to is perhaps the mill where offending
slaves were traditionally punished, and where a muzzle would
prevent them from spitting. An old man is addressing his slave
about his son's borrowing money for a girl.

TUNICULARIA (F 76–78)

Tunicularia *("The Tunic Play")* is probably named after a tunic that had some role to play in the plot, like the palla [*"cloak"*] in Plautus' Menaechmi *("The Two Menaechmuses")*. Alternatively, it could refer to a female tunic

76 (103–104 R.³) Varro, *Ling.*7.107–8

apud Naevium . . . [108] in Tunicularia:

꘎   ecbolicas aulas quassant

quae eiciuntur, a Graeco verbo ἐκβολή [*ed. Ald.*: exbole *codd.*] dictum.

     ecbolicas *Kent*: exbolas *codd.*

77 (105 R.³) Fest., p. 166.11–22 L.

NAUCUM ait Ateius Philologus poni pro nugis. . . . et Naevius in Tunicularia:

꘎   eius noctem nauco ducere

TUNICULARIA (F 76–78)

maker. Little can be deduced about the plot from the re-
maining fragments. F 77 suggests a love intrigue of some
kind, whereas the longest fragment, F 78, probably comes
from a polemical prologue by the author.
  Comm.: Spaltenstein 2014, 278–88.

76 Varro, *On the Latin Language*

Naevius . . . [108] in *The Tunic Play*:

> they break the rejected pots[1]

ecbolicas ["rejected"; a *hapax legomenon*] are those which
are to be thrown away, from the Greek word ἐκβολή
["throwing out"].

[1] "Breaking rejected pots" is perhaps a proverb, like "bringing
coals to Newcastle."

77 Festus

Ateius the Grammarian[1] says that *naucum* ["worthless"] is
put for *nugae* ["a trifle"]. . . . And Naevius in *The Tunic
Play*:

> to consider a night of hers worthless

[1] L. Ateius Praetextatus, known as Ateius Philologus, was a
first-century BC grammarian and literary historian, a contempo-
rary of Cicero (see Funaioli 1907, 136–41; Suet. *Gram. et rhet.*
10, with Kaster 1995, 138–48 ad loc.).

78 (99–102 R.³) Fest., p. 260.16–22 L.

PENEM antiqui codam vocabant . . . dictus est forsitan a pendendo. Naevius in Tunicularia:

ia⁶
                                Theodotum
cum Apella comparas qui Compitalibus
sedens in cella circumtectus tegetibus
Lares ludentes peni pinxit bubulo?

significat peniculo grandi, id est coda.

1–3 Theodotum / cum Apella comparas qui Compitali-bus / sedens *Umphenbach*: Theodotum compellas qui aras Com-pitalibus / sedens *cod.*   3 circumtectus *C. O. Mueller*: cir-cumtectuas *cod.*

COMICA INCERTA (F 79–108)

Seven of these fragments (two from Cicero F 79 and F 80, two from Varro F 83 and F 84, two from Nonius F 100 and F 101, and one from Donatus F 104) are all clearly as-signed to Naevius, but their titles as transmitted are all corrupt. They are generally assigned to palliatae [*"come-dies in Greek dress"*] *on account of their style and content. The content of F 100, a list of meats, probably spoken by a slave or a parasite, makes its comic origin probable. In his presentation of F 104, Donatus speaks of comic poets.*

78 Festus

The ancients called a tail *penis* ["tail/penis"] . . . perhaps said from *pendere* ["hang"]. Naevius in *The Tunic Play*:

> Theodotus,
> do you compare him with Apelles, Theodotus, who
> on the feast of the Crossroads,
> seated in a cellar screened round with matting,
> painted the household gods at play with a bull's tail?[1]

he means with a big brush, that is a tail.

[1] The text of this fragment is much disputed, and the one printed here is based on a conjecture by Umphenbach. Apelles was a famous Greek painter of the Hellenistic period. The comparison with the little-known painter Theodotus suggests the fragment comes from Naevius' prologue to the play in which he compares himself with Apelles at the expense of a rival whom he implicitly compares with the insignificant Theodotus (see Spaltenstein 2014, 282).

PLAYS OF UNCERTAIN OR
UNKNOWN TITLE (F 79–108)

The single word in Varro F 83 gives no real clue to its context, but if the conjectured title Fretum *("The Strait") in Varro's F 84 is correct, the play could have been based on the common comic theme of a shipwreck. In F 79 and F 80, provided from the same play* † Ludus † *("The Lydian" or possibly "The Trick/Game") by Cicero, the content is concerned with contemporary politics and could come from either a* fabula palliata *or a* fabula praetexta *["drama on a Roman theme"]. In all the remaining fragments, the play-wright's name Naevius is mentioned, but no title is given. Their content suggests a comic context.*

79 (*Praet.* 7 R.[3]) Cic. *Sen.* 20

quodsi legere atque audire voletis externa, maximas res publicas ab adulescentibus labefactatas, a senibus sustentatas et restitutas reperietis:

ia[8]?   cedo qui vestram rem publicam tantam amisistis tam
          cito?

sic enim percontantur, ut est in Naevii poetae Ludo [*vel* posteriori libro *codd.*]: respondentur . . . [F 80].

80 (*Praet.* 8 R.[3]) Cic. *Sen.* 20

sic enim percontantur, ut est in Naevi poetae Ludo [*vel* posteriori libro *codd.*]: respondentur et alia et hoc in primis:

ia[8]   proveniebant oratores novi, stulti adulescentuli

81 (107 R.[3]) Varro, *Ling.* 5.153

in circo primum unde mittuntur equi, nunc dicuntur carceres, Naevius OPPIDUM appellat . . . quod ad muri spe-

Comm.: Spaltenstein 2014, 289–308. Lit.: Molinelli 2008 (F 101).

79 Cicero, *On Old Age*

But if you wish to read and hear of foreign examples, you will find the greatest states to have been undermined by young men and to have been supported and restored by old men:

> tell me how you ruined a state as mighty as yours so quickly[1]

For this is the question, as it is found in the poet Naevius' play † *Ludus* †: answers are made: . . . [F 80].

[1] Naevius appears to be commenting in these two fragments (F 79 and F 80) on the politics of his day. Both passages support the thesis that the old are better than the young when it comes to government. The genre is uncertain: Ribbeck[1] considered it a comedy, named after its chief slave Lydus, but Ribbeck[2] reassigned it to a *praetexta*. The title *Ludus* is uncertain; it could mean *The Lydian* or *The Trick/Game*.

80 Cicero, *On Old Age*

For this is the question, as it is found in the poet Naevius' play † *Ludus* †: other answers are made and this in particular:

> new orators came forth, stupid young men

81 Varro, *On the Latin Language*

In the circus the place from which the horses are sent off at the start is now called *carceres* ["stalls"], but Naevius

ciem [*C. O. Mueller*: a muris partem *codd.*] pinnis [*Laetus*: pennis *codd.*] turribusque [*Aug.*: turribus qui *codd.*] carceres olim fuerunt, scripsit poeta:

ia[8]   dictator ubi currum insidit pervehitur usque ad
        oppidum

De metro cf. De Melo 2019, 780.

82 (120 R.[3]) Varro, *Ling.* 7.53

apud Naevium:

ia[6]   risi egomet mecum cassabundum ire ebrium

cassabundum a cadendo.

83 (35[2] R.[3]) Varro, *Ling.* 7.54

in [Plauti] *Menaechmis* [797]: "inter ancillas sedere iubeas, lanam carere." idem hoc est verbum in † *Cemetria* † [Commotria *Turnebus*: Cosmetria *C. O. Mueller*: Demetria *Goetz / Schoell*] Naevii:

    carere

carere a carendo, quod eam tum purgant ac deducunt, ut careat spurcitia.

Cf. *Praetext.* F 3.

---

[1] The name of the play is corrupt. Editors suggest alternatives such as *Commotria* ("*The Hairstylist*"), *Cosmetria* ("*The Chamber Maid*"), or *Demetria* [a girl's name].   [2] It is not clear which form of the word occurred in this play.

calls it *oppidum* ["town"] . . . Because the stalls once had pinnacles and towers like a wall, the poet wrote:

> when the dictator[1] sits in the chariot, he is driven
>   right up to the town[2]

[1] Possibly T. Manlius Torquatus, who was made *dictator comitiorum ludorumque faciendorum causa* ["dictator for organizing elections and games"] in 208 BC.   [2] Perhaps from a comic prologue, referring to the games at which the play is being put on. Otherwise, the fragment could be part of a play on Roman themes, a *fabula praetexta* or *togata*. There is, however, no firm evidence that Naevius wrote comedies on Roman themes, *togatae*.

82 Varro, *On the Latin Language*

In Naevius:

> I laughed to myself [to see him] tottering along
>   drunk[1]

cassabundum ["tottering"] from *cadere* ["fall over"].

[1] Perhaps spoken by a comic slave, describing his drunken master to a third person.

83 Varro, *On the Latin Language*

In *The Two Menaechmuses* [Plautus, *Menaechmi* 797]: "Please tell him to sit among the maids and to card wool." This same word is in the *Cemetria*[1] of Naevius:

> to card[2]

carere ["to card"] comes from *carere* ["to lack"], because then they clean the wool and spin it out, so that it may lack dirt.

84 (129 R.[3]) Varro, *Ling.* 7.70

in *Truculento* [Plaut. *Truc.* 495] "sine virtute argutum civem mihi habeam pro praefica." ‹PRAEFICA› [*add. Aldus*] dicta, ut Aurelius scribit [Funaioli 1907, 90, F 11], mulier ab luco quae conduceret [*Spengel*: conduceretur *codd.*] quae ante domum mortui laudes eius canerent [*Spengel*: caneret *codd.*] . . . quibus testimonium est quod † fretum est † [*codd.*: in Freto est: *Goetz / Schoell*: Freto inest *Canal*: tritum est *Buecheler*: facetum est *Ribbeck*] Naevii:

tr[8]   haec quidem hercle, opinor, praefica est; nam mortuum collaudat

Claudius scribit [Funaioli 1907, 98, F 8]: "quae praeficeretur ancillis, quemadmodum lamentarentur, praefica est dicta." utrumque ostendit a praefectione praeficam dictam.

hercle *codd.*: mehercle *Paul. Fest.*   nam *codd.*: quae sic *Paul. Fest.*: quasi *Ribbeck*[1]

Cf. Paul. *Fest.*, p. 250.5–8 L.

84 Varro, *On the Latin Language*

In *The Truculentus* [Plautus, *Truculentus* 495]: "I would consider an eloquent citizen without bravery like a woman hired to lead the mourning." <*praefica*> ["woman leading the mourning"], as Aurelius[1] writes, is the name given to a woman from the grove,[2] who hired women to sing the praises of a dead man in front of his house . . . witness to these customs is what is <in *The Strait*> [so Goetz / Schoell][3] of Naevius:

> Indeed, I think, this woman is a leading mourner; for
> she praises a dead man

Claudius writes:[4] "the woman who was put in charge [*praeficeretur*] of the slave girls, [to show them] how they should lament, was called a *praefica* ["woman leading the mourning"]." Both passages show that the *praefica* was called from *praefectio* ["being put in charge"].

[1] Aurelius Opillius, a grammarian active at the turn of the second and first centuries BC (see Funaioli 1907, 90, F 11; Suet. *Gram. et rhet.* 6, with Kaster 1995, 110–16 ad loc.).

[2] That is the grove of Venus Libitina, goddess of death and funerals.

[3] It is unclear what stood here in the text. The most likely option, given the genitive "of Naevius" is a play name, is possibly *Fretum* ["*The Strait*"]. A play of that name is attributed to Plautus at Gell. *NA* 3.3.7, who adds that some think it is not by Plautus. If that were the title here, it could perhaps have been a comedy about a merchant who was supposed to have been shipwrecked in a dangerous sea strait.

[4] The mid-first-century BC grammarian Servius Clodius (Funaioli 1907, 98, F 8; Suet. *Gram. et rhet.* 3.1–3, with Kaster 1995, 70–80 ad loc.).

85 (136 R.³) Fronto, *Ad M. Caesarem et invicem libri,*
Ep. 2.5.2 (p. 26.12–16 van den Hout)

. . . istae litterae ad me tuae . . . non satis proloqui possum,
ut animum meum gaudio in altum sustulerint, desiderio
flagrantissimo incitaverint, postremo quod ait Naevius
[*codd.*: Novius *Augustin.*]:

ia⁶   . . . animum amore capitali conpleverint

conpleverint *edd.*: conpleverunt *codd.*

86 (111–12 R.³) Fronto, *Ad M. Caesarem et invicem libri,*
Ep. 2.8.1 (p. 28.14–16 van den Hout)

haec enim olim incommoda regibus solis fieri solebant, at
enim nunc adfatim sunt quei et regum filiis,¹ ut Naevius
ait:

tr⁷   linguis faveant atque adnutent . . . et subserviant

lac. proposuit Ribbeck¹ metri causa   et ‹animis› subser-
viant *Buecheler*

¹ quei et regum filiis *Naevio attribuunt van den Hout et edd.*
plerique, exceptis Ribbeck³ et Marmorale

87 (108–10 R.³) Gell. *NA* 7.8.5–6

Cf. T 9.

85 Fronto, *Correspondence* [Marcus Aurelius to Fronto]

. . . I cannot express sufficiently how your letters to me . . . have raised my heart on high with joy and have stirred it with most ardent desire, finally, as Naevius[1] says:

. . . they have filled my heart with deadly love[2]

[1] Although all manuscripts have Naevius, some editors print Novius. The two names are often confused. [2] Possibly from the speech of a comic *adulescens* ("young man"), whose love is rendered dangerous by the opposition of his father or a rival.

86 Fronto, *Correspondence* [Marcus Aurelius to Fronto]

In the past such inconveniences as these used to happen only to kings, but now there are plenty of men who also in the case of kings' sons,[1] as Naevius says:

hold their tongues and nod assent . . . and act as underlings[2]

[1] The phrase *quei et regum filiis* ["also in the case of kings' sons"] is made part of Naevius' play by most editors, though this attribution is questioned by Ribbeck[3] and Marmorale (1953).
[2] Warmington (1936, 147) thinks this line (to which he adds "also in the case of kings' sons") could come from a tragedy, but a general phrase about flatterers would suit the popular rhetoric of comedy.

87 Gellius, *Attic Nights*

Cf. T 9.

88 (117 R.[3]) Paul. *Fest*., p. 10.1–3 L.

APLUDA est genus minutissimae paleae frumenti sive panici, de qua Naevius:

ia[6]   non hercle apluda est hodie quam tu nequior

Cf. Mai 1836, 54.

89 (118 R.[3]) Paul. *Fest*., p. 26.18–19 L.

ALEONEM aleatorem, Naevius:

tr[7]   pessimorum pessime, audax, ganeo, lustro,[1] aleo

   [1] Cf. *Com.* F 108.

Cf. Mai 1836, 30.

90 (124 R.[3]) Paul. *Fest*., p. 31.3–4 L.

BILBIT factum est a similitudine sonitus, qui fit in vase. Naevius

ia[6]?   . . . bilbit amphora

inquit.

88 Paul the Deacon, *Epitome of Festus*

apluda ["chaff"] is a kind of very small husk from wheat or millet, about which Naevius says:

> not even chaff, by god,[1] is more worthless today than
>   you[2]

[1] The interjection *hercle* (lit., "by Hercules") is restricted in comedy mainly to male speakers.   [2] The context is uncertain. Since the speaker is likely to be male, perhaps a comic father is criticizing his son.

89 Paul the Deacon, *Epitome of Festus*

aleo ["gamester"; rare form] for *aleator* ["gambler"; classical form], Naevius:

> most wicked of the wickedest men, you impudent
>   glutton, you vagabond, you gambler[1]

[1] The list of insults would apply best perhaps to a comic parasite, but slaves and *adulescentes* ("young men") could equally well provide the butt for such abuse.

90 Paul the Deacon, *Epitome of Festus*

bilbit ["gurgles"; rare and ante-classical] is formed from the similarity of sound which is made in a wine jar. Naevius says:

> . . . the wine jar gurgles[1]

[1] Spoken perhaps by a comic drunkard. The sound referred to is that made by new wine fermenting in its jug (cf. Mai 1836, 67).

91 121–21[1–2] R.[3]

a Paul. *Fest.*, p. 51.10–13 L.

COCUM et pistorem apud antiquos eundem fuisse accepimus. Naevius,

tr[7]   cocus

inquit

> edit Neptunum, Cererem . . .

significat per Cererem panem, per Neptunum pisces, per Venerem holera.

> Neptunum, Cererem: *Gloss.* 5.521, 565; *Mai* 1836, *131*; *edd.*: Neptunum Venerem Cererem *codd.*

b *Gloss.* 5.521

Ceres frumentum vel panem, Liber vitem vel vinum, Venus libidinem vel olera, Neptunus aquam vel pisces, Vulcanus ignem vel solem significat: "cocus edit Neptunum . . ."

tr[7]   cocus edit Neptunum Cererem . . .
        et Venerem expertam Vulcanum, Liberumque
            obsorbuit
        pariter.

id est cocus comedit pisces et panem et olera cocta ad ignem et vinum pariter bibit.

> 2 obsorbuit *Gloss.* 5.565, *Ribbeck[1]*: absorbuit *codd.*, *Warmington.*

91[1]

a Paul the Deacon, *Epitome of Festus*

cocus ["a cook"] and *pistor* ["a miller/baker"] we have learned was the same thing among the ancients. Naevius

> a cook

he says

> ate Neptune, Ceres . . .

By Ceres he means bread, by Neptune fish, and by Venus vegetables.

b *Glossaria Latina*

Ceres means corn or bread, Liber the vine or wine, Venus desire or vegetables, Neptune water or fishes, Vulcan fire or sun:

> a cook ate Neptune, Ceres . . .
> and Venus that had known Vulcan and Liber too he
>   gulped down
> all at once.

That is the cook ate fishes, and bread, and vegetables cooked on the fire, and at the same time drank wine.

[1] Two entries in the *Glossaria Latina* (5.521 and 5.565) quote all three lines, but with no attribution. Paul the Deacon quotes only the first line, but gives the author as Naevius. Mai (1836, 131) quotes "a cook . . . Venus," but attributes the lines wrongly to Ennius. The passage seems to come from a comedy in which a cook is described as having eaten the meal he had prepared for his guests and having drunk their wine.

92 (113 R.[3]) Paul. *Fest.*, p. 103.11–13 L.

LIBERALIA Liberi festa, quae apud Graecos dicuntur Διο-
νύσια. Naevius:

tr^7 libera lingua loquemur ludis Liberalibus

loquemur *edd.*: loquimur *codd.*

93 (122 R.[3]) Fest., p. 228.1–7 L.

PETIMINA in umeris iumentorum ulcera . . . eo nomine
autem, et inter duos armos suis quod est aut pectus appel-
lari solitum testatur Naevius in descriptione suillae, cum
ait:

ia^6 . . . petimine porcino qui meruerat

porcino *Dalecamp*: piscino *codd.*

92 Paul the Deacon, *Epitome of Festus*

Liberalia the festival of Liber, which among the Greeks is called Dionysia. Naevius:

> we will speak with a free tongue[1] at Liber's Games[2]

[1] The first person is unlikely to refer to Naevius himself, speaking for example in a prologue, since it is not in the usual meter for a prologue (iambic senarius) and the Games referred to were not an occasion for dramatic performance in Rome. More likely, in the body of the play a low-status character such as a slave allows himself freedom of speech on the pretext that it is the Dionysia / Liberalia festival (cf. *Tarentilla* F 65).   [2] The festival of Liber (god of wine, equivalent of Bacchus / Greek Dionysus) took place in Rome annually on March 17. Naevius could be using the term as a Roman equivalent to Dionysia in the Greek original. Here it allows a wordplay on the god's name Liber and the Latin word for "free" (*liber*).

93 Festus

petimina ["ulcers"] are sores on the shoulders of beasts of burden . . . And that the same word[1] was accustomed to be applied also to the space that lies between the two fore-quarters of a pig or its breast is witnessed by Naevius in a description of pork when he says:

> . . . who had procured with a joint of pork[2]

[1] Festus seems to be dealing with two homonyms: one that refers to ulcers, the other (in Naevius) that refers to a part of a pig.   [2] The mention of food suggests a connection with a comic cook or parasite. The context is too minimal to decide on the exact meaning of *meruerat* ["had procured"]; other possibilities include "had deserved," "had earned," or even "had completed his military service."

94 (116 R.[3]) Fest., p. 238.20–23 L.

PERSIBUS [*Scaliger*: persicum *codd.*] peracutum significare videtur . . . Naevius:

tr[7]   et qui fuerit persibus † carpenti adstratio † . . .

carpenti adstratio *cod.*: cum argenti adest oratio *Ribbeck*

Cf. Naevius, *Demetrius, Com.* F 35; Plaut. *Fab. Inc.* 24 (De Melo 2013, 470); Varro, *Ling.* 7.107.

95 (126–27 R.[3]) Fest., pp. 318.32–20.1 L.

RUTABULUM est, quo rustici in proruendo igne, panis coquendi gratia ⟨utuntur⟩ [*add. edd.*] . . . Naevius [*edd.*: Navius *codd.*: Novius *Aug.*] obscenam uiri partem describens:

tr[7]   vel quae sperat se nupturam viridulo adulescentulo,
ea licet senile tractet detritum rutabulum?

1 viridulo *Ribbeck*[1]: viri *cod.*   adulescentulo *Ursinus*:
adulescentulos *cod.*   2 detritum *L. Mueller, metri causa*:
retritum *cod.*

96 (128 R.[3]) Fest., p. 372.2–7 L.

SONTICUM MORBUM in XII [2.2, cf. Warmington 1938, *ROL* 3, 434–35] significare ait Aelius Stilo certum cum

---

[1] See *Twelve Tables* 2.2 in Warmington 1938 (*ROL* III, 434–35).   [2] Aelius Stilo was an early first-century BC Stoic grammarian, teacher of Varro and Cicero, and commentator on early Latin religious and legal texts such as the *Carmen Saliare* ("Salic

94 Festus

persibus[1] ["very cunning"; from *per*- intensive, "very," and *sibus*, "cunning"] seems to mean "very clever" . . . Naevius:

> and a man who will be very clever . . .[2]

[1] On the meaning and derivation of this word, see F 35. It is uncertain whether both fragments refer to the same passage of *Demetrius*.   [2] The end of the line is corrupt and incomprehensible in the manuscripts.

95 Festus

rutabulum ["poker"] is what country people ⟨use⟩ in poking up a fire for baking bread . . . Naevius, describing the obscene part of a man:

> again, she who hopes to marry a virile young man,
> is she to handle an old man's worn-out poker?[1]

[1] The context is uncertain. Perhaps spoken by a comic old man who wants to marry a younger woman.

96 Festus

sonticum morbum ["serious disease"; excusing a person from attending at the law courts] in the *Twelve Tables*[1] [Rome's earliest law code] Aelius Stilo[2] says means a certi-

Hymn") and the *Twelve Tables*. Fragments in Funaioli 1907, 51–76; see also Suet. *Gram. et rhet.* 3.1–2, with Kaster 1995, 68–80 ad loc.

iusta causa; quem nonnulli putant esse, qui noceat, quod
sontes significat nocentes. Naevius ait:

*tr*⁷   sonticam esse oportet causam, quam ob rem perdas
mulierem

97 (123 R.³) Fest., p. 434.11–13 L.

SANDARACAM [*Paul. Fest.*: SANDERACAM *Fest.*] . . . <colo-
ris genus> [*suppl. ex epit. Pauli*], quod Graeci sa<ndycem>
[*suppl. edd.*] . . . Naevius:

?   meru<la sandaracino ore>

<la . . . ore> *suppl. ex epit. Pauli*

Cf. Paul. *Fest.*, p. 435.2–3 L.

98 (130–31 R.³) Fest., p. 494.17–19 L.

at antiqui tam etiam pro tamen usi sunt, ut Naevius:

*ia*⁶?   . . . quid si taceat? dum videat, tam sciat
quid scriptum sit . . .

fied disease with a just cause. Some think it means a disease which harms, because *sontes* ["guilty men"] means men who do harm. Naevius says:

> you must have a genuine case[3] for ruining a woman[4]

[3] *sontica causa* ("a genuine case") is a legal expression for a valid reason.   [4] There is no clear indication of whether this fragment comes from a comedy or a tragedy. If the former is the case, it could be spoken by a comic husband wishing to rid himself of his wife.

97 Festus

sandaraca ["red"] . . . ‹is a kind of color›, which the Greeks [call] *sa‹ndyx›* ["red dye"] . . . Naevius:

> a blackbird ‹with a red beak›[1]

[1] The red color referred to does not correspond exactly to the yellow of a real blackbird's beak. Perhaps this is a comic metaphor referring to a courtesan with makeup.

98 Festus

But the ancients used *tam* ["so"] even instead of *tamen* ["still"], as Naevius:

> . . . what if he remains silent? Provided he sees, he
>   could still know
> what has been written . . .[1]

[1] The context and speaker (or speakers) remain unclear. A character is shown some writing, but remains silent.

99 (114 R.³) Fest., p. 500.17–18 L.

TINTINNIRE est apud Naevium hoc modo:

ia⁸   tantum ibi molae crepitum faciebant, tintinnabant
        compedes

Cf. Paul. *Fest.*, p. 501.7–8 L.

100 (65 R.³) Non., pp. 150.40–51.2 M. = 220 L.

PRAECISUM et OMASUM partes carnis et viscerum. Nae-
vius † Herularia † [Erularia *Bothe*: Nervularia *Ritschl*]:

tr⁷?   . . . praecisum omasum pernam callos glires glandia

        callos *Onions*: gallus *codd.*   glires *Bentinus*: glifis
    codd.   glandia *ed. princ.*: grandia *codd.*

101 (25 R.³) Non., p. 155.24–26 M. = 228 L.

PROSPICA et DESPICA, intenta et contemplata. Naevius
† Assitogiola † [Astiologa *vel* Astrologa *Ribbeck¹⁻²*: Agita-
toria *Iunius*]:

?   hac sibi prospica, hac despica

potest ergo prospicus et despicus dici.

        hac . . . hac *Bothe*: ac . . . ac *codd.*

---

¹ The title *Assitogiola* in the manuscripts of Nonius makes no
sense. Ribbeck¹⁻² suggests *Astiologa* ("*The Clever-Speaking Girl*")
and *Astrologa* ("*The Lady Fortune Teller*"), both of which are
possible but unprovable. Earlier, Junius had suggested *Agitatoria*
("*The Play of the Charioteer*").

99 Festus

tintinnire ["to jangle"; fourth conjugation] occurs in this form [*tintinnabant*, "they jangled"; first conjugation] in Naevius:[1]

the mills made such a noise there, the fetters jangled[2]

[1] Both forms occur occasionally in later Latin, but are rare.

[2] Wearing fetters and working in a mill are typical slave punishments.

100 Nonius

praecisum ["cutlet"] and *omassum* ["tripe"] are parts of meat and offal. Naevius † in *Herularia* †:[1]

. . . cutlets, tripe, ham, pork rinds, dormice, sweetbreads

[1] If the title in Nonius stands in its corrected form of *Erularia* (as suggested by Bothe), it would mean something like *"The Play of the Little Master."* Ritschl suggested *Nervularia* (*"The Rope Play"*). This was also the title of a now lost play by Plautus (see Gell. *NA* 3.3.6); cf. Plautus' play title *Rudens* (*"The Rope"*).

101 Nonius

prospica ["looking ahead"] and *despica* ["looking down"] mean looking eagerly and contemplating. Naevius in † *Assitogiola* †:[1]

here she was looking up ahead, there she was looking down

so one can say *prospicus* and *despicus* [as adjectives].

102 (115 R.[3]) Non., pp. 200.14–29 M. = 294–95 L.

COLLUM neutri est generis. . . . collus masculino [genere]
. . . Naevius † cor † [codd.: Colace *Iunius*: *fort.* Corollaria
Ribbeck[1]]:

tr[7]   . . . utrum scapulae plus an collus habeat calli nescio

habeat calli *Hermann*: calli habeat *codd.*

103 (135 R.[3]) Non., p. 207.14–21 M. = 305 L.

GUTTUR neutri est generis. . . . masculino . . . Naevius:

ia[6]   ingurgitavit usque ad imum gutturem

104 (95 R.[3]) Donat. ad Ter. *Ad.* 521.1–2

"et istoc si quid potis est rectius": si mortem significaret
[Syrus], non conveniret adulescentem [Ctesiphonem]
"ita" dicere . . . [521.2] quamquam eiusmodi adulescentes
inducant comici, ut Naevius in Tribacelo [*Ribbeck*: Triba-
selo *codd.*: Triphallo *Bothe*]:

ia[6]   deos quaeso ut adimant et patrem et matrem meos

Cf. Plaut. *Most.* 233.

---

[1] The Donatus manuscripts have the form *Tribaselus*, which
makes no sense. Ribbeck[1–2] suggests *Tribacelus*, referring to an
effeminate priest of Cybele (Gk. βάκηλος + prefix *tri-*), as in
Triphallus (F 75), a title suggested also for this play by Bothe.

102 Nonius

collum ["neck"] is neuter in gender. . . . *collus*[1] masculine
. . . Naevius . . . :[2]

> . . . whether my shoulder blades or my neck have
> thicker skin, I do not know[3]

[1] Regular early Latin form until Cicero, when neuter *collum*
becomes the norm.   [2] The word *cor* in the manuscripts after
Naevius could conceal a play title such as *Colax* ("*The Flatterer*":
F 18–21) or *Corollaria* ("*The Garland Play*": F 22–29).
[3] The speaker is most likely to be a comic slave, complaining
of being beaten.

103 Nonius

guttur ["throat"] is of neuter gender.[1] . . . masculine . . .
Naevius:

> he swallowed it down to the bottom of his gullet[2]

[1] The gender of *guttur* is neuter in classical Latin, but mascu-
line in early Latin until the time of Varro.   [2] Perhaps a de-
scription of a parasite or other comic glutton. However, a meta-
phorical use of "swallowing" a story or a lie cannot be ruled out.

104 Donatus, *Commentary on Terence*

"and something even better than that if possible": if
[Syrus] means his death, it would not be fitting for the
young man [Ctesipho] to say "yes" . . . [521.2] although
comic poets bring on stage young men of this kind, like
Naevius in † *Tribaselus*[1] †

> I beg the gods to remove both my father and my
> mother

255

105 (137–38 R.[3]) Diom., *GL* I, p. 343.11–13

item "amo" veteres inchoativo modo "amasco" dixerunt
. . . Naevius:

ia[6]   . . . nunc primulum
       amasco . . .

106 (125 R.[3]) Diom., *GL* I, p. 374.1–4

"aio" verbum inusitatam habet declinationem, de cuius
imperativo non nulli ambigebant. verum dictum est "ai,"
ut Naevius alicubi:

ia[6]   an nata est sponsa praegnans? vel ai vel nega.

   an nata est *Prisc.*: an est nata *codd. Diom.*

Cf. Prisc., *GL* II, pp. 494.14–15; 541.20–21.

107 (134 R.[3]) Glossogr. Vatic., p. 175 Mai 1836

DEPUIRE verberare. Naevius:

ia[6]   . . . depuit me miseram ad necem

105 Diomedes

In the same way the ancients used *amasco*[1] ["I begin to love"] as the inchoative form of *amo* ["I love"] . . . Naevius:

> . . . now for the first time
> I am beginning to love . . .[2]

[1] The inchoative form *amasco* is attested only here.
[2] The sentence would suit a young man in love, but other comic speakers would be possible.

106 Diomedes

The verb *aio* ["I say"] has unusual forms. Some people were in doubt about its imperative. In fact, it is pronounced *ai*[1] ["say"], as Naevius [has it] somewhere:

> my daughter, she who is engaged, is pregnant? Admit it or deny it.[2]

[1] The imperative form *ai* is attested only here.
[2] Pregnancy outside marriage is a common comic theme. Perhaps here an outraged father addresses a young man, but other contexts are possible.

107 Vatican glossographer

depuire ["to beat"] means to flog. Naevius:

> . . . he is beating me, poor girl, to death[1]

[1] A female character of low status describes being beaten.

108 (119 R.³) Glossogr. Vatic., p. 313 Mai 1836

LUSTRO . . . ille qui vagus est et nihil agit nisi fora lustrat, unde Naevius de quodam:

ia^6 vagus

inquit

          est et lustro . . .

Cf. *Com.* F 89

108 Vatican glossographer

lustro ["vagabond," occurs only here and in *Com*. F 89]
. . . a man who is a vagrant and does nothing but wander
round [*lustrat*][1] the markets. Hence Naevius says of some-
one:

he is a vagrant and a vagabond . . .

[1] The compiler seeks to derive *lustro* from *lustrare* ["to wan-
der"], whereas it is more likely to be derived from *lustrum*
["brothel"] and *lustrari* ["to haunt brothels"].

TRAGOEDIAE (F 1–54)

Only half the number of fragments (54) survive from Nae-
vius' tragedies as they do from his comedies (108). Comedy
seems to have been his preferred dramatic genre. Five of
Naevius' seven named tragedies have titles that had been
used by the classical fifth-century tragedians Aeschylus,
Sophocles, and Euripides, namely Andromacha, Danae,
Hector, Iphigenia, *and* Lycurgus. *Whether these plays*
were derived directly from these predecessors is incapa-
ble of proof. In the remaining two, Equus Troianus *and*
Hesiona, *Naevius includes themes from the Trojan cycle*
that have no known Greek tragic models. Such themes,
which are to recur in the Bellum Punicum, *would have*
been of special interest to the Romans, given their belief
that they were descended partly from Trojan fugitives. An-
other characteristic of Naevian tragedy, perhaps more Ro-
man than Greek in tone, is the depiction on stage of gods
and the confrontation between gods and men, as with
Liber in Lycurgus *and Jupiter in* Danae.

ANDROMACHA (F 1)

There is some doubt as to whether this fragment should be
assigned to a tragedy by Naevius (Ribbeck[1]; Warmington,
ROL II, 110–11; Klussmann 1843, 184; Schauer, Naevius

TRAGEDIES (F 1–54)

The majority of Naevius' fragments from named tragedies are provided by Nonius (35 out of 41), with single examples provided by Cicero, Festus, Gellius, Macrobius, Priscian, and Servius. Of the thirteen remaining unnamed tragic fragments, three each come from Festus / Paulus and Isidore, two each from Cicero and Varro, and one each from Jerome, Nonius, and Servius. Nonius, then, with thirty-six fragments, is our best source for Naevian tragedy, whereas Charisius, who was our best source for his comedies, provides no tragic fragments.

For more details on Naevius' Greek-based tragedies, see Introduction to Naevius: Works.

Bibl.: Mette 1964, 50–54; De Rosalia 1989, 87–95; Manuwald 2001, 101–11. Comm.: Spaltenstein 2014, 309–645; Schauer 2012, 67–115. Lit.: Ribbeck 1875, 44–62; Waszink 1972, 924–27; Manuwald 2011, 196–97.

ANDROMACHA (F 1)

F 1 TrRF) or to a comedy by Novius (Servius Danielis; Bothe 1834; Ribbeck[2–3]). Ribbeck[2–3] thought the simile contained in the fragment to be more comic than tragic in

style. However, the tragic associations of the name An-
dromache would make it an improbable title for an Atellan
farce, whereas a picturesque simile, especially in an ad-
dress to a child, cannot be excluded from Naevius' tragic
style (cf. the popular wordplay in F 16). Tragedies of the
same title were composed in Greek by Euripides and An-
tiphon (55 F 1 TrGF), and similar material is found in
Euripides' Hecuba and Troades. In Latin, Livius Andron-
icus treated the subject of the capture and remarriage of
Andromache after the Trojan War in his play Hermiona
(Trag. 23 R.²⁻³ = F 15 FRL), and Ennius composed his
tragedy Andromacha *(Trag. F 23–33 FRL) on the same*
theme. Accius' Astyanax *(Trag. 164 R.²⁻³ = 131–54 War-*

1 (Novius *Atell.* 4ᵃ⁻ᵇ R.³) Serv. Dan. ad Verg. *Georg.* 1.266

FISCINA genus est vasis, id est corbulae brevis, quas per-
ferunt qui arbusta vindemiant . . . Naevius [*Commelinus:*
Novius *codd.*] in Andromacha:

ia^6 quod tu, mi gnate, quaeso ut in pectus tuum
        demittas, tamquam in fiscinam vindemitor

2 in fiscinam vindemitor *Bothe*: vindemiator in fiscinam *codd.*

DANAE (F 2–12)

Aeschylus wrote a trilogy on the subject of Danae, followed
by a satyr play Diktyulkos *(F 46–49 TrGF). Sophocles also*
composed a tragedy named Danae *(F 165–70 TrGF) and*
an Acrisius *treating the exile of Danae (F 60–76 TrGF),*
which may or may not have been the same play. Two fur-
ther unassigned fragments of Sophocles (F 46, 50 TrGF)

*mington) dealt with related material. The fragment is too
short for it to be attributed safely to a particular context,
but if the play followed the same plot as Euripides'* An-
dromache *and Livius Andronicus'* Hermiona, *the address
to a son, if spoken by Andromache, would fit well her ad-
dress to her son by Pyrrhus shortly before she sacrifices
herself to save him; so Spaltenstein 2014 ad loc., who com-
pares Euripides'* Andromache *415ff.:* μέμνησο μητρός
. . . [*"remember your mother . . ."*]. *Servius Danielis at-
tributes the play to the comedian Novius, which most edi-
tors change to Naevius. The two names are often confused
(see Spaltenstein 2014, 62–63).*

Comm.: Spaltenstein 2014, 312–18.

1 Servius Danielis, *Commentary on Virgil*

fiscina ["a fruit basket"] is a type of container, that is a
shallow basket, which those who harvest grapes carry . . .
Naevius in *Andromache*:

> this, my son, I ask you to press deep into your heart,
> as the harvester presses grapes into a basket

DANAE (F 2–12)

may have belonged to his Danae. *We also know of a* Danae
*by Euripides (F 316–30a TrGF). In Latin there is a single
fragment belonging to a play of this name by Livius An-
dronicus (Trag. 19 R.*[2–3] *= F 13 FRL), which some would
assign to Naevius.*

Danae was the daughter of Acrisius and Aganippe.

*Since it was fated that she would kill her father, Acrisius
had her locked up in a stone dungeon. Jupiter fell in love
with her and descended into her dungeon in the form of a
shower of gold. From their union was born Perseus. Acri-
sius banished mother and child to sea in a wooden ark. It
came to land on the island of Seriphos, where the pair were
rescued by a fisherman and taken to king Polydectes, who
subsequently married Danae. When Acrisius learned of
this, he went to Seriphos to bring Danae and Perseus
home. On arrival, he was accidentally killed by a discus*

2 (12 R.³) Non., p. 110.19–21 M. = 157 L.

FULGORIVIT, fulgorem fecit vel fulmine afflavit. Naevius
Danae [*Junius:* sane a *codd.*]:

ia⁶   suo sonitu claro fulgorivit Iuppiter

3 (10 R.³) Non., pp. 123.33–24.16 M. = 178–79 L.

ICIT significat percutit, ab ictu . . . Naevius Danae:

ia⁶   . . . quae quondam fulmine icit Iuppiter

4 (11 R.³) Non., p. 138.13–15 M. = 201 L.

MANUBIAS, manus exuvias [*Quicherat:* exubiae *codd.*].
Naevius Danae:

ia⁶?   . . . manubias subpetat pro me . . .¹

¹ De versu *cf. Ribbeck³.*

---

¹ For this meaning of *manubiae,* see *OLD* s.v. *manubiae* 3.
² Perhaps Danae asks Jupiter to support her protestation of
innocence with a crack of thunder.

thrown by Perseus, thus fulfilling the ordinance of fate. The details of the myth are to be found in Apollod. Bibl. 2.4.1.3, Hyg. Fab. 63, and Servius' commentary on Verg. Aen. 7.327 and 8.345.

The action of Naevius' play concerns Jupiter (F 2–5) and his visit to Danae's dungeon (F 11–12), the discovery of his rape of Danae and her pregnancy (F 6, 8, 10), and her banishment by Acrisius (F 7, 9).

Comm.: Spaltenstein 2014, 319–67. Lit.: Di Salvo, 1972; Morelli 1974; Lefèvre 2000.

2 Nonius

fulgorivit ["he lightened"], he made a flash or blasted with a thunderbolt. Naevius in *Danae*:

> Jupiter lightened with his own loud sound[1]

[1] Perhaps in response to Danae's request in F 4.

3 Nonius

icit ["he struck"] means "he smote," from *ictus* ["a blow"] . . . Naevius in *Danae*:

> . . . which once Jupiter struck with a thunderbolt

4 Nonius

manubias ["thunderbolts"],[1] equipment of the hand. Naevius in *Danae*:

> . . . let [Jupiter] provide his thunderbolts on my behalf[2] . . .

5 (2 R.^{3}) Non., p. 186.24–25 M. = 274 L.

VALENTIA, fortitudo. Naevius Danae:

ia^6 omnes formidant homines eius valentiam

     homines *Vossius*: hominis *codd.*

6 (4 R.^{3}) Non., p. 262.24–28 M. = 401 L.

CONFIDENTIA, constantia . . . Naevius in Danae:

tr^7 excidit orationis omnis confidentia

7 (9 R.^{3}) Non., pp. 290.31–91.7 M. = 449 L.

EXIGERE est excludere . . . Naevius Danae:

ia^6 . . . indigne exigor patria innocens

8 (7 R.^{3}) Non., pp. 305.23–6.7 M. = 475–76 L.

FAMA est rursus infamia . . . Naevius ⟨Danae⟩ [*suppl. ex Non., p. 518.2 M. = 833 L.*]:

ia^8 desubito famam tollunt[1] si quam solam videre in via

     videre *Non., p. 518.2 M. = 833 L.*: videmus *Non., p. 306.7 M. = 476 L.*

[1] Cf. Enn. *Trag.* 8.3 *FRL*.

Cf. Non., p. 518.1–2 M. = 833 L.

5 Nonius

valentia ["strength"], might. Naevius in *Danae*:

> all men fear his[1] might

[1] Probably Jupiter's.

6 Nonius

confidentia ["confidence"], steadfastness . . . Naevius in *Danae*:

> all confidence of speech was lost[1]

[1] Perhaps referring to Danae on the discovery of her pregnancy.

7 Nonius

exigere ["drive out"] means exclude . . . Naevius in *Danae*:

> . . . undeservedly am I, an innocent woman, driven
> out of my homeland[1]

[1] The speaker is Danae.

8 Nonius

fama ["fame"] can also mean infamy . . . Naevius ‹in *Danae*›:

> they suddenly raise a scandal if they have seen a
> woman alone in the street

9 (8 R.³) Non., p. 366.1–4 M. = 581 L.

PRETIUM pro praemio . . . Naevius Danae:

tr^7 quin ut quisque est meritus, praesens pretium pro
        factis ferat

10 (5 R.³) Non., p. 456.20–25 M. = 731 L.

COMPOTEM in bonam partem solum accipi putatur, cum
et in malam positum sit . . . Naevius Danae:

tr^7 . . . eam nunc esse inventam probri
        compotem scis

  1 probri *Mercier*: probris *L. Mueller*: propris *vel* propriis
codd.   De versu *cf. Ribbeck[1]*.

11 (3 R.³) Non., pp. 469.34–70.1 M. = 753 L.

CONTEMPLA . . . Naevius Danae:

ia^6 contemplo placide formam et faciem virginis

       contempla *Ribbeck[1]*

12 (6 R.³) Non., pp. 503.38–4.3 M. = pp. 809–10 L.

LAVIT pro lavat . . . Naevius Danae:

tr^7 . . . auri rubeo fonte lavere ⟨me⟩ memini manum

     auri *Delrius*: animi *codd.*   rubeo *Buecheler*: iubeo
codd.   me *add. Grotius*

Cf. Ter. *Eun*. 584–85.

---

  [1] The text is uncertain, and this interpretation is conjectural.
As reconstructed here, the line would refer possibly to Danae's
remembering Jupiter's appearance to her in the form of a shower
of gold. In Greek mythology, beginning with Hesiod, Zeus made

9 Nonius

pretium ["recompense"] for reward . . . Naevius in *Danae*:

> indeed, as each man deserves, he should take the
> immediate recompense for his deeds[1]

[1] A general statement to be taken in the context of Danae's punishment by Acrisius.

10 Nonius

compotem ["sharing in"] is thought to be used only in a good sense, although it has also been used in a bad sense . . . Naevius in *Danae*:

> . . . and now you know she has been found to be
> a partaker in unchastity

11 Nonius

contempla ["view"] . . . Naevius in *Danae*:

> I quietly view the maiden's form and face[1]

[1] The speaker is probably Jupiter.

12 Nonius

lavit ["washes"] for *lavat* [a change of conjugation, third for classical Latin first] . . . Naevius in *Danae*

> . . . I remember washing my hand in a glowing
> fountain of gold[1]

Danae pregnant by descending on her in her prison as a shower of gold; cf. Pindar, *Pythians* 12.17–18; Sophocles, *Antigone* 944–45; Menander, *Samia* 586–97; Terence, *Eunuchus* ("The Eunuch") 584–85 (probably derived from Menander's *Eunuch*).

EQUUS TROIANUS (t 1; F 13)

We have four Latin fragments from a play entitled "The
Trojan Horse": one from Livius Andronicus (Trag. 20–22
R.$^{2-3}$ = F 14 FRL), the present one from Naevius, and two
of uncertain authorship (Trag. Inc. 7–8 R.$^{2-3}$). It is possible
that all the fragments belong to one play by Livius An-
dronicus or Naevius. There is no surviving Greek play of
this title, although Sophocles' Sino (F 542–44 TrGF) may
have contained related material.

The wooden horse was built by the Greek Epeus after

t 1 Cic. *Fam.* 7.1.2

quid enim delectationis habent sescenti muli in "Clytaem-
nestra" [Acci] aut in "Equo Troiano" [Naevi] creterrarum
tria milia aut armatura varia peditatus et equitatus in ali-
qua pugna?

13 (13 R.^{3}) Macrob. *Sat.* 6.1.38 (ad Verg. *Ecl.* 3.49: "num-
quam hodie effugies, veniam quocumque vocaris")

Naevius in Equo Troiano:

ia^8   numquam hodie effugies quin mea manu moriare . . .

EQUUS TROIANUS (t 1; F 13)

ten years of inconclusive fighting at Troy. It was filled with Greek warriors; and the Trojan king Priam, thinking the Greeks had gone home leaving this offering for Minerva, had the horse taken into Minerva's temple, ignoring the warnings of Cassandra. The warriors were let out by the Greek Sino during the night and proceeded to take possession of the city.

Comm.: Spaltenstein 2014, 369–85. Lit.: Rostagni 1916; Erskine 1998; Suerbaum 2000a.

t 1 Cicero, *Letters to Friends*

For what pleasure is provided by six hundred mules in *Clytemnestra* [of Accius], or in *The Trojan Horse* [of Naevius][1] three thousand water bowls, or the various armaments of the infantry and cavalry in some battle?

[1] Cicero does not specify whether he is speaking of the play by Livius Andronicus (*Trag.* F 14 *FRL*) or by Naevius. As the word *creterra* ("water bowl") is attested twice in Naevius (*Trag.* F 41; *BP* F 25), but not in Livius Andronicus, it is generally accepted that the play by Naevius is referred to here.

13 Macrobius, *Saturnalia* (on Virgil, "this time you will never escape; I will meet you, wherever you call me to")

Naevius in *The Trojan Horse*:

this time you will never escape; rather you will die by my hand . . .[1]

[1] Spoken perhaps by Menelaus, threatening Helen after the fall of Troy.

HECTOR PROFICISCENS (F 14–15)

The play, named only in Priscian (F 15), appears to have dealt with the theme of Hector's farewell to his parents, wife, and son before his departure for battle. The theme derives ultimately from Homer, Iliad 6, where Hector addresses farewells to his mother, wife, and son, but not, as here, to his father, Priam. The subject had been treated in Greek by the second of the two authors named Astydamas (i.e., Astydamas II) in a tragedy called Hector *(60 F 1[h]–*

14 (15 R.[3]) Cic. *Tusc.* 4.67

aliter enim Naevianus ille gaudet Hector:

tr[7]   laetus sum laudari me abs te, pater, a laudato viro

aliter ille apud Trabeam [Trab. *Com.* 1–5 R.[2–3]].

Cf. Cic. *Fam.* 5.12.7, 15.6.1; Sen. *Ep.* 102.16.

15 (14 R.[3]) Prisc., *GL* II, p. 400.1–4

ADORIOR et ADORIO . . . Naevius in Hectore proficiscente:

tr[7]   tunc ipsos adoriant, ne qui hinc Spartam referat
         nuntium

      qui *Hermann*: quis *codd.*

HECTOR PROFICISCENS (F 14–15)

2[a] TrGF). *Naevius' source for "Hector's Departure" is uncertain and could have been a now-missing Alexandrian play. F 14 is now unanimously assigned to the same play of Naevius by modern editors, although Cicero does not give its title, and in the past the fragment had been assigned by Bothe (1834) to Ennius'* Hectoris Lytra *(Enn. Trag. F 56–71 FRL).*
    Comm.: Spaltenstein 2014, 386–93.

14 Cicero, *Tusculan Disputations*

The famous Hector of Naevius expresses his joy differently:

> I am happy to be praised by you, father, a man
>   praised [by others]

from the Hector of Trabea [Trab. *Com.* F 1–5 R.[2–3]].

15 Priscian

adorior and *adorio* ["attack"; in deponent and active forms] . . . Naevius in *Hector's Departure*:

> then let them attack those warriors, so that no one
>   can bring back news from here to Sparta[1]

[1] Probably spoken by Hector as battle commander.

FRL VI: NAEVIUS

HESIONA (F 16)

The myth of Hesione is recounted in Hyg. Fab. 89. She was a Trojan princess, daughter of Laomedon and sister of Priam. When Laomedon had refused to pay Apollo and Poseidon for building the walls of Troy, the gods sent a plague and a sea monster to destroy the city. Oracles promised Laomedon relief if he exposed Hesione to be devoured by the sea monster. Hercules offered to save her in

16 (*Aesiona* 1 R.[3]) Gell. *NA* 10.25.3

admonendum existimo "lingulam" veteres dixisse gladiolum oblongum in speciem linguae factum, cuius meminit Naevius in tragoedia Hesiona. versum Naevi opposui:

tr[7] ne mihi gerere morem videar lingua, verum lingula

ne mihi *Bentley*: sine mi *codd.*

Cf. Varro, *Ling.* 7.107; Mart. 14.120.

IPHIGENIA (F 17)

Tragedies with this title in Greek are known from Aeschylus (F 94 TrGF), Sophocles (F 305–12 TrGF), Euripides ("Iphigenia among the Taurians" and "Iphigenia at Aulis"), and Polyidus? (78 F 1–2 TrGF [Ἰφιγένεια ἡ ἐν Ταύροις?]) and in Latin from Ennius (Trag. F 82–88 FRL). The myth involves the story of Agamemnon's daughter Iphigenia, who was to be sacrificed at Aulis in order to enable the Greeks to sail to Troy. She was rescued

274

HESIONA (F 16)

*return for her hand in marriage. Having slain the monster,
however, Hercules was refused Hesione's hand and, in re-
venge, attacked Troy, slew Laomedon, and gave Hesione
as a prize to his comrade in arms, Telamon. No other Greek
or Latin play with this title is known, and Naevius may
have based his play on a lost Hellenistic Greek original.*
  Comm.: *Spaltenstein 2014, 394–99.*

16 Gellius, *Attic Nights*

I think I should remind you that the ancients used the
term *lingula* of a small oblong sword, fashioned in the
form of a tongue, which Naevius mentions in the tragedy
Hesione. I have brought forward the verse of Naevius:

> lest I should seem to indulge myself with words,[1]
>   rather than with my sword[2]

  [1] Literally, "with my tongue"; a play on words between *lingua*
("tongue") and *lingula* ("sword").   [2] The line is perhaps spo-
ken by Hercules, threatening Laomedon.

IPHIGENIA (F 17)

*by Diana, who whisked her off to Tauris in a cloud and
made her the priestess of her temple there (Apollod.* Epit.
3.21–22; Hyg. Fab. *98; Dict. 1.20–23). The model for Nae-
vius' play is probably Euripides' "Iphigenia among the
Taurians," which tells of Iphigenia's duties of sacrificing
any foreigners that come to king Thoas' kingdom of Tauris.
When her brother Orestes comes with Pylades to steal
the statue of Artemis, at the behest of Apollo, they are*

captured and sent to Iphigenia for sacrifice. Iphigenia rec-
ognizes her brother, and the pair plan their escape by sea
with Pylades and the sacred statue. Thoas attempts to

17 (16 R.³) Non., p. 370.19–24 M. = 589 L.

PASSUM, extensum, patens . . . Naevius Iphigenia:

tr⁷   passo velo vicinum, Aquilo, Orestem in portum fer
         foras

   velo *Iunius*: vel hoc *codd.*   velo vicinum, aquilo *Rib-*
beck³: me vicinum aquilo *Maehly*: hoc vicinum aquilone
codd.   Orestem in portum *Ribbeck³*: hinc in portum *War-*
mington: (h)ortum *codd.*

LYCURGUS (F 18–41)

Various accounts of the resistance of Lycurgus to the in-
troduction of the worship of Dionysus (Bacchus, referred
to by Naevius by his Latin title Liber, see F 33) into his
kingdom of Thrace are extant. Homer (Iliad 6.130–40) tells
how for attacking the nurses of Dionysus Lycurgus was
blinded by Zeus and subsequently died. Fragments from
two tetralogies on the subject of Lycurgus are known from
Greek tragedy, one by Aeschylus (T 67 and F 123b TrGF)
and one by Polyphrasmon (7 F 1 TrGF). A satyr play on
the subject by Timocles is known by name only (86 T 2
TrGF). The Bacchae of Euripides and Stasiastae ("The
Rebels") by Accius (Trag. 604 R.²⁻³) contained related ma-
terial. Apollodorus (Bibl. 3.5.1 = 3.35) tells how Lycurgus
chased Dionysus into the sea on his journey through
Thrace and took his Bacchants and satyrs prisoner. These

pursue and kill them, but is prevented from doing so by Athena, who subsequently sets up Iphigenia as priestess of Artemis in Greece.

Comm.: Spaltenstein 2014, 400–422.

17 Nonius

passum ["full"], stretched out, spread open . . . Naevius in *Iphigenia*:[1]

> North wind, carry Orestes away with full sail to the
>   nearby port

[1] This is the only fragment securely assigned to *Iphigenia*, but the text is far from certain.

LYCURGUS (F 18–41)

were suddenly set free, and Lycurgus, gripped by a Dionysiac frenzy, mistook his son Dryas for a vine and killed him. A famine overtook the land, and the inhabitants fled, leaving their king in chains on mount Pagaeus, where Dionysus had him torn to pieces by horses. A slightly different version is given in Hyginus (Fab. 132), *where Lycurgus, having attempted to rape his mother while drunk, subsequently tried to destroy all vines. Again he was seized by a Dionysiac frenzy, killed his wife and son, and was exposed by Dionysus on Mount Rhodope to be devoured by panthers. According to Diodorus Siculus* (3.65), *Dionysus, having been tricked by Lycurgus, who massacred all his followers, defeated Lycurgus in a pitched battle, blinded, tortured, and killed him, and had him replaced on the Thracian throne by Charops, who introduced Dio-*

nysiac worship to the country. It is uncertain which Greek play Naevius took as his model. In general, scholars have seen the first (Edonoi) or second (Bassarai) play of Aeschylus' tetralogy as its ultimate source (see TrRF p. 90; Bednarek 2021, 158). Elements common to all versions, such as the arrival of Dionysus and his followers in Thrace, their pursuit by Lycurgus, and the revenge of the god, are clearly to be seen in the remaining fragments. However,

18 (50 R.³) Fest., p. 208.29–36 L.

OBSTINATO obfirmato, perseveranti . . . Naevius in Lycurgo:

?   vos qui astatis obstinati

19 (26–28 R.³) Non., p. 6.15–17 M. = 10 L.

INLICERE est proprie inlaqueare. Naevius Lycurgo:

ia⁶   alii
     sublime in altos saltus inlicite . . .
     ubi bipedes volucres lino linquant lumina

    1 alii *Scaliger*: alis *codd.*   2 sublime *edd.*: sublimen *codd.*

Bednarek (2021, 155–58) sees no evidence in Naevius' play for the pursuit and capture of Liber and posits an ending in which Lycurgus is lured to his death. The scene is probably set in front of Lycurgus' palace.

Comm.: Spaltenstein 2014, 423–519. Lit.: Duentzer 1837; Traina 1953b (F 21); Bertini 1972; Mariotti 1974; Lattanzi 1994; Suerbaum 2000a; Bednarek 2021, 121–42, 155–59.

18 Festus

obstinato means "firm," "steadfast" . . . Naevius in *Lycurgus*:

> you who stand there steadfast[1]

[1] The fragment is too short for the exact context to be known.

19 Nonius

inlicere ["to lure"] is literally "to ensnare." Naevius in *Lycurgus*:

> you others
> lure them on high into the lofty glades . . .
> where through flaxen traps the two-footed birds may
>   leave the light of day[1]

[1] Lycurgus gives orders for the capture of the Bacchants (cf. F 34). Alternatively, Bednarek (2021, 123–26) argues that the fragment comes from the end of the play, in which Lycurgus and his followers are lured to their blinding and death in the mountains.

20 (24–25 R.³) Non., p. 9.16–19 M. = 14 L.

MUTUS onomatopoeia est incertae vocis, quasi mugitus. nam mutus sonus est proprie, qui intellectum non habet. Naevius Lycurgo:

ia^6 ducite
    eo cum argutis linguis mutas quadrupedes

    2 cum *ed. Ald. 1513*: tum *codd.*

21 (29–30 R.³) Non., p. 14.15–19 M. = 21 L.

VITULANTES veteres gaudentes dixerunt . . . Naevius Lycurgo:

ia^6 ut in venatu vitulantis ex suis
    locis nos mittant poenis decoratas feris

    2 decoratas *Ribbeck¹*: decoratus *codd.*

22 (35 R.³) Non., p. 73.16–17 M. = 102 L.

ACRIMONIA est animi vivacitas. Naevius Lycurgo:

tr^7 ne ille mei feri ingeni atque animi acrem acrimoniam

20 Nonius

mutus ["dumb"] is an onomatopoeia of a vague utterance, like lowing. For a dumb sound is literally one that has no sense. Naevius in *Lycurgus*:

> lead them
> there, like dumb beasts with shrill tongues[1]

[1] A description of the Bacchants being led into captivity, raising loud but unintelligible cries, like dumb animals (cf. F 27).

21 Nonius

The ancients said *vitulans*[1] ["rejoicing"] for "happy" . . . Naevius in *Lycurgus*:

> in order that they may send us, rejoicing in the hunt,
> away from their territory, adorned with savage
>   punishments[2]

[1] The word recurs in *Clastidium* (*Praet.* F 1), where its etymology is discussed in the context of the quotation.
[2] The Bacchants refer to Lycurgus' plans to expel them from his country.

22 Nonius

acrimonia ["bitterness"] is liveliness of mind.[1] Naevius in *Lycurgus*:

> yes, he [shall feel] the harsh bitterness of my wild
>   heart and mind[2]

[1] Nonius chooses the wrong meaning of *acrimonia* here, explaining it as "liveliness" rather than "bitterness."   [2] The speaker is perhaps Lycurgus in confrontation with Liber.

23 (46–47 R.^{3}) Non., p. 84.31–34 M. = 120 L.

CETTE significat dicite vel date, ab eo quod cedo. Naevius
Lycurgo:

ia^6 proinde huc Dryante regem prognatum patre
Lycurgum cette

1 proinde huc Dryante *Ribbeck, edd.*: proin Dryante *Iunius*:
proindustriantte *codd.*

24 (45 R.^{3}) Non., p. 109.21–23 M. = 156 L.

FIMBRIAE sunt omnis extremitas. ‹Naevius Lycurgo . . .
FLORA› [*lacunam sign. ed. 1583:* ‹Naevius . . . FLORA›
suppl. Lindsay] Naevius Lycurgo:

tr^7 . . . ut videam Vulcani opera haec flammis fieri
flora

25 (33 R.^{3}) Non., p. 124.31–32 M. = 180 L.

IGNOTAE, id est insciae. Naevius Lycurgo:

?   ignotae iteris sumus; tute scis

ignotae *Non., p. 124.32 M. = 180 L.*: ignoti *Non., p. 485.5 M.
= 778 L., Prisc., GL II, p. 229.5*

Cf. Non., p. 485.3–5 M. = 778 L.; Prisc., *GL* II, p. 229.1–5.

---

1 In two of the three quotations of this line (Non., p. 485.5 =
778 L.; Prisc., *GL* II, p. 229.5), the adjective *ignoti* ("ignorant")
is masc. pl., but in one (Non., p. 124.31–32 M. = 180 L.) it is fem.
pl. (*ignotae*). It is difficult to tell which is correct. In the case of
the masc. pl., the speaker could be Liber, using a generalizing
plural for himself and his male and female followers. In the case
of the fem. pl., the female Bacchants could be the speakers.

23 Nonius

cette means "say" or "give," from the verb *cedo* ["give"].
Naevius in *Lycurgus*:

> then bring here the king, born of his father Dryas,
> Lycurgus[1]

[1] The victorious Liber orders Lycurgus to be brought before
him.

24 Nonius

fimbriae ["fringe"] is the extremity of anything. <Naevius
in *Lycurgus* . . . *flora* ["bright"]> Naevius in *Lycurgus*:[1]

> . . . that I[2] may see these things[3] through the agency
>   of Vulcan become
> bright[4] with flames

[1] There is a problem with Nonius' text (a lacuna was first
marked in the 1583 edition), as *fimbriae* is not mentioned in the
quotation. Lindsay's supplement <Naevius in *Lycurgus* . . . *flora*>
is unsatisfactory, as the meaning of *flora* is not explained. It is
possible, however, that this explanation did exist, but has also
been lost.   [2] The speaker is probably Liber. For other pos-
sibilities, see Bednarek 2021, 133–34.   [3] "These things"
perhaps refer to Lycurgus' palace.   [4] *florus* is here an adjec-
tive meaning "bright colored" (cf. *TLL* 6.1.927.28).

25 Nonius

ignotae ["ignorant"; fem. pl. nom.] that is not knowing.
Naevius in *Lycurgus*:

> we are ignorant[1] of the road, you know it

26 (37–38 R.[3]) Non., p. 124.33–35 M. = 180 L.

INIURIE dictum pro iniuriose. Naevius Lycurgo:

tro[7] (A) oderunt di homines iniuros. (B) egone an ille
  iniurie
facimus?

1 iniuros *Bothe*: iniustos *Havet*: iniuriose *codd.*

27 (44 R.[3]) Non., p. 159.5–9 M. = 234 L.

PECUA et pecuda ita ut pecora veteres dixerunt . . . Nae-
vius . . . Lycurgo:

ia[6] sine ferro ut pecua manibus ad mortem meant

pecua *Mercier*: pecora *codd.*   ut pecua manibus *War-
mington*: pecora manibus ut *codd.*

28 (18 R.[3]) Non., p. 191.12–18 M. = 281 L.

ANGUES masculino genere . . . Naevius Lycurgo:

ia[6] alte iubatos angues in sese gerunt

iubatos *Junius*: iugatos *codd.*

26 Nonius

iniurie ["unjustly"; *hapax legomenon*] said for *iniuriose*.
Naevius in *Lycurgus*:

> (A) The gods hate unjust men. (B) Is it I or he who
> act unjustly?[1]

[1] Speaker (B) is probably Lycurgus, referring perhaps to
Liber as "he." The identity of speaker (A) is uncertain (possibilities are a subject of Lycurgus or the chorus).

27 Nonius

the ancients said *pecua* ["cattle"] and *pecuda* [both anteclassical] for *pecora* . . . Naevius . . . in *Lycurgus*:

> without the use of arms as cattle go to death led by
>   the hand[1]

[1] As in F 20, the captured Bacchants, being led without resistance into captivity, are described as cattle.

28 Nonius

angues ["snakes"] in the masculine gender[1] . . . Naevius in
Lycurgus:

> high [on their necks?] they carry crested snakes upon
>   themselves[2]

[1] Both genders are attested in classical Latin, but the masculine is more common.   [2] Probably a description (by the
messenger) of the Bacchants (cf. F 30, 37).

29 (39 R.³) Non., pp. 191.31–92.1 **M.** = 282 L.

AMNEM . . . feminino [genere] . . . Naevius Lycurgo:

*tr*⁷   sed quasi amnis celeris rapit sed tamen inflexu
       flectitur

celeris *Ribbeck*²: cis *codd.*

30 (19 R.³) Non., p. 192.29–32 **M.** = 283 L.

ARVA . . . feminino [genere]. Naevius Lycurgo {lib. II}
[*secl. edd.*]:

*ia*⁶   . . . quaque incedunt omnes arvas obterunt

31 (20 R.³) Non., p. 213.10–11 **M.** = 314 L.

MELOS genere neutro. Naevius Lycurgo:

*ia*⁶?   . . . suavisonum melos

32 (31–32 R.³) Non., pp. 224.37–25.4M. = 333 L.

SCHEMA . . . neutro [genere]. Naevius Lycurgo:

29 Nonius

amnis ["river"] . . . in the feminine [gender][1] . . . Naevius in *Lycurgus*:

> but like a swift river it rushes on and yet twists and
> turns[2]

[1] Both genders are attested in classical Latin, but the masculine is more common.   [2] The context is uncertain, but Liber could be addressing Lycurgus, advising flexibility.

30 Nonius

arva ["field"] . . . in the feminine [gender]. Naevius in *Lycurgus*:

> . . . wherever they walk they crush all the [planted]
> fields[1]

[1] Probably part of a messenger speech describing the Bacchants (cf. F 28, 37).

31 Nonius

melos ["melody"] in the neuter gender. Naevius in *Lycurgus*:

> . . . sweet-sounding melody[1]

[1] Without any context it is impossible to tell whether this is part of a choral song or a messenger speech.

32 Nonius

schema ["attire"] . . . in the neuter [gender]. Naevius in *Lycurgus*:

ia^6
                                        pergite
          thyrsigerae Bacchae Bacchico cum schemate

2 bacchae *Ribbeck[1]*: bacchae modo *codd.*

33 (36 R.[3]) Non., pp. 258.38–59.7 M. = 395 L.

CONTENDERE significat comparare . . . Naevius in Ly-
curgo:

tr^7 cave sis tuam contendas iram contra cum ira Liberi

34 (21–23 R.[3]) Non., pp. 322.35–23.3 M. = 506 L.

INGENIO veteres dixerunt . . . sua sponte vel natura. Nae-
vius Lycurgo:

ia^6 vos qui regalis corporis custodias
          agitatis, ite actutum in frundiferos locos,
          ingenio arbusta ubi nata sunt, non obsitu

3 arbusta ubi nata *Scaliger*: arbusto vineta *codd.*

35 (48 R.[3]) Non., pp. 334.25–37 M. = 526–27 L.

LIQUIDUM rursum significat molle et fluxum . . . Naevius
Lycurgo:

288

proceed
wand-bearing Bacchants in Bacchic attire[1]

[1] Probably spoken by the leader of a chorus of Bacchants. However, Bednarek (2021, 129) sees a reference to Lycurgus and his attendants being disguised as Bacchants.

33 Nonius

contendere ["to compete"] means to compare . . . Naevius in *Lycurgus*:

beware of setting up your anger in competition with
the anger of Liber[1]

[1] Perhaps spoken by Liber in a final confrontation with Lycurgus.

34 Nonius

The ancients said *ingenio* ["naturally"] . . . in the sense of "of one's own accord" or "by nature." Naevius in *Lycurgus*:

you whose duties are to guard the royal person
go straightaway to the leaf-bearing places
where the trees have sprung up naturally, not through
planting[1]

[1] Lycurgus bids his guards search for the Bacchants in the woods (cf. F 19). Bednarek (2021, 128–29) argues for an address by Liber to Lycurgus' attendants, asking them to take him to a place where he will meet his end entangled by vines.

35 Nonius

liquidus ["liquid"; adj.] also means "soft" and "flowing" . . . Naevius in *Lycurgus*:

*ia*⁶   iam solis aestu candor cum liquesceret

cum *edd.*: cui *codd.*

36 (17 R.³) Non., p. 476.6–10 M. = 763 L.

TUTANT . . . Naevius Lycurgo:

*ia*⁶   tuos qui celsos terminos tutant . . .

37 (34 R.³) Non., p. 481.23–29 M. = 772 L.

POTIOR illam rem pro illa re potior . . . Naevius Lycurgo:

*ia*⁶   dic quo pacto eum potiti: pugnan an dolis?

pugnan an *Bothe*: pugna an *codd.*

38 (40 R.³) Non., p. 487.6–10 M. = 782 L.

timor et TIMOS . . . Naevius Lycurgo:

*ia*⁶   iam ibi nos duplicat advenientis timos pavos

now when the white [frost] was melting in the sun's
  heat[1]

[1] Perhaps from a messenger speech in which the Bacchants
are described as still sleeping at dawn (cf. Eur. *Bacch.* 678).

36 Nonius

tutant ["they guard"] . . . Naevius in *Lycurgus*:

those who guard your lofty borders[1] . . .

[1] Probably from a messenger speech announcing the arrival
of Liber and his followers (cf. F 27, 29).

37 Nonius

potior ["I get"] that thing [accusative] instead of *potior* ["I
get"] that thing [ablative] . . . Naevius in *Lycurgus*:

say how you got him, by fighting or trickery[1]

[1] Lycurgus asks how Liber was captured.

38 Nonius

timor ["fear"], also in the form *timos* [*hapax legomenon*]
. . . Naevius in *Lycurgus*:

there and then fear and terror bend us double as we
  arrive[1]

[1] Possibly the guards recount their initial meeting with the
Bacchants?

39 (49 R.[3]) Non., p. 503.16–27 M. = 808 L.

ab eo quod est fervit breviato accentu FERVERE facit . . .
Naevius Lycurgo:

ia[6]   late longeque transtros nostros fervere

transtros nostros *Ribbeck*[2–3]: trans nostros *codd.*: Thraces nostros *Bothe*

40 (43 R.[3]) Non., p. 540.3–7 M. = 866 L.

PATAGIUM, aureus clavus qui pretiosis vestibus inmitti
solet . . . Naevius Lycurgo:

tr[7]   pallis patagiis crocotis malacis mortualibus

Cf. Non., p. 548.24–32 M. = 880 L.

41 (41–42 R.[3]) Non., p. 547.22–25 M. = 878 L.

CRETERRA[1] est quam nunc situlam vocant. Naevius Ly-
curgo:

[1] Cf. *Equus Troianus* t 1; *BP* F 25.

39 Nonius

From the verb *fervit* ["it burns"] comes *fervere* ["to burn"]
with shortened vowel[1] . . . Naevius in *Lycurgus*:

> that far and wide our crossbeams burn[2]

[1] That is, Naevius uses *fervo, fervere* [third conjugation] for
classical Latin *ferveo, fervere* [second conjugation].

[2] A description of the fire threatened by Liber in F 24, spoken
by Lycurgus or one of his attendants.

40 Nonius

patagium ["border"] a golden stripe that is accustomed to
be sewn into expensive garments . . . Naevius in *Lycurgus*:

> gowns with decorated borders, saffron tunics, soft
> clothes of death[1]

[1] A description of the Bacchants' attire? Why "clothes of
death" should be mentioned is uncertain. *Mortualia* were origi-
nally funeral dirges, noted for their silliness; thus, the phrase
could simply sum up the clothes described as "soft fripperies,"
without any reference to death. Alternatively, Bednarek (2021,
129–30), retaining the interpretation "clothes of death," sees a
reference to Lycurgus and his followers being lured to their death
in Bacchic attire.

41 Nonius

creterra ["bowl"][1] is what we now call a bucket. Naevius
in *Lycurgus*:

[1] For this unusual word, derived ultimately from the Greek
krater ("mixing bowl") and occurring also in the forms *crater* and
crater, cf. *The Trojan Horse* t 1.

tr^7 namque ludere ut laetantis inter sese vidimus
         praeter amnem, aquam creterris sumere ex fonte . . .

1 namque ludere ut *Vossius*: nam vel ludere *vel* nam ut ludere *codd.*   sese *Vossius*: se *codd.*   2 aquam creterris sumere *Ribbeck*²: creterris sumere aquam *codd.*

Cf. Non., p. 84.12–13 = 119 L.

TRAGICA INCERTA (F 42–54)

In many cases it is impossible to tell whether the fragments in question come from tragedy or comedy. The sources

42 (62 R.³) Cic. *Orat.* 152

omnes poetae praeter eos qui ut versum facerent saepe hiabant, ut Naevius:

ia^6 vos qui adcolitis Histrum fluvium atque algidam

qui *codd.*: ques *vel* queis *vel* quis *Ritschl*

43 (61 R.³) Cic. *Orat.* 152

omnes poetae praeter eos qui ut versum facerent saepe hiabant, ut Naevius [F 42] . . . et ibidem:

ia^6 quam numquam vobis Grai atque barbari

---

[1] Cicero's "in the same" suggests the fragment comes from the same play as F 42, but Warmington assigns it to the *Incerta* (Naevius, *Trag. Inc.* 33) and not to *Iphigenia*, to which he assigns F 42.

> for when we saw them happily playing with one
>   another
> by the riverside, taking water in bowls from the
>   stream . . .[2]

[2] Another description of the Bacchants (cf. F 28, 30, 32, 37, 40).

UNASSIGNED TRAGIC FRAGMENTS
(F 42–54)

give no indication of title or genre. Listed here are the fragments whose style or content suggests tragedy.
    Comm.: Spaltenstein 2014, 619–45.

42 Cicero, *Orator*

All poets [avoid hiatus] except those who often allow hiatus to make up the verse, like Naevius:

> you who live by the river Danube and the region of
>   cold[1]

[1] Warmington (Naevius, *Trag.* 23 *ROL*) associates this fragment with the tragedy *Iphigenia*, although Cicero does not mention the play.

43 Cicero, *Orator*

All poets [avoid hiatus] except those who often allow hiatus to make up the verse, like Naevius [F 42] . . . and in the same:[1]

> which never to you have Greeks and foreigners

44 (54 R.[3]) Varro, *Ling.* 7.53

apud Naevium [*Fab. Inc.* F 82] . . . idem:

tr[7]   in pedibus diabathra habebat, erat amictus epicroco

utrumque vocabulum [*diabathrum et epicrocum*] Grae-
cum.

> pedibus *Rhollandellus ed. 1475*: pecudibus *codd.*   pedi-
> bus diabathra *De Melo 2015*: diabathra pedibus *codd.*

45 (56 R.[3]) Varro, *Ling.* 7.92

apud Naevium:

ia[6]   circumvenire video ferme iniuria

ferme dicitur quod nunc fere.

> circumvenire *Ribbeck[1]*: ciccum venire *codd.*: eccum venire
> *edd.*: circumveniri *Ribbeck[2–3]*   video *codd.*: videor *Rib-
> beck[2–3]*

46 (58 R.[3]) Fest., pp. 172.16–74.1 L.

NUME⟨RO⟩ . . . ⟨pro nimium diceba⟩nt [*suppl. Lindsay ex
epit. Pauli*] . . . apud Naevium:

tr[7]   neminem vidi qui numero sciret quicquid scito opus

> quicquid scito opus *vel* opust *edd.*: qui quod scit id est opus
> *codd.*   opus *codd.*: opust *Scaliger, edd. plerique*

Cf. Paul. *Fest.*, p. 173.4 L.

44 Varro, *On the Latin Language*

In Naevius [*Fab. Inc.* F 82] . . . the same:

> he had slippers on his feet, he was wrapped in a
>   saffron gown[1]

Both words [*diabathrum*, "slippers," and *epicrocum*, "saffron gown"] are Greek.

[1] Possibly a description of Liber at his capture (from *Lycurgus*); both items of clothing are normally worn by women. Both words (*diabathrum*, "slippers," and *epicrocum*, "saffron gown") are Greek loans, suggesting eastern effeminacy. Warmington includes this line in the *Lycurgus* fragments (Naevius, *Trag.* 43), as does Bednarek (2021, 130), who suggests it could come from a description of Lycurgus at his death.

45 Varro, *On the Latin Language*

in Naevius:

> I see it [or he/she?] tricks [me?][1] almost with
>   injustice

ferme ["almost"] is said for what now is *fere*

[1] The text of the first part of the line is uncertain; other possibilities are "look, I see him coming" or "I see [him] surrounded."

46 Paul the Deacon, *Epitome of Festus*

numero ["fully"] ‹is what they used to say for *nimium*› ["too much"] . . . in Naevius:

> I have seen no one who knew fully whatever ought to
>   be known

47 (51 R.[3]) Paul. *Fest.*, p. 248.20–21 L.

PARTUS et pro nascendo ponitur et pro parato. Naevius:

?   male parta male dilabuntur

    male parta male *edd.*: male male parta *codd.*   dilabun-
tur *edd.*: delabuntur *codd.*

Cf. Plaut. *Poen.* 844; Cic. *Phil.* 2.65; Ps.-Acro ad Hor. *Carm.*
3.24.61.

48 (60 R.[3]) Fest., p. 384.16–19 L.

‹SUMM›USSI dicebantur ‹murmuratores› [*suppl. ex epit.*
Pauli]. Naevius:

ia[8]   odi

inquit

        ‹summussos; pro›inde aperte dice ‹quid sit›
            ‹quod› times

    ‹summussos pro›*et*‹quid sit›*suppl. ex epit. Pauli*   quod
add. Ursinus   times *om. Paul.*

Cf. Paul. *Fest.*, p. 385.1–2 L.

49 (53 R.[3]) Non., p. 205.23–28 M. = 302 L.

FRETUM neutri tamen generis esse volumus . . . masculini
. . . Naevius:

ia[6]   dubii faventem per fretum introcurrimus

47 Festus

partus is said both for "birth" [noun] and for "acquired" [participle]. Naevius:

> things acquired in a bad way disappear in a bad way[1]

[1] Such a proverb could be equally well at home in comedy; cf. Plautus, *Poenulus* ("The Little Carthaginian") 844.

48 Festus

⟨Murmurers⟩ are said to be *summ⟨ussi⟩* ["mutterers"]. Naevius says:

> I hate mutterers; so say plainly ⟨what it is that⟩ you
>   fear[1]

[1] Given the lack of context, the fragment could come either from a comedy or from a tragedy.

49 Nonius

Nevertheless, we want *fretum* ["strait"] to be of the neuter gender . . . masculine gender [mainly ante-classical] . . . Naevius:

> in doubt we run inside the welcoming[1] strait[2]

[1] A possible play on the Greek εὔξεινον πόρον, "Euxine Strait," i.e., a strait welcoming to strangers.   [2] Warmington assigns this fragment to *Iphigenia* (Naevius, *Trag.* 22). The fragment is probably not connected with Naevius' comedy *Fretum* ("The Strait": *Com. Inc.* 84).

50 (57 R.³) Serv. Dan. ad Verg. *Aen.* 4.267

EXSTRUIS a struice . . . Naevius nominativo singulari:

?   struix malorum

51 (*Com.* 106 R.³) Hieron. *Ep.* 60.14

Naevius poeta:

ia⁶   pati

inquit,

> necesse est multa mortales mala

mortales *cod.*, *Sauppe*: mortalem *codd.*

52 (52 R.³) Isid. *Orig.* 5.26.17

praepositionem "inter" pro "e" ponebant. Naevius:

?   mare interbibere

. . . id est ebibere

53 (59 R.³) Isid. *Orig.* 12.1.30

Latini [bovem] TRIONEM vocant eo quod terram terat, quasi terionem. Naevius:

ia⁶   . . . trionum hic moderator rusticus

50 Servius Danielis, *Commentary on Virgil*

exstruis ["you heap up"] from *struix* ["a heap"] . . . Naevius in the nominative singular:

> a heap of evils

51 Jerome, *Letters*

Naevius the poet says:

> mortals must bear many evils

52 Isidore, *Origins*

They used to put the preposition *inter* for *e*. Naevius:

> to drink down the sea

. . . that is [*interbibere*] for *ebibere* ["drink down"].

53 Isidore, *Origins*

Latin speakers call the plow ox *trio* because it wears away [*terat*] the earth, as if it were *terio*.[1] Naevius:

> . . . here is a rustic driver of plow oxen[2]

[1] *terio* is a hypothetical form invented by Isidore, to explain the etymology of *trio* from *tero*. Cf. Varro *Ling.* 7.74, who invents the form *terriones* in order to derive *triones* from *terra* ("earth").

[2] Although Isidore does not name the play, Warmington assigns this fragment to *Iphigenia* (Naevius, *Trag.* 20) because of its similarity with Eur. *Iph. Taur.* 236–37, in which the chorus speak of the approach of a herdsman bringing news (of the arrival of Orestes and Pylades). However, the content of this fragment is too general for this attribution to be certain.

54 (55 R.[3]) Isid. *Orig.* 14.8.27

CONFRAGES loca in qua undique venti currunt ac sese frangunt. ut Naevius ait:

ia[6]
                                    . . . in montes ⟨confrages⟩
        ubi venti frangebant locum

  1 confrages *suppl. Klussmann*

Cf. Schol. ad Luc. 6.126; Paul. *Fest.*, p. 35.21 L.

54 Isidore, *Origins*

confrages ["exposed places"] places where the winds run together from all sides and break themselves. As Naevius says:

> . . . into the mountains, into ‹the exposed places›,
> where the winds break the landscape

PRAETEXTAE (F 1–5)

Naevius was perhaps the first Latin dramatist to turn from adapting Greek tragedies and comedies to composing plays on native Roman historical and mythological themes, known as fabulae praetextae. *In this he was followed by Ennius, from whom we have fragments of two* praetextae, *the* Ambracia *and the* Sabinae *(Enn. Praet. F 1–5 FRL). In general, plays from this specifically Roman dramatic genre are rare. We know of only around 15 titles of* prae-textae, *as compared with over 140 titles on Greek-based*

CLASTIDIUM (F 1–2)

The play takes as its subject the contemporary battle at Clastidium in Cisalpine Gaul in 222 BC. The consul Marcus Claudius Marcellus relieved the town, which was being besieged by the Gauls, and killed their leader, Viridomarus. On his return to Rome Marcellus was awarded a triumph and received the spolia opima, *a rare and prestigious distinction (on the historical background see Polybius 2.34; Livy,* Epit. 20; *Valerius Maximus 3.2.5; Plutarch,*

PRAETEXTAE (F 1–5)

themes from Roman authors (see Ribbeck 1875, 33). Of Naevius' five surviving fragments, two come from a contemporary historical play, Clastidium, *and three from a play based on Rome's foundation myth,* Romulus *sive* Lupus.

Bibl.: *Suerbaum 1994, 2002, 2003; Manuwald 2001 [2004], 93–101. Comm.: Spaltenstein 2014, 523–48. Lit.: Grauert 1847; De Durante 1966; Manuwald 2001, 134–61; Kragelund 2002; Boyle 2006, 83–87; Feeney 2016, 108.*

CLASTIDIUM (F 1–2)

Marc. *4.5). The two fragments preserved by Varro come from the happy aftermath of the victory. The play could have been put on at the funeral games for Marcellus in 208 BC or in 205 BC, when his son dedicated the temple to Honor and Courage that Marcellus had vowed at Clastidium, but there is no firm evidence for either date (see Marmorale 1967, 129–30; Goldberg 1995, 32–33; Bernstein 2000; Lehmann 2002, 101n41).*

1 (1 R.³) Varro, *Ling.* 7.107

apud Naevium . . . in Clastidio:

?   vitulantes

a Vitula

Cf. *Trag.* F 21.

2 (2 R.³) Varro, *Ling.* 9.78

in vocabulis casuum possunt item fieri ‹iacturae› [*suppl. Goetz / Schoell*] . . . ac reponi quod aberit, ubi patietur natura et consuetudo . . . ut in hoc apud Naevium in Clastidio:

ia⁶   vita insepulta laetus in patriam redux

ROMULUS SIVE LUPUS (t 1; F 3–5)

The legend of Romulus and the she-wolf and its connection with Rome's foundation story was probably known before the time of Naevius (see Leo 1913, 90 and n. 1). There are

1 Varro, *On the Latin Language*

in Naevius . . . in *Clastidium*:

> uttering a cry of joy[1]
>
> from [the goddess] Vitula[2]

[1] The verb *vitulo* is rare and ante-classical (also at Plautus, *Persa* ["The Persian"] 254, and Ennius, *Trag. Inc.* F 201 *FRL*). The word is also used in Naevius, *Trag.* F 21. Here it describes perhaps the Romans rejoicing at their victory, but with no context this must remain uncertain.   [2] A goddess of joy according to Macrobius, *Saturnalia* 3.2.11, attested only here. De Melo (2019, 1032) sees *Vitula* as an abstraction based on the verb rather than the other way round.

2 Varro, *On the Latin Language*

In words <losses> of cases can come about . . . and what is lacking can be replaced,[1] when nature and usage allow . . . as in this [verse] of Naevius in *Clastidium*:

> with his life unburied, happy, restored to his fatherland[2]

[1] In the example, the adjective *redux* ("restored") is found only here in the nominative singular, and so is a lacking form, which, according to Varro, Naevius has replaced or innovated.   [2] The line probably describes the safe return to Rome of Marcellus from the battle of Clastidium.

ROMULUS SIVE LUPUS (t 1; F 3–5)

no fragments in the Bellum Punicum *that refer specifically to this legend, but it would be unusual if it were not touched upon also in this epic that dealt with the early history of Rome. Whether the double title referred to a single play has been hotly debated in the past, but now it is generally agreed that it did (see Tandoi 1974). Festus refers only to "The Wolf" (F 5), and Varro (F 3 and F 4) to "Romulus." The remains are too meager to allow us to reconstruct the plot. Donatus (t 1) suggests a scene in*

t 1 Donat. ad Ter. *Ad.* 537

nam falsum est, quod dicitur intervenisse lupum Naevianae fabulae alimonio Remi et Romuli, dum in theatro ageretur.

3 (3 R.[3]) Varro, *Ling.* 7.54

carere a carendo, quod eam [lanam] tum purgant ac deducunt, ut careat spurcitia; ex quo carminari dicitur tum lana, cum ex ea carunt [*Neukirch, edd.*: carent *codd.*] quod in ea haeret neque est lana, quae in Romulo Naevius appellat asta ab Oscis:

asta

Cf. *Com. Inc.* F 83.

which a wolf suckles the infants Romulus and Remus, while F 3 suggests a later stage of the legend in which an Etruscan king lends Romulus aid against the king of Alba Longa.

Comm.: Spaltenstein 2014, 536–48. Lit.: Beare 1949; Alfonsi 1967 (F 5); Tandoi 1974; 1975 (F 5); Bettini 1981 (F 5).

t 1 Donatus, *Commentary on Terence*

For it is false, what is said, that a wolf burst in upon the feeding of Romulus and Remus in a play of Naevius when it was being acted in the theater.

3 Varro, *On the Latin Language*

[The verb] *carere* ["to card"] is from *carere* ["to lack"],[1] because then they clean [the wool] and spin it out, so that it may lack dirt. From this wool is said to be carded at the time when they card out of it what is attached to it and is not wool, things which in his *Romulus* Naevius calls *asta* ["impurities"] from the Oscans.[2]

impurities[3]

[1] The verb *caro* ["card"] (more correctly *carro*) is not connected with *careo* ["lack"].   [2] Possibly a reference to the spinning duties of the Sabine women, who were traditionally thought to have been abducted to become the wives of the first inhabitants of Rome.   [3] The etymology and exact meaning of this word, which Varro claims is Oscan, are unknown. It is uncertain what form the word took in Naevius' play. The preceding neut. pl. relative *quae* ["things which"] suggests that *asta* is plural.

4 (4 R.³) Varro, *Ling.* 7.107

multa apud poetas reliqua esse verba quorum origines possint dici, non dubito, ut apud Naevium . . . in Romulo:

consponsus

contra sponsum rogatus.

<con>sponsus *Popma, Neukirch, edd.*: sponsus *codd.*

Cf. Varro, *Ling.* 6.69–70: spondet enim qui dicit a sua sponte "spondeo." <qui> spo<pondit [*Spengel*] est sponsor. qui idem [*ed. Ven.*: quidem *codd.*] <ut> [*add. Augustinus*] faciat obligatur sponsu [*Spengel*: sponsus *codd.*], consponsus. [70] hoc Naevius significat cum ait "consponsi."

5 (5–6 R.³) Fest., p. 334.8–12 L.

REDHOSTIRE, referre gratiam, Naevius in Lupo:

*tr*⁷   rex Veiens regem salutat Viba Albanum Amulium
        comiter senem sapientem: contra redhostis? min
            salust?

1 rex *Ribbeck*²⁻³: vel *cod.*   salutat *Scaliger*: saltant *cod.*   Viba *Buecheler*: vibae *cod.*   amulium *Scaliger*: mulium *cod.*   2 comiter *Scaliger*: comitem *cod.*   min salust *Ribbeck*²⁻³: menalus *cod.*

4 Varro, *On the Latin Language*

I do not doubt that there are many words left among the poets whose origins can be told, for example in Naevius . . . in *Romulus*:

> cosurety[1]

one who is asked to make a counterpromise.

[1] We are not sure which form of the word *consponsus* Naevius used in the *Romulus*, but if Varro's comments at 6.70 refer to the same passage, it could well have been the plural *consponsi* ["cosureties"].

Cf. Varro, *On the Latin Language* 6.69–70: For that man *spondet* ["makes a promise"] who says from his own *sponte* ["free will"] *spondeo* ["I promise"]. The man who *spopondit* ["has made a promise"] is a *sponsor* ["surety"]. The man who is obliged by his *sponsus* ["promise"] to do the same is a *consponsus* ["cosurety"]. [70] This is what Naevius means when he says *consponsi* ["cosureties"].

5 Festus

redhostire ["to requite"; rare and ante-classical], to repay a favor, Naevius in *The Wolf*:

> Viba,[1] king of Veii,[2] salutes Alban Amulius,[3]
> a wise old man, in kindly fashion. Do you repay my
>   favor? Do you wish me well?

[1] The name of this Etruscan king is uncertain. His role in the play was perhaps to help Romulus kill Amulius.

[2] An Etruscan city to the north of Rome.

[3] A legendary king of Alba Longa, who had ordered the infants Romulus and Remus to be thrown into the Tiber. Naevius mentions him also at *Bellum Punicum* F 10.

VARIA (F 1–3)

SATURA (F 1)

A Satura ("Medley") was an ancient form of stage enter-
tainment with songs and dances performed to flute accom-
paniment (cf. Livy 7.2.7: "[Native Roman actors] per-
formed medleys, full of musical measures, with songs

1 Fest., p. 306.25–30 L.

QUIANAM pro quare, et cur, positum est apud antiquos, ut
Naevium . . . in Satyra:

?   quianam Saturnium populum pepulisti

Cf. Liv. 7.2.7: [histriones Romani] impletas modis saturas des-
cripto iam ad tibicinem cantu motuque congruenti peragebant.

CUM METELLIS ALTERCATIO (F 2)

A verse of Naevius, said to have been found insulting by
the leading Roman family, the Metelli, is quoted in the fifth
century AD by Ps.-Asconius in a comment on Cicero's Ver-
rine Orations (T 5). This source also provides a one-verse
reply by the Metelli in the Saturnian meter. Caesius Bassus
in the first century AD also mentions the quarrel and

VARIOUS (F 1–3)

SATURA (F 1)

*written out to flute accompaniment and with appropriate
gesture"). This type of drama existed in Rome before Liv-
ius Andronicus introduced Greek-based tragedy and com-
edy. F 1 is our only evidence for Naevius' working in such
a genre.*

1 Festus

quianam ["why ever"?; ante-classical form] is put for
quare and *cur* [both classical Latin for "why"?] among the
ancients, such as Naevius . . . in his *Medley*:

> Why ever did you expel the Saturnian[1] people?

[1] The people of the legendary Golden Age of Saturn, who
were expelled by Jove.

CUM METELLIS ALTERCATIO (F 2)

*quotes the reply from the Metelli, but not Naevius' original
verse (T 6). The verse by Naevius, quoted in T 5, is more
likely to have been in iambic than in Saturnian meter, but
its exact context as a dramatic fragment or as a freestand-
ing verse is unknown. Why this verse angered the Metelli
is a matter of debate; see further Introduction to Naevius:
Life; Works; and cf. T 5 and 6.*

2 Schol. (Ps.-Ascon.) ad Cic. *Verr.* 1.29.16–21

Cf. T 5, T 6.

NAEVI EPIGRAMMA (F 3)

There is some discussion as to whether this epitaph was genuinely written by Naevius. Courtney (1993, 48) sees it as the work of an overzealous imitator, as do Marmorale (1967, 140–41) and Lehmann (2002, 104–5). The epitaph

3 Gell. *NA* 1.24.1–2

Cf. T 7.

2 Ps.-Asconius, Scholia to Cicero, *Verrine Orations*

Cf. T 5, T 6.

NAEVI EPIGRAMMA (F 3)

is very close in content to that of Plautus, quoted in the same passage of Gellius, and Gellius' source for both seems to be Varro's lost De poetis. *There are good general discussions in Suerbaum (1968, 31–42), who sees it as possibly genuine, and Gruen (1990, 92–93).*

3 Gellius, *Attic Nights*

Cf. T 7.

BELLUM PUNICUM
(t 1–13; F 1–47)

According to Cicero (t 2), Bellum Punicum ("The Punic War") was a product of Naevius' old age. Its division into books, as reflected in our sources, did not originate with Naevius, who wrote it in one continuous unit, but was the work of the later mid-second-century BC grammarian C. Octavius Lampadio (t 6). The poem represents an important new development in Latin epic, as it moves away from Livius Andronicus' adaptation of Homer's Odyssey *and takes as its subject matter a purely Roman theme, the First Punic War between Rome and Carthage (264–241 BC). It does not, however, depart completely from Homeric material, as the first three books combine the Punic War with a narrative of the destruction of Troy and the flight to Italy of Aeneas and his followers. In this way the first truly Roman epic can be seen to have its roots in Homeric themes, which were nevertheless relevant to recent Roman history. The Romans believed that their state had been founded by fugitives from Troy. Furthermore, the question of the treatment by the Greeks of the defeated Trojans had relevance for Rome's treatment of her defeated enemies in the Punic War. Divisions between myth and history would not*

BELLUM PUNICUM
(t 1–13; F 1–47)

have been as clear-cut to the Roman as to a modern audience. The Trojan War and its aftermath, including the settlement of Italy by Aeneas and his comrades, would have been considered just as much a historical event as the First Punic War. The only difference would have been one of chronology. The Trojan War was an event in the distant past, whereas Naevius had firsthand experience of fighting in the First Punic War (t 7). The conflict between Rome and Carthage could also have been considered to have its roots in the strained relations between Dido and the fugitive Aeneas (BP F 7). This is not made explicit in the surviving fragments, but Virgil's later treatment of the subject in the Aeneid, *which to some extent must have been influenced by Naevius (t 11, 14), certainly brings these themes to the fore.*

For a more detailed analysis of the Bellum Punicum *and its narrative structure, see Introduction to Naevius: Works.*

Comm.: Flores 2014; Viredaz 2020, 220–371. Lit.: Fleckeisen 1861; Fraenkel 1935; Rowell 1947; Strzelecki 1957–58; Barchiesi 1963; Mazzarino 1965; 1966; Goldberg 1995, 51–52, 73–82; Farrell 2005; Biggs 2020, 53–94.

TESTIMONIA (t 1–13)

t 1 Cic. *Brut.* 75–76 [= T 2 Livius Andronicus; T 18 Ennius]

tamen illius, quem in vatibus et Faunis adnumerat Ennius, bellum Punicum quasi Myronis opus delectat. [76] sit Ennius sane, ut est certe, perfectior; qui si illum, ut simulat, contemneret, non omnia bella persequens primum illud Punicum acerrimum bellum reliquisset. sed ipse dicit cur id faciat. "scripsere," inquit, "alii rem vorsibus" [Enn. 7 *Ann.* F 1a *FRL*]; et luculente quidem scripserunt, etiam si minus quam tu polite. nec vero tibi aliter videri debet, qui a Naevio vel sumpsisti multa, si fateris, vel, si negas, surripuisti.

t 2 Cic. *Sen.* 49–50

nihil est otiosa senectute iucundius . . . [50] quid in levioribus studiis, sed tamen acutis, quam gaudebat Bello suo Punico Naevius, quam Truculento Plautus, quam Pseudolo?

TESTIMONIA (t 1–13)

t 1 Cicero, *Brutus*

The *Bellum Punicum* of that man whom Ennius counts among the soothsayers and Fauns gives pleasure like a work of Myron[1] does. [76]. Granted that Ennius is more polished, as he certainly is: yet, if Ennius really despised him, as he pretends, he would not, in recounting all our wars, have left aside that first, most bitter, Punic war. But he himself tells us why he does so. "Others," he says, "have written about the thing in verse" [Enn. 7 *Ann.* F 1a *FRL*]; and indeed they did write about it splendidly, even if with less polish than you. Nor indeed should you think otherwise, you who have taken much from Naevius, if you admit it, or, if you deny it, have stolen much from him.

[1] Myron of Eleutherae, an Athenian sculptor of the mid-fifth century BC.

t 2 Cicero, *On Old Age*[1]

Nothing is more pleasant than a leisurely old age . . . [50] What of [those men who were engaged in] light yet intellectually demanding studies? What joy did Naevius take in his *Bellum Punicum*, what joy Plautus in his *Truculentus* and *Pseudolus*?

[1] The dialogue *On Old Age*, dedicated to Cicero's friend Atticus, is set in the year 155 BC. The speaker of this passage is Marcus Porcius Cato, then aged eighty-four, in dialogue with P. Scipio Africanus Minor (b. 185 BC, consul 148 BC and 146 BC) and Caius Laelius (b. about 190 BC, consul 140 BC).

t 3 Varro, *Ling*. 5.43

Aventinum aliquot de causis dicunt. Naevius ab avibus, quod eo se ab Tiberi ferrent aves.

t 4 Varro, *Ling*. 5.53

[Palatium] a pecore dictum putant quidam; itaque Naevius "Balatium" appellat.

Cf. Paul. *Fest.*, p. 245.9–10 L.; Serv. *Aen.* 8.51.

t 5 Hor. *Epist*. 2.1.53–54

Naevius in manibus non est et mentibus haeret
paene recens? adeo sanctum est vetus omne poema.

t 3 Varro, *On the Latin Language*

Aventinum ["The Aventine" hill] they say is so called from a number of reasons. Naevius says it is named from *aves* ["birds"], because birds go there from the Tiber.[1]

[1] Varro does not name the work, but the subject matter, like that of t 4, suggests it comes from Rome's foundation myth dealt with in Book 3 of the *Bellum Punicum*.

t 4 Varro, *On the Latin Language*

Palatium ["The Palatine" hill] some think is said from *pecus* ["sheep"]; and so Naevius calls it *Balatium* ["The Bleating" hill].[1]

[1] Varro does not name the work, but the subject matter, like that of t 3, suggests it comes from Rome's foundation myth dealt with in Book 3 of the *Bellum Punicum*.

t 5 Horace, *Epistles*

> Is not Naevius in our hands[1] and does he not cling to
>   our minds[2]
> [as if] almost contemporary? So sacred is every old
>   poem.[3]

[1] In written form.   [2] As memorized verses.   [3] Horace does not name the work, but the reference is most likely to the *Bellum Punicum*, still studied as a school text in Horace's day.

t 6 Suet. *Gramm. et rhet.* 2.2 [= T 70 Ennius]

hactenus tamen imitati, ut carmina parum adhuc divulgata
vel defunctorum amicorum vel si quorum aliorum probas-
sent diligentius retractarent ac legendo commentandoque
etiam ceteris nota facerent: ut C. Octavius Lampadio
Naevi *Punicum bellum*, quod uno volumine et continenti
scriptura expositum divisit in septem libros.

Cf. Non., p. 170.17–19 M.= 250 L.: Santra de Verborum Antiqui-
tate III: "quod volumen unum nos lectitavimus, et postea inveni-
mus septemfariam divisum."

t 7 Gell. *NA* 17.21.44–45

Cf. T 11.

t 6 Suetonius, *Lives of Illustrious Men. Grammarians and Rhetoricians*

Still, they imitated him [Crates of Mallos[1]] only this far, that they carefully reviewed poems that had been little circulated up till then, either those of dead friends or of any others they approved, and by reading and commenting on them made them known to others as well. This is what C. Octavius Lampadio[2] did in the case of Naevius' *Bellum Punicum*, which he divided into seven books, it having previously been set out as one single continuous book roll.

Cf. Nonius: Santra[3] in his *On the Antiquity of Words* Book 3 [says]: "which we had often read as a single volume and later we found divided into seven."

[1] A Greek grammarian who taught in Rome in the mid-second century BC; see Funaioli 1907, x; Suet. *Gram. et rhet.* 2.1 (with Kaster 1995, 58–61 ad loc.).   [2] A grammarian of the mid-second century BC; see Funaioli 1907, 21–22; Suet. *Gram. et rhet.* 2.2 (with Kaster 1995, 64–66 ad loc.).   [3] A contemporary of Varro, writing in the mid-first century BC (see Funaioli 1907, 384–89). Although Naevius is not named by Nonius, the seven-fold division of books in Santra probably refers to Naevius' *Bellum Punicum*. Santra seems to have been Suetonius' source for this (see Kaster 1995, 64–66; Zetzel 2018, 20–21).

t 7 Gellius, *Attic Nights*

Cf. T. 11.

t 8 Fest., p. 156.20–22 L.

‹primus eam [navalem coronam] accepit C.› Atilius bel‹lo Punico primo, ut a Naevio narra›tum est in car‹mine Belli Punici›.

locum restituit Cichorius

t 9 Lactant. *Div. inst.* 1.6.7–9

M. Varro . . . in libris rerum divinarum . . . ait . . . [8] Sibyllas decem numero fuisse . . . [9] quartam Cimmeriam in Italia, quam Naevius in libris belli Punici, Piso in annalibus nominet.

t 10 Serv. Dan. ad Verg. *Aen.* 1.170

novam . . . rem Naevius bello Punico dicit, unam navem habuisse Aeneam, quam Mercurius fecerit.

t 11 Serv. Dan. ad Verg. *Aen.* 1.198

totus hic locus [Verg. *Aen.* 1.198–207] de Naevio belli Punici libro translatus est.

t 8 Festus

‹The first man to win [a naval crown] was C.› Atilius, in ‹the First Punic War, as is told by Naevius› in his song ‹of *The Punic War*›.[1]

[1] The text of this fragment is so damaged that neither the poet's name nor the title of the work remains. The restored readings printed here derive from a conjecture by Cichorius (1922, 34–35). He suggests it refers to the mention in Naevius' *Bellum Punicum* of a naval crown (Festus' lemma), awarded to C. Atilius Serranus at the naval battle of Mylae in 260 BC. Earlier commentators identified the Atilius in question with M. Atilius Regulus at the sea battle at Economus in 256 BC or with A. Atilius Calatinus for one of his naval battles around Sicily in the years 258/7 BC.

t 9 Lactantius, *Divine Institutes*

M. Varro . . . in his *Books on Divine Matters* . . . says . . . [8] that the Sibyls were ten in number . . . [9] the fourth is the "Cimmerian" in Italy, which Naevius in his books on *The Punic War* and Piso in his *Annals* mention by name.

t 10 Servius Danielis, *Commentary on Virgil*

Naevius says something . . . new in *The Punic War*, namely that Aeneas had one ship which Mercury had built.

t 11 Servius Danielis, *Commentary on Virgil*

This whole passage [Verg. *Aen.* 1.198–207] is taken from Naevius' book on *The Punic War*.

t 12 Serv. Dan. ad Verg. *Aen.* 1.273

Naevius et Ennius Aeneae ex filia nepotem Romulum conditorem urbis tradunt.

Cf. Serv. ad Verg. *Aen.* 1.273.

t 13 Serv. Dan. ad Verg. *Aen.* 4.9

"Anna soror": cuius filiae fuerint Anna et Dido, Naevius dicit.

t 14 Schol. ad Verg. *Aen.* 7.123 [*Cod. Paris. Lat.* 7930]

"Anchises fatorum arcana reliquit": divinitatem Anchisae assignat, qui ubique divinus dicitur. Naevius enim dicit Venerem libros futura continentes Anchisae dedisse.

LIBER I (t 15–16; F 1–6)

It used to be thought that the first two books of the work were concerned with the mythical history of Aeneas' wanderings from Troy to Italy and the founding of Rome and Carthage, but in recent years it has become clear that Book 1 begins with the story of the First Punic War down until the year 262 BC. Two of the fragments, specifically assigned in our sources to Book 1, deal with events from the First Punic War, namely F 1, an expedition led by Manius Valerius in the second year of the war (263 BC), and F 4, the sack of Agrigentum in 262 BC. At this point the narration of the war is interrupted, and the mythical history begins and continues until the beginning of Book 4, where the narrative of the war is taken up again. Both the testi-

t 12 Servius Danielis, *Commentary on Virgil*

Naevius and Ennius say that Aeneas' grandson, Romulus, born from his daughter [Ilia], was the founder of the city.

t 13 Servius Danielis, *Commentary on Virgil*

"sister Anna": Naevius tells us whose daughters Anna and Dido were.

t 14 Scholia to Virgil

"Anchises left behind the secrets of the fates": He [Virgil] assigns divinity to Anchises, who is everywhere said to be divine. For Naevius says that Venus gave to Anchises books containing the events of the future.

BOOK I (t 15–16; F 1–6)

monia attached to Book 1 deal with events on the mythical voyage from Troy to Italy: a visit to the island of Prochyta (t 15) and the storm at sea with Venus' appeal to Jupiter to aid the Trojans (t 16). All the remaining fragments securely attributed to Book 1 come from this mythical section: F 2 deals with the flight from Troy of Aeneas, Anchises, and their followers; F 5, whose attribution to Book 1 is in doubt, probably deals with the concerns of Jupiter or Venus for the Trojans in flight; and F 3, with an encounter on their journey with primitive peoples. F 6 possibly concerns Aeneas' relief at the end of the storm at sea, though the exact context remains uncertain. Various fragments listed under Fragmenta Incerta, *since they are not*

*assigned to any particular book in our sources, may well
have come from Book 1 on the grounds of their contents.
F 26, an address to the Muses, may, on the analogy of in-
vocations to the Muses in Homer (Il. 1.1; Od. 1.1), Ennius
(1 Ann. F 1 FRL), and Virgil (Aen. 1.8), have come from
the beginning of Book 1. What appears to be a formal
declaration of war (F 34) could come from the beginning
of the Carthaginian war narrative, although other con-
texts, including the making of treaties, are also possible;*

Testimonia (t 15–16)

*Aeneas' voyage from Troy to Italy with Anchises and his
followers, the storm at sea, his visit to the Sibyl and to the*

t 15 Serv. Dan. ad Verg. *Aen.* 9.712

"Prochyta alta tremit": . . . hanc [insulam] Naevius in
primo belli Punici de cognata Aeneae nomen accepisse
dicit.

t 16 Macr. *Sat.* 6.2.31

in primo Aeneidos [Verg. *Aen.* 1.81–296] tempestas de-
scribitur et Venus apud Iovem queritur de periculis filii et
Iuppiter eam de futurorum prosperitate solatur. hic locus
totus sumptus a Naevio est ex primo libro belli Punici. illic
enim aeque Venus Troianis tempestate laborantibus cum
Iove queritur et sequuntur verba Iovis filiam consolantis
spe futurorum.

*F 35, probably from a similar context to F 3, namely, en-
counters with primitive tribes; F 24 and 29 probably come
from Venus' address to Jupiter mentioned in t 15; F 40, on
the wives of Anchises and Aeneas leaving Troy, clearly
comes from the same context as F 2; F 45, Anchises' prayer
to Neptune, comes probably from either before or after the
voyage from Troy.*

   *Lit.: Wimmel 1970 (F 4); Pasoli 1974 (F 3); Godel 1978
(F 3).*

Testimonia (t 15–16)

*island of Prochyta occur in the testimonia attested specifi-
cally for Book 1.*

t 15 Servius Danielis, *Commentary on Virgil*

"high Prochyta trembles": . . . This [island] Naevius says
in Book 1 of *The Punic War* took its name from a kins-
woman of Aeneas.[1]

  [1] The commentator suggests that Prochyta (mod. Procida)
was renamed Aenaria, after Aeneas' relative, but that name was
actually given to the neighboring island of Ischia.

t 16 Macrobius, *Saturnalia*

In Book 1 of the *Aeneid* [Verg. *Aen.* 1.81–296] a storm is
described, and Venus complains to Jupiter about her son's
danger, and Jupiter consoles her concerning the prosper-
ity of the future. This whole passage is taken from Book 1
of Naevius' *Punic War*. For there in the same way, when
the Trojans are suffering in a storm, Venus complains to
Jupiter, and there follow the words of Jupiter comforting
his daughter with hope of the future.

Fragmenta (F 1–6)

F 1: *Manius Valerius leads part of the army on an expedition in Sicily. Manius Valerius was consul in 263 BC; so the reference is to an event in the second year of the First Punic War (264–241 BC). The fragment must come chron-*

1 (3 Bl.) Charis., *GL* I, p. 128.17–19 = p. 163 B.

EXERCITI Gn. Naevius belli Punici libro I:

Manius Valerius

2   consul partem exerciti in expeditionem
       ducit

1 M' (*i.e.*, *Manius*) *Merula*: M (*i.e.*, *Marcus*) *codd.*, *Keil,
Barwick*

De metro cf. Strzelecki 1964, 2.

F 2: *After the siege of Agrigentum (F 4), still within Book 1, Naevius breaks off the war narrative and inserts an interlude on Aeneas' leaving Troy after the sack of the city, his wanderings by sea, his arrival in Italy, and the founda-*

2 (6 Bl.) Serv. Dan. ad Verg. *Aen.* 2.797

sane adamat poeta ea quae legit diverso modo proferre.
Naevius belli Punici primo de Anchisa et Aenea fugienti-
bus haec ait:

4   eorum sectam sequuntur multi mortales

BELLUM PUNICUM: BOOK I

Fragments (F 1–6)

*ologically after the formal declaration of war, if that is
what is referred to in F 34. On the historical background,
see Barchiesi 1962, 393–94; Viredaz 2020, 222–23; Biggs
2020, 80–81.*

1 Charisius

The form *exerciti* ["of the army"; archaic genitive on the
analogy of second declension forms, for classical *exercitus*]
is found in Cn. Naevius, *The Punic War*, Book 1:

> Manius Valerius,
> the consul, leads part of the army on an   2
> expedition

*tion of Rome. The narrative of the war against Carthage
is not resumed until Book 4. In F 2 Aeneas and his family
are followed by many others leaving Troy and taking their
gold with them.*

2 Servius Danielis, *Commentary on Virgil*

Indeed our author likes to produce what he has read in a
different way. Naevius in Book 1 of *The Punic War* says
this about Anchises and Aeneas in flight:[1]

> many mortals follow their path   4

[1] It is uncertain whether the three verses quoted here form a
continuous text or are separated from each other in Naevius'
poem.

ecce hoc est "invenio admirans numerum" [Verg. *Aen.* 2.797]

5   multi alii e Troia strenui viri

ecce hi sunt "animis parati" [Verg. *Aen.* 2.799]

6   ubi foras cum auro illinc exibant

ecce et "opibus instructi" [Verg. *Aen.* 2.799: animis opibus-que parati].

   6 illinc *Vossius*: illic *codd.*

Cf. Cic. *Sest.* 97; Schol. Veron. ad Verg. *Aen.* 2.717.

De metro cf. Barchiesi 1962, 364.

F 3: Probably a description of primitive tribes met with by the Trojans on their journey. The reference could be to the primitive tribes of Latium (so Klussmann 1843, 44), but since Aeneas does not reach Italy until Book 3, the passage would have to come from a speech by Jove assuring Venus

3 (10 Bl.) Macrob. *Sat.* 6.5.9 (ad Verg. *Aen.* 10.551 "silvi-colae Fauno")

silvicolae Fauni. Naevius belli Punici libro primo:

7   silvicolae homines bellique inertes

F 4: This fragment, assigned by Priscian to Book 1, prob-ably comes from a description of the bas-reliefs on the east pediment of the temple of Agrigentum depicting a fight

Here are Virgil's words "I marveling find a great number" [Verg. *Aen.* 2.797]

    many other determined men from Troy   5

Here are Virgil's words "ready in mind" [Verg. *Aen.* 2.799]

    when they went outdoors away from there with gold   6

Here again is Virgil's "laden with wealth" [Verg. *Aen.* 2.799]

about the Trojans' future in Italy (see t 15, F 5). Other explanations are possible. Marmorale (1950, 240) sees a reference to tribes met on the coast of North Africa by the Trojans after the storm at sea; Barchiesi (1962, 379–80) thinks the line refers to primitive peoples met in Sicily on the voyage from Troy.

3 Macrobius, *Saturnalia* (on Virgil, "to the wood-haunting Fawn")

"Wood-haunting fawns." Naevius in Book 1 of *The Punic War*:

    wood-haunting men and unskilled in war   7

between the giants (Gigantomachy) (cf. Diod. 13.82.4, and see Bergk 1842, 191). Alternative interpretations, involving other works of art (on a shield or a ship), are possible

333

(see lists in Goldberg 1995, 52n47; Viredaz 2020, 240), but less likely. The town of Agrigentum in Sicily was besieged and sacked by the Romans as part of their campaign against the Carthaginians in 262 BC and was retaken by the Carthaginians in 254 BC, when the Roman garrison took refuge in the temple. The west pediment of the same temple had a depiction of the flight from Troy, which could

4 (8 Bl.) Prisc., *GL* II, pp. 198.6–99.2

[primae] declinationis femininorum genetivum etiam in -as more Graeco solebant antiquissimi terminare . . . Naevius in carmine belli Punici I:

8   inerant signa expressa, quo modo Titani,
        bicorpores Gigantes magnique Atlantes
10   Runcus atque Porpureus, filii Terras

pro "Terrae." in eodem [F 5]: . . .

10 Runcus *Vahlen*: rhumcus *vel* rhuncus *vel* runcus. *codd.*

Cf. Prisc., *GL* II, p. 217.10–13.

F 5: This fragment is assigned to the same work as F 4 by Priscian. It is unclear whether he means also to the same book. It is too general in tone to place exactly in the narrative. The mention of the "fortune of men" suggests the speaker could be a god. It may refer to Jupiter pondering the fortune of men after an appeal to him by Venus to help the Trojans in their flight (cf. t 15, F 24 and 29, and see

have formed a connection with the mythical section of the Bellum Punicum *(Goldberg 1995, 51–52). The motif of a description of temple reliefs is taken up later in epic by Virgil in his description of the pictures in Dido's temple in Carthage at* Aen. *1.466ff., depicting the fall of Troy, which leads into Aeneas' narrative of the flight from Troy in* Aen. *2.*

4 Priscian

The very ancients also used the termination *-as* [archaic already in Naevius' time] in Greek fashion for feminine genitives of the [first] declension [*-ae* in classical Latin] . . . Naevius in his song of *The Punic War*, Book 1:

> Figures were depicted on it showing how the Titans,   8
> double-bodied Giants, and the great Atlases,
> Runcus and Porpureus,[1] sons of Earth   10

using *Terras* for *Terrae* ["of Earth"; gen.]. In the same [F 5] . . .

[1] Domesticated Latin equivalents for the Greek giants' names Ῥοῖτος or Ῥοῖκος and Πορφυρίων (see Mariotti 1955, 62–63).

Strzelecki 1959, 36–37; Flores 2014, 26–27). Alternatively, the thoughts could be those of Venus herself or even of a person from the historical narrative. There is no indication in the fragment whether the speaker is male or female. The fragment's attachment to Book 1 and its context must remain in doubt.

5 (18 Bl.) Prisc., *GL* II, pp. 198.6–99.2

[primae] declinationis femininorum genetivum etiam in -as more Graeco solebant antiquissimi terminare . . . Naevius in carmine belli Punici I [F 4] . . . in eodem:

11   ei venit in mentem hominum fortunas

pro "fortunae."

6 (21 Bl.) Prisc., *GL* II, pp. 242.20–43.1

inquies . . . cuius etiam simplex in usu invenitur trium generum. Naevius in carmine belli Punici I [*codd.*: Punici II *Hertz*]

12   iamque eius mentem fortuna fecerat quietem

LIBER II (F 7–9)

Three fragments are securely assigned to Book 2. Two of them (F 8 and F 9) deal with a council or procession of the gods, perhaps to decide the fate of the Trojans following Venus' appeal to Jupiter at the end of Book 1 (cf. t 15). This interpretation was first proposed by Leo (1913, 82) and is shared by most modern critics. The third is F 7, in which Aeneas is questioned about his departure from Troy. The context of F 7 may be Aeneas' arrival in Carthage after the

5 Priscian

The very ancients also used the termination *-as* [archaic already in Naevius' time] in Greek fashion for feminine genitives of the [first] declension [*-ae* in classical Latin] . . . Naevius in his song of *The Punic War*, Book 1 [F 4] . . . In the same:

> the fortune of men came into his [or: her] mind 11

using *fortunas* for *fortunae* ["fortune"; gen. sg.].

6 Priscian

inquies ["unquiet"; adj.] . . . whose simple form [*quies*, "quiet"; adj.] is also found used in all three genders. Naevius in his song of *The Punic War*, Book 1:[1]

> and now fortune had made his [or: her][2] mind quiet 12

[1] Hertz prints *II* [Book 2] in his edition, but the *codd.* clearly read *I* [Book 1] (Viredaz 2020, 249).   [2] The gender of the person referred to is not distinguished in the Latin pronoun *eius*, but the most likely reference is to Aeneas, in his relief after escaping the storm at sea. Given the uncertainty about the reference of the pronoun, this must remain conjectural.

BOOK II (F 7–9)

storm at sea, with which Book 1 may have ended (see F 6), and his questioning by Dido, though the gender of the speaker is left uncertain in the Latin. The exact location of the storm at sea in Naevius is also unclear and may have preceded an arrival either in Prochyta or in North Africa.

Lit.: Mariotti 1955, 38–39 (F 7); Serrao 1965 (F 7); Paratore 1970 (F 7); Scarsi 1987 (F 7).

7 (20 Bl.) Non., p. 474.5–9 M. = 760 L.

PERCONTA. Novius Malevolis . . . Naevius Belli Punici lib. II [*Merula*: I *codd.*]:

13 blande et docte percontat Aenea quo pacto
   Troiam urbem liquerit

  13 Aenea *Fleckeisen*: Aeneas *codd.*   14 liquerit *codd.*
Non., p. 335: reliquisset *codd. Non.*, p. 474

Cf. Non., pp. 334.38–35.4 M. = 527 L.

8 (24 Bl.) Macrob. *Sat.* 6.5.8 (ad Verg. *Aen.* 3.75. "quam pius Arquitenens")

hoc epitheto usus est Naevius belli Punici libro secundo:

15 deinde pollens sagittis inclitus arquitenens
   sanctus Iove prognatus Pythius Apollo

  16 sanctus *Vahlen*: sanctusque *codd.*   Iove *Buecheler*:
Delphis *codd.*

Cf. F 41.

9 (22 Bl.) Prisc., *GL* II, pp. 231.13–32.5

non est tamen ignorandum, quod etiam . . . hic et haec puer vetustissimi protulisse inveniuntur . . . Naevius in II belli Punici:

17 prima incedit Cereris Proserpina puer

7 Nonius

perconta ["ask"; active form for classical deponent]. Novius in *The Evil Men* (53/4 R[3]) . . . Naevius in *The Punic War*, Book 2:

> with charm and skill she [or: he?] asks how Aeneas 13
> left the city of Troy[1]

[1] The gender of the speaker is not given in the Latin, but the adverb *blande* ["with charm"] would suit a female, and the best candidate is Dido. Cf. Venus' description of Dido's charming words to Aeneas at Verg. *Aen.* 1.670–71: *hunc Phoenissa tenet Dido blandisque moratur / vocibus* ("Him Phoenician Dido holds back and delays with charming words"). For Dido's questioning of Aeneas on his escape from Troy, cf. Verg. *Aen.* 1.750–56. Naevius, like Virgil after him, could have seen in the disastrous love affair of Aeneas and Dido a prefiguration of the hatred between Rome and Carthage (see Mariotti 1955, 38–39).

8 Macrobius, *Saturnalia* (on Virgil, "whom the pious Archer [*Arquitenens*] God")

Naevius used this epithet [*Arquitenens*, "bow wielding"] in Book 2 of his *Punic War*:

> then mighty with arrows, the famous bow bearer, 15
> holy son of Jupiter, Pythian Apollo

Cf. F 41.

9 Priscian

One must not forget that . . . the oldest writers are found using *puer* ["child"; normally masculine "boy" in classical Latin] as both masculine and feminine . . . Naevius in Book 2 of *The Punic War*:

> first comes Proserpina, the child of Ceres 17

LIBER III (F 10–11)

*The reference to Amulius in F 10 shows that the book is set
in Italy and so deals with the final episode in the mytho-
logical inset on Aeneas' travels from Troy to Rome via
Carthage, which began in Book 1. Two fragments, F 10
and F 11, are assigned by the sources to Book 3. The first
refers to Amulius, the king of the Albans, thanking the gods
on some occasion. The second describes some favorable*

10 (26 Bl.) Non., p. 116.31–5 M. = 167 L.

GRATULARI, gratias agere . . . Naevius Belli Punici lib. III:

18   isque susum ad caelum sustulit suas:
      rex Amulius divis gratulabatur

18 isque *codd.*: manusque *Stephanus, Merula*   suas *sc.*
manus, *cf. Ennius, Inc. Ann. F 147 FRL*   18–19 suas
res / *codd.*: suas / rex *Mariotti*   19 rex *Stephanus, edd.*: res
codd.   Amulius *Bentinus*: ammulus *codd.*   divis gra-
tulabatur *Lindsay*: gratulabatur divis *codd.*

11 (25 Bl.) [Prob.] ad Verg. *Ecl.* 6.31 (vol. 3.2, p. 336.5–12
Th.-H.)

. . . quod poeta Ennius Anchisen augurium [*Skutsch:* -ii
codd.] ac per hoc divini quiddam habuisse praesumit
sic "doctus†que Anchisesque Venus quem pulcra dea-
rum / fari donavit, divinum pectus habere" [Enn. 1 *Ann.*
F 12 *FRL*]. Naevius belli Punici libro tertio sic:

BOOK III (F 10–11)

omen observed by Anchises and a sacrifice made by him perhaps shortly after his arrival in Italy with Aeneas, although the exact context for this fragment cannot be securely pinned down.

Lit.: M. Barchiesi 1963 (F 10); Morelli 1965; 1989 (F 10); Bettini 1981 (F 10).

F 10: The Alban king Amulius gives thanks to the gods.

10 Nonius

gratulari means "to give thanks" . . . Naevius in *The Punic War*, Book 3:

> and he raised his [hands] aloft to heaven: 18
> king Amulius gave thanks to the gods.

F 11: A good augury appears to Anchises, who institutes a sacrifice.

11 [Probus], *Commentary on Virgil*

. . . because the poet Ennius assumed that Anchises knew the art of augury and through this had something of the divine will. Thus [Enn. 1 *Ann.* F 12 *FRL*]: "learned Anchises, to whom Venus, splendid among goddesses, gave the gift of prophecy and a divine heart." So Naevius in Book 3 of *The Punic War*:

20   postquam avem aspexit in templo Anchisa,
      sacra in mensa Penatium ordine ponuntur;
      immolabat auream victimam pulchram.

Cf. Schol. Veron. ad Verg. *Aen*. 2.687 (vol. 3.2, p. 427.1–5 Th.-H.).

LIBER IV (F 12–16)

*With Book 4 the narrative returns to the First Punic War,
dealing with the events of the years around 257 BC. Five
fragments (F 12–16) are assigned by our sources to this
book. F 13 deals with the destruction by the Roman army
of the island of Malta. We know that this expedition was
led by C. Atilius Regulus, consul of 257 BC (see Cichorius
1922, 39, and cf. Orosius,* Hist. *4.8.5: "Atilius the consul
laid waste and destroyed the noble Sicilian islands of Li-*

12 (38 Bl.) Non., p. 76.3–5 M. = 106 L.

ATROX crudum. Naevius Belli Poenici lib. IV [IV *pars
codd., Strzelecki, Mariotti, Flores*: III *pars codd., Lindsay*]

23   simul atrocia proicerent exta ministratores

      proicerent *codd*.: porricerent *Iunius*

Cf. Paul. *Fest*., p. 17.11–12 L.

After Anchises observed a bird in the heaven's   20
     quadrant,
on the table of the Household Gods sacred offerings
     were placed in order;
he sprinkled[1] [for sacrifice] a beautiful golden[2] victim.

[1] The verb *immolare* refers technically to the sprinkling of a victim with salted meal (*mola salsa*) prior to sacrifice, rather than to the sacrifice itself.   [2] The adjective refers probably to the horns of the victim, covered in gold leaf before sacrifice, rather than to the color of the victim.

BOOK IV (F 12–16)

para and Malta"). The remaining fragments refer to military or religious actions which are too general to assign to any historical event. If in F 16 praetor *is taken in its technical sense, referring to a Roman magistrate, the only year in which the* praetor urbanus *held a military command was in 260 BC, but other interpretations of this word are possible.*

F 12: A description of a religious sacrifice.

12 Nonius

atrox means *crudus* ["raw"]. Naevius in *The Punic War*, Book Four[1]:

at the same time the attendants should throw forth   23
     the raw innards

[1] The manuscripts of Nonius are divided between Book 3 and Book 4, and this fragment could come from either. The sacrifice described could be as much at home in the military context of Book 4 as in the mythological context of Book 3. Most modern editors place it in Book 4.

13 (37 Bl.) Non., p. 90.24–27 M. = 129 L.

CONCINNARE conficere vel colligere. Naevius Belli Poe-
nici lib. IV:

24 transit Melitam
Romanus exercitus, insulam integram urit,
populatur, vastat, rem hostium concinnat

versus disposuit Leo (1905), p. 45 n. 4: alii aliter

14 (40 Bl.) Non., p. 97.13–19 M. = 138 L.

DANUNT dant . . . Naevius Belli Poenici lib. IV:

27 . . . eam carnem victoribus danunt

15 (41 Bl.) Non., p. 183.16–17 M. = 269 L.

VICISSATIM, per vices. Naevius Belli Punici lib. IV:

28 vicissatim volvi victoriam . . .

volvi *codd.*: volui *trisyll. vel* volvier *Lindsay*

F 13: The Roman army under C. Atilius Regulus crosses over to Malta and destroys the island [257 BC].

13 Nonius

concinnare ["to finish off"] means *conficere* ["to upset"] or *colligere* ["to appropriate"]. Naevius in *The Punic War*, Book 4:

> the Roman army 24
> crosses to Malta, burns the whole island,
> lays it waste, devastates it and finishes off the affairs
>   of the enemy

F 14: A victory feast. The exact context, public games or a military victory, remains uncertain.

14 Nonius

danunt [ante-classical form for classical] *dant* ["they give"] . . . Naevius in *The Punic War*, Book 4:

> . . . that meat they give to the victors 27

F 15: The report of a battle.

15 Nonius

vicissatim [ante-classical form] means *per vices* ["by turn," "from one to the other"]. Naevius in *The Punic War*, Book 4:

> that the victory rolls from one to the other . . . 28

F 16: The taking of auspices.

16 (39 Bl.) Non., p. 468.20–32 M. = 751 L.

AUSPICAVI pro auspicatus sum . . . Naevius Belli Poenici lib. IV:

29   virum praetor advenit, auspicat auspicium
      prosperum

> 29 virum *codd.*: verum *Iunius*   advenit *Merula*: adve-
> niet *codd.*: adveneit *Lindsay*

LIBER V

Ex libro V nulla fragmenta extant.

LIBER VI (F 17–20)

Four fragments have been assigned to this book. The source for them all is Nonius. Of these, F 20 seems to refer to Publius Claudius Pulcher, consul in 249 BC. F 17 refers to the renewal in 248 BC of the treaty of 263 BC between the Romans and Hiero of Syracuse. F 19 comes possibly

16 Nonius

auspicavi ["I took auspices"; ante-classical perfect active form] for *auspicatus sum* [perfect deponent form, normal in classical Latin] . . . Naevius in *The Punic War*, Book 4:

the leader[1] of men comes and takes auspicious   29
auspices

[1] Literally, "praetor." The word is probably not used in its technical sense of the magistrate known as the urban praetor, but simply means leader in its etymological sense of one who leads the way. Cichorius (1922, 32–33) and Altheim (1961, 102–3) interpret the word in its technical sense, referring to the military command of the urban praetor in 260 BC. Mariotti (2001, 67–70) takes *virum praetor* as a calque on the Homeric ἄναξ ἀνδρῶν, meaning "leader of men."

BOOK V

No fragments or testimonia have been transmitted that relate to this book.

BOOK VI (F 17–20)

from a council of the Carthaginians, talking about the Romans in the seventeenth year of the war [247 BC]. F 18 could refer to any Roman military operation against the Carthaginians at this period.

F 17: By the renewal in 248 BC of a treaty between the Romans and Hiero of Syracuse, Hiero is allowed to retain his kingdom.[1]

[1] See Cichorius 1922, 49–50.

17 (43 Bl.) Non., pp. 210.41–11.7 M. = 311 L.

LOCA . . . masculini [generis] . . . Naevius Belli Punici lib. VI:

31   convenit regnum simul atque locos ut haberent

18 (45 Bl.) Non., p. 267.17–21 M. = 408 L.

CENSERE significat existimare . . . Naevius Poenici Belli lib. VI:

32   censet eo venturum obviam Poenum

19 (44 Bl.) Non., p. 325.6–7 M. = 510 L.

ILICO, in eo loco. Naevius Belli Poenici lib. VI:

33   septimum decimum annum ilico sedent

F 20: The arrogant treatment of the legions described here probably refers to the actions of Publius Claudius Pulcher in 249 BC at Lilybaeum (cf. Diod. 24.3, and see Cichorius 1922, 45; Altheim 1961). Naevius, a native of Campania,

17 Nonius

loca ["places"; neut. pl.] . . . are of the masculine [gender] . . . in Naevius *The Punic War*, Book 6:

> it is agreed that they should retain their kingdom   31
> together with their lands

18 Nonius

censere means "to think" . . . Naevius in *The Punic War*, Book 6:

> he thinks that the Carthaginian will come[1] there to   32
> meet him

[1] The verb probably refers to coming together in battle, but could possibly indicate a more friendly meeting. The context is uncertain; various possibilities are discussed by Viredaz (2020, 300–302).

F 19: The year is 247 BC. The speaker must be Carthaginian, possibly in a council.

19 Nonius

ilico ["there"] means "in that place." Naevius in *The Punic War*, Book 6:

> this is the seventeenth year that they [the Romans]   33
> have been camped there

may have served under him in the legio Campana *("Campanian legion") at the disastrous naval battle of Drepanum in the same year (see Marmorale 1967, 27).*

20 (42 Bl.) Non., p. 515.8–11 M. = 828 L.

SUPERBITER . . . Naevius Belli Poenici lib. VI:

34   superbiter contemtim conterit legiones

Cf. Non., pp. 515.38–16.2 M. = 830 L.; Plaut. *Poen.* 537.

LIBER VII (F 21–22)

*The historical background to this book is provided by
F 21, which, although the text is corrupt, refers to the
treaty made by Q. Lutatius Catulus, consul of 241 BC,
with the Carthaginians after the Roman naval victory off
the Agates islands. F 22 probably refers to a Sicilian de-
mand for the return of hostages by the Romans. It is un-
clear whether the two fragments mentioned together by
Nonius come from the same context, and Book 7 is men-
tioned only in connection with the first. Whether F 22 re-
fers to the same treaty as F 21 or whether it goes back to
the treaty with Hiero in 248 BC (cf. F 17) and so possibly
belongs to Book 6 is a matter of debate. Flores (2014, 132–*

21 (47 Bl.) Non., p. 474.17–19 M. = 760 L.

PACISCUNT. Naevius Belli Poenici lib. VII:

20 Nonius

superbiter ["haughtily"; ante-classical for classical *superbe*]. . . . Naevius in *The Punic War*, Book 6:

> haughtily and contemptuously he wore down the 34
>   legions

BOOK VII (F 21–22)

33) argues for the first option, while Viredaz (2020, 298–300) prefers the second. Varro's statement, as reported by Gellius in t 6, that Naevius told in the Bellum Punicum *of his own participation in the First Punic War, probably belongs to this final seventh book. It had been a poetic practice, going back to the Greek Alexandrian period, for poets to include at the end of their work some personal information about themselves in a so-called "sphragis," or signature. This practice is followed in later Roman poetry by, for example, Virgil (Georg. 4.559ff.), Horace (Carm. 3.30), Propertius (1.22), and Ovid (Am. 3.15).*

F 21 The Carthaginians led by Hamilcar Barca agree to a preliminary pact with Q. Lutatius Catulus in 241 BC.[1]

[1] See Polyb. 1.62.8. This pact was subsequently rejected by the Roman assembly and replaced by one less favorable to the Carthaginians (see Polyb. 1.63.1–2).

21 Nonius

paciscunt ["they agree"]. Naevius in *The Punic War*, Book 7:

35   id quoque paciscunt, ut moenia sint quae
         Lutatium reconcilient, captivos plurimos

    35 ut moenia *Merula*: moenia *codd.*   36 reconcilient
Merula: reconciliant *codd.*

22 (46 Bl.) Non., pp. 474.17–21 M. = 760–61 L.

PACISCUNT. Naevius Belli Poenici lib. VII [F 21] . . . idem:

37   Sicilienses paciscit obsides ut reddant

BELLI PUNICI SEDIS INCERTAE FRAGMENTA (F 23–47)

*There remain a further twenty-four fragments that can be
assigned to* The Punic War *on the grounds of meter and
content, but where the source texts give no book number
and refer only to Naevius (marked *) or to Naevius in* The
Punic War *(marked **). Scholars differ as to whether F 30,
38, and 43 belong to the historical narrative of* The Punic
War *or to the mythological story of Aeneas. Mention of*

* = nominat Naevium; ** = nominat Naevium et Bellum Punicum
(sine libri numero)

> this they [the Carthaginians] also agree, in order that   35
>   their obligations should be
> such as to reconcile Lutatius, that they [should
>   return] many captives

22 Nonius

paciscunt ["they agree"]. Naevius in *The Punic War*, Book
7 [F 21] . . . the same:

> he[1] agrees that they [the Romans] should give back   37
>   their Sicilian hostages

[1] Whether the subject is the Lutatius Catulus of F 21, refer-
ring to the treaty of 241 BC, or some other Roman concerned
with the earlier treaty of 248 BC is unclear.

UNPLACED FRAGMENTS OF THE
BELLUM PUNICUM (F 23–47)

*elephants in F 23 makes it clear that the reference there is
to the Punic War, and the famine mentioned in F 42 is more
likely to refer to various episodes in the historical war
when either the Romans or the Carthaginians suffered this
fate.*

*   Lit.: Borghini 1979 (F 32); Bleckmann 1998 (F 34, 38);
Molinelli 2004 (F 47).*

*23 (55 Bl.) Varro, *Ling.* 7.39

apud Naevium:

38   atque prius pariet locusta Lucam bovem

Luca bos elephans. cur ita sit dicta, duobus modis inveni scriptum. nam et in Cornelii commentario erat ab Libycis Lucas, et in Vergilii ab Lucanis Lucas.

Cf. Isid. *Orig.* 12.2.14–15.

*24 (15 Bl.) Varro, *Ling.* 7.51

Naevius:

39   patrem suum supremum optumum appellat

supremum ab superrumo dictum.

*23 Varro, *On the Latin Language*

in Naevius:

> and sooner will a locust give birth to a Lucan cow[1]   38

A *Luca bos* ["Lucan cow"] means an elephant. Why it was called thus, I have found recorded in two ways. For in the commentary of Cornelius *Lucas* ["Lucan"] was derived from *Libyci* ["Libyans"] and in that of Vergilius *Lucas* was derived from *Lucani* ["Lucanians"].

[1] The fragment is generally scanned as a Saturnian and attributed to the *Bellum Punicum*. However, since it is also possible to scan it as an incomplete trochaic septenarius, a dramatic context, from comedy or tragedy, cannot be ruled out. The identity of the commentators mentioned by Varro, Cornelius, and Vergilius, is uncertain, and it is unclear which work they were commenting on. Lehmann (2002, 107–8) suggests that Cornelius could refer to the grammarian Cornelius Epicadus, a freedman of Sulla, and that Vergilius could refer to M. Vergilius, tribune of the plebs in 87 BC.

*24 Varro, *On the Latin Language*

Naevius:

> she [or: he?] calls upon her [or: his?][1] father, the   39
>   highest and best

supremum "highest" is derived from *superrumus*

[1] The subject is not marked for gender in the Latin and could be either masculine or feminine. It could describe Venus' appeal to Jupiter on behalf of the Trojans in Book 1 (cf. t 15, F 29). Certainly, the epithets "highest and best" are those customarily applied to Jupiter (known in Rome as *Optimus Maximus*), and he is the father of Venus.

*25 (31 Bl.) Caesius Bassus, *GL* VI, pp. 265.8–66.3

de saturnio versu dicendum est, quem nostri existimave-
runt proprium esse Italicae regionis, sed falluntur. a Grae-
cis enim varie et multis modis tractatus est, non solum a
comicis, sed etiam a tragicis. nostri autem antiqui, ut vere
dicam quod apparet, usi sunt eo non observata lege nec
uno genere custodito . . . apud Naevium poetam hos rep-
peri idoneos:

40   ferunt pulchras creterras aureas lepistas

pulchras creterras *Mar. Vict., Sacerd.*: pulchros pateras *Caes.*
Bass.   aureas *Sacerd.*: aereas *Caes. Bass.*: aureasque *Mar.*
Vict.

Cf. Mar. Vict., *GL* VI, p. 139.8; Mar. Plot. Sacerd., *GL* VI,
p. 531.7.

*26 (1 Bl.) Caesius Bassus, *GL* VI, pp. 265.8–66.3

de saturnio versu dicendum est, quem nostri existimave-
runt proprium esse Italicae regionis, sed falluntur. a Grae-
cis enim varie et multis modis tractatus est, non solum a
comicis, sed etiam a tragicis. nostri autem antiqui, ut vere
dicam quod apparet, usi sunt eo non observata lege nec
uno genere custodito . . . apud Naevium poetam hos rep-
peri idoneos . . . [F 25] et alio loco:

*25 Caesius Bassus

I must speak of the Saturnian meter, which our country-
men thought was native to the Italian region, but they are
mistaken. In fact, it was used by the Greeks in many and
various ways, not only by the comic poets, but also by the
tragedians. Our ancient poets, to speak truly what seems
clear, used this meter without observing fixed rules or
keeping to a single type . . . I have found these suitable
examples in Naevius:

> they carry beautiful bowls and golden drinking cups[1]   40

[1] The passage could refer to the reception of the Trojans by
Dido in Carthage (Book 2). Alternatively, it could refer to the
rescue of valuable objects from the flames of Troy (Book 1). The
words for "bowl" (*creterra*) and "drinking cup" (*lepista*) are Greek
loanwords, a rarity in Naevius (see Barchiesi 1962, 366; Feeney
2016, 72). On *creterra* see Trag. F 41 n. 1 and cf. *Equus Troia-
nus* t 1.

*26 Caesius Bassus

I must speak of the Saturnian meter, which our country-
men thought was native to the Italian region, but they are
mistaken. In fact, it was used by the Greeks in many and
various ways, not only by the comic poets, but also by the
tragedians. Our ancient poets, to speak truly what seems
clear, used this meter without observing fixed rules or
keeping to a single type . . . I have found these suitable
examples in Naevius . . . [F 25] and in another place:

41   novem Iovis concordes filiae sorores

   novem *in marg.*: navem *codd.*

Cf. Hes. *Theog.* 60–61; Mar. Vict., *GL* VI, p. 139.10, 29; Ter.
Maur., *GL* VI, p. 400.2514.

**27 (30 Bl.) Gell. *NA* 5.12.6–7

Iovis Diiovis dictus est et Lucetius, quod nos die et luce
quasi vita ipsa afficeret et iuvaret. [7]

42   Lucetium

autem Iovem Cn. Naevius in libris Belli Poenici appellat.

Cf. Serv. ad Verg. *Aen.* 9.567.

you[1] nine concordant sisters, daughters of Jupiter[2]   41

[1] It is assumed the Muses are being addressed (vocative) in an invocation, but the case could be either vocative or nominative. If nominative, it is impossible to determine the context.

[2] Possibly from an appeal to the Muses by Naevius at the beginning of his work (see the discussion at Book 1). However, such addresses are not restricted to the opening of works in Homer (cf. *Il.* 2.491–92) and Hesiod (cf. *Theog.* 964, 1022). Livius Andronicus addressed his Muse in the opening of his *Odysseia* (*Od.* F 1 *FRL*) as *Camena* in the singular. Naevius' Muses are plural. Whether he called them *Camenae* or *Musae* we do not know, but Terentianus Maurus (*GL* VI, p. 400.2514: "as when some writer refers to the *Camenae* as nine sisters") suggests he may have used *Camenae*. Naevius' "nine concordant sisters, daughters of Jupiter" is very close to Hesiod's reference to the nine like-minded daughters born by Mnemosyne to Zeus (Hes. *Theog.* 60–61: "[Mnemosyne] bore nine daughters, all of one mind [cf. "concordant"], whose hearts were set upon song").

**27 Gellius, *Attic Nights*

Jove was called *Diiovis* and *Lucetius* ["light bringer"] because he blesses and helps us with day and light, as if with life itself.

light bringer[1]   42

is what Cn. Naevius calls Jupiter in his books on *The Punic War*

[1] The context of this reference to Jove as "light bringer" is uncertain.

**28 (57 Bl.) Fest., p. 158.7–10 L.

‹N›EMUT nisi etiam vel ‹nempe. Naevius in carmine Bell›i Punici [*suppl. Scaliger*]:

43   nemut . . . aerumnas

Cf. Paul. *Fest.*, p. 159.3 L.

**29 (16 Bl.) Fest., p. 306.25–28 L.

QUIANAM pro quare et cur positum est apud antiquos, ut Naevium in carmine Punici belli:

44   summe deum regnator, quianam genus odisti?

genus odisti *Leo 1905, 47n2*: genus isti *cod.*: genuisti *Scaliger*: me genuisti *Havet*

*30 (54 Bl.) Paul. *Fest.*, p. 333.2–3 L.

RUMITANT rumigerantur. Naevius:

45   simul alius aliunde rumitant inter se

se *Augustinus, Leo 1905, 30n10*: sese *codd.*

Cf. Fest., p. 332.6–8 L.

**28 Festus

‹n›emut means "unless indeed" or ‹"indeed." Naevius in his song› of *The Punic War*:

> unless indeed . . . troubles 43

**29 Festus

The word *quianam* is placed for *quare* and *cur* [all meaning "why?"] by the ancients, as for example Naevius in his song of *The Punic War*:

> highest ruler of the gods, why then do you hate my 44
> race?[1]

[1] Probably an appeal by Venus to Jupiter on behalf of the storm-tossed Trojans in Book 1 (cf. t 15 and F 24). The first half of the line may be based on the Homeric ὕπατε κρειόντων ("highest of the gods"), used at *Od.* 1.45, by Pallas Athene in an address to her father, Zeus (see Feeney 2016, 164–65). The word "hate" is conjectural; the reading of the manuscripts is corrupt.

*30 Paul the Deacon, *Epitome of Festus*

rumitant, they exchange rumors. Naevius:

> at the same time they exchange rumors among 45
> themselves, from here and there[1]

[1] Perhaps from the historical section describing either the worries of the soldiers or the reaction of the Senate in Rome.

**31 (58 Bl.) Fest., p. 406.8–15 L.

SUPPARUS ⟨puellare dicebatu⟩r vestimen⟨tum lineum, quod et s⟩ubucula ap⟨pellabatur. . . . :

46   ⟨sup⟩parum

puni⟨ceum vestimentum ita vo⟩cat Naevius de ⟨bello Puni⟩co

  sic suppl. Scaliger et Ursinus

Cf. Paul. *Fest.*, p. 407.6–7 L.

*32 (50 Bl.) Fest., p. 418.8–16 L.

STUPRUM pro turpitudine antiquos dixisse apparet . . . Naevius:

47   seseque ei perire mavolunt ibidem
   quam cum stupro redire ad suos popularis

  47 ei *Scaliger, Ursinus*: i *cod.*

Cf. Paul. *Fest.*, p. 419.1–2 L.

*33 (51 Bl.) Fest., p. 418.8–18 L.

STUPRUM pro turpitudine antiquos dixisse apparet . . . Naevius [F 32] . . . item:

49   sin illos deserant fortissimos viros
   magnum stuprum populo fieri per gentis

Cf. *Dub. Nom.*, *GL* V, p. 591.12–13.

---

[1] Possibly a speech in a political assembly. As in F 32, the context could be Regulus' speech before the Senate in 255 BC,

**31 Festus

supparus ["tunic"] <was the name for an item of girl's linen> clothing, <which was also called> *subacula* ["under-tunic"]. . . . :

> a tunic 46

Naevius names in this way [*supparus*] <a Carthaginian garment in his *Punic War*>.[1]

[1] The text of Festus is very corrupt, and the attribution to the *Bellum Punicum* relies on conjectural readings. Cf. *Com.* F 50.

*32 Festus

It is clear that the ancients used the word *stuprum* ["disgrace"] for shamefulness . . . Naevius:

> and they prefer to perish on the spot 47
> than to return with shame to their fellow countrymen[1]

[1] This could come from almost any battle context. Bleckmann (1998, 65–67) suggests a speech before the Senate by Regulus after his defeat in 255 BC.

*33 Festus

It is clear that the ancients used the word *stuprum* ["disgrace"] for shamefulness . . . Naevius [F 32] . . . and again:

> but if they should desert them, those bravest of men, 49
> there would be great shame for the people
> throughout the nations[1]

but there can be no certainty about this, and the fragment would fit a number of wartime contexts.

*34 (35 Bl.) Paul. *Fest.*, p. 425.4–8 L.

SAGMINA dicebant herbas verbenas, quia ex loco sancto carpebantur [*Mercklin*: arcebantur *codd.*] legatis proficiscentibus ad foedus faciendum bellumque indicendum; vel a sanciendo, id est confirmando. Naevius:

51   scopas atque verbenas sagmina sumpserunt

   scopas *Scaliger*: scapos *vel* scapas *codd.*

Cf. Fest., pp. 424.34–26.4 L.; Serv. Dan. ad Verg. *Aen*. 12.120.

**35 (56 Bl.) Fest., p. 428.33–36 L.

‹SARRARE › [*Tovar 1968*: sardare *cod., epit. Pauli*] intellegere . . . ‹Nae›vius Belli Pu‹nici libro [*suppl. ex epit. Pauli*]:

52   quo›d bruti nec satis ‹sarrare queunt›

   suppl. ex epit. Pauli   sarrare *Varro, Ling. 7.108, Tovar 1968*: sardare *cod. et epit. Pauli*

Cf. Paul. *Fest.*, p. 429.8–9 L.

---

¹ This form is conjectural, based on the same form at Varro *Ling.* 7.108. The manuscripts of Festus and Paul the Deacon have *sardare* (which would be a *hapax legomenon*), which is probably

*34 Paul the Deacon, *Epitome of Festus*

They used the term *sagmina* ["sacred tufts"] for vervain herbs because they were gathered from a sacred place when ambassadors were setting out to make a treaty or to declare war; or from *sancire* ["sanctify"], that is confirming. Naevius:

> they took twigs and vervain as sacred tufts[1]   51

[1] Perhaps from a description of the formal declaration of war on the Carthaginians in Book 1. Priests named *fetiales* represented the Roman people in their dealings with other nations. By holding a bunch of sacred herbs, they were made inviolable. Historically, the declaration of the First Punic War took place in the year 264 BC (see the discussion at Book 1). In addition to being appropriate for a declaration of war, the fragment would also suit contexts of treaty making (so Schwarte 1972), such as in 263 BC with Hiero of Syracuse or in 241 BC with the Carthaginians.

**35 Festus

Naevius uses ‹*sarrare*[1] to mean› "understand" in his ‹book› of *The Punic War*:

> because[2] they are brutish and ‹cannot understand›   52
> enough[3]

based on an error by Paul, who may have connected the word wrongly with the Sardinians.   [2] *quod* is translated here as a conjunction ["because"], but it could also be a relative ["a thing which"].   [3] Possibly a description of the early inhabitants of Italy, from the mythological section in Book 3, or of primitive tribes met earlier in the voyage from Troy (cf. F 3). However, contexts from the historical section of the epic cannot be ruled out.

*36 (60 Bl.) Fest., p. 482.7–11 L.

TOPPER significare ait Artorius[1] cito . . . citius; sic C⟨n.⟩ Naevi⟨us⟩:

53   . . . ⟨topper⟩ capesset flammam Volcani

Cn. Naevi: . . . topper capesset *Vahlen 1854*: C. naevicapesset *cod.*   flammam *cod.*: flamma *Havet*

[1] Cf. Funaioli 1907, 481 F 3.

**37 (32 Bl.) Non., pp. 197.12–17 M. = 289–90 L.

CASTITAS et CASTIMONIA generis feminini. masculini . . . Naevius carmine Punici Belli:

54   res divas edicit, praedicit castus

*38 (59 Bl.) Non., p. 214.7–8 M. = 315 L.

METUS masculino. feminino Naevius:

55   magnae metus tumultus pectora possidit

magnae *Lindsay*: magni *codd.*

---

[1] The anxieties described could come from either the mythological or the historical section of the epic. The expression is too general for a more precise context to be identified.

*36 Festus

topper Artorius[1] says means "quickly" . . . More quickly;
thus Cn. Naevius:

> . . . <more quickly> it will take Vulcan's flame[2]   53

[1] Probably the rhetorician C. Artorius Proculus, a late first-
century BC source for Verrius Flaccus on rare lexical items, men-
tioned by Quintilian at *Inst.* 9.1.2 (see Funaioli 1907, 480–81).

[2] The meter of this line is not easily identified as the text is
corrupt, so that it could come from either a dramatic or an epic
context. The propagation of fire would perhaps better fit military
contexts, and so an attribution to *The Punic War* seems more
likely; however, a tragic reference to the burning of Lycurgus'
palace by Liber (cf. *Trag.* F 24 and 39) cannot be ruled out.

**37 Nonius

The words *castitas* ["chastity"] and *castimonia* ["chaste-
ness"] are feminine in gender. Naevius in his song of *The
Punic War* uses the masculine [*castus* = "rules of chastity";
a rare and mainly ante-classical form]:

> he declares sacred matters, he proclaims rules of   54
> chastity[1]

[1] Possibly a reference to the leading role of Anchises in reli-
gious matters, although other contexts are possible.

*38 Nonius

metus ["fear"] in the masculine gender. In the feminine
gender [an ante-classical usage] Naevius:

> a tumult of great fear takes possession of their hearts[1]   55

**39 (52 Bl.) Donat. ad Ter. *Andr.* 55

PLERIQUE OMNES ἀρχαϊσμὸς est. nam errat, qui "pleri-que" παρέλκον intellegit, aut qui subdistinguit "plerique" et sic infert "omnes." hoc enim pro una parte orationis dixerunt veteres eodem modo, quo Greaci πάμπολλα et Latini "plus satis." Naevius in bello Punico:

56   plerique omnes subiguntur sub unum iudicium

*40 (5 Bl.) Serv. Dan. ad Verg. *Aen.* 3.10

"litora cum patriae lacrimans": amat poeta quae legit im-mutata aliqua parte vel personis ipsis verbis proferre. Nae-vius enim inducit uxores Aeneae et Anchisae cum lacrimis Ilium relinquentes his verbis:

57   amborum uxores
        noctu Troiad exibant capitibus opertis,
        flentes ambae abeuntes lacrimis cum multis

    58 Troiad *Vossius*: Toiade *codd.*

**39 Donatus, Commentary on Terence

plerique omnes ["almost all"] is an archaism. For whoever thinks *plerique* is superfluous is wrong, as is the man who separates off *plerique* and emphasizes *omnes*. For the ancients used *plerique omnes* as a single part of speech in the same way as the Greeks use πάμπολλα ["very many"] and the Romans *plus satis* ["more than enough"]. Naevius in *The Punic War*:

> almost all are brought under a single judgement[1]   56

[1] Possibly describing the outcome of a council of war or meeting of the Senate.

*40 Servius Danielis, *Commentary on Virgil*

"when in tears [I leave] my country's shores": our poet likes to reproduce what he has read with some changes in wording or even of the characters speaking. For Naevius introduces the wives of Aeneas and Anchises leaving Troy in tears with these words:

> the wives of both   57
> left Troy at night with their heads covered,
> both weeping as they went away with many tears[1]

[1] This fragment refers to the wives of Aeneas and Anchises leaving Troy. Although Servius Danielis gives no book number, the context is the flight from Troy in the mythical excursus in Book 1 (cf. F 2). Virgil makes no mention in his *Aeneid* narrative of Anchises' wife. His son Aeneas was the product of his affair with the goddess Venus.

*41 (62 Bl.) Macrob. *Sat.* 6.5.8 (ad Verg. *Aen.* 3.75: "quam pius Arquitenens")

hoc epitheto usus est Naevius belli Punici libro secundo [F 8]: . . . idem alibi:

60   cum tu arquitenens, sagittis pollens dea

> dea *codd.*: dea deana *Fleckeisen*: deana *Buecheler*

**42 (49 Bl.) Prisc., *GL* II, pp. 152.17–53.8

ACER et . . . , quamvis "acris' et . . . plerumque faciant . . . feminina, in utraque tamen terminatione communis etiam generis inveniuntur prolata. . . . Naevius in carmine belli Punici:

61   fames acer augescit hostibus . . .

Cf. Prisc., *GL* II, pp. 229.20–30.4.

**43 (23 Bl.) Prisc., *GL* II, pp. 235.20–36.1

invenitur tamen etiam simplex DECOR DECORIS paenultima correpta apud vetustissimos . . . Naevius in carmine belli Punici:

62   magnam domum decoremque ditem vexerant

aliter enim iambus stare non potest.

Cf. Mai 1836, 165.

---

1 Possibly a reference to the pillaging by the Romans of the temple of Aphrodite at Eryx in 244 BC (Polyb. 2.7.10; cf. Cichorius 1922, 52–54; Altheim 1961, 115–17). Alternatively, M. Barchiesi (1962, 538–39), replacing *ditem* ["rich'] with *Ditem* ["Dis," god of the underworld], sees a reference in the mythological section to his horses carrying back (*vexerant*) Dis to his home (*domum*),

*41 Macrobius, *Saturnalia* (on Virgil, "whom the pious Archer [*Arquitenens*] God")

Naevius used this epithet [*Arquitenens*, "bow wielding"] in Book 2 of his *Punic War* [F 8]: . . . And the same author [uses it] elsewhere:

> when you, archer goddess, powerful with your   60
> arrows[1]

[1] A reference to Diana in some unknown context.

**42 Priscian

acer ["keen"] and . . ., although they frequently produce *acris* and . . . as feminines, are still found in use also expressing the common gender in both terminations. . . . Naevius in the song of *The Punic War*:

> keen hunger [*acer* as fem.] grows for the enemy[1] . . .   61

[1] This could come from any of a number of siege narratives in the epic. Cichorius (1922, 29–30) sees a reference to Hannibal's troops being besieged by the Romans at Agrigentum in 262 BC.

**43 Priscian

The simple form *decor, decoris* ["beautiful"] is found in very old writers with the penultimate syllable short . . . Naevius in the song of *The Punic War*:

> they had carried away the great dwelling, beautiful   62
> and rich[1]

Otherwise the iambic foot would not scan.

possibly after the council of the gods in Book 1. Priscian's mention of an iambic foot suggests he may have considered this a fragment from drama and not from the epic in Saturnians.

**44 (36 Bl.) Prisc., *GL* II, p. 249.3–7

hic et haec Samnis, huius Samnitis . . . huius neutrum Naevius SAMNITE protulit in carmine belli Punici:

63 Samnite

Cf. Prisc., *GL* II, p. 338.2.

**45 (9 Bl.) Prisc., *GL* II, pp. 351.25–52.5

inveni MARUM pro "marium," qui tamen in rarost usu genetivus, apud Naevium in carmine belli Punici:

64 senex fretus pietati deum adlocutus
   summi deum regis fratrem Neptunum
66 regnatorem marum

  64 pietati *vel* pietate *codd.*: pietatei *Vahlen*

**46 (48 Bl.) Isid. *Nat. rer.* 44.3

FLUSTRA sunt motus maris sine tempestate fluctuantis velut Naevius in bello Punico sic ait:

67 onerariae onustae stabant in flustris

ut si diceret in salo.

Cf. Paul. *Fest.*, p. 79.11–12 L.

---

[1] Possibly a description of the Roman fleet sent to reinforce Roman troops besieging Lilybaeum in 249 BC (cf. Polyb. 1.53–54) and destroyed by the Carthaginians. Other naval contexts from the war narrative are possible.

**44 Priscian

Samnis ["Samnite"] in the nominative masculine and feminine, the genitive is *Samnitis*. The neuter of this word Naevius wrote as *Samnite* in his song of *The Punic War*.

Samnite   63

**45 Priscian

I have found *marum* ["of the seas"; genitive plural] for *marium*, a form of the genitive (plural) which is rare nevertheless, in Naevius in his song of *The Punic War*:

the old man[1] reliant on his piety addressed the god,   64
Neptune, the brother of the highest king of the gods,
ruler of the seas   66

[1] Possibly a reference to a prayer to the sea god by old Anchises before or after the voyage from Troy, in the mythical section of the book (see the discussion at Book 1). Other contexts for a prayer by Anchises to Neptune (e.g., the storm at sea, cf. t 15; a safe arrival in Africa or Italy) are also possible. Even an address to Neptune by some senior figure (*senex*) in the military narrative of *The Punic War* cannot be ruled out.

**46 Isidore, *On the Nature of Things*

flustra ["calm water"] means the motion of the sea as it undulates when there is no storm, as Naevius says in his *Punic War*:

the loaded merchant ships stood in the calm water[1]   67

as if he said at sea.

*47 (19 Bl.) Isid. *Orig.* 19.22.20

CITROSA, quasi concrispa ad similitudinem citri. Naevius:

68   pulchraque ‹vasa› ex auro vestemque citrosam

      vasa *suppl. Reichardt*

Cf. Macrob. *Sat.* 3.19.5; Paul. *Fest.*, p. 37.19 L.

*47 Isidore, *Origins*

citrosa ["citrus scented"], as if "curled" like citrus wood.
Naevius:

> and beautiful <vases> from gold and citrus-scented[1]   68
>   clothing[2]

[1] The interpretation of *citrosus* as "citron-scented" in Naevius
is given by Macrobius, *Saturnalia* 3.19.5. Cf. Paul. *Fest.*, p. 37.19
L.   [2] Perhaps a list of items either saved from Troy or pil-
laged by the Greeks (cf. Verg. *Aen.* 2.763–66). Others see it as a
list of costly items rescued from Troy and given to Dido as a gift
by Aeneas (cf. Verg. *Aen.* 1.647–56); cf. F 25.

CAECILIUS

INTRODUCTION

LIFE AND NAME

Of the life of Caecilius we know little for certain. Jerome dates the peak of his career in 179 BC (T 18), which would suggest a birthdate in the late 220s, and asserts he was an Insubrian Gaul, reportedly from Milan. Gellius claims that in earlier times "Statius" was a "slave name" (*servile nomen*) and that therefore the poet was originally called "Statius" (T 16). Combining these reports, many scholars have favored the idea that the poet was a war captive, taken during Roman military activities in the north, although two quite different reconstructions have been offered. During an earlier campaigning phase, Rome temporarily took control of Milan in 222.[1] If captured and enslaved then to a Roman of the *gens* Caecilius, the future poet would have been at most a very young child. Later fighting led to the final seizure and dissolution of Gallic control of Milan in 194,[2] and a Gaul of fighting age could certainly have been taken prisoner in those years. Gellius is wrong to imply, however, that Statius is solely a slave name even in the days of the middle Republic. It is well

[1] Polybius 2.34.15. According to Livy 5.34 Gallic invaders had founded Milan in 391 BC.
[2] Livy 34.46.1.

attested as a Samnite name, and Robson (1938) has argued that it is more plausible that the future poet was born to an Oscan-speaking family (possibly relocated to settle in the north as the Gauls were being pushed out), later coming to Rome under the patronage of a Caecilius, rather than as a native Gallic speaker, learning Latin only as an enslaved adult and yet quickly becoming one of Rome's leading comic poets. Cicero claims that Caecilius spoke Latin "badly" (T 5, *male*), but is nonetheless ready to call him "perhaps" the greatest of the comic poets (T 6, *fortasse*). Differing presumptions about ethnicity and ease of language acquisition compete here (Oscan, the language of the Samnites, is closely related to Latin, unlike any Gallic dialect), and certainty is not possible.

Almost all our sources from the beginning name the poet simply as Caecilius, although our second oldest, Volcacius Sedigitus, a scholar-poet writing at the beginning of the first century BC, calls him Caecilius Statius (T 2). Gellius further asserts that the name Statius, imposed by an owner on the enslaved man, only later became a kind of cognomen (T 17, *quasi*), though elsewhere he too names the poet simply as Caecilius (T 18). Only Jerome in his *Chronicle* names him as "Statius Caecilius" (T 19), otherwise dubbing him simply Caecilius (T 20). The mobility of the name, now nomen, now cognomen, argues for its non-Latin origin.

Once at Rome, Caecilius became a close comrade of Ennius (T 19, *contubernalis*); indeed, if we take the word in its root sense of soldiers bunking together, it would imply that the older and the younger poets shared their living space for a time. Warmington even speculates that Caecilius chose to specialize in comedy because his friend

Ennius excelled in tragedy.[3] The actor / manager L. Ambivius Turpio, in the prologue speech to Terence's *Hecyra*, claims he supported the poet's early career when some of Caecilius' plays were driven off the stage or gained a hearing only with difficulty (T 1).[4] In his later career, however, Caecilius was clearly Rome's leading comic poet, even if there are historical problems with Suetonius' story that the young Terence was required to read his first play to the aged Caecilius before the aediles would accept the play for staging (T 13).

This anecdote of poetic succession, a story pattern beloved in ancient biographical traditions, conflicts with the accepted chronology for the successive deaths of Ennius and Caecilius. Jerome tells us that Caecilius died just a year after his older friend Ennius (T 19),[5] and Cicero places the death of Ennius in 169 BC.[6] Terence's first play,

---

[3] Warmington 1938, xxvii: "thus the two poets were able to be friends without being rivals in the same sphere." Ennius wrote a very few comedies (Ennius, *Comedies* F 1–6 *FRL*). On the other hand, they may simply have needed to share living expenses, as some sources including Cic. *Sen.* 14 (= Ennius T 33 *FRL*) indicate Ennius endured poverty in his old age.

[4] Some would attribute this to the allegedly poor quality of his Latin (perhaps while still mastering the language if we accept the adult enslavement narrative?), but the fragments themselves do not bear this out.

[5] Ritschl (1845, 183 n.) argues from Cicero's failure to list Caecilius among the *longaevi* that he was not of the same generation as Ennius.

[6] Cic. *Brut.* 78 (= Ennius T 19 *FRL*) and Cic. *Sen.* 14 (= Ennius T 33 *FRL*), i.e., in the consulship of Quintus Marcius Philippus and Gnaeus Servilius Caepio. Jerome's chronology, however,

The Woman of Andros, was staged at the *Ludi Megalenses* of 166 BC.[7] The aediles who bought Terence's play for the games were not yet in office before Caecilius died. It is certainly not impossible that the younger poet might have met and even shared some of his work with Caecilius before the latter's death, but Caecilius cannot have been the official arbiter of what was staged in 166. He was buried near the Janiculum.

WORKS AND RECEPTION

Fragments attributed to Caecilius are associated with some forty titles in our sources, although a few of these may be variant titles for a single play, notably *Hypobolimaeus ("The Changeling")*. Caecilius seems to have looked particularly to Menander for models; sixteen of his play titles are among those attested for Menander, thirteen of them known only for Menander among the poets of Greek New Comedy. Latin titles such as *Exul ("The Exile")*, *Meretrix ("The Prostitute")*, *Portitor ("The Customs Officer")*, and *Triumphus ("The Triumph")* look back to the style of Plautus, although only one, *Rastraria ("A Play about a Hoe")*, and that reported as an alternate or additional title

places the death of Ennius in 168 BC (*Ab Abr.* 1849, p. 140a Helm = Ennius T 99 *FRL*). Reggiani (1977) argues for the possibility of placing the death of Ennius even later.

[7] *didascalia Andria*: *acta ludis megalensibvs M. Fulvio M'. Glabrione aedilibus curulibus . . . facta I M. Marcello C. Sulpicio cos.* ("acted at the Megalensian Games in the curule aedileship of Marcus Fulvius and Manius Glabrio . . . [his] first play, in the consulship of Marcus Marcellus and Gaius Sulpicius").

for a *Hypobolimaeus* ("*The Changeling*"), uses the pattern very frequent in Plautus and other earlier comic poets (cf. *Asinaria*, *Vidularia*, and Naevius' *Carbonaria*). Other titles come from Greek character names (*Davus*, *Hymnis*), Greek loan words such as *Epicleros* ("*The Heiress*"), *Epistathmos* ("*The Quartermaster*"), *Plocium* ("*The Necklace*"), and even a Greek phrase, *Exhautuhestos* ("*A Legend in His Own Mind*"), and look forward to the usages of Terence. Though no single source gives both titles, it seems very likely that one of his plays was known both as *Obolostates* as well as *Faenerator* ("*The Moneylender*"). While Greek names and terms among Caecilius' preserved titles may seem to point forward toward Terence's practices and away from Plautus (whose only Greek titles are personal names), such titles are also well represented in the remains of Naevius' comedies; so, no straight line of evolution in the practices of the *comoedia palliata* can be drawn.

While almost none of Caecilius' plots can be reconstructed in any detail, transmitting authors give us some sense for three of his titles. Aulus Gellius' comparison of Caecilius' *Plocium* ("*The Necklace*") with its Menandrian source material provided the only detailed insight into Roman comedy's methods of adaptation until the discovery of the papyrus with remnants of Menander's *Dis Exapaton* ("*Twice a Swindler*") F 1 (LCL 132: 148–68). Gellius provides us with the longest fragments of *Plocium*, but we would not be able to guess much of its apparently familiar plot of rape, recognition, and generational tensions without Gellius' summary. So too for the *Hypobolimaeus* ("*The Changeling*"), which is likely one play, though perhaps two or three with similar titles, and the *Synephebi* ("*Fellow Recruits*"), for both of which Cicero's comments along with his quotations suggest plots with young men deceiving their fathers for money to finance their erotic enterprises.

Familiar comic devices attested by individual fragments suggest other standard plot elements, but do not suffice to reconstruct wholes. The *Carine* (*"The Carian Woman"* or *"The Carian Mourner"*) included a recognition by tokens; we guess the title item of *Plocium* (*"The Necklace"*) had the same function, but no fragment shows that. Both *Fallacia* (*"Deceit"*) and *Imbrii* (*"Imbrians"*) may have had a double plot, in the case of the latter based on a plot summary for the likely Menandrian original.

Other fragments show the presence of familiar comedy character types: e.g., the parasite in *Asotus* (*"The Libertine"*) F 7, the cook in *Chrysion* F 1, the domineering Roman *matrona* in *Plocium* (*"The Necklace"*) F 1, and both harsh (F *Inc.* 2) and indulgent (*Synephebi* / *"Fellow Recruits"* F 1) fathers. The title characters of *Chrysion* and *Hymnis* were hetaeras. Slaves feature in most plays, often threatened with familiar violence—for instance in *Fallacia* (*"Deceit"*) F 6 and F 7, *Harpazomene* (*"The Ravished Woman"*) F 3—but there is evidence for characters playing against type, such as the slave in love in *Syracusii* (*"Syracusans"*) F 2 and Saturnalian inversion of masters and slaves in *Symbolum* (*"The Token"*) F 1.

Some structural features can be inferred. Several fragments have been claimed to be part of Caecilian prologues, often simply for containing background narrative. The likeliest example may be *Plocium* (*"The Necklace"*) F 14, where a joking reference to an "actor's augury" might fit well in a prologue negotiating to win the audience's goodwill for the coming performance. Other fragments hint at metatheatrical self-consciousness, as when a character in an unknown play (F *Inc*. 9a) compares himself to "all the old fools in comedies." *Titthe* (*"The Wet Nurse"*) F 6 sounds like preparation for an eavesdropping scene, perhaps even functioning as a miniature play-within-the-play.

Caecilius certainly enjoyed and employed the humor of particularly Roman references in the Greekish Caeciliopolis he fashioned for the plays' action. The sole F 1 of *Exhautuhestos* (*"A Legend in His Own Mind"*) describes characters acting like a troop of gladiators. A number of these Roman touches are particularly military, e.g., the oak crown (F *Inc*. 17), a decury in *Asotus* (*"The Libertine"*) F 6, and recruitment to fill out a century in *Triumphus* (*"The Triumph"*) F 2. Indeed, a play entitled *The Triumph*, even if metaphorical for a more domestic victory, must have sounded particularly Roman for a *comoedia palliata*.

Caecilius was valued for varying qualities after his lifetime. Cicero both disparaged the quality of his Latin (T 5; cf. F *Inc*. 10 with Cicero's remarks to Atticus) and praised him as perhaps the Romans' best comic poet (T 6). Horace lauded his substance in comparison to Terence's artistry (T 10), while Varro singled out both Caecilius' superiority in plotting (T 8) and ability to arouse emotion in the audience (T 9). Quintilian approved of drama along with other literature as a pleasurable variation in oratory (T 14) but thought Roman comedy fell far short of Athenian and put a little distance between himself and earlier authorities who had praised Caecilius (T 15).

The earliest preserved critical ranking of Roman comic poets, by Volcacius Sedigitus, firmly places Caecilius first (T 2), ahead of Plautus and several rungs above Terence. Others later concurred in this high evaluation. Deufert (2002, 71–74), however, has pointed out that Volcacius sharply divides his list between the lower ranking poets and the first three, who, moreover, appear in reverse chronological order. In addition to picking up on Hellenistic scholarship that ranked Greek dramatists (in part based on didascalic records of victories), the initial triad of Naevius, Plautus, and Caecilius may also reflect a notion that Naevius was the innovator of comedy at Rome, Plautus the great developer of the art in the next generation, and Caecilius the culmination of the form, from which subsequent poets declined. Later, Terence would often muscle his way into the first rank. Deufert also notes that Cicero quotes Caecilius four times more often than Plautus (and all but one Plautus quotation from the same moralizing play, *Trinummus*), but Terence twice as often as Caecilius, perhaps reflecting the interest in these poets by more elite readers in the late Republic. The career of the actor Roscius shows Plautus was still being staged in the last century BC, but we have no hard evidence of performances of Caecilius by then.

THE ARRANGEMENT OF
MATERIAL IN THIS EDITION

The fragments of the comedies of Caecilius are presented in alphabetical order of title, individually numbered thereunder, following the edition of Guardì 1974. The title of his *Carine* ("The Carian Woman" or "The Carian Mourner"), given thus in the transmitting sources, is alphabetized in this form. Fragments from plays of unknown title (*Incerta*) follow in chronological order of the source text. One fragment identified by Guardì (2001) after the publication of his edition is here numbered F *Inc*. 44.

TESTIMONIA (T 1–20)

T 1 Ter. *Hec*. 14–23

      in eis quas primum Caecili didici novas
15   partim sum earum exactus, partim vix steti.
      quia scibam dubiam fortunam esse scaenicam,
      spe incerta certum mihi laborem sustuli,
      easdem agere coepi ut ab eodem alias discerem
      novas, studiose ne illum ab studio abducerem.
20   perfeci ut spectarentur: ubi sunt cognitae,
      placitae sunt. ita poetam restitui in locum
      prope iam remotum iniuria advorsarium
      ab studio atque ab labore atque arte musica.

T 2 (= T 4 Ennius; T 10 Naevius) Volcacius Sedigitus, *Carm.* F 1 *FPL*[4] (p. 113), ap. Gell. *NA* 15.24

Sedigitus in libro, quem scripsit de poetis, quid de his sentiat, qui comoedias fecerunt, et quem ex omnibus praestare ceteris putet ac deinceps, quo quemque in loco et honore ponat, his versibus suis demonstrat:

TESTIMONIA (T 1–20)

T 1 Terence, *The Mother-in-Law*

(actor/manager Ambivius Turpio speaking) When I first put on new plays by Caecilius, I was driven off the stage in some of them and struggled to hold my ground in others. I realized that a theatrical career was a precarious one; success was uncertain, and the only certainty was toil. But I set myself to revive these same plays in order to obtain other new ones from the same author; I was very eager that he should not be discouraged from his profession. I managed to get the plays performed, and, once they were known, they were a success. In this way I restored the playwright to his place, when the attacks of his opponents had practically driven him from his profession and from his craft and from the dramatic art.

T 2 Volcacius Sedigitus[1] in Gellius, *Attic Nights*

In the book he wrote about poets, Sedigitus demonstrates in the following verses what he thinks of those who wrote comedies, and whom he believes to surpass all others, and finally to which position of honor he assigns each individual:

---

[1] Volcacius Sedigitus, an early Roman scholar-poet, ca. 100 BC (*RE* Volcatius 6). See Funaioli 1907, 82–83; Courtney 1993, 93–96.

multos incertos certare hanc rem vidimus,
palmam poetae comico cui deferant.
eum meo iudicio errorem dissolvam tibi,
ut, contra si quis sentiat, nihil sentiat.

5 Caecilio palmam Statio do comico.
Plautus secundus facile exuperat ceteros.
dein Naevius, qui fervet, pretio in tertiost.
si erit, quod quarto detur, dabitur Licinio.
post insequi Licinium facio Atilium.

10 in sexto consequetur hos Terentius.
Turpilius septimum, Trabea octavum optinet,
nono loco esse facile facio Luscium.
decimum addo causa antiquitatis Ennium.

5 do comico *vel* do cominico *vel* dominico *codd.*: do mimico
ed. Juntina, Gronovius: do comicum *Rocca*   13 antiquitatis
causa decimum addo *Courtney*

T 3 (= T 2 Naevius) Cic. *Rep.* 4.11

sed Periclen . . . violari versibus et eos agi in scaena non
plus decuit, quam si Plautus, inquit, noster voluisset aut
Naevius Publio et Gnaeo Scipioni aut Caecilius Marco
Catoni maledicere

Cf. August. *Civ.* 2.9.

"We see that many debate this matter, being uncertain to which comic poet they should assign the victory palm. By my judgment, I will resolve this uncertainty for you, so that, if anyone thinks otherwise, that opinion has no value. I give the victory palm to the comic poet Caecilius Statius. Plautus, in second place, easily surpasses the others. Then Naevius, who is passionate, is in third position. If there is something to give to the one in fourth place, it will be given to Licinius. I have Atilius following Licinius. In sixth place Terence will follow them, Turpilius holds seventh, Trabea eighth position. I easily put Luscius [Lanuvinus] in ninth place. As the tenth poet I add Ennius by virtue of his antiquity."

T 3 Cicero, *On the Republic*

but for Pericles . . . to be insulted in verse and for these verses to be recited on stage was no more proper, he said,[1] than for our own Plautus or Naevius to have wished to abuse Publius and Gnaeus Scipio,[2] or for Caecilius to have wished to vilify Marcus Cato[3]

[1] Spoken in the dialogue by P. Cornelius Scipio Aemilianus Africanus Minor (185/84–129 BC; cos. 147 BC and 134 BC, censor 142 BC).   [2] P. Cornelius Scipio (cos. 218 BC; *RE* 330) and his brother Cn. Cornelius Scipio Calvus (cos. 222 BC; *RE* 345) both fought the Carthaginians in Spain in 218–211 BC, dying separately in battle in 211.   [3] Marcus Porcius Cato the Elder ("the Censor," 234–149 BC; cos. 195 BC, censor 184 BC).

T 4 Cic. *Att*. 1.16.15

epigrammatis tuis, quae in Amaltheo posuisti, contenti erimus, praesertim cum et Thyillus nos reliquerit et Archias nihil de me scripserit; ac vereor ne, Lucullis quoniam Graecum poëma condidit, nunc ad Caecilianam fabulam spectet.

---

¹ In Greek myth the foster mother or nurse of the infant Zeus in Crete. In some versions Almathea is a goat nursing the infant, in others a nymph employing the goat. When the goat breaks one of its horns, Almathea fills the horn with fruit and herbs, presents it to Zeus, and he in turn places goat and horn among the stars (see Ovid, *Fasti* 5.115–28). The horn is then the origin of the idea of the cornucopia.   ² An epigrammatist, also mentioned by Cicero in *Letters to Atticus* 1.9.2. *Anth. Pal.* 6.170 (LCL 67: 386) and 7.223 (LCL 68: 126) are attributed to him.   ³ Aulus Licinius Archias, a poet originally from Syria, who came to Rome, eventually acquired citizenship and was then successfully de-

T 5 Cic. *Brut*. 258

mitto C. Laelium P. Scipionem; aetatis illius ista fuit laus tamquam innocentiae sic Latine loquendi—nec omnium tamen, nam illorum aequalis Caecilium et Pacuvium male locutos videmus—. . .

T 4 Cicero, *Letters to Atticus*

I shall content myself with your epigrams, which you placed in the shrine of Almathea,[1] especially since Thyillus[2] has deserted me and Archias[3] has written nothing about me; in fact, I'm afraid that, since he [Archias] has written a Greek poem for the Luculli,[4] he is now looking toward Caecilian drama.[5]

fended by Cicero in 62 BC (in his *Pro Archia*) against a charge of having gained the citizenship illegally.   [4] L. Licinius Lucullus (cos. 74 BC; *RE* 104) and family. This Licinius Lucullus had significant victories in the east (Plutarch, *Life of Lucullus* 28.8), eventually was allowed to triumph (63 BC, perhaps the theme of Archias' poem; Lucullus was his patron), but eventually retired to live in luxury.   [5] Shackleton Bailey (LCL 7, p. 91 n. 18) suggests this means Archias was considering writing a historical drama about one of the Caecilii Metelli (related to Licinius Lucullus), but a *fabula praetexta* seems unlikely at this period, compared to a comedy in the style of Caecilius Statius.

T 5 Cicero, *Brutus*

I pass over C. Laelius[1] and P. Scipio:[2] the great distinction of that period was integrity of character as much as speaking pure Latin—though not of all men, for we see that their contemporaries Caecilius and Pacuvius spoke badly—. . .

[1] C. Laelius Sapiens (cos. 140 BC; *RE* Laelius 3).   [2] P. Cornelius Scipio Aemilianus Africanus minor (185/84–129 BC; cos. 147, 134, censor 142 BC; *RE* Cornelius 335).

T 6 (= T 23 Ennius) Cic. *Opt. gen.* 2

itaque licet dicere et Ennium summum epicum poetam, si cui ita videtur, et Pacuvium tragicum et Caecilium fortasse comicum.

T 7 (= T 28 Ennius) Cic. *Fin.* 1.4

iis igitur est difficilius satisfacere qui se Latina scripta dicunt contemnere. in quibus hoc primum est in quo admirer, cur in gravissimis rebus non delectet eos sermo patrius, cum idem fabellas Latinas ad verbum e Graecis expressas non inviti legant. quis enim tam inimicus paene nomini Romano est qui Enni Medeam aut Antiopam Pacuvi spernat aut reiciat, quod se isdem Euripidis fabulis delectari dicat, Latinas litteras oderit? Synephebos ego, inquit, potius Caecili aut Andriam Terenti quam utramque Menandri legam?

T 8 Varro, *Sat. Men.* 399 B.

in quibus partibus in argumentis Caecilius poscit palmam, in ethesin Terentius, in sermonibus Plautus.

T 9 Varro, *Ling.* F 40 Fun. (Char. *GL* I, p. 241.28 = p. 315 B.)

ἤθη, ut ait Varro de Latino sermone libro V, nullis aliis servare convenit, inquit, quam Titinio, Terentio, Attae; πάθη vero Trabea Atilius Caecilius facile [*fort.* facillime?] moverunt.

TESTIMONIA

T 6 Cicero, *The Best Kind of Orator*

Therefore, one may say that Ennius is the greatest epic poet, if he seems so to anyone, and Pacuvius the greatest tragic poet, and Caecilius [Statius] perhaps the greatest comic poet.

T 7 Cicero, *On Ends*

It is therefore more difficult to satisfy those who say they scorn writing in Latin. As for them, the first thing that amazes me is this: why does their native language not please them in very serious matters, when the same people are not unwilling to read Latin plays translated word for word from Greek ones? Who is so hostile to practically the very name "Roman" that he despises and rejects Ennius' *Medea* or Pacuvius' *Antiopa* because he says he finds pleasure in the corresponding plays of Euripides but hates Latin literature? "Shall I," he says, "read Caecilius' *Synephebi* or Terentius' *Andria* in preference to either of these comedies by Menander?"

T 8 Varro, *Menippean Satires*

In these matters, Caecilius wins the prize for his plots, Terence for his characters, Plautus for language.

T 9 Varro, *On the Latin Language*

As Varro says in Book 5 of *On Latin Speech*, it is agreed that character delineation (*ethos*) is nowhere else better maintained than in Titinius, Terence, and Atta; on the other hand Trabea, Atilius, and Caecilius easily aroused audience emotions (*pathos*).

T 10 Hor. *Ep.* 2.1.57–59

> dicitur Afrani toga convenisse Menandro,
> Plautus ad exemplar Siculi properare Epicharmi,
> vincere Caecilius gravitate, Terentius arte.

T 11 Hor. *Ars P.* 52–55

> . . .
> et nova fictaque nuper habebunt verba fidem, si
> Graeco fonte cadent parce detorta. quid autem
> Caecilio Plautoque dabit Romanus ademptum
> 55 Vergilio Varioque?

T 12 Vell. Pat. 1.17.1

in Accio circaque eum Romana tragoedia est; dulcesque Latini leporis facetiae per Caecilium Terentiumque et Afranium subpari aetate nituerunt.

T 13 Suet. *Vita Ter.* 2 (Suet. *Reliq.*, pp. 28–29 Rufferscheid)

scripsit comoedias sex, ex quibus primam "Andriam" cum aedilibus daret, iussus ante Caecilio recitare, ad cenantem cum venisset, dictus est initium quidem fabulae, quod erat

---

[1] Junior officials in charge of public games, which could include play performances.

TESTIMONIA

T 10 Horace, *Epistles*

They say the toga of Afranius suited Menander; Plautus races after the example of Sicilian Epicharmus. Caecilius wins the prize for substance, Terence for art.

T 11 Horace, *The Art of Poetry*

. . . and words, though new and of recent make, will win acceptance, if they spring from a Greek fount and are drawn therefrom but sparingly. Why indeed shall Romans grant this license to Caecilius and Plautus, and refuse it to Virgil and Varius[1]?

[1] L. Varius Rufus (*RE* 21), ca. 74–14 BC, author of epic and a tragedy, *Thyestes*, produced at Octavian's Actian Games in 29 BC, for which Varius was awarded a million sesterces.

T 12 Velleius Paterculus, *Compendium of Roman History*

Roman tragedy centers in and around Accius; and the sweet pleasantry of Latin humor reached its zenith in practically the same age under Caecilius, Terence, and Afranius.[1]

[1] L. Afranius (*RE* 5), active in the second half of the second century BC, author of comedies in Roman dress (*fabulae togatae*).

T 13 Suetonius, *Lives of Illustrious Men, Terence*

He [Terence] wrote six comedies, and when he offered the first of these, the *Andria*, to the aediles,[1] they ordered him first to read it to Caecilius. When he came to Caecilius' house, he found him at dinner. Because he was shabbily dressed, it is said Terence sat down on a bench near the

395

contemptiore vestitu, subsellio iuxta lectulum residens legisse, post paucos vero versus invitatus ut accumberet cenasse una, dein cetera percucurrisse non sine magna Caecilii admiratione.

T 14 (= T 65 Ennius) Quint. *Inst.* 1.8.11

nam praecipue quidem apud Ciceronem, frequenter tamen apud Asinium etiam et ceteros qui sunt proximi, videmus Enni Acci Pacuvi Lucili Terenti Caecili et aliorum inseri versus, summa non eruditionis modo gratia sed etiam iucunditatis, cum poeticis voluptatibus aures a forensi asperitate respirant.

T 15 Quint. *Inst.* 10.1.99–100

in comoedia maxime claudicamus. licet Varro Musas, Aeli Stilonis sententia, Plautino dicat sermone locuturas fuisse si Latine loqui vellent, licet Caecilium veteres laudibus ferant, licet Terenti scripta ad Scipionem Africanum referantur (quae tamen sunt in hoc genere elegantissima, et plus adhuc habitura gratiae si intra versus trimetros

---

1 L. Aelius Stilo (*RE* 144), born ca. 150 BC, wide-ranging scholar. He made a catalogue of the twenty-five plays of Plautus that he regarded as genuine (see Suetonius, *De grammaticis* 3, with Kaster 1995, 68–80; cf. Cicero, *Brutus* 205).

2 Terence, *Adelphoe* 15–21, alludes in his prologue to a malicious report that he has been helped by *homines nobiles*. Some

dining couch and read the beginning of his play. But after just a few verses he was invited to join the dinner party, and afterward ran through the rest of the play to Caecilius' considerable admiration.

T 14 Quintilian, *The Orator's Education*

Particularly in Cicero, but frequently also in Asinius[1] and others who are nearest [in time], we find inserted lines from Ennius, Accius, Pacuvius, Lucilius, Terence, Caecilius and others for the sake not only of the learning shown but also of the pleasure given, when the ears can relax from the forensic asperities through poetic delights.

[1] C. Asinius Pollio (76 BC–AD 4; cos. 40 BC), supporter of Caesar, historian, builder of Rome's first public library.

T 15 Quintilian, *The Orator's Education*

It is in comedy that our steps most falter. True, Varro (quoting the view of Aelius Stilo)[1] held that the Muses would have talked like Plautus if they had chosen to speak Latin; true, older critics extol Caecilius; true, Terence's works are attributed to Scipio Africanus[2] (and they are in fact the most elegant of their kind, and would have possessed even more attraction if they had been written

took this to mean Scipio Aemilianus and friends gave help in writing the plays (Cicero, *Att.* 7.3.10, even suggests C. Laelius as a contributor: see F *Inc.* 10) rather than simple patronage, but whether this was precisely the charge is unclear, let alone whether Terence did have ghostwriters.

397

stetissent): [100] vix levem consequimur umbram, adeo ut
mihi sermo ipse Romanus non recipere videatur illam
solis concessam Atticis venerem, cum eam ne Graeci qui-
dem in alio genere linguae optinuerint.

T 16 (= T 76 Ennius) Fronto, *Ad M. Caesarem et invicem
libri, Ep.* 4.3.2 (pp. 56.18–57.1 van den Hout)

quamobrem rari admodum veterum scriptorum in eum
laborem studiumque et periculum verba industriosius
quaerendi sese commisere, oratorum post homines natos
unus omnium M. Porcius eiusque frequens sectator C.
Sallustius, poetarum maxime Plautus, multo maxime Q.
Ennius eumque studiose aemulatus L. Coelius nec non
Naevius, Lucretius, Accius etiam, Caecilius, Laberius
quoque.

T 17 Gell. *NA* 4.20.12–13

"Statius" autem servile nomen fuit. plerique apud veteres
servi eo nomine fuerunt. [13] Caecilius quoque, ille co-
moediarum poeta inclutus, servus fuit et propterea nomen
habuit "Statius." sed postea versum est quasi in cogno-
mentum, appellatusque est "Caecilius Statius."

wholly in trimeters):[3] [100] nevertheless, we barely achieve a faint shadow, and I have come to think that the Latin language is incapable of acquiring that grace which was vouchsafed uniquely to the Athenians—for the Greeks too failed to achieve it in any other dialect of their language.

[3] A curious view, as even Menander did not write wholly in trimeters. Donald Russell aptly quotes Richard Bentley's view (*Schediasma de metris Terentianis*) on the orator's taste: "Q. evidently wanted Terence's plays, which begin with trimeters in the first scene, to go on in the same metre to the end. You would think he had never seen a stage, never attended a comic performance."

T 16 Fronto, *Correspondence*

For that reason only a few of the old writers devoted themselves to the toil, study, and risk of seeking out words more industriously: of orators from the beginnings of mankind, uniquely Marcus Porcius [Cato] and his frequent follower Sallust, of poets especially Plautus, most especially Quintus Ennius, and Lucius Coelius,[1] who zealously emulated him, and also Naevius, Lucretius, Accius as well, Caecilius and also Laberius.[2]

[1] The historian L. Coelius Antipater (2nd cent. BC; *RE* 7).
[2] The mime writer Decimus Laberius (ca. 106–43 BC).

T 17 Gellius, *Attic Nights*

Now Statius was a slave name. In old times there were many slaves of that name. [13] Caecilius too, the famous comic poet, was a slave and as such called Statius. But afterward this was made into a kind of surname, and he was called Caecilius Statius.

T 18 (= T 84 Ennius) Gell. *NA* 17.21.49

neque magno intervallo postea Q. Ennius et iuxta Caeci-
lius et Terentius et subinde et Pacuvius et Pacuvio iam
sene Accius clariorque tunc in poematis eorum obtrectan-
dis Lucilius fuit.

T 19 (= T 98 Ennius) Hieron. *Ab Abr.* 1838 [179 a.C.]
(p. 138b Helm)

Statius Caecilius comoediarum scriptor clarus habetur,
natione Insuber Gallus et Ennii primum contubernalis.
quidam Mediolanensem ferunt. mortuus est anno post
mortem Ennii et iuxta Ianiculum sepultus.

T 20 (= T 100 Ennius) Hieron. *In Mich.* 2, praef.

si enim criminis est Graecorum benedicta transferre, ac-
cusentur Ennius et Maro, Plautus [Ter. *An.* 18–19], Cae-
cilius et Terentius, Tullius quoque et ceteri eloquentes
viri, qui non solum versus, sed multa capita et longissimos
libros ac fabulas integras transtulerunt.

T 18 Gellius, *Attic Nights*

Not much later [after the visit of Carneades to Rome] were Ennius and soon after Caecilius and Terence[1] and then also Pacuvius and, when Pacuvius was already old, Accius, and then, rather famous for criticizing their poems, Lucilius.

[1] Gellius' absolute chronology is faulty, perhaps through relying on memory, although the sequence of poets is correct. Ennius, Caecilius, and Terence died in 169, 168, and 159 BC, respectively, while Carneades, head of the Academy, participated in Athens' diplomatic mission to Rome in 155 BC.

T 19 Jerome, on the year 179 BC

Caecilius Statius, a writer of comedies, is considered famous, an Insubrian Gaul by nationality and at first a comrade of Ennius. Some say he was from Milan. He died a year after the death of Ennius and is buried by the Janiculum.

T 20 Jerome, *Commentary on Micah*

For if it is a crime to translate what the Greeks have expressed well, Ennius and Maro [Virgil] should be accused, Plautus [Ter. *An.* 18–19], Caecilius, and Terence, also Tullius [Cicero] and other eloquent men, who have translated not only verses, but also many chapters and very long books and entire plays.

TESTIMONIA DUBIA (T 21–22)

T 21 Porph. ap. Euseb. *Praep. evang.* 10.3.13 (465d)

Πορφυρίου ἀπὸ τοῦ αʹ τῆς φιλολόγου ἀκροάσεως·
"ὅπου γε καὶ Μένανδρος τῆς ἀρρωστίας ταύτης ἐπλή-
σθη, ὃν ἠρέμα μὲν ἤλεγξε διὰ τὸ ἄγαν αὐτὸν φιλεῖν
Ἀριστοφάνης ὁ γραμματικὸς ἐν ταῖς παραλλήλοις
αὐτοῦ τε καὶ ἀφ᾽ ὧν ἔκλεψεν ἐκλογαῖς; Λατῖνος δὲ ἐξ
βιβλίοις, ἃ ἐπέγραψε Περὶ τῶν οὐκ ἰδίων Μενάνδρου,
τὸ πλῆθος αὐτοῦ τῶν κλοπῶν ἐξέφηνε· καθάπερ ὁ
Ἀλεξανδρεὺς Φιλόστρατος Περὶ τῆς τοῦ Σοφοκλέους
κλοπῆς πραγματείαν κατεβάλετο. Κεκίλιος δὲ ὥς τι
μέγα πεφωρακὼς ὅλον δρᾶμα ἐξ ἀρχῆς εἰς τέλος Ἀν-
τιφάνους τὸν Οἰωνιστὴν μεταγράψαι φησὶ τὸν Μέ-
νανδρον εἰς τὸν Δεισιδαίμονα."

T 22 Isid. *Orig.* 8.7.7

duo sunt autem genera comicorum, id est, veteres et novi.
veteres qui et ioco ridiculares extiterunt ut Plautus, Accius
[*fort.* Caecilius?], Terentius. novi qui et satirici, a quibus
generaliter vitia carpuntur, ut Flaccus, Persius, Iuvenalis
vel alii.

---

[1] The tragedian Accius certainly does not belong in this list.
Deufert (2002, 259n113) suggests his name may have displaced
that of Caecilius, a more familiar member of the comic triad.

TESTIMONIA DUBIA (T 21–22)

T 21 Porphyry in Eusebius, *Preparation for the Gospel*

From Book 1 of Porphyry's *Lecture on Philology*: "When even Menander was full of this weakness, though Aristophanes the Grammarian because of liking [Menander] so much exposed him gently in his parallel extracts from him and quotations of those he stole from. Latinus[1] in six books he wrote *On Things Not Menander's Own* revealed the mass of his plagiarisms. In the same way Philostratus of Alexandria assembled a study *On the Plagiarism of Sophocles*. And Caecilius,[2] as though having made a great discovery, says that Menander rewrote an entire play from beginning to end, Antiphanes' *Bird Seer*, into his own *Superstitious Man*."

[1] A Greek grammarian of unknown date.

[2] Earlier scholarship identified this source as Caecilius of Calacte, a Greek rhetorician active in Rome under Augustus, and this is cited as F 164 Ofenloch. There is no clear evidence, however, that Caecilius of Calacte ever wrote about drama. Others have taken this as evidence that Caecilius Statius not only discussed his Greek comic predecessor's use of previous comedy but may also have done so in a prologue to one of his own plays.

T 22 Isidore, *Origins*

There are two kinds of comic poets, that is, the old and the new. The old, who exposed ridiculous characters to joking, such as Plautus, Accius [Caecilius?],[1] Terence. The new are also called satirists, by whom vices are generally reviled, such as Flaccus [Horace], Persius, Juvenal, and others.

FABULAE PALLIATAE

AETHRIO (F 1–5)

Variant readings of the title occur, with Aethrio *and* Etherio *(both translated as "The Ethereal") the most common. The title character might be Jupiter, and the fact that someone takes counsel with Mercury in F 4 might strengthen that possibility. A plot resembling Plautus'* Amphitruo, *with a Jupiter come to earth is one possibility*

1 (1 R.[3]) Non., p. 536.8–11 M. = 859 L.

PROSUMIA: navigii genus. Caecilius . . . Aethrione:

ia^6 de nocte ad portum sum provectus prosumia

    a portu *Quicherat*   profectus *vel* provectus *codd.*

Cf. Paul. *Fest.*, p. 252.18 L.

2 (2 R.[3]) Fest., pp. 172.16–74.10 L.

NUME⟨RO: . . . pro nimium diceba⟩nt . . . at Panurgus Antonius haec ait: NUMERO nimium cito, celeriter nimium . . . Caecilius in Aethrione:

ia^6 (A) ei perii! (B) quid ita? (A) numero venit. (B) fuge
    domum!

COMEDIES

AETHRIO (F 1–5)

(and two manuscript readings give a variant title of Amphitrio*), but may be no more than a guess. F 5 suggests a helper character at work.*

Bibl.: *Schlüter 1884, 4; Negro 1919, 35–36; Perutelli 2002, 11–18, 27–30; Livan 2005, 28–29, 47–48.*

1 Nonius

prosumia ["spy ship"]: a kind of ship. Caecilius . . . in *The Ethereal*:

> by night I was carried into the port by spy ship

2 Festus

They said *numero* for "too much" . . . But Panurgus Antonius says this: *numero* means very quickly, very swiftly . . . Caecilius in *The Ethereal*:

> (A) I'm done for! (B) How's that? (A) He's come very
>   quickly. (B) Run off home!

---

perii *vulgo*: peri *cod., corr. Augustinus in mg.*   domum]
modo *coni. Kiessling*

3 (3 R.[3]) Fest., p. 196.31–36 L.

ORAE extremae partes terrarum, id est maritimae dicun-
tur, unde et vestimentorum extremae partes, quae quidem
et primae dici possunt. Caecilius in Aethrione usus est pro
initio rei, cum ait:

ia^6 oram reperire nullam qua expediam queo

    qua *Spengel*: qua me *Carrio*: quam *cod.*   expediar *War-*
mington

4 (4 R.[3]) Fest., p. 454.8–11 L.

SENTINARE: satagere, dictum a sentina, quam multae
aquae navis cum recipit periclitatur. . . . Caecilius in
⟨A⟩ethrione:

tr^7 cum Mercurio capit consilium postquam sentinat
      satis

Cf. Paul. *Fest.*, p. 455.18–21 L.

5 (5 R.[3]) Diom., *GL* I, p. 386.17–19

apud veteres reperimus †id quod nolumus, non vultis† ut
est in Aethrione apud Caecilium:

tr^7 actutum, voltis, empta est; noltis, non empta est.

    post vultis *lacunam indicat Keil*   id quod non vultis nol-
tis *edd. vett.*   ut est in Aethrione apud Caecilium *Keil*: est
in etherione apud lucilium *codd.*   actutum *recenti manu*
adscriptum in cod.: actiuum *codd.*   emta noltis *cod.*

406

3 Festus

orae denotes the furthest parts of the earth, that is, sea-coasts, therefore also the outermost parts of garments, which can also be called first parts. Caecilius in *The Ethereal* used the term for the beginning of something, when he says:

> I can't find any brink to start out from

4 Festus

sentinare: to have one's hands full, derived from *sentina* ["bilgewater"]; when a low-riding ship[1] takes on bilgewater, it is in danger. . . . Caecilius in *The Ethereal*:

> after shipping enough water,[2] he forms a plan with
> Mercury

[1] *multae aquae* seems to describe a ship displacing lots of water and therefore low to the water line.   [2] Paulus gives the same derivation of *sentinare* but suggests it means emptying the bilge to escape danger.

5 Diomedes

In old writers we find *noltis* for "you don't want,"[1] as in *The Ethereal* of Caecilius:

> Right away, you want her, she's bought; you don't
> want her, she's not bought.

[1] The form *nolumus* ("*we* do not want") does not make sense in this context, nor does a posited lacuna easily solve the problem. The sense needed is clear, and the translation reflects the text printed by early editions.

ANDRIA (F 1)

The title in the manuscripts of Nonius is written as Andrea, which might reflect either a Greek title Ἀνδρία (Andria: "The Woman of Andros") or Ἀνδρεία (Andreia: "Courage" or "Manliness"). Menander certainly wrote an Andria (F 34–49 K.-A.), which, along with his Perinthia ("Woman of Perinthos"), Terence used as the basis of his comedy entitled Andria (Ter. And. 13). It is generally thought less

1 (6 R.³) Non., p. 152.18–23 M. = 223 L.

PUTIDUM: putre. . . Caecilius Andria:

ia⁶   conducit navem putidam

Andreia *Dziatzko*: andrea *codd.*   putidam *cod.*, *edd.*:
putridam *rell.*, *Ribbeck*, *Lindsay*

ANDROGYNOS (F 1–2)

Titles related to Androgynos ("The Man / Woman") are known from both Old and New Comedy in Greece. Eupolis wrote an Ἀστράτευτοι ἢ Ἀνδρόγυναι ("Draftdodgers" or "Men / Women"), where the pairing suggests that ἀνδρόγυνος implied avoidance of masculine duties. Perhaps more, the definition in the Suda of ἀνδρόγυνος included τὰ ἀνδρῶν ποιῶν, τὰ γυναικῶν πάσχων ["performing the functions of men, experiencing the functions of women"], a possible theme of insult in Old Comedy, but the thirteen surviving fragments (F 35–47 K.-A.) do not illuminate the plot. Menander wrote an Ἀνδρόγυνος ἢ

ANDRIA (F 1)

likely that Terence would have done so if his predecessor Caecilius had based one of his plays on a Menandrean Andria *(but see below on the possible source for Caecilius'* Synaristosae*). The evidence that Menander might have written an* Andreia *is a variant in manuscripts of Stobaeus.*

Bibl.: Schlüter 1884, 4; Webster 1950, 77–78; Reggiani 1977; Camilloni 1985, 212; Manuwald 2011, 235n113.

1 Nonius

putidum: for *putre* ["rotten"] . . . Caecilius in *The Woman of Andros*:

he hires a clapped-out ship

ANDROGYNOS (F 1–2)

Κρής *("The Man / Woman" or "The Cretan"), equally obscure (F 50–56 K.-A.), though it may have featured a mercenary soldier from Crete. Others have thought of a plot similar to Terence's* Eunuch, *in which a young man might have disguised himself as a girl. A twelfth-century Latin comedy, the* Alda *of William of Blois, in which a boy dresses as a girl to gain access to a protected girl, claims to derive from Menander. Elements of its plot might derive from a prose summary of Menander (Menander, Ἀνδρό-γυνος test. ii K.-A.).*

Bibl.: Schlüter 1884, 4; Neumann 1953; Frassinetti 1979, 78–79; Camilloni 1985, 212; Livan 2005, 61–62.

1 (7 R.³) Fest., pp. 494.33–96.2 L.

TAENIAS Graecam vocem sic interpretatur Verrius ut dicat ornamentum esse laneum capitis honorati, ut sit apud Caecilium in Androgyno:

ia⁶   sepulchrum plenum taeniarum ita ut solet

   "uti solet *vel* ut adsolet *praestat fortasse*" *Ribbeck*³

2 (8 R.³) Fest., pp. 416.35–18.7 L.

STOLIDUS, stultus. . . . et Caecilius in Hypobolimaeo . . . et in Androgyno:

tr⁷   sed ego stolidus; gratulatum med oportebat prius.

   med *Bothe*: me *cod.*   oportebat *Augustinus*: oporteat
cod.: tibi me oportebat *Umpfenbach*

ASOTUS (F 1–7)

Asotus (*"The Libertine"*) *is a Greek loan word occurring as an adjective only in Cicero. In Greek New Comedy, Timostratus wrote an* Ἄσωτος (*F 1 K.-A.*), *while his predecessors Antiphanes (F 48 K.-A.) from Middle Comedy*

1 (9–10 R.³) Non., p. 517.10–19 M. = 832 L.

DESUBITO . . . Caecilius Asoto:

ia⁸   nam ego duabus vigiliis transactis duco desubito
      domum

   nam] eam *Scaliger*   ducor *vir doctus in ed. Bas.*

410

1 Festus

Verrius[1] explains *taenias* as a Greek word meaning a wool adornment for the head to give honor, as found in Caecilius in *The Man / Woman*:

> a tomb festooned with headbands, as is the custom

[1] M. Verrius Flaccus (ca. 55 BC?–ca. AD 20?; *RE* Verrius 2), scholar and tutor to Augustus' grandsons, Gaius and Drusus; author of the lost *De verborum significatu*, epitomized by Festus.

2 Festus

stolidus ["stupid"], idiotic. . . . And Caecilius in *The Changeling* (F 3) . . . and in *The Man / Woman*:

> But I'm an idiot! I should have congratulated you before.

ASOTUS (F 1–7)

and Euthycles (F 1 K.-A.) from Old Comedy each wrote an Ἄσωτοι *("Libertines"). Timostratus is perhaps a more likely source, but nothing can be reconstructed of the plot.*
Bibl.: Schlüter 1884, 4–5; Negro 1919, 36; Camilloni 1985, 212; Perutelli 2002, 19.

1 Nonius

desubito ["suddenly"] . . . Caecilius in *The Libertine*:

> for after the second watch I suddenly take [her?] home

2 (14 R.³) Non., p. 258.11–12 M. = 393 L.

CALLET etiam dictum a callositate. Caecilius Asoto:

ia⁶   tu iam callebis, ille festus desidet

tu *codd.*, *ed. princ.*: tunc *cod.*: tum *rell.*: tun *Ribbeck*   fes-
tum *Palmer*: fessus *Scaliger*

3 (13 R.³) Non., p. 471.11–16 M. = 756 L.

POPULAT. est et passivum populatur . . . Caecilius Asoto:

ia⁶?   iamdudum depopulat macellum

4 (11–12 R.³) Non., p. 474.2–4 M. = 760 L.

MUTUET: mutuum sumat. Caecilius Asoto:

ia⁶   (A) ad amicos curret mutuatum. (B) mutuet mea
       causa.

5 (17 R.³) Non., pp. 474.35–75.7 = 762 L.

OPINO pro opinor . . . Caecilius Asoto:

tr⁷?   nil fore opino inter me atque illum

nihil *posito trochaeos discripserunt Spengel, Ribbeck*: me
codd.: mea *rell.*

6 (15 R.³) Non., p. 139.18–21 M. = 203 L.

MERITISSIMO. . . . Caecilius Asoto:

ia⁶   meritissimo hic me eiecit ex hac decuria!

eicit *cod.*

2 Nonius

callet ["is experienced"] can also have a meaning from hardness of skin, being calloused. Caecilius in *The Libertine*:

> now you'll toughen up, he'll succumb to partying

3 Nonius

populat ["ravages"]. There is also a deponent form *populatur* . . . Caecilius in *The Libertine*:

> he's long since been plundering the meat market

4 Nonius

mutuet: "let him take out a loan." Caecilius in *The Libertine*:

> (A) He'll run to his friends to get a loan. (B) Let him take out a loan on my behalf.

5 Nonius

opino for *opinor* ["I think"] . . . Caecilius in *The Libertine*:

> I believe there will be nothing between him and me

6 Nonius

meritissimo ["most deservedly"]. . . . Caecilius in *The Libertine*:

> He threw me out of this troop[1] most deservedly!

[1] *decuria* could be a military unit of ten, a group of judges, or a political unit. Cf. Plautus, *Persa* 143: *exigam hercle ego te ex hac decuria* ("by Hercules, I'll toss you out of this troop").

413

7 (16 R.³) Non., p. 507.5–6 M. = 815 L.

EDIM pro edam. Caecilius Asoto:

ia⁶?   nihilne nihil tibi esse quod edim?

> nihilne nihil tibi *cod.*: nihil nehil tibi *vel* nihilne tibi *rell.*

CARINE (F 1–2)

Carine *("The Carian Mourner") is more likely to have been drawn from the* Καρίνη *("The Carian Woman," F 201–3 K.-A.) of Menander than that of Antiphanes (F 112–13*

1 (104–5 R.³) Fest., p. 352.1–3 L.

RELUERE: resolvere, repignerare. Caecilius in Carine:

ia⁶   ut aurum et vestem, quod matris fuit,
    reluat, quod viva ipsi opposivit pignori

> 2 opposivit *Scaliger*: opposuit *codd.*

2 (= 106–7 R.³) Fest., p. 416.31–35 L.

STALAGMIUM genus inaurium videtur significare. Caecilius in Karine cum ait:

ia⁶   tum ex aure eius stalagmium
    domi habeo.

> 1 tum *Augustinus*: ium *cod.*: *fort.* iam *Lindsay*

Cf. Paul. *Fest.*, p. 417.5–6 L.

7 Nonius

edim for *edam* ["I might eat"]. Caecilius in *The Libertine*:

> (Parasite?) Nothing—you really have nothing for me
> to eat?

CARINE (F 1–2)

K.-A.). Carian women were well known as professional
mourners, and the Καρικά μέλη ["Carian songs"] were
the distinctive dirges they performed.
  Bibl.: Schlüter 1884, 5–6; Boscherini 1999, 103.

1 Festus

reluere ["to redeem"]: to release, to redeem from a pledge.
Caecilius in *The Carian Mourner*:

> in order that s/he may redeem the jewelry and
>   clothing, belonging to the mother,
> which she in her lifetime deposited with me as a
>   pledge

2 Festus

stalagmium ["pendant"] seems to indicate a kind of ear-
ring. Caecilius in *The Carian Mourner* says:

> Then I have the gold drop-earring from her (?) ear
> at home.

CARINE VEL CRATINUS (F 3)

Several manuscripts of Priscian (the only source for this
fragment) give an impossible form for the play title, while
others attribute it to a Cratinus. *The latter would be the*
only evidence for a play with the Greek comic poet Crati-

3 (108–9 R.[3]) Prisc., *GL* II, p. 282.11–15

CONCORS, CONCORDIS. antiquissimi tamen solebant gene-
tivo similem proferre nominativum. Caecilius in Cratino:

bacch[3]	modo fit obsequens hilarus comis
bacch[4]	communis concordis, dum id quod petit potitur.

crastino *vel* crastino *codd.*: cratino *rell.*: Charino *Bothe*:
Carine *Meineke, Guardì*   1 hilaris *vel* hilares *vel* ilarus
codd.   comes *codd.*: commonis *cod.*

CHALCIA (F 1–2)

Chalcia *("The Bronzesmiths' Festival") borrows for its title*
the Greek term Χαλκεῖα, *also known to be the title of*
a play by Menander. Harpocration (p. 304.12 Dindorf)
gives one source saying the festival was native to Ath-
ens and included other craftsmen, though especially the

1 (18–19 R.[3]) Non., p. 464.21–24 M. = 743 L.

PARERE etiam viros dici posse Caecilius auctor est Chal-
ciis:

tr[7]	ait hic vicinus, se eas peperisse, et vobis datum.

CARINE VEL CRATINUS (F 3)

*nus as title character. Although we know Cratinus staged
a version of himself under his own name as the leading
character of his play, "The Wineflask" (Πυτίνη), Meineke,
followed by Guardì, emended the text to* Carine, *a play
title that is otherwise attested.*

3 Priscian

concors, concordis ["harmonious, agreeing"]. The earliest
writers, however, tended to employ a nominative of the
same form as the genitive. Caecilius in *Cratinus*:

> Sometimes he becomes accommodating, cheerful,
>   friendly,
> affable, agreeable—until he gets what he wants.

CHALCIA (F 1–2)

*bronzesmiths. One of the three surviving Menander frag-
ments (F 400 K.-A.) mentions in its plot an old man in
love. Caecilius' F 1 suggests a concealed birth in his plot.
The scene was likely Athens.*
   Bibl.: Schlüter 1884, 5; Camilloni 1985, 212–13.

1 Nonius

parere ["to give birth"] can also be said of men, as Caeci-
lius does in *The Bronzesmiths' Festival*:

> This neighbor says he gave birth to them, and a gift
>   was made to you.

id prudenter mutuatum ab Homero: αὐτὰρ Γλαῦκος ἔτικτεν ἀμύμονα Βελλεροφόντην [*Il.* 6.155].

ait] sat *codd. corr.*, *Gravert*: at *Spengel*: scit *Havet*: at ait *L. Mueller*   se eas peperisse *Iunius*: se asperisse *codd.*: se has peperisse *Buecheler*   et] id *L. Mueller*: it *in app. Lindsay*

2 (20–21 R.[3]) Non., p. 491.23–26 M. = 789 L.

SONITI et SONU pro sonitus et sono . . . Caecilius Chalciis:

tr[7]?   num quid nam fores fecere soniti?

num quid nam *Gravert*: nam quid nam *codd.*: nam quid *Bothe*: nam quid iam *vel* nam quid nunc *Spengel*: numquid iam *vel* nunc quidnam *Ribbeck*   facere *codd.*: fecere *rell.*

CHRYSION (F 1)

The title is a Greek female personal name, the diminutive of Χρυσίς *("Chrysis"). Chrysion is not recorded as a Greek comedy title, but the very productive Middle Comedy poet Antiphanes wrote a* Χρυσίς *(F 223–24 K.-A.), whose title character was a renowned hetaera, and the personal name occurs for an old hetaera in Timocles'*

1 (22–24 R.[3]) Gell. *NA* 6.17.3–13

quis adeo tam linguae Latinae ignarus est quin sciat eum dici obnoxium, cui quid ab eo cui esse obnoxius dicitur incommodari et noceri potest, ut qui habeat aliquem noxae, id est culpae suae, conscium? . . . [13] qua vero ille grammaticus finitione usus est, ea videtur in verbo tam

This is a learned borrowing from Homer: "and Glaucus begot incomparable Bellerophon" [*Il.* 6.155].

2 Nonius

soniti ["noise"; genitive] for *sonitus* and *sonu* [ablative] for *sono* . . . Caecilius in *The Bronzesmiths' Festival*:

Have the doors resounded at all?

CHRYSION (F 1)

Orestautocleides *("Autocleides as Orestes," F 27 K.-A.). Eubulus wrote a* Χρυσίλλα *("Chrysilla"), also likely a hetaera name, whose one surviving fragment is a complaint about marriage (F 115 K.-A.). Chrysion ("Goldie") in this play is almost certainly a hetaera, though young or old we cannot say, and there is certainly a party going on. Bibl.: Schlüter 1884, 5; Cipriani 2010, 118–21.*

1 Gellius, *Attic Nights*

Who then is so ignorant of the Latin language as not to know that one is called "obnoxious" who can be inconvenienced or injured by another, to whom he is said to be "obnoxious" because the other is conscious of his *noxa*, that is to say, of his guilt? . . . [13] In fact that grammarian, by using this definition, seems to have observed in such a

multiplici unam tantummodo usurpationem eius notasse,
quae quidem congruit cum significatu quo Caecilius usus
est in Chrysio in his versibus:

ia[6]   . . . quamquam ego mercede huc conductus tua
         advenio, ne tibi me esse ob eam rem obnoxium
         reare; audibis male si male dicis mihi

1 conductus *codd.*: adductus *cod.*   3 dicis *codd.*: dixis
Carrio

DARDANUS (F 1)

Menander wrote a Δάρδανος, but its four fragments
(F 102–5 K.-A.) tell us nothing of the plot nor prove it was
Caecilius' source material. While Zeus fathered the epony-
mous founder of Dardania (Hom. Il. 20.215), the name in
Menander and Caecilius more likely designates an en-
slaved character from that still-barbarian region, called by

1 (25 R.[3]) Non., p. 392.15–18 M. = 628 L.

SPISSUM significat tardum . . . Caecilius Dardano:

ia[6]   nihil spei ego credo: omnis res spissas facit.

nihil (nil *Ribbeck*) spei ego credo *Lindsay, Ribbeck*[3]: nihil ego
spei credo *codd.*: nihil rei ego credo *cod.*: nil re ego spe credo *L.*
Mueller

complex word only one of its uses—a use which indeed agrees with how Caecilius employed it in these verses in the *Chrysion*:

(Cook?) . . . although I'm arriving here under
    contract to you,
don't think that I'm therefore under your control;
if you defame me, you'll get defamation in return

DARDANUS (F 1)

his ethnic rather than a personal name. As the title character, he should play a significant role in the plot, perhaps aiding a young master. Pliny the Elder (HN 30.2.9) claims that Democritus excavated books on magic from the tomb of "Dardanus of Phoenicia," so someone passing himself off as a magician might be a possible title character as well.
  Bibl.: Schlüter 1884, 6; Cipriani 2010, 121–24.

1 Nonius

spissum means slow. . . Caecilius in *Dardanus*:

I put no trust in hope: she makes everything tardy.

DAVUS (F 1)

Davus *is a typical slave name in Roman comedy (from Greek* Δᾶος, *also originally a barbarian ethnic name), so much so that Galen (Nat. Fac. 2.67 K.) refers to "Davuses and Getases" as archetypal deceivers of their masters. As*

1 (= 26 R.[3]) Fest., p. 254.24–28 L.

PROBRUM: stuprum, flagitium . . . Caecilius in Davo:

ia[6]   ea tum compressa parit huic puerum, sibi probrum

DEMANDATI (F 1)

The title Demandati *("Those Entrusted") indicates those put in another's charge, most likely young men still in tutelage.*

1 (27 R.[3]) Non., pp. 123.33–24.8 M. = 178 L.

ICIT significat percutit, ab ictu . . . Caecilius Demandatis:

tr[7]   si umquam quisquam vidit quem catapulta aut balista
         icerit

DAVUS (F 1)

only one fragment is preserved under this title for Caeci-lius, there is a small possibility that the titular name is an error for Dardanus.

Bibl.: Spengel 1829, 5; Lascu 1969; Hanses 2020, 238.

1 Festus

probrum ["disgrace"]: dishonor, shame . . . Caecilius in *Davus*:

> having been raped, she then produced a son for him, dishonor for herself

DEMANDATI (F 1)

Bibl.: Schlüter 1884, 7.

1 Nonius

icit means "strikes," from *ictus* ["blow"] . . . Caecilius in *Those Entrusted*:

> if ever anyone has seen someone struck by a catapult or crossbow

EPHESIO (F 1)

Ephesio *is generally taken to be a personal name. Menander wrote an* Ἐφέσιος *("The Ephesian"), in one of whose fragments (150 K.-A.) a character imagines being sold at auction, probably as a prisoner of war. If this was Caecilius' source material for* Ephesio, *it is not clear why he changed an ethnic name into the personal name.*[1] *Antiphanes in Middle Comedy as well as Posidippus and Simylus each wrote an* Ἐφεσία *("The Ephesian Woman"). A Greek in-*

1 (28–29 R.[3]) Non., p. 1.2–5 M. = 3 L.

SENIUM est taedium et odium . . . Caecilius in Ephesione:

ia[6]   tum equidem in senecta hoc deputo miserrumum,
sentire ea aetate eumpse esse odiosum alteri.

1 equidem] quidem *codd. Cic.: om. Non.*   senecta *Cic.:*
senectute *Non.*   2 eumpse esse *Fleckeisen:* eum se esse
Cic.: eum ipsum esse *Non.:* eumpseum esse *Lindsay:* ipsum esse
Bothe

Cf. Cic. *Sen.* 25 (*Plocium* F 9; F *Inc.* 2 FRL).

EPICLEROS (F 1–2)

The legal term Ἐπίκληρος *("The Heiress") was a popular title in Greek comedy, with examples written by Antiphanes (F 94 K.-A.), Heniochus (Suda s.v. η 392), Alexis (F 78–80 K.-A.), Menander (F 129–36 K.-A.), Diphilus (F 40 K.-A.), and Diodorus (F 2 K.-A.), as well as a Latin comedy by Turpilius (Com. 50–71 R.[3] = F 1–13 Rychlewska). Two ancient sources differentiate a first and a second*

EPHESIO (F 1)

scription (IG II² 2323.151) records a victory at Athens for
the comic poet Crito with an Ἐφεσίοι ("The Ephesians").
Bibl.: Schlüter 1884, 7; Camilloni 1985, 213.

1 Camilloni (1985, 213) appealingly suggests *ne* was not the
ending of the personal name in the ablative, but a particle begin-
ning the quotation; then the title would be not *Ephesio* but *The
Ephesian*, just as in Menander.

1 Nonius

senium means loathing and disgust . . . Caecilius in *Eph-
esio*:

> Then in old age I think this is the worst:
> when a man of that age feels himself repulsive to
> another.

EPICLEROS (F 1–2)

*Ἐπίκληρος by Menander, but Ἐπίκληρος may also have
been an alternative title for the play we know as Ἀσπίς
("The Shield"). The theme was so popular because of the
Athenian law that provided for the sole heiress to her fa-
ther's property to be married to her nearest male relative
or his designate. The plots of Menander's* Aspis *as well as
Terence's* Phormio *and* Adelphoe *turn on this issue. Which*

425

if any of the Greek comedies might have been Caecilius'
source for his own Epicleros *is unrecoverable. It has been*
suggested that Caecilius F Inc. 33 and 37 also came from
this play.

1 (30–31 R.[3]) Prisc., *GL* II, p. 354.7–12

apud antiquos "hic" et "haec memoris" et "hoc memore"
proferebatur. in quo testis est Caper antiquitatis doctissi-
mus inquisitor. ostendit enim Caecilium in Epiclero sic
protulisse:

ia[6]   itane Antipho est inventus profluvia fide?
itanest inmemoris, itanest madida memoria?

    1 invenitur *"quod duo codd. altero exhibent loco"* Spengel:
inventus *codd. utroque loco*: est inventus *Bothe*   est[1] *om.*
cod.   proflu*u*a *cod.*: profluia *Ribbeck*   2 madida]
medida *codd.*

Cf. Prisc., *GL* II, p. 235.13–14.

2 (32 R.[3]) Prisc., *GL* II, p. 514.15–17

invenitur tamen etiam CLAUDEO, sed et CLAUDO pro
CLAUDICO . . . Caecilius in Epiclero:

ia[6]   an ubi vos sitis, ibi consilium claudeat?

    ubi] ibi *cod.*   an ubi non sitis *vel* ubi nec sitis *Ribbeck*[3]

Cf. Mai 1836, 107, 142.

COMEDIES: EPICLEROS

Bibl.: Schlüter 1884, 7–8; Oppermann 1939, 124; Webster 1950, 97–98; Frassinetti 1979, 79–80; Camilloni 1985, 213.

1 Priscian

In archaic writers *memoris* ["mindful"] occurs as both masculine and feminine singular and *memore* as neuter [in place of *memor*]. Caper, a very learned researcher of earlier usage, gives evidence of this. For he reports Caecilius used it thus in *The Heiress*:

> Is Antipho really found out as a slippery character?
> Is he so forgetful, is his memory so soggy?

2 Priscian

The form *claudeo* [archaic form: "I limp, falter"] is found, as well as *claudo*, for *claudico* . . . Caecilius in *The Heiress*:

> Is it a fact that, wherever you are, there good counsel
>   goes limping?

427

EPISTATHMOS (F 1)

Epistathmos *is usually translated "The Quartermaster."*
Posidippus wrote an Ἐπίσταθμος,[1] *from which one frag-*
ment (11 K.-A.) survives, a list of supplies. The speaker of

1 (33 R.[3]) Prisc., *GL* II, p. 334.13–18

"hic" et "haec celer" vel "celeris" et "hoc celere." . . . Cae-
cilius in Epistathmo:

ia[6]   si properas, escende huc meam navem: ita celeris est.

properas *cod. corr.:* prosperas *cod.*   escende *vel* ex-
scende *Gulielmius:* extende *codd.*   meam *cod., Ribbeck:* in
meam *rell., Spengel*   navim *codd.*   caeleris *cod.*

EPISTULA (F 1–2)

Alexis *wrote an* Ἐπιστολή *("Letter"), and this was an*
alternative title for the Ἄσωτοι *("Libertines") of Euthycles*
in Old Comedy (see Asotus*). Machon of Sicyon, who pro-*
duced his plays at Alexandria (Ath. 14.664a), also wrote
an Ἐπιστολή, *while Timocles, one of the last poets of*
Middle Comedy, was the author of an Ἐπιστολαί *("The*

EPISTATHMOS (F 1)

the sole fragment here owns or has hired a ship and thus is not the mere "Quartermaster" of the title.
    Bibl.: Schlüter 1884, 8.

[1] The Greek term means "one stationed at the door," which explicitly includes "quartermaster" in the military sense, but also anyone in charge of guarding or dispensing goods of value.

1 Priscian:

celer ["swift"] and *celeris* both occur for masculine and feminine singular as well as *celere* for neuter. . . . Caecilius in *The Quartermaster*:

> If you're in a hurry, climb aboard my ship here: she's
>   quite fast.

EPISTULA (F 1–2)

Letters"). A fabula togata by Afranius likewise entitled Epistula *("The Letter") is also attested. It is likely that the title letter played a significant role in Caecilius' plot, but nothing else can be recovered.*
    Bibl.: Schlüter 1884, 8; Leo [2]1912, 313; Monaco 1965; Camilloni 1985, 213; De Nonno 1997.

1 (34–35 R.³) Fest., p. 118.1–3 L.

MANTARE saepe manere. Caecilius in Epistola:

ia⁷?   (A) iamne adeo? manta! (B) iam hoc vide; caecus
              animum . . .
              . . . adventus angit.

> *personas distinxit Ribbeck*   1 iamne] iam me *Aldus*: iam
> ore *Ursinus*: iamque *Bothe*   iam] iam ne *cod.*: nam *Al-*
> *dus*   2 caecu's *Ribbeck*²   *post* animum *lacunam mini-*
> *mum viginti litterarum indicavit Ursinus*

2 (37 R.³) Prisc., *GL* II, p. 229.10–12

IOVIS nominativo quoque casu invenitur. Caecilius in
Epistula:

ia⁶   nam novus quidem iam deus repertus est Iovis

> novus *codd.*: nobis *Ribbeck*   equidem *Osann, quem Rib-*
> *beck est secutus*   iam *post* quidem *add. Brugmann*   nam
> nobis equidem novus repertust Iovis deus *coni. Ribbeck*

EXHAUTUHESTOS
(ΕΞ ΑΤΤΟΤ ΕΣΤΩΣ) (F 1)

*The title is a Greek phrase and a conjecture for unreadable
terms in our only source, Donatus, based on the analogy
of Terence's play title (and transcribed Greek phrase)
Heauton Timoroumenos ("The Self-Tormentor").[1] It means
a man relying entirely on himself, so presumably exces-
sively self-confident and a leading figure in the play. Note
the reference to the Roman institution of gladiators in a
play in Greek dress with Greek title.*

430

1 Festus

mantare means to wait repeatedly. Caecilius in *The Letter*:

> (A) Now already? Wait up! (B) Look at that now. This
> unforeseen arrival . . .
> . . . chokes his brain.

2 Priscian

Iovis ["Jupiter"; genitive form in classical Latin] also oc-
curs in the nominative. Caecilius in *The Letter*:

> for now indeed a new god has been discovered: Jove

EXHAUTUHESTOS
(ΕΞ ΑΥΤΟΥ ΕΣΤΩΣ) (F 1)

*Bibl.: Schlüter 1884, 8–9; Camilloni 1985, 214–15;
Cipriani 2003, 65–70; Livan 2005, 79–80.*

[1] Other proposed readings of the mistranscribed Greek title
include *Eratosthenes* (Schlüter 1884; Cipriani 2003), *Eranosthe-
nes* (Cipriani 2003), and *Hecate* (Camilloni 1985), none otherwise
known among Caecilius' titles.

1 (38–39 R.³) Donat. ad Ter. *Ad.* 668

"praesens praesenti eripi": adiuvant significationem haec
ex abundanti addita . . . sic Caecilius in Exhautuhestoti:

ia⁶   ⟨est⟩ haec caterva plane gladiatoria
cum suum sibi alius socius socium ⟨sauciat⟩.

1 est *ante* haec *add. Ribbeck, post Bergk*   plena *codd.,*
corr. Lindenbrog   2 sauciat *add. Stephanus*

EXUL (F 1–2)

Before Caecilius' Exul ("The Exile"), Alexis wrote a Φυγάς
("Refugee"), Philemon an Ἄπολις *("Stateless"), Nicostra-*
tus an Ἀπελαυνόμενος *("Driven Away"), and Theophilus*
an Ἀπόδημοι *("Those Abroad"), any of which might con-*
ceivably have been translated as "Exile" in Latin, although

1 (40 R.³) Non., p. 75.21–22 M. = 106 L.

ABSCONDIT pro abscondidit. Caecilius Exule:

tr⁷   nam hic in tenebris intus sese abscondit.

abscondidit *cod.*: abscondit *rell., Lindsay*

2 (41 R.³) Non., p. 369.29–34 M. = 588 L.

PUTARE: animo disputare . . . Caecilius Exule:

ia⁸   non haec putas, non haec in corde versantur tibi?

tibi *codd.*: ti *rell.*: in corde tibi versatur *cod.*

1 Donatus, *Commentary on Terence, The Brothers*

"taken in person from him personally": These verbal re-
dundancies emphasize the meaning . . . so Caecilius in *A
Legend in His Own Mind*:

> This is obviously a troop of gladiators,
>   when each comrade stabs his own comrade in his own
>   interest.

EXUL (F 1–2)

*Alexis and Philemon are the best known, and thus perhaps
more likely as source material for Caecilius' play. The first
fragment may suggest someone ordered into exile who
sought not to go, but a plot is unrecoverable.*
    Bibl.: Schlüter 1884, 9.

1 Nonius

abscondit ["he hid away"; alternative form] for *abscondidit*.
Caecilius in *The Exile*:

> For this man hid himself away in the shadows within.

2 Nonius

putare ["to think"]: to debate within the mind . . . Caecilius
in *The Exile*:

> Don't you ponder these things, aren't they turning
>   over in your heart?

FALLACIA (F 1–7)

The title Fallacia *("Deceit") possibly reflects* Καταψευδό-
μενος *("The False Accuser"), a known play in the works of
Alexis, Philemon, Menander, and Sosipater, or Menander's*
Ἄπιστος *("The Distrustful Man"),*[1] *whose one surviving
fragment (F 1 K.-A.) suggests a plan to deceive an old man,
though some have suggested the* Apistos *might rather be
the source for Plautus'* Aulularia. *Naevius wrote a* Dolus
as well. The typical slave name Parmeno (F 6) suggests

1 (42–43 R.[3]) Non., p. 512.1–13 M. = 823 L.

DURITER pro dure . . . Caecilius Fallacia:

ia[6]   (A) nam quam duriter
  vos educavit atque asperiter!
                             (B) non negat.

  2 educavi *codd.*   atque asperiter *Bothe*: atque aspere
codd.: asperque *Scaliger*   1–2 nam quin duriter / Vos edu-
carit *Bothe*: nam quin duriter / Atque aspere vos educarit *Gravert*

2 (44–45 R.[3]) Non., p. 511.27–31 M. = 823 L.

ALIQUANTISPER. . . . Caecilius Fallacia:

ia[6]   nam si illi, postquam rem paternam amiserant,
       egestate aliquantisper iactati forent

     1 amiserunt *dub. in app. Ribbeck*   2 iactatio *cod.*

434

FALLACIA (F 1–7)

someone who might have aided sons or wards brought up harshly (F 1–2) in deceiving the father figure in pursuit of a more luxurious life (F 3).

    Bibl.: Schlüter 1884, 9; Negro 1919, 36; Webster 1950, 121; Argenio 1965, 270–73; Gaiser 1966, 191–94; Camilloni 1985, 214; Manuwald 2011, 241.

[1] Cf. Theophrastus, *Characters* 18: ἀπιστία.

1 Nonius

duriter ["severely"; archaic form] for *dure* . . . Caecilius in *Deceit*:

              (A) How severely he brought you up, indeed how harshly!
              (B) He doesn't deny it.

2 Nonius

aliquantisper ["for some time"]: . . . Caecilius in *Deceit*:

for if, after they had lost their paternal inheritance, they were driven about for some time in poverty

3 (46 R.³) Non., p. 127.22–23 M. = 185 L.

INCURSIM pro celeriter. Caecilius Fallacia:

tr^7 nullus sum nisi meam rem iam omnem propero
        incursim perdere.

4 (47–48 R.³) Non., p. 430.10–15 M. = 694 L.

INIURIA a contumelia hoc distat. iniuria enim levior res
est. . . . Caecilius Fallacia:

tr^7 facile aerumnam ferre possunt si inde abest inuria;
        etiam iniuriam, nisi contra constant contumeliam.

1 possum *L. Mueller*   2 misi *codd.*   constant *codd.*   et iniuriam si contra constant *cod.*   contumelia *Bothe*: contumeliam *codd.*   si citra constat contumeliam *cod.*, *Fr. Hermann*

5 (51–52 R.³) Non., p. 511.27–34 M. = 823 L.

ALIQUANTISPER . . . Caecilius Fallacia:

ia^7 (A) velim paulisper te opperiri.
    (B) quantisper?
                    (A) non plus triduum.

1 operiri *codd.* (operari *cod.*): opperiri *edd.*

6 (50 R.³) Non., p. 147.24–25 M. = 215 L.

OSSICULATIM: ut si minutatim. Caecilius Fallacia:

tr^7 ossiculatim Parmenonem de via liceat legant.

hosticulatim *cod.*   parmenon est *ut videtur cod.*

3 Nonius

incursim for quickly. Caecilius in *Deceit*:

> I'm done for—unless I hurry up and ruin my whole
> estate in a rush.

4 Nonius

iniuria differs from affront in this way: injury is a lesser
matter. . . . Caecilius in *Deceit*:

> They can easily bear hardship if it is without injury;
> even injury, unless they are faced with affronts.

5 Nonius

aliquantisper ["for a little while"] . . . Caecilius in *Deceit*:

>   (A) I'd like you to wait a little while.
> (B) How little?
>   (A) Not more than three days.

6 Nonius

ossiculatim ["bit by bony bit"]: as if it were piecemeal.
Caecilius in *Deceit*:

> Let them pick Parmeno up from the road bonemeal-
> style.

7 (49 R.³) Non., p. 514.7–8 M. = 826 L.

PUGNITUS pro pugnis. Caecilius Fallacia:

tr⁷   nisi quidem qui sese malit pugnitus pessum dari

    nisi quis est qui se *Madvig*   sese *Guietus, Bothe, Ribbeck*: se *codd., Lindsay*

GAMOS (F 1)

Antiphanes, Sophilus, Diphilus, and Philemon all wrote plays entitled Γάμος *("The Marriage"). In Latin, Pomponius and Laberius both used the Latin title* Nuptiae

1 (53 R.³) Fest., p. 486.19–22 L.

TOXICUM dicitur cervari‹um venenum, quo› quidam perungere sagitta ‹s ›... Caecilius Gamo:

ia⁶   ut hom‹inem. . . › toxico transegerit

    hom . . . *cod.*: hom‹inem miserum› *Scaliger*: hom‹inem amoris› *Spengel*

HARPAZOMENE (F 1–6)

Prior to Caecilius' play of the same name, Antiphanes wrote a Ἁρπαζομένη *(likewise "The Ravished Woman") and Philemon a play either entitled* Ἁρπαζομένη *or* Ἁρπαζόμενος *("The Kidnapped Man").[1] Caecilius' play is reported under both titles, but* Harpazomene *("The Ravished Woman") is both more frequent and seems more likely. The fragments are consistent with the story of a*

7 Nonius

pugnitus for "by means of fists." Caecilius in *Deceit*:

> except someone who prefers to hit the dirt through a
> knock-out

GAMOS (F 1)

*("Marriage") for plays of theirs. The sole fragment here is
presumably metaphorical.*
   Bibl.: Schlüter 1884, 9–10.

1 Festus

toxicum is the name for deer-wort poison, with which
some . . . anoint arrows. Caecilius in *The Marriage*:

> so that he shot the fellow with arrow poison

HARPAZOMENE (F 1–6)

*young man in love (threatened by someone in F 6), but we
have no details.*
   *Bibl.: Schlüter 1884, 10; Argenio 1965, 270; Boscherini
1999, 110; Perutelli 2002, 19–22; Cipriani 2003, 71–75;
Livan 2005, 12–18.*

[1] The feminine form in either language certainly implies abduction for sexual purposes; the masculine form of the title might
not.

1 (54–55 R.^{3}) Non., p. 155.18–19 M. = 228 L.

PULCRITAS pro pulcritudo. Caecilius Harpazomene:

ia^6 di boni,
quid illud est pulchritatis!

creticos exhibit L. Mueller, quem Lindsay secutus est: di boni!
quid *e.q.s.*

2 (56 R.^{3}) Non., p. 200.16–24 M. = 294 L.

COLLUS masculine . . . Caecilius Harpazomene:

ia^6?   hunc collum Ludo praecidi iube!

Ludo *L. Mueller*: Lydo *Warmington*: ludo *vulgo*   pre-
cipi *cod.*   iude *cod.*

3 (57–58 R.^{3}) Charis., *GL* I, p. 144.17–19 = p. 183 B.

SCHEMA quasi monoptoton sit, proinde declinasse Caeci-
lium in Ἀρπαζομένῳ denotatur:

ia^6?   utinam † tescioli † te schema sine cruribus
videam . . .

pro schemate.

pisciculi *Ribbeck*: bestiolae *Maehly*   to schema *Ribbeck*:
te sine schema *ed. princ.*: te servoli schema *Buecheler*   utinam
inquit tescioli schematä sine *cod.*   te sciole istac schema
olim Ribbeck

1 Nonius

pulcritas ["beauty"; alternative earlier form] for *pulcritudo* ["pulchritude"]. Caecilius in *The Ravished Woman*:

> Great gods!
> What beauty that is!

2 Nonius

collus ["neck"; normally neuter *collum*] in the masculine . . . Caecilius in *The Ravished Woman*:

> Have this neck cutlet carved for Sport![1]

[1] The manuscript reading *Ludo* or *ludo* is a dative of purpose, implying a feast celebrating (perhaps personified) play. Warmington suggests *Lydo*, the Lydian (slave?), perhaps doing the carving.

3 Charisius

Caecilius treated *schema* ["form"; a Greek loan word] as if it were an indeclinable noun in *The Kidnapped Man*:

> if only I could see you without legs, in the form of
> †. . .† . . .

in place of *schemate*.[1]

[1] Caecilius uses *schema* as an ablative feminine singular; *schema* is normally a neuter third declension noun, whose ablative singular is *schemate*.

4 (59–60 R.[3]) Non., pp. 10.10–22 M. = 15–16 L.

INLEX et EXLEX est qui sine lege vivat . . . Caecilius Harpazomene:

ia^6? quid narras barbare cum indomitis moribus,
inlitterate inlex?

> 1 cum indomitis *codd.*: indomitis cum *Ribbeck*   2 inlex
> hi sunt *cod.*: inlex es *codd. rell.*, *Spengel, Lindsay*: inlegis *Buecheler*: inlex inlitterate *Brugmann*: inlex Sisenna Hist. *L. Mueller,*
> *fort. recte*

5 (61 R.[3]) Non., p. 128.12–13 M. = 186 L.

INEPTITUDO pro ineptia. Caecilius Harpazomene:

tr^7 qui, homo ineptitudinis cumulatus, cultum oblitus es?

> qui *codd.*: quid *Mercerus*: equi (*id est* ecqui) *Ribbeck*: qui tu
> *L. Mueller*   cultrum *Bothe, Schlüter*

6 (62–63 R.[3]) Donat. ad Ter. *Eun*. 671

"quid vestis mutatio": sic veteres . . . Caecilius Ἁρπαζομένῃ:

tr^7 quid tibi aucupatio est
argumentum aut de meo amore verbificatio est patri?

> 1 aucupatio *ed. princ.*: acceptio *codd., Wessner*   est *om.*
> *cod., edd. vett.*   2 de meo amore *codd.*: meo *om. ed. princ.,*
> *del. Luchs, Ribbeck*

4 Nonius

inlex and *exlex* describe one who lives lawlessly . . . Caecilius in *The Ravished Woman*:

> What are you reporting so barbarously, with your wild
>   ways,
> you illiterate outlaw?

5 Nonius

ineptitudo ["folly"; alternative earlier form] for *ineptia*. Caecilius in *The Ravished Woman*:

> How, you heap of folly, did you forget your manners?

6 Donatus, *Commentary on Terence, The Eunuch*

"Why this change of garb": So earlier writers . . . Caecilius in *The Ravished Woman*:

> Why are you bird-snaring[1]
> for proof or fabricating words for my father about my
>   affair?

[1] Donatus is interested in Caecilius' creation of a substantive ending in *-tio*, of which there are many more in Terence. See Livan 2005, 94.

HYMNIS (F 1–9)

The title Hymnis *is a female personal name; Menander wrote a* Ὕμνις *(F 362–71 K.-A.), most likely a hetaera name, as in Lucian* (Dial. meret. *13). The plot in Caecilius would then include a young man in love with the title character (perhaps expressing himself in F 3), to the disapproval of his father (F 5). How F 1 might fit into the plot*

1 (64–65 R.[3]) Diom., *GL* I, p. 383.10–14

quod vulgo OBSEPIO dicimus veteres OBSIPIO dixerunt. Caecilius in Hymnide:

ia[8]   habes
  Miletida; ego illam huic despondebo et gnato saltum
    obsipiam.

1 habes *codd.*: abis *cod.*   2 Miletida *Bothe, Ribbeck*: m. iletidam *codd.*: mulierculam *cod.*: Melitidem *Betini*   despondebo *cod.*   et gnato *Spengel*: et ex nato *vel* et ex tanto *vel* ex nato *codd.*   saltum *codd.*: tum *vel* saltem *rell.*

Cf. Plaut. *Cas.* 922.

2 (66–67 R.[3]) Non., pp. 78.30–79.3 M. = 110 L.

BLATERARE, confingere per mendacia. . . . ‹BLANDITIES› Caecilius Hymnide:

ia[6]   sine † blanditiae nihil agit
    in amore inermus

blandities *add. Onions*   1 blanditiae *codd., corruptum videtur*: sine blaterare *Vettori*: desine blanditias blatere *Osann*:

HYMNIS (F 1–9)

is quite unclear: the father should be speaking, but the
woman of Milos, if eligible for marriage, should not be the
same as the title character, and how her betrothal would
impede the son's plans is opaque.

Bibl.: Schlüter 1884, 10–11; Argenio 1965, 270; Frassi-
netti 1979, 80–81; Camilloni 1985, 215; Austin 1999, 47–
49; Boscherini 1999, 109, 113; Cipriani 2010, 124–28.

1 Diomedes

We standardly say *obsepio* ["hedge in"]; past generations
said *obsipio*. Caecilius in *Hymnis*:

> you have
> the woman of Milos; I shall betroth her to this man
> and trap my son in the woods.

2 Nonius

blaterare ["to babble"] is to fabricate through falsehoods.
. . . *blandities* ["blandishment"] Caecilius in *Hymnis*:

> an unarmed man in love achieves nothing
> without blandishment

---

sine blandirier *Stowasser*: sine blande blaterem *prop. in app.*
Lindsay   agis *L. Mueller*

3 (71 R.³) Non., p. 135.2–3 M. = 196 L.

LUCULENTITATEM a luculento. Caecilius Hymnide:

*tr*⁷   . . . vide luculentitatem eius et magnificentiam!

> em *ante* vide *add. Ribbeck*   luculentitem *cod.*: luculen-
> tiam *in senario Buecheler*   eius *om. Bothe*

4 (70 R.³) Cic. *Fin*. 2.22

atqui reperiemus asotos primum ita non religiosos ut
"edint de patella," deinde ita mortem non timentes ut illud
in ore habeant ex Hymnide:

*tr*⁷   mihi sex menses satis sunt vitae; septimum Orco
       spondeo.

5 (68–69 R.³) Non., p. 134.11–17 M. = 195 L.

LICITARI: congredi, pugnare . . . Caecilius Hymnide:

*ia*⁷   (P.?)   quae
       narrare inepti est ad scutras ferventis.
       (F.?)   quin machaera
       licitari adversum ahenum coepisti sciens.

> 2 ad *add. Ribbeck*   3 licitari *edd.*: licitaria *codd.*   ahe-
> num *edd.*: aeneum *codd.*

3 Nonius

luculentitas ["splendor"] from *luculentus* ["splendid"].
Caecilius in *Hymnis*:

> . . . Look at her splendiferousness and magnificence!

4 Cicero, *On Ends*

Yet we shall find profligates in the first place so devoid of
religious scruples that they "will eat the food from the
paten," and secondly so fearless of death as to be always
quoting the lines from the *Hymnis*:

> Six months of life are enough for me; the seventh I
> pledge to Death.[1]

[1] Apparently adapted by Lucilius, *Satires* F 659 Warmington:
qui sex menses vitam ducunt, Orco spondent septimum ("those
who drag out their life for six months, pledge the seventh to
Death").

5 Nonius

licitari ["to bid, contend for"]: to join battle, to fight . . .
Caecilius in the *Hymnis*:

> (Father?)   It's stupid
> to talk to steaming kettles.
> (Son?)   Well, you've begun
> to take up sword against bronze, as well you know.[1]

[1] Talking to a steaming kettle may resemble our "talking to a
brick wall," but since cooking pots were mostly bronze, the son
can twist the metaphor.

6 (72 R.³) Fest., p. 182.30–34 L.

NICTARE et oculorum et aliorum membrorum nisu saepe aliquid conari, dictum est ab antiquis . . . Caecilius in Hymnide:

*tr*⁷ garruli sine dentes iactent, sine nictentur perticis.

garruli medentes *cod. corr. Scaliger*

7 (73 R.³) Fest., p. 454.30–33 L.

SENIUM, a senili acerbitate et vitiis dictum, posuit Caecilius in Hymnide:

*tr*⁷ sine suam senectutem ducat usque ad sen‹i›um
        sorbilo.

usque *Bentley*: utique *cod., Lindsay*   sen‹i›um *edd.*: senum *cod.*   sorbilo *Bentley*: sorbitio *cod.*: sorbito *Spengel*: sonticum *Gravert*

8 (74 R.³) Fest., p. 254.19–21 L.

PRODEGERIS, consumpseris, perdideris, ut Caecilius in Hymni‹de›:

*tr*⁷ prodigere est cum nihil habeas te inrid‹er›ier.

est *cod.*: et *Ribbeck*   te *cod.*: ted *Neue*   inridier *cod., Ribbeck, corr. Dacerius*

9 (74¹ R.³) Charis., *GL* I, p. 207.20–24 = p. 269 B.

nudius tertius Caecilius in Hymnide . . . significat autem "nunc est dies tertius."

? nudius tertius

6 Festus

nictare ["to blink, twitch"] is to try something often, both
by an effort of eyes and other body parts, said by earlier
writers . . . Caecilius in the *Hymnis*:

> Let the babblers flap their jaws, let them wobble with
> their canes.

7 Festus

senium ["senility"], derived from the tartness and faults of
old age, used by Caecilius in *Hymnis*:

> Let him extend his old age all the way to senility, a
> drop at a time.

8 Festus

prodegeris ["you have squandered"], "you've used up,"
"destroyed" . . . for example, Caecilius in *Hymnis*:

> Dissipation is when you have nothing—and they
> laugh at you.

9 Charisius

Caecilius uses *nudius tertius* in *Hymnis* . . . it means, how-
ever, "now is the third day."

> the third day

HYPOBOLIMAEUS (SUBDITIVOS)
(t 1–3, F 1–8)

Plays entitled Ὑποβολιμαῖος *("The Changeling") were written by Alexis (F 246 K.-A., making a political reference to Ptolemy II), Cratinus the Younger,[1] Eudoxus, Philemon, and Menander (F 372–87 K.-A.); most assume Menander's play lies behind that of Caecilius.*

Four play titles reported for Caecilius include the borrowed Greek term Hypobolimaeus *("The Changeling") or its archaic Latin equivalent* Subditivos, *both masculine substantives that mean "substituted person"; in ancient comedy that is a term for a suppositious child or changeling, although here it may simply mean that the designated young man was given to a foster father to raise. Three of these titles—*Hypobolimaeus *("The Changeling"),* Hypobolimaeus Chaerestratus *("The Changeling Chaerestratus"), and* Hypobolimaeus Rastraria *("The Changeling: A Play about a Hoe") seem likely to be variant reports of a single play whose plot involved the young man Chaeres-*

t 1 Varro, *Rust.* 2.11.11

neque non quaedam nationes harum [caprarum] pellibus sunt vestitae, ut in Gaetulia et in Sardinia. cuius usum apud anticos quoque Graecos fuisse apparet, quod in tragoediis senes ab hac pelle vocantur διφθερίαι et in comoediis qui in rustico opere morantur, ut aput Caecilium in Hypobolimaeo habet adulescens, apud Terentium in Heautontimorumeno senex.

HYPOBOLIMAEUS (SUBDITIVOS)
(t 1–3, F 1–8)

*tratus being raised in the country, although that conclu-
sion relies on the belief that Cicero in one of his speeches
confused the name of the young man raised in the country
with that of his brother who was raised in the city (nota-
bly, Cicero adds parenthetically "I think, that is his
name"). Guardì numbers the fragments of these as three
separate plays, and that arrangement is followed here. The
fourth reported title is* Hypobolimaeus Aeschinus *("The
Changeling Aeschinus"), and this suggests a separate play,
with Aeschinus as its protagonist.*

Bibl.: Teuffel 1858, 4–5; Schlüter 1884, 11–12; Faider
1908–9, 334; Negro 1919, 28–31, 36–37; Argenio 1965,
257–65; Frassinetti 1979, 80–83; Camilloni 1985, 215–17;
Gaiser 1987–88; Perutelli 2002, 22–26; Livan 2005, 89–90;
Cipriani 2010, 128–31, 154–55; Hanses 2020, 101, 126–
27.

[1] Also under the title Ψευδυποβολιμαῖος, *"The False Change-
ling"* (F 10 K.-A.), which seems a bit of overkill.

t 1 Varro, *On Agriculture*

Some tribes are clad in (goats') skins, for example, in Gae-
tulia and Sardinia. The ancient Greeks also have this cus-
tom, as is shown by the fact that the old men in tragedies
are called "jerkin wearers" from this goat skin, and also
men in comedies working in rural tasks, such as the young
man in Caecilius' *Changeling*, and the old man in Ter-
ence's *The Self-Tormentor*.

t 2 Cic. *Rosc. Am.* 46

etquid tandem tibi videtur, ut ad fabulas veniamus, senex
ille Caecilianus minoris facere Eutychum filium rusticum,
quam illum alterum, Chaerestratum? (nam, ut opinor, hoc
nomine est) alterum in urbe secum honoris causa habere,
alterum rus supplicii causa relegasse?

t 3 Schol. Gronov. ad Cic. *Rosc. Am.* 46

apud Caecilium comoediographum inducitur pater qui-
dam qui habebat duos filios, et illum, quem odio habebat,
secum habebat, quem amabat, ruri dedit.

1a (75 R.^{3}) Non., pp. 178.14–17 M. = 261–62 L.

TETULIT: tulit. . . . Caecilius Hypobolimaeo:

ia^6 aerumnam pariter tetulisti meam

1b Quint. *Inst.* 1.10.18

apud Menandrum in Hypobolimaeo senex, qui reposcenti
filium patri velut rationem inpendiorum quae in educa-
tionem contulerit exponens psaltis se et geometris multa
dicit dedisse.

nam mecum *suppl. Ribbeck ante* aerumnam

---

1 Not the boy's father, but a countryman entrusted with the
young man's upbringing. If such a character appeared in Caeci-
lius' version, this line might be part of his exchange with the boy's
father.

COMEDIES: HYPOBOLIMAEUS (SUBDITIVOS)

t 2 Cicero, *Pro Sexto Roscio Amerino*

To take an example from the stage, I ask you whether you really think that the old man in the play of Caecilius thinks less of the son Eutychus, who lives in the country, than of the other, Chaerestratus[1] (for, I think, that is his name); that he keeps the one with him in the city as a token of esteem, while he has sent the other into the country as a punishment?

[1] Warmington believed, based on Festus (p. 186.30–32 L.) and Quintilian (*Inst.* 1.10.18), that "Cicero has interchanged the names, and that the country-reared son was Chaerestratus, and the town-reared son Eutychus."

t 3 Scholia Gronoviana to Cicero, *Pro Sexto Roscio Amerino*

In a play of Caecilius the comic poet a certain father appears on stage who had two sons, and the one he disliked he kept at home with him and the one whom he loved he consigned to the country.

1a Nonius

tetulit ["he endured"; earlier form] for *tulit*. . . . Caecilius in *The Changeling*:

> you have endured my hardship equally with me

1b Quintilian, *The Orator's Education*

The old man[1] in Menander's *The Changeling*, who, in giving an account as it were to the boy's real father (who is claiming him back) of the expenses he has incurred on his education, says that he has paid large sums to teachers of the lyre and teachers of geometry.

453

2 (76 R.[3]) Prisc., *GL* II, pp. 199.17–200.6

SCHEMA pro schemate. . . . Caecilius in Hypobolimaeo:

ia[6]   filius in med incedit satis hilara schema.

med *Bothe*: me *codd.*   incendid *cod.*   hilaria *cod.*:
hilari *codd. rell.*   schaema *cod.*: scema *rell.*   filius meus
in me incedit ‹eccum› sat h. s. *Ribbeck*[2]: filius ‹meus eccum›
incedit in me sat h. s. *Ribbeck*[3]: ‹tum› filius in me incedit s. h. s.
Umpfenbach

3 (77 R.[3]) Fest., pp. 416.35–18.5 L.

STOLIDUS, stultus. . . . et Caecilius in Hypobolimaeo:

ia[6]   abi hinc tu, stolide; vis ille ut tibi sit pater.

illi *cod., corr. Augustinus*: ille *Bothe*: vis *vel* visne illi *Ribbeck*:
dic illi *Buecheler*

4 (78 R.[3]) Non., p. 514.31–32 M. = 828 L.

IRACUNDITER. Caecilius Subditivo:

ia[6]   quaeso ne temere hanc rem agas ne iracunditer.

agas et ne *codd.*: et *om. ed. princ., edd.*

5 (79–80 R.[3]) Gell. *NA* 15.9.1

vere ac diserte Caecilius hoc in Subditivo scripsit:

ia[7]   nam hi sunt inimici pessumi, fronte hilaro, corde
           tristi
ia[6]   quos neque ut adprendas neque uti dimittas scias.

2 adprendas *Non., edd.*: ad prebendas *cod.*: adprehendas *rell.*
Gell.   uti dimittas *Spengel*: ut mittas *codd. Gell.*: ut vitare
cod. Non.: vitare *rell. Non.*

2 Priscian

schema ["form"; here treated as a first declension feminine ablative] for *schemate*.[1] . . . Caecilius in *The Changeling*:

My son advances toward me in quite festive form.

[1] *schema* is normally a neuter third declension noun, whose ablative singular is *schemate*; cf. *Harpazomene* F 3 *FRL*.

3 Festus

stolidus ["stupid"], idiotic. . . . And Caecilius in *The Changeling*:

Get out of here, you idiot; you want *that* man for your father.

4 Nonius

iracunditer ["angrily"]: Caecilius in *The Changeling*:

Please don't handle this matter heedlessly or irascibly.

5 Gellius, *Attic Nights*

Correctly and elegantly[1] Caecilius wrote this in *The Changeling*:

The worst enemies have cheerful faces and bitter hearts:
you don't understand how to hold onto them nor how to get rid of them.

[1] Gellius is defending the use of *frons* as a masculine noun (cf. Corbeill 2015, 44–45).

Cf. Non., pp. 204.26–5.2 M. = 301 L.

6 (81 R.[3]) Charis., *GL* I, p. 132.4–5 = p. 169 B.

HEBEM. Caecilius in Ὑποβολιμαίῳ:

ia[6]?   subito res reddent hebem.

     reste reddent *ed. princ.*: res te *Bothe*

7 (82 R.[3]) Fest., p. 486.5–10 L.

‹TUGU›RIA a tecto appellantur . . . ‹Caecilius in Hypo›bolimaeo:

ia[6]   habita ‹bat**** tugurio pau›perculo

     habitaba‹t in tuguriolo pau›perculo *suppl. Ribbeck*: tugurio sine operculo *Ursinus*: tugurio nullo operculo *C. O. Mueller*

8 (84 R.[3]) Fest., p. 340.17–22 L.

RAVIM anti‹qui dicebant pro raucitate.› . . . ‹. . . Caeciliu›s in Hypobolimaeo:

?   prius ‹quam**ad ravim**› . . . citam feceris

     citam *ut vid. cod.*   prius ‹ad ravim deposcat sane quam conten›tam feceris *suppl. Ribbeck*[3]: prius / ‹ad ravim poscaris quam place›ntam feceris *Ursinus*: prius / ‹ad ravim poscas quam place›ntam feceris *Gravert*: prius ‹ad ravim procaris quam me place/ntam feceris *Dacerius*: ‹ad ravim› prius ‹poscaris quam place›ntam feceris *Spengel*: prius ‹ad ravim poscase panem quam place›ntam feceris *Ribbeck*[1–2]

6 Charisius

hebem ["slow, dull"; earlier form for *hebetem*]. Caecilius in *The Changeling*:

> The situation will immediately slow him down.

7 Festus

tuguria ["huts"] are named after *tectum* ["shelter, roof"] . . . Caecilius in *The Changeling*:

> s/he was living in an impoverished hovel[1]

[1] Possibly from a prologue.

8 Festus

ravim the ancients said for *raucitas* ["hoarseness"]. . . . . . .
Caecilius in *The Changeling*:

> before you make . . . to hoarseness

HYPOBOLIMAEUS AESCHINUS (F 1)

1 (92 R.³) Gell. *NA* 15.14.1–5

apud Q. Metellum Numidicum in libro accusationis *In Valerium Messalam* tertio nove dictum esse adnotavimus. [2] verba ex oratione eius haec sunt [*Orat.* 58 F 8 *FRL*]: "cum sese sciret in tantum crimen venisse atque socios ad senatum questum flentes venisse, sese pecunias maximas exactos esse." [3] "sese pecunias," inquit, "⟨maximas⟩ exactos esse" pro eo quod est "pecunias a se esse maximas exactas." [4] id nobis videbatur Graeca figura dictum . . . [5] Caecilius ⟨quo⟩que eadem figura in Hypobolimaeo Aeschino usus videtur:

ia⁶   ego illud minus nihilo exigor portorium.

id est "nihilominus exigitur de me portorium."

nihilo *codd. Gell. et Non.*: nilo *Fleckeisen, Ribbeck*

Cf. Non., p. 106.21–22 M. = 152 L.

HYPOBOLIMAEUS CHAERESTRATUS (F 1)

1 (85 R.³) Fest., p. 180.27–32 L.

at NOXA peccatum, aut pro peccato poena . . . Caecilius in Hypobolimaeo Chaerestrato:

ia⁶   nam ista quidem noxa muliebre est magis quam viri.

istaec *Gravert*   muliebrem et *cod,. corr. Bothe*: muliebris est *Ursinus*: muliebrist *C. O. Mueller*: mulierist *Gravert*: mulieris magis quam viri est *Meineke*

HYPOBOLIMAEUS AESCHINUS (F1)

1 Gellius, *Attic Nights*

In Quintus Metellus Numidicus, in the third book of his *Accusation of Valerius Messala*, I have made note of a novel expression. [2] The words of his speech are as follows [*Orat.* 58 F 8 *FRL*]: "When he knew that he had incurred so grave an accusation, and that our allies had come to the senate in tears, to make complaint that they had been exacted enormous sums of money." [3] He says "that they had been exacted enormous sums of money," instead of "that enormous sums of money had been exacted from them." [4] This seemed to me an imitation of a Greek idiom[1] . . . [5] Caecilius seems also to have used that form of expression in his *Changeling Aeschinus*:

That tariff I nonetheless am exacted.

That is: "the tariff is nonetheless exacted from me."

[1] An error by Gellius: this double accusative construction is native to Latin.

HYPOBOLIMAEUS CHAERESTRATUS (F 1)

1 Festus

But *noxa* ["harm"], an error or a penalty for error . . . Caecilius in *The Changeling Chaerestratus*:

For that's more a woman's sort of error than a man's.

HYPOBOLIMAEUS RASTRARIA (F 1–6)

1 (86 R.[3]) Non., p. 147.6–7 M. = 214 L.

OBSORDUIT obsolevit. Caecilius Hypobolimaeo Rastraria:

ia[6]   obsorduit iam haec in mea aerumna miseria.

obsorduit *codd.*: obsurduit *Ribbeck*   mea *Fleckeisen*: me *codd.*

2 (87 R.[3]) Non., p. 505.29–30 M. = 813 L.

MANTAT pro manet. Caecilius Hypobolimaeo Rastraria:

ia[6]   in voltu eodem, in eadem mantat malitia.

3 (88 R.[3]) Non., p. 176.6–8 M. = 259 L.

SINGULATIM et SINGILLATIM a singulis. Caecilius Hypo-
bolimaeo Rastraria:

ia[6]   hos singulatim sapere, nos minus arbitror.

nos singulatim sapere non minus *Bothe*

4 (89 R.[3]) Non., p. 40.1–4 M. = 58 L.

RABERE dictum est a rabie . . . Caecilius Hypobolimaeo
Rastraria:

tr[7]?   rabere se ait

HYPOBOLIMAEUS RASTRARIA (F 1–6)

1 Nonius

obsorduit ["has become soiled"]: "has worn out." Caecilius in *The Changeling: A Play about a Hoe:*

> This misery has already worn out in my hardship.

2 Nonius

mantat ["is waiting"] for *manet* ["remains"]. Caecilius in *The Changeling: A Play about a Hoe:*

> He abides in the same look, the same spite.

3 Nonius

singulatim and *singillatim* [both "one by one"] from *singuli* ["one at a time"]. Caecilius in *The Changeling: A Play about a Hoe:*

> I consider these men wise individually, ourselves less so.

4 Nonius

rabere ["to rave"] is derived from *rabies* ["madness"] . . . Caecilius in *The Changeling: A Play about a Hoe:*

> he claims he's raving

5 (90 R.[3]) Non., p. 89.14–15 M. = 127 L.

COEPERE: incipere. Caecilius Hypobolimaeo Rastraria:

ia[6]   (A) ere, obsecro, hercle, desine! (B) mane, coepiam.

obsecro *Spengel*: obscuro *codd.*

6 (91 R.[3]) Non., p. 16.14–17 M. = 23 L.

LACTARE est inducere vel mulgere, vellere, decipere . . .
Caecilius Hypobolimaeo Rastraria:

tr[7]   quod prolubium, quae voluptas, quae te lactat
largitas?

Cf. Ter. *Ad.* 985.

IMBRII (F 1–8)

*Prior to Caecilius' Imbrii ("The Imbrians"), Menander
wrote an Ἴμβριοι ("Imbrians," F 190–*192 K.-A.).
P.Oxy. 1235 tells us the play was written for the Dionysia
of 302/1 BC, but kept from being staged by the tyrant
Lachares. It includes a partial plot summary about two
poor men working together on the island of Imbros who
married twin sisters. The speaker of F 7 refers to his*

1 (93 R.[3]) Non., p. 159.5–20 M. = 234 L.

PECUA et PECUDA ita ut pecora veteres dixerunt . . . Cae-
cilius Imbriis:

ia/tr   et homini et pecudibus omnibus

pecudibus *codd.*, *Lindsay*: pecubus (*vel* pecudis) *Spen-
gel*   et hominibus et pecudis *Gravert*

5 Nonius

coepere ["to begin"]: "to start." Caecilius in *The Change-ling: A Play about a Hoe:*

> (A) Master, please, by Hercules, stop! (B) Hang on,
>   I'm just getting going.

6 Nonius

lactare ["to wheedle"] is "to lead on or to milk, pluck, deceive" . . . Caecilius in *The Changeling: A Play about a Hoe:*

> What desire, what pleasure, what lavishness is
>   milking you dry?

IMBRII (F 1–8)

brother and F 2 to a pregnancy, which would fit such a plot. The reference in F 4 implies returning to a homeland elsewhere, so the "Imbrians" of the title may have been political or economic exiles from elsewhere (Athens?), granted a happy homecoming in the end.

Bibl.: Schlüter 1884, 12–13; Argenio 1965, 276; Frassinetti 1979, 83–84; Cipriani 2010, 156–57.

1 Nonius

pecua and *pecuda* ["cattle"; earlier forms] are used by early writers for *pecora* . . . Caecilius in *The Imbrians:*

> for man and all cattle

2 (94–95 R.³) Non., p. 188.11–13 M. = 276 L.

UTER pro uterus . . . Caecilius Imbriis:

*tr*⁷   nunc uter
crescit, non potest celari.

3 (99 R.³) Fest., p. 210.11–15 L.

OBSTIPUM, oblicum. . . . Caecilius in Imbris:

*ia*⁸   resupina obstipo capitulo sibi ventum facere tunicula.

   obstito *codd., corr. Gifanius*   ventum] iunctim *cod. (non
ed. princ.)*   cunicula *codd., corr. Ursinus*

4 (100 R.³) Prisc., *GL* II, p. 231.13–18

"hic puerus" . . . vetustissimi protulisse inveniuntur . . .
Caecilius in Imbris:

*tr*⁷   age age i puere, duc me ad patrios fines decoratum
      opipare!

   age age i puere *codd.*: i *om. rell.*   duc *cod., Spengel*: duce
codd.

Cf. Mai 1836, 390, 407.

5 (96–97 R.³) Prisc., *GL* II, p. 512.24–13.6

EXPERGISCOR experrectum facit quamvis vetustissimi
etiam "expergitus" dicebant . . . Caecilius analogiam pro-
tulit in Imbriis:

2 Nonius

uter ["belly, womb"; earlier nominative form] for *uterus*
. . . Caecilius in *The Imbrians*:

> Now her belly
> swells; it can't be hid.

3 Festus

obstipum ["bent"], slanting. . . . Caecilius in *The Imbrians*:

> On her back, her little head awry, she fans herself
> with her little tunic.

4 Priscian

puerus ["boy"; earlier form, nom. masc.] is found in the
earliest writers . . . Caecilius in *The Imbrians*:

> Come along, lad, move: lead me to my homeland
> richly decked out![1]

[1] Or "to be richly decked out," if *decoratum* is supine.

5 Priscian

expergiscor ["I awake"] forms the perfect participle *exper-
rectus*, although the earliest writers also said *expergitus*
. . . Caecilius offers a parallel in *The Imbrians*:

tr^7?   surdo mihi
        dormitum suadet ut eam quisquam? et si ego
            obdormivero,
        tute idem ubi eris experrectus?

> 1 surdo mihi *Fleckeisen*: mihi surdo *Ribbeck¹*: mihi sordo *cod.*:
> mihi sordi *codd. rell.*: mihi sordida *Lipsius 1 Krehlii*: mihi sordido
> *ed. Ven. 1*: mihi sobrio *coni. Buecheler*: dum sorbilo *coni. in app.*
> *Ribbeck³*: socordi mihi *Brakman*   2 dormitum *e.q.s. codd.*,
> *Guardì*: dormitum ut eam quisquam suadet *Ribbeck²⁻³*: suadet
> ut eam quisquam dormitum *Warmington*   3 idem *add.*
> *cod.*   ubi eris *cod.*: uberius *cod.*: ibi eris *Putsch*

6 (98 R.³) Non., p. 194.7–11 M. = 285 L.

BALNEAE generis feminini. . . . Caecilius in Imbris:

tr^7?   quid? mihi non sunt balneae?

> in Imbris *codd.*: infoebis *cod.*: Synephebis *Lindsay*

7 (101–2 R.³) Non., pp. 524.18–25.24 M. = 843 L.

TURBAM et TURBAS diversam volunt habere significa-
tionem, ut sit turba populi conventus, turbae turbationes.
nos contra lectum invenimus et indiscrete positum et pro
turbis turbam . . . Caecilius in Imbriis:

ia^8 mirum adeo, nisi frater domi ebriatus turbam
            aliquam dedit.

> ebriatus *Buecheler*: ebrius *codd.*

> Though I'm deaf to the appeal,
> is anyone trying to get me to go to sleep? Even if I do
>   sleep,
> you there, when will you be wide awake?

6 Nonius

balneae ["baths"] feminine gender.[1] . . . Caecilius in *The Imbrians*:

> What? Don't I have baths?

[1] According to Varro (*Ling.* 9.68), in the classical period *balneum* was used for a private bath, *balneae* for the public baths. Perhaps the distinction is just developing in Caecilius' time, and the older speaker is offended by correction or denial.

7 Nonius

turba ["crowd"] and *turbae* ["tumult"] should have different meanings, where *turba* is a gathering of the people and *turbae* uproar. In fact, we have found *turba* and *turbae* used indiscriminately . . . Caecilius in *The Imbrians*:

> It will be amazing if my drunken brother hasn't
>   created some uproar at home.

8a (103 R.[3]) Non., p. 465.1–6 M. = 744 L.

GRUNDIRE . . . etiam hominum esse grunditum Caecilius
[in] Imbriis designavit:

> in *vel om. codd.*

8b Diom., *GL* I, p. 383.20–22

grunnit porcus dicimus; veteres grundire dicebant, ut sit
instans grudio: Caecilius:

ia[6]   cruento ita ore grundibat miser

MERETRIX (F 1–2)

For Caecilius' title Meretrix *("The Prostitute"), the closest
Greek term would be* Ἑταίρα *("Hetaera"), but no Greek
comedy so entitled is known. The Roman authors Turpilius
and Novius, however, both wrote plays entitled* Hetaera,

1 (110 R.[3]) Non., p. 536.8–9 M. = 859 L.

PROSUMIA: navigii genus. Caecilius Meretrice:

ia[6]   Cypro gubernator propere vertit prosumiam.

> Cupro *Buecheler*: Cypro *Lindsay*: cui pro *codd.*: cui progu-
> bernator *edd. vett., Bothe, Spengel*: cum ultro *Ribbeck*   vertit
> propere *dub. in app. Lindsay*

Cf. Paul. *Fest.*, p. 252.18 L.

8a Nonius

grundire ["to grunt"] . . . Caecilius in *The Imbrians* has shown that grunting is also used of human beings:

8b Diomedes

We say "a pig grunts"; earlier writers used *grundire* when one is groaning insistently: Caecilius:

> even with mouth so bloody the poor man was
> grunting

MERETRIX (F 1–2)

while Pomponius wrote a Postribulum *("The Brothel"). It has been suggested that Caecilius and Turpilius worked from the same Greek original.*
    Bibl.: Schlüter 1884, 13.

1 Nonius

prosumia ["spy ship"]: a kind of ship. Caecilius in *The Prostitute*:

> The helmsman quickly turned the spy ship away from
> Cyprus.

2 (111–12 R.³) Non., p. 202.12–14 M. = 297 L.

CANDELABRUM generis neutri, ut saepe. masculini Caecilius Meretrice . . . :

*tr*⁷   . . . memini ibi candelabrum ligneum ardentem

    ibi fuisse (*vel* videre) *Ribbeck*: invenit inibit *Buecheler*: illic *Gravert*   ligneum *Bothe, Spengel*

NAUCLERUS (F 1–3)

The title Nauclerus *("The Shipmaster") is a Greek loanword.*[1] *Menander wrote a* Ναύκληρος *("Shipmaster"), as did Eudoxus (F 1 K.-A.), while Nausicrates wrote a* Ναύκληροι *("Shipmasters," F 1 K.-A.). The Menander fragments (246–51 K.-A.) reveal the safe return of a ship, and some play with tragic language, but not enough to reconstruct its plot or Caecilius' play, though likely based on*

1 (= 113 R.³) Non., pp. 505.35–6.5 M. = 813 L.

AUDIBO pro audiam . . . Caecilius Nauclero:

*an*⁷   nunc abeo; audibis praeterea si dicis "filia redeat."

    nunc abeo] num habeo *Spengel*: non habeo *Bothe*: nunc ab eo *Buecheler*   dicis *codd.*: dices *Buecheler*: ditis *Ribbeck*³   si eius redeat filia *vel* si redierit filia *Ribbeck*¹⁻²: sed vin redeat filia? *Gravert*

2 (114 R.³) Non., p. 126.27–28 M. = 183 L.

INFELICENT . . . Caecilius Nauclero:

2 Nonius

candelabrum ["lamp stand"] is often neuter. Caecilius uses masculine gender in *The Prostitute*:

> . . . I remember a wooden lamp stand shining there

NAUCLERUS (F 1–3)

Menander's. Naevius wrote a Nautae *("The Sailors," F 50 FRL).*
> *Bibl.: Schlüter 1884, 13; Webster 1950, 73n1.*

[1] It also appears in Plautus, *Mil.* 1110, and there are some postclassical usages, but it is supplanted by *gubernator* ("captain, helmsman") in classical Latin.

1 Nonius

audibo ["I shall hear"; earlier future form] for *audiam* [classical future form] . . . Caecilius in *The Shipmaster*:

> I'm going now; you'll hear hereafter if you say "Let the daughter come back."

2 Nonius

infelicent ["may they curse"] . . . Caecilius in *The Shipmaster*:

tr^7 ut te di omnes infelicent cum male monita memoria!

ut dedi *codd.*   infelicitent *codd.*, *corr. Guietus, def. Bue-*
cheler   monita] molita *codd.*: merita *cod.*, *L. Mueller*   in-
felicent male moenita *Spengel*

3 (115 R.[3]) Non., p. 12.21–26 M. = 19 L.

SUPPILARE est involare vel rapere: a pilorum raptu; unde
et furtum passi conpilari dicuntur. . . . Caecilius Nauclero:

ia^6 subpilat vestem atque ornamenta omnia

subpilat vestem aurum *vel* subpilat vestem *Onions*: sub-
pilatum est eum *codd.*: suppilatum est aurum *coni. Bothe,*
Spengel, Ribbeck: suppilatum est aurum argentum atque
Maehly   ormenta *cod.*

NOTHUS NICASIO (F 1–3)

Before Caecilius' Nothus Nicasio ("The Illegitimate Nica-
sio"), Philemon wrote a Νόθος *(F 51–53 K.-A.), meaning*
at Athens the offspring of a legally unrecognized union. A
masculine name Νικασίος *seems unknown in the* Lexicon
of Greek Personal Names, *although there are two in-*
stances of a feminine Νικασία, *and a slave named Nicasio*
appears in Afranius, Tog. 189 R.[3]. *The title might suggest*
a plot centered on achieving recognition of legitimate birth

May all the gods plague you with your
misremembered memory![1]

[1] *infelicent* occurs in Plautus, *Cas.* 246, *Merc.* 436, *Rud.* 885
and 1225, *Epid.* 13, and *Poen.* 449. Cf. Menander, *Epitrepontes*
425: ὡς ... ὁ Ζεὺς ἀπολέσαι ("may Zeus destroy"), and Antipha-
nes, F 190.3 K.-A.: ὅσα Ποσειδῶν ἀπολέσαι ("may Poseidon
destroy").

3 Nonius

suppilare ["to pilfer"] means "to fly at" or "to snatch at,"
from pulling out hair; so those who have suffered a theft
are said to be fleeced. .... Caecilius in *The Shipmaster*:

s/he fleeces (someone) of clothing and all accessories

NOTHUS NICASIO[1] (F 1–3)

*and thus citizen status for the title character, but the frag-
ments offer no indication of this. F 1 may refer to a money
pouch carried around the neck, with some role in the plot.*
    *Bibl.: Schlüter 1884, 14; Harrison 1968, 61–70; Mac-
Dowell 1978, 99; Boscherini 1999, 112.*

[1] Warmington suggests that the addition of the personal name
to this title may mean that Caecilius may have written another
play simply entitled *Nothus* ("*The Illegimate Offspring*").

1 (116 R.[3]) Non., p. 97.25–26 M. = 138 L.

DECOLLARE: ex collo deponere. Caecilius Notho Nicasione:

ia[8] habes, vide; tibi tradidi; in tuo collo est. decolles
   cave.

   viden *vel* vide em *coni. Ribbeck*: habes quidem tibi *L. Mueller*

2 (117 R.[3]) Non., pp. 324.34–25.3 M. = 509 L.

ILICO: significat statim, mox . . . Caecilius Notho Nicasione:

cr ilico ante ostium hic erimus.

3 (118 R.[3]) Non., p. 325.6–13 M. = 510 L.

ILICO: in eo loco . . . Caecilius Notho Nicasione:

cr? manete ilico!

   manet *cod.*

OBOLOSTATES VEL FAENERATOR
(F 1–7)

Obolostates ("*The Moneylender*") is simply transliterated
from Greek Ὀβολοστάτης,[1] a small-time moneylender (a
"weigher of obols"). The double title is not preserved together in our sources but reconstructed on the belief that
Caecilius would not have written two different plays with
essentially the same title. The borrowed Greek title seems

1 Nonius

decollare ["behead" in classical Latin] means to unburden from the neck.[1] Caecilius in *The Illegitimate Nicasio*:

> You've got it, see! I've handed it over to you; it's on your neck. Just don't unburden your neck.

[1] This unique example in Caecilius may be his own joke by literalization: *decollare* as "take off from" rather than "take off at the neck."

2 Nonius

ilico ["there," but also "instantly"] means at once, very soon . . . Caecilius in *The Illegitimate Nicasio*:

> We'll be in front of the door here at once.

3 Nonius

ilico ["there"]: "in that place" . . . Caecilius in *The Illegitimate Nicasio*:

> Stay there!

OBOLOSTATES VEL FAENERATOR
(F 1–7)

a guarantee of a specific Greek source play, but no such title is recorded for Greek comedy. Nicostratus wrote a Τοκιστής *("The Usurer"), which is also the alternative title for Alexis'* Καταψευδόμενος *(cf. Caecilius' Fallacia). Recorded among Plautus' lost plays is a Faeneratrix ("The Woman Moneylender," F 1–2 De Melo). F 1–2 might*

express the despair of a young lover; the Laches addressed
in F 4 could be the titular moneylender. Schlüter also at-
tributed F Inc. 6 to this play.

1 (119–20 R.³) Non., p. 508.7–13 M. = 817 L.

REPERIBITUR pro reperietur . . . Caecilius Obolostate:

tr⁸   nunc enimvero est cum meae morti remedium
       reperibit nemo.

    Obolostate *Mercier*: obolo *codd.*   nunc nunc enim vero
in senario Bergk: meae quum *in senario Bothe, Spengel*

2 (121 R.³) Non., p. 279.24–42 M. = 430 L.

DEPONERE est desperare: unde et depositi desperati di-
cuntur . . . Caecilius in Obolostate:

tr⁷   depositus modo
    sum anima, vita sepultus sum.

    2 animo *dub. in app. Ribbeck*   vita *codd.*: vivos L. Muel-
ler   sum² *del. Ribbeck*   1–2 depositus anima modo,
vita sepultus sum *Spengel*: depositus anima, vita modo sepultu'
sum *Bothe*

3 (= 122–23 R.³) Fest., p. 376.25–33 L.

⟨SILICERNIUM dicitur cena fu⟩ nebris, quam ⟨Graeci
περίδειπνον v⟩ocant. . . . ⟨. . . Caecilius Ob⟩olostate:

tr⁷   cre⟨didi silicernium eiu⟩s me esse esurum

    Graeci περίδειπνον *Mueller*   cre⟨18 *litt.*⟩ş me esse
esurum *cod., litteras quae in cod. non apparent habet Paulus*

Bibl.: Schlüter 1884, 14–15; Argenio 1965, 274; Cipriani 2010, 131–33.

[1] The term occurs in Aristophanes' *Clouds* 1155 and Antiphanes' *Neottis*, F 166 K.-A.

1 Nonius

reperibitur ["it will be found"; earlier future form] for *reperietur* [classical future form] . . . Caecilius in *The Moneylender*:

> Now assuredly is when no one will find an antidote
>   for my death.

2 Nonius

deponere ["to cast down"] is "to despair of": thus the desperate are called downcast . . . Caecilius in *The Moneylender*:

> Just now I was
> cast down in spirit, buried while alive.

3 Festus

silicernium is the name for the funeral feast, which the Greeks call . . . περίδειπνον . . . Caecilius in *The Moneylender*:

> I was sure I was about to dine on his funeral feast

Cf. Paul. *Fest.*, p. 377.4–7 L.

4 (126–28 R.³) Non., p. 277.28–36 M. = 426 L.

DELICA est aperi et explana. . . . Caecilius Obolostate:

ia⁶

(A) si linguas decem
habeam, vix habeam satis te qui laudem, Lache.
(Laches) immo vero haec ante solitus sum. res
delicat.

1 decem *Bentinus*: dete *codd*.   2 Lache *Mercier*: ache
codd.   3 vero ante haec *Bothe*: antehac *Spengel*

Cf. Non., p. 98.6–7 M.= 139 L.

5 (124–25 R.³) Non., p. 154.10–12 M. = 226 L.

POPULATIM. Caecilius Obolostate:

ia⁶   (A) ego perdidi te, qui omnes perdo servolos
populatim.
(B) quaeso, ne ad malum hoc addas malum.

1 perduo *Bothe*: perdito *coni. Ribbeck*   perdo servolos
L. Mueller: servos perdo *codd*.

6 (132–33 R.³) Non., pp. 149.27– 50.4 M. = 218 L.

PENICULAMENTUM a veteribus pars vestis dicitur . . . Cae-
cilius Feneratore:

ia⁶   volat exsanguis, simul anhelat
peniculamentum ex pallio datur.

1 exsanguis *Bothe*: sanguis *codd*.   2 ex pallio datur *Bue-
cheler*: et pallio datur *codd.*: e pallio datur *Lindsay*: et palliolatur
Iunius: et pallio *del. Bothe, Spengel*

478

4 Nonius

delica ["clear up"] means "clarify" and "explain." . . . Cae-
cilius in *The Moneylender*:

(A) If I had ten tongues,[1]
I would scarcely have enough to praise you, Laches.
(Laches)[2] No indeed, I'm long accustomed to such.
The situation makes that clear.

[1] Epic style: cf. Homer, *Iliad* 2.488–89: πληθὺν δ᾽ οὐκ ἂν ἐγὼ
μυθήσομαι οὐδ᾽ ὀνομήνω, / οὐδ᾽ εἴ μοι δέκα μὲν γλῶσσαι, δέκα
δὲ στόματ᾽ εἶεν ("I could not tell or name the throng, not even if
I had ten tongues and ten mouths"). Later Latin poets tend to
inflate this to one hundred tongues (e.g., Verg. *Aen.* 6.665; Pers.
5.2).   [2] Speaker attribution is uncertain: *res delicat* could be
a reply from Laches' interlocutor.

5 Nonius

populatim ["among all nations, everywhere"]. Caecilius in
The Moneylender:

(A) I've ruined you, just as I ruin young slaves
everywhere.
(B) Please, don't pile this evil onto evil.

6 Nonius

peniculamentum ["tail, train"] in older writers is the name
for a part of a garment . . . Caecilius in *The Moneylender*:

He flies along ghostly pale, gasping at the
same time, the tail end of his cloak trailing.

7 (134 R.³) Non., p. 543.20–24 M. = 872 L.

PELVIS: sinus aquarius in quo varia pelluuntur . . . Caecilius in Feneratore:

tr⁷   pelvim sibi poposcit

PAUSIMACHUS (F 1–5)

The title is not an uncommon Greek personal name, meaning "one who halts the fighting," but no homonymous Greek comedy is known. A father tries to forbid his son's

1 (135 R.³) Non., p. 515.24–25 M. = 829 L.

RARENTER. Caecilius Pausimacho:

ia⁶   edepol voluntas homini rarenter venit.

voluptas *Palmer, Bothe, Spengel*

2 (136–37 R.³) Non., p. 127.13–19 M. = 184 L.

IAMDIU pro olim. Caecilius Pausimacho:

ia⁶   (*Meretrix*) libera essem iam diu
si istoc habuissem ingenio amatores mihi.

1 libera *Iunius in marg.*: liber *codd.*   2 si ston habuissem ingenio *vel* si ston (*om.* habuissem ingenio) *vel* habuissem ingenio siston *codd.*: si istoc habuissem ingenio *Onions*: si isto *Mercier*: si sto *Lachmann*: si stoc *Roth*

7 Nonius

pelvis ["basin"]: a water bowl in which various things are washed . . . Caecilius in *The Moneylender*:

> s/he demanded a washbasin for herself/himself

PAUSIMACHUS (F 1–5)

affair (F 4), presumably with the hetaera who speaks in F 2.

Bibl.: Schlüter 1884, 15; Negro 1919, 34; Boscherini 1999, 107; Livan 2005, 18–49.

1 Nonius

rarenter ["rarely"; ante- and post-classical]. Caecilius in *Pausimachus*:

> By Pollux, free will rarely comes to a person.

2 Nonius

iamdiu ["this long time"] for "some time ago." Caecilius in *Pausimachus*:

> (*Hetaera*) I would have been a free woman some time
>   ago
> if I had had lovers of that character.

3 (138 R.[3]) Non., p. 548.16–18 M. = 879 L.

MOLOCHINUM: a Graeco, color flori similis malvae. Caecilius Pausimacho:

ia^6 carbasina molochina ampelina

molichina *cod.*   ampelina *Bentinus*: amperina *vel* amperita *vel* amperinta *codd.*

4 (139–40 R.[3]) Non., pp. 334.2–13 M. = 524–25 L.

LIMARE etiam dicitur coniungere . . . Caecilius Pausimacho:

ia^6 (*Pater*)   hoc a te postulo,
ne cum meo gnato posthac limassis caput.

2 meo] eo *codd.*   limassis *Bentinus*: limasses *codd.*

5 (140[1] R.[3]) Non., p. 3.3–13 M. = 5 L.

VELITATIO dicitur levis contentio: dicta ex congressione velitum . . . Caecilius Pausimacho:

?   velitatio *vel* velitari

PHILUMENA (F 1–2)

Philumena *is a woman's name (meaning "Beloved"), borne also by a young wife in Terence's* Hecyra. *No Greek source comedy is known.*

3 Nonius

molochinum ["mauve"]: from the Greek, a color similar to the mallow flower. Caecilius in *Pausimachus*:

> light green garb, mallow purple, vine colored[1]

[1] Probably describing female dress, possibly as worn by hetaeras (cf. F 2).

4 Nonius

limare ["to file, polish"] also used for "to join together" . . . Caecilius in *Pausimachus*:

> (Father)   This I demand from you,
> that you not put your head together with my son after
>   this.

5 Nonius

velitatio ["skirmishing"] means a light skirmish, derived from the encounter of light-armed troops . . . Caecilius in *Pausimachus*:

> skirmish (or) to skirmish[1]

[1] Nonius mentions the play by name alone, without direct quotation from Caecilius, leaving unclear whether the noun or a verb form appeared in the play text.

PHILUMENA (F 1–2)

Bibl.: Schlüter 1884, 15; Jannaconne 1946, 56–57.

1 (141 R.^{3}) Non., p. 197.24–27 M. = 290 L.

CORBES. "corbulas" Varro *de Re Rustica* lib. I . . . Caecilius
Philumena:

ia^6?   qui panis soli corbulam

quid? *L. Mueller*   soli *codd.*: solidi *Ribbeck*

2 (141^1 R.^{3}) Non., p. 304.24–36 M. = 473 L.

FACTIO iterum significat opulentiam abundantiam et no-
bilitatem . . . Caecilius Philumena:

tr^7?   ita eorum famam occultabat factio

filiumena ita *cod.*: filium in alta *rell., corr. Gravert*: lata *Iunius*:
altam *Bothe*   ita eorum] facinorum *Madvig*   occata-
bat *cod.*   *fort.* Caecilius Philumena * * * * idem Plocio

PLOCIUM (F 1–20)

Gellius tells us that Caecilius based his Plocium *("The
Necklace") on Menander's* Πλόκιον *("The Little Neck-
lace," F 296–310 K.-A.). The passages Gellius discusses
offered the only opportunity to study Roman adaptation
of Greek comedy in detail until the rediscovery of frag-
ments of Menander's* Δὶς Ἐξαπατῶν *("The Double De-
ceiver"), which parallel sections of Plautus'* Bacchides.

*More of the plot can be reconstructed than for any other
fragmentary Roman comedy, but not all details of Menan-
der's plot need have appeared in Caecilius' version. Before
the play opens, a young man from a rich household has
raped and impregnated a girl from a poor family during
a night festival, though neither can recognize the other*

1 Nonius

corbes ["baskets"]. Varro uses *corbulae* ["baskets"; diminutive form in earlier writers] in the first book of *On Farming* . . . Caecilius in *Philumena*:

> who . . . a small basket of bread for one alone

2 Nonius

factio ["group acting together"] also denotes opulence, abundance, and renown . . . Caecilius in *Philumena*:

> thus their renown overshadowed their bad reputation

PLOCIUM (F 1–20)

thereafter. Subsequently, the two have become betrothed. Her father is ignorant of the girl's pregnancy, although the women of the household must have helped in concealing it (as in Terence's Hecyra*). On the eve of the wedding (the day of the play's action), the girl gives birth, and her cries lead a male slave in the household (Parmeno in Menander, but his name in Caecilius is not known) to discover the truth. As a "good slave" (loyal to the head of household), he reveals the situation to the girl's father (F 4–7 may come from this discussion). Presumably the father of the girl in turn communicates the news to the father of the young man (Laches in Menander, unknown in Caecilius), though still hoping that the wedding can go forward (perhaps with* *an undertaking to expose the child). The groom's family refuses (F 12–13; possibly the mother plays a key role here). The father of the girl resolves on a public lawsuit and departs for the forum (F 16–17). The necklace of the title must have been the key recognition token by which the identity of the young man as previous rapist was discovered, though where and how this happened we do not know. Perhaps the slave who revealed the crisis also aided in the discovery, especially if he discusses his (imminent?) freedom in F 19.*

The longest fragments are least revelatory of plot, but more devoted to character painting. F 1 shows the transformation of Menander's rich heiress (an epikleros *named Crobyle), married to keep control of her money within the family, into the more stereotypical* uxor dotata *(wife married for her rich dowry) that her Romanized husband complains of. Caecilius has also transformed Menander's iambic trimeter of ordinary speech into a polymetric song, or* canticum, *trimming away elements specific to Menander's plot in favor of much more emotional and imagistic expression of the husband's enslavement to the wife's money. F 2 continues in this vein: the husband complains to an elderly neighbor (generally assumed to be a typical* senex, *though conceivably the father of the girl?), but details of the wife's control of property, husband, and children in Menander are replaced by a graphic vignette of the Roman wife seeking to determine if the husband has come home drunk. These complaints must have preceded the revelation of the birth. F 8 parallels a speech by the slave Parmeno in Menander, lamenting the state of his impoverished master; Caecilius' more compact lines might be spoken by the slave but could also be given by the girl's father. Gellius sepa-*

rately informs his readers that the (in his view richly nuanced) speech by Parmeno as he overhears the girl's birth pangs in Menander becomes far less moving (and perhaps shorter?) in Caecilius, who may have trimmed the slave's part and transferred some of his reflections elsewhere. Either of the old men could complain about old age in the words of F 9.

The play undoubtedly ended with the renewed wedding and legitimation of the newborn child. More intriguing may be the very beginning, if F 14 comes from a prologue. An actors' augury to divine the play's future success makes a very Roman appeal to the audience for their approval in a manner much more Plautine than Terentian.

Bibl.: Teuffel 1858, 4–5; Wordsworth 1874, 317, 595–96; Schlüter 1884, 15–17; Leo ²1912, 101, 192–94; Negro 1919, 40–48; Allinson 1921, 428–33; Fraenkel 1922, 159, 231 [Fraenkel 2007, 105, 158]; Pascal 1926, 168–77; Webster 1950, 99–100; Duckworth 1952, 47–48; Webster 1955, 160; Beare 1964, 78; Thomas and Lee 1965, 954; Williams 1968, 363–66; Segal ¹1968; ²1987, 23–24, 26; Marzullo 1973, 85–104; Questa 1974; Traina 1974, 41–53; Wright 1974, 120–26; Frassinetti 1979, 84–85; Gentili 1979, 49–54; Pociña 1981–83, 70–73; Camilloni 1985, 218–19; Skutsch 1985; Jocelyn Jan. 1985; Jocelyn Mar. 1985; Negri 1990; Seele 1992; Riedweg 1993; Lennartz 1994, 89–94; Jensen 1997, 368–78; Scafuro 1997, 294 and n. 35; Boscherini 1999, 105, 111; Chiarini 2004, 85–87; Livan 2005, 78–79 et passim; Monacelli 2005, 65–78; Cipriani 2010, 133–40; Manuwald 2011, 235–36, 241; Richlin 2017, 277–78; Hanses 2020, 111, 176.

1 (142–57 R.³) Gell. *NA* 2.23.5–10

Caecili Plocium legebamus; hautquaquam mihi et qui
aderant displicebat. [6] libitum est Menandri quoque Plo-
cium legere, a quo istam comoediam verterat. [7] sed
enim postquam in manus Menander venit, a principio sta-
tim, di boni, quantum stupere atque frigere quantumque
mutare a Menandro Caecilius visus est! Diomedis hercle
arma et Glauci non dispari magis pretio existimata sunt.
[8] accesserat dehinc lectio ad eum locum in quo maritus
senex super uxore divite atque deformi querebatur, quod
ancillam suam, non inscito puellam ministerio et facie
haut inliberali coactus erat venundare suspectam uxori
quasi paelicem. nihil dicam ego, quantum differat; versus
utrimque eximi iussi et aliis ad iudicium faciundum ex-
poni. [9] Menander sic [F 296 K.-A.]:

> (Λα.) ἐπ᾽ ἀμφότερα νῦν ἡ ᾽πίκληρος ἡ κ‹αλή›
> μέλλει καθευδήσειν. κατείργασται μέγα
> καὶ περιβόητον ἔργον· ἐκ τῆς οἰκίας
> ἐξέβαλε τὴν λυποῦσαν, ἣν ἐβούλετο,
> 5 ἵν᾽ ἀποβλέπωσιν πάντες εἰς τὸ Κρωβύλης
> πρόσωπον ᾖ τ᾽ εὔγνωστος οὖσ᾽ ἐμὴ γυνή
> δέσποινα. καὶ τὴν ὄψιν, ἣν ἐκτήσατο·
> ὄνος ἐν πιθήκοις, τοῦτο δὴ τὸ λεγόμενον,
> ἔστιν. σιωπᾶν βούλομαι τὴν νύκτα τήν
> 10 πολλῶν κακῶν ἀρχηγόν. οἴμοι Κρωβύλην

1 Gellius, *Attic Nights*

We were reading Caccilius' *Necklace*, which I and those present much enjoyed. [6] We decided to read also the *Necklace* of Menander, from which Caecilius had translated that comedy. [7] But after Menander came to hand, right from the beginning, great gods! how inert and tedious Caecilius seemed, and how much he had changed from Menander! Really, the armor of Diomedes and that of Glaucus were not more different in value.[1] [8] We had then read to the place where the old husband was complaining about his wealthy and unsightly wife, because he had been forced to sell his female slave, a talented girl with by no means servile looks, because the wife suspected she was his mistress. I won't describe how great the difference was; I've had the lines of both poets excerpted and give them to others to judge. [9] Here's Menander [F 296 K.-A.]:

> (Laches) In both ways now my grand heiress wife
> will sleep soundly. She's accomplished a great
> and famous deed: she tossed the girl who was
>   upsetting her
> out of the house, just as she wished,
> so that everyone who looks Crobyle in the face   5
> will know for sure that my wife
> rules. And what a face she possesses!
> She's the ass among the monkeys: that's the saying.
> I dare not speak about the nighttime,
> the origin of so many evils. Poor me,   10

---

[1] In Homer (*Il.* 6.234ff.), Diomedes, discovering an old guest-friendship, proposes exchanging his bronze for the gold armor of Glaucus.

λαβεῖν ἔμ᾽, εἰ καί δέκα τάλαντ᾽ ‹ἠνέγκατο,[1]
τὴν› ῥῖν᾽ ἔχουσαν πηχέως· εἶτ᾽ ἐστὶ τό
φρύαγμά πως ὑπόστατον; ‹μὰ τὸν› Δία
τὸν Ὀλύμπιον καὶ τὴν Ἀθηνᾶν, οὐδαμῶς.
15   παιδισκάριον θεραπευτικὸν δὲ καὶ λόγου
† τάχιον· ἀπαγέσθω δέ. τισαρανπισαγαγοι.[2]

[10] Caecilius autem sic:

an   (A) is demum miser est qui aerumnam suam nesciat
      occulta re ferre:
         ita me‹d› uxor forma et factis
         facit, si taceam, tamen indicium.
         quae, nisi dotem, omnia quae nolis
5   habet: qui sapiet, de me discet,
         qui quasi ad hostis captus, liber
         servio salva urbe atque arce.
an[7] quae, mihi quidquid placet, eo privat vi:‹volt› vix me
      servatam.

---

[1] {ἐ}με καί ‹δώ›δεκα τάλαντα ‹φερομένην Holford-Strevens
[2] τίς ἄρ᾽ ἀντεισαγάγοι Holford-Strevens (cf. Holford-Strevens 2020b, 43).
1 qui *codd.*: quia *rell.*   nesciat *Ribbeck*: nequit *codd.*:
nescit *cod.*   occulta re *Leo, Lindsay, Ribbeck*: occultare
codd., edd.   ferre *multis corruptum videtur, secl. Pighi*:
efferre *Spengel*: foris *Ribbeck*   2 me *codd., corr. Questa*
6 captus liber *cod.*: libere captus *cod.*: captus libere *codd. rell.,
Pighi*   7 atque] et *Pighi*   8 priuatu uim me seruatum
codd., corr. Traina: privatum it me servatum *Thysius*: privatum it
me servatam ‹velim›? *Ribbeck*: eo privat vi: ‹volt› vix me serva-
tam *Guardì: alii alia*

for marrying Crobyle, even if she did bring 10 talents
    along—
and a foot-long nose. Well, then, is her temper
somehow to be endured? No, by Zeus
the Olympian and Athena, in no way!
That little slave girl was a willing worker, quicker   15
than you could ask. But she's the one to go. [corrupt
    text]

[10] Caecilius however writes this:

It's a really wretched man, who can't bear his own
    hardship in secret:
      so my wife treats me in looks and deeds;
      if I shut up, it's still proof.
      She has everything you wouldn't want her to—   5
      except the dowry. If you're smart, learn from me.
      Enslaved just like a prisoner of war,[2] I'm a free
      man—
and a slave, though my city and citadel's
    unsacked.[3]
Anything I like, she takes from me by force. She
    scarcely wants me to live.

[2] The military image is particularly Roman (Fraenkel 1922,
223), but the power of a rich wife is a familiar topos in Greek
comedy (cf. Menander, F 802, 805 K.-A., and Alexis, F 150 K.-A.).

[3] Perhaps paratragic: cf. Ennius, *Andromacha*, F 23b.6 *FRL*:
arce et urbe orba sum ("I am bereft of citadel and city").

dum ego eius mortem inhio, egomet vivo mortuus
    inter vivos.

tr[7] 10   ea me clam se cum mea ancilla ait consuetum, id me
    arguit;

ita plorando orando instando atque obiurgando me
    obtudit,

bacch[3]   eam uti venderem. nunc credo inter suas

ia[6]   aequalis et cognatas sermonem serit:

cr[4]   "quis vestrarum fuit integra aetatula,

cr 15   quae hoc idem a viro

impetrarit suo, quod ego anus modo

effeci, paelice ut meum privarem virum?"

wilam   haec erunt concilia hodie; differor sermone miser.

    9 dum ego eius *Non.*: *om.* ego *codd. Gell.*   inhio] inibo
codd. Non.   11 orando *codd.*: atque orando *cod.*, *del. Rib-*
beck   13 et *codd.*: atque *cod.*, *del. Ribbeck*   14 nostrarum
codd. nonnulli   15 idem] itidem *vulgo*: item *Pighi*
    18 differor] differar *Ribbeck*   miser] misere *Ribbeck*

Cf. Non., p. 502.11–12 M. = 806 L.

2 (158–162 R.[3]) Gell. *NA* 2.23.11–19

praeter venustatem autem rerum atque verborum in duo-
bus libris nequaquam parem, in hoc equidem soleo ani-
mum attendere, quod quae Menander praeclare et appo-
site et facete scripsit, ea Caecilius ne qua potuit quidem
conatus est enarrare, [12] sed quasi minime probanda
praetermisit et alia nescio quae mimica inculcavit, et illud
Menandri de vita hominum media sumptum simplex et
verum et delectabile nescio quo pacto omisit. idem enim
ille maritus senex cum altero sene vicino colloquens et

I'm pining for her death, and I live like a corpse
    among the living.
She says I've been secretly familiar with my slave girl,   10
    she accuses me;
with such bawling, begging, bugging, and berating,
    she beat me down,
so that I sold the girl. Now I suspect among her
friends and relatives she's spreading this story:
"Which of you women, even in tender youth,
could have gotten this from her husband,   15
the very thing that I, an old woman,
managed—stripping my man of his mistress?"
That'll be today's conclaves: poor me, I'm shredded
    by gossip.

2 Gellius, *Attic Nights*

Moreover beyond the elegance of subject matter and
diction, by no means the same in the two works, I tend
to notice this also: the things that Menander wrote very
clearly and appropriately and wittily were those Caecilius
did not try to relate fully, even where possible; [12] but he
has passed them by as if unworthy of attention, and has
stuffed in some mime material; and what Menander took
from everyday life, simple, accurate and delightful, some-
how Caecilius has missed. For example, that same elderly
husband, chatting with an elderly neighbor, and praying

uxoris locupletis superbiam deprecans haec ait [F 297 K.-A.]:

(Λα.) ἔχω δ' ἐπίκληρον Λάμιαν· οὐκ εἴρηκά σοι
τουτὶ γάρ; (A) οὐχί. (Λα.) κυρίαν τῆς οἰκίας
καὶ τῶν ἀγρῶν καὶ †πάντων ἄντ' ἐκείνης†
ἔχομεν. (A) Ἄπολλον, ὡς χαλεπόν. (Λα.)
    χαλεπώτατον.
ἅπασι δ' ἀργαλέα 'στίν, οὐκ ἐμοὶ μόνῳ,
υἱῷ, πολὺ μᾶλλον, θυγατρί.
                    (A) πρᾶγμ' ἄμαχον λέγεις.
(Λα.) εὖ οἶδα.

[13] Caecilius vero hoc in loco ridiculus magis quam personae isti quam tractabat aptus atque conveniens videri maluit. sic enim haec corrupit:

ia⁶   (A) sed tua morosane uxor quaeso est? (B) quam
       rogas?
       (A) qui tandem? (B) taedet mentionis, quae mihi
       ubi domum adveni, adsedi, extemplo savium
       dat ieiuna anima. (A) nil peccat de savio;
5   ut devomas vult quod foris potaveris.

[14] quid de illo quoque loco in utraque comoedia posito existimari debeat manifestum est, cuius loci haec ferme sententia. [15] filia hominis pauperis in pervigilio vitiata est. [16] ea res clam patrem fuit, et habebatur pro virgine. [17] ex eo vitio gravida mensibus exactis parturit. [18] servus bonae frugi, cum pro foribus domus staret et propin-

for relief from his domineering rich wife, says [F 297 K.-A.]:

> (Laches) I'm married to a monster heiress; didn't I
>   tell you
> this? (A) No. (La.) She rules the house
> and the farms and †everything†
> we own. (A) By Apollo, that's harsh. (La.) The
>   harshest.
> She's a pain to everyone, not just me,
> to our son, much more so, to our daughter.
>   (A) You mean an unwinnable position.
> (La.) I know.

[13] Here Caecilius preferred to play the clown rather than fit and accommodate himself to this particular character he was handling. This is how he ruined the passage:

> (A) Tell me, is your wife moody? (B) How can you
>   ask?
> (A) Well then? (B) I hate to talk about it: when I
> come home, I sit down, right away she kisses me
> with her starving bad breath.[1] (A) That kiss is no
>   mistake;
> she wants you to vomit up what you drank away from
>   home.

[14] It is clear what the view ought to be about that scene also, found in both comedies, of which this is more or less the idea: [15] a poor man's daughter was raped during a nighttime religious vigil. [16] Her father knew nothing of it, and she was considered a virgin still. [17] Pregnant from the rape, she gave birth at full term. [18] An honest slave, who happens to be standing in front of the house door,

quare partum erili filiae atque omnino vitium esse obla-
tum ignoraret, gemitum et ploratum audit puellae in
puerperio enitentis: timet, irascitur, suspicatur, miseretur,
dolet. [19] hi omnes motus eius affectionesque animi in
Graeca quidem comoedia mirabiliter acres et illustres,
apud Caecilium autem pigra istaec omnia et a rerum dig-
nitate atque gratia vacua sunt.

1 quam] va *Ribbeck*: me *Traina*   rogas *cod.*: errogas *vel*
erogas *vel* me rogas *rell.*   2 qui *codd.*: quas qui *cod.*   3 adsedi
Non.: ac sedi *codd. Gell.*   4 nil *cod.*: ni(c)hil *codd.*   5 foris
cod.: toris *vel* thoris *rell.*   potaveris *ed. Ven. 1472*: putaveris
codd.

3 (163 R.³) Non., p. 314.21–22 M. = 491 L.

nam et GRAVITER multum intellegitur. Caecilius Plocio:

ia⁶   placere occepit graviter, postquam emortuast.

hoccoepit *cod.*   emortuast *Ribbeck*: emortuas *codd.*: est
mortua *cod.*

4 (164–65 R.³) Gell. *NA* 3.16.3–4

hoc idem tradit etiam Menander, poeta vetustior, huma-
narum opinionum vel peritissimus; versus eius super ea re
de fabula Plocio posui [F 307 K.-A.]: γυνὴ κυεῖ δέκα
μῆνας. sed noster Caecilius cum faceret eodem nomine

1 The remainder of the original Menander quotation is miss-
ing.

ignorant both of the imminent delivery of his master's daughter, and completely unaware of the rape, hears the cries and weeping of the girl in labor. He expresses fear, anger, suspicion, pity, and sorrow. [19] All his emotions and changes of feeling are wonderfully vivid and manifest in the Greek comedy; in Caecilius, however, the same things are all dull and devoid of the dignity and grace fit for these matters.

1 The Romans believed that fasting could cause bad breath: cf. Plautus, *Merc.* 574 (*ieiunitatis plenus, anima foetida*); Ovid, *Ars am.* 3.277; and Martial 4.4.7–8.

3 Nonius

graviter ["seriously"] is also understood to mean "much." Caecilius in *The Necklace*:

> She started to please me a lot, once she was dead.1

1 The problem for the father of the young man in the play is that his rich wife is still alive. If he speaks this line, it would refer to a deceased first wife, but the neighbor or the father of the girl might be more likely (and in the latter case there would be no mother in the house from whom to conceal her pregnancy, only female slaves).

4 Gellius, *Attic Nights*

The earlier poet Menander, a man well versed in popular opinions, relates the same thing. I note here his verse on that subject from his play *The Little Necklace* [F 307 K.-A.]: "A woman is pregnant for ten months."1 But our Caecilius, when he wrote a comedy with the same title and

et eiusdem argumenti comoediam ac pleraque a Menan-
dro sumeret, in mensibus tamen genitalibus nominandis
non praetermisit octavum, quem praeterierat Menander.
Caecilii versus hisce sunt:

tr^7 (A) soletne mulier decimo mense parere?

                       (B) pol nono quoque
etiam septimo atque octavo.

1 insoletne *codd.*, *corr. Hertz*: insuetne *Bothe*   nono
quoque *cod.*: nonoque *codd.*

5 (166 R.^{3}) Non., p. 84.3–4 M. = 118 L.

COMMEMORAMENTUM. Caecilius Plocio:

ia^6 pudebat credo commemoramentum stupri.

6 (167 R.^{3}) Non., p. 153.12–13 M. = 224 L.

PROPERATIM, id est properanter. Caecilius:

ia^6 properatim in tenebris istuc confectum est opus.

istuc *cod.*: tunc *rell.*

Cf. Non., p. 155.4–5 M. = 227 L. (. . . Caecilius Plocio . . .).

the same plot and borrowed most of the material from Menander, when counting out the months of pregnancy, did not leave out the eighth, as Menander had.[2] Here are Caecilius' lines:

(A) Does a woman usually give birth in the tenth month?
              (B) Yes, by Pollux, and in the ninth and also the seventh and the eighth months.

[2] Greek medicine believed that an eight months' child did not survive, whereas both a seven months' and a nine months' child were likely to (Hippocrates, *Eight Months' Child* VII 436 Littré). Romans of Caecilius' time may not have shared this view, accounting for his addition. Cf. Plautus, *Amph.* 482.

5 Nonius

commemoramentum ["reminder, mention"; ante-classical]. Caecilius in *The Necklace*:

I think there was shame in any mention of the rape.

6 Nonius

properatim ["speedily"; ante-classical] is the same as *properanter*. Caecilius:

That job was done hurriedly in the shadows.

7 (168 R.[3]) Non., p. 209.13–14 M. = 308 L.

INSOMNIUM . . . feminini . . . Caecilius Plocio:

ia[7]   consequitur comes insomnia;
ea porro insaniam affert.

2 aufert *cod.*

8 (169–72 R.[3]) Gell. *NA* 2.23.20–21

post ubi idem servus percontando quod acciderat reppe-
rit, has aput Menandrum voces facit [F 298 K.-A.]:

(ΠΑΡΜ.) ὦ τρὶς κακοδαίμων, ὅστις ὢν πένης
  γαμεῖ
καὶ παιδοποιεῖθ'. ὡς ἀλογιστός ἐστ' ἀνήρ,
ὃς μήτε φυλακὴν τῶν ἀναγκαίων ἔχει,
μήτ' ἂν ἀτυχήσας εἰς τὰ κοινὰ τοῦ βίου
5 ἐπαμφιέσαι δύναιτο τοῦτο χρήμασιν,
ἀλλ' ἐν ἀκαλύπτῳ καὶ ταλαιπώρῳ βίῳ
χειμαζόμενος ζῇ, τῶν μὲν ἀνιαρῶν ἔχων
τὸ μέρος ἁπάντων, τῶν δ' ἀγαθῶν οὐδὲν μέρος·
ὑπὲρ γὰρ ἑνὸς ἀλγῶν ἅπαντας νουθετῶ.

[21] ad horum sinceritatem veritatemque verborum an
aspiraverit Caecilius consideremus. versus sunt hi Caecili
trunca quaedam ex Menandro dicentis et consarcinantis
verba tragici tumoris:

7 Nonius

insomnium . . . also feminine gender . . . Caecilius in *The Necklace*:

> Insomnia followed as a companion;
> then that brought on madness.

8 Gellius, *Attic Nights*

Later, when the same slave by his questions has found out what happened, in Menander he [Parmeno] makes this speech [F 298 K.-A.]:

> (Par.) How triply wretched is the poor man who
>   marries
> and has children. How unreasonable is the man,
> who keeps no watch for his necessities,
> nor when unfortunate in the affairs of life
> could use his money to cloak the fact.   5
> Instead in a storm he lives a bare and
> wretched life, sharing indeed in all
> troubles, but with no share of good things.
> I'm hurting for one person—but warning all.

[21] Let's consider whether Caecilius approached the sincerity and truth of these words. Here are the verses of Caecilius, offering some maimed bits of Menander patched with tragic bombast:

ia^6 is demum infortunatus est homo
pauper qui educit in egestatem liberos,
cui fortuna et res ut est continuo patet.
nam opulento famam facile occultat factio.

1 infortunatus est *cod.*: est infortunatus *rell.*

3 ut est *codd.*: est ut *Spengel*: utu est *Ribbeck¹*: nuda est
Ribbeck²⁻³   4 famam *codd.*: famem *cod.*   facile *cod.*:
facilem *rell.*

Cf. *Philumena* F 2.

9 (173–75 R.³) Cic. *Sen.* 25

melius Caecilius de sene alteri saeculo prospiciente, quam
illud idem:

ia^6 edepol, senectus, si nil quicquam aliud viti
adportes tecum, cum advenis, unum id sat est
quod diu vivendo multa quae non volt videt.

1 si nil *Fruterius*: si nihil *codd. Cic.*: ut si nihil *codd. Non.*: etsi
nil *Bothe*: ut nil *Onions*   aliud *cod.*: ad aliud *cod.*   quic-
quam *et* viti *om. Non. unus cod.*

3 quod diu] diu qui *Manutius*   volt *vel* vol *vel* vult *codd.*

Cf. Non., p. 247.4–6 = 371 L. (. . . Caecilius Plocio . . .).

10 (176 R.³) Non., p. 97.13–21 M. = 138 L.

DANUNT, dant . . . Caecilius Plocio:

ia^6 patiere quod dant, quando optata non danunt.

patiere] potiere *vel* patere *Bothe*: potiere *Ribbeck¹⁻²*

> So wretched indeed is the man who
> in his poverty begets children for a life of want.
> His misfortune and actual state lie constantly open to
> view.
> A rich man's disrepute his friends readily conceal.

9 Cicero, *On Old Age*

Caecilius had a better thought about an old man looking out for the next generation[1] when he wrote that:

> By Pollux, Old Age, if you bring no other defects
> with you, when you come, this one's enough:
> by living long a man sees much he doesn't want to.

[1] Cicero has just quoted Caecilius, *Synephebi* F 2: "He plants trees to benefit another age."

10 Nonius

danunt ["they give"; ante-classical] is the same as *dant* . . . Caecilius in *The Necklace*:

> You will endure what they [the gods?] grant, since
> they do not grant your desires.

503

11 (177 R.[3]) Donat. ad Ter. *An.* 805

"quando ut volumus non licet": et ad praesentis et ad prae-
teritae vitae excusationem pertinet ista responsio, qua
purgatur voluntas in quaestu meretricio Chrysidis. Caeci-
lius in Plocio:

ia[6]   vivas ut possis, quando non quis ut velis.

   non quis *Fabricius*: nequit *codd. fere omnes*: nequis *cod., ed.
princ.*: nec quis *Ribbeck*: nequeas *Seyffert*: nequitur *Spengel*

12 (178–79 R.[3]) Non., p. 297.35–36 M. = 462 L

EXTOLLERE, differre. Caecilius Plocio:

tr[7]   abi intro atque istaec aufer; tamen hodie extollat
           nuptias.

   aufer *vulgo*: aufert *codd.*: aufer, si *Ribbeck*: auferto: tam
Bothe: adfer tamen, ut hodie *L. Mueller*   extollet *dub. in
app. Ribbeck*

13 (180 R.[3]) Non., p. 484.24–34 M. = 778 L.

SUMPTI pro sumptus. Caecilius Plocio:

ia[7]   quid hoc futurum obsonio est, ubi tantum sumpti
           factum?

   est *Bothe*: et *codd.*

11 Donatus, *Commentary on Terence, The Woman of Andros*

"since we can't live how we will": This answer tends to excuse both her past and present life, whereby Chrysis' choice in the business of prostitution disappears. Caecilius in *The Necklace*:

> Live as you are able, when you can't live as you wish.[1]

[1] Cf. Menander, *Andria?*, F *47 K.-A. (= *Monost.* 273 J.): ζῶμεν γὰρ οὐχ ὡς θέλομεν, ἀλλ᾽ ὡς δυνάμεθα ("let's live not as we wish, but as we can"), perhaps proverbial.

12 Nonius

extollere ["to lift up"], to put off. Caecilius in *The Necklace*:

> Go in and get rid of that stuff; still, let him put off the wedding today.

13 Nonius

sumpti ["expense"; ante-classical genitive] for *sumptus* [classical genitive]. Caecilius in *The Necklace*:

> What's to be done with this feast, when so much has been spent on it?

14 (181–82 R.[3]) Non., p. 468.20–29 M. = 751 L.

AUSPICAVI pro auspicatus sum . . . Caecilius Plocio:

ia[6]   insanum auspicium! <num> aliter histrionium est
atque ut magistratus publice cum auspicant?

1 hospitium *codd.*   num *add. Lindsay:* haud *Spen-
gel*   histrionium *Guietus:* istrionium *codd.*   insanum!
auspicium *Leo:* insanum auspicium:: <num> aliter *Slater*
2 publicitus cum auspicant *Maehly:* publice quando auspicant
Bothe: publice quoque auspicant *Spengel:* auspicant cum publice
L. Mueller: publicae rei cum auspicant *Ribbeck*

15 (183 R.[3]) Non., p. 164.21–22 M. = 242 L.

RARENTER pro rare. Caecilius Plocio:

tr[8]?   tu nurum non vis odiosam tibi esse quam rarenter
videas?

16 (184 R.[3]) Non., p. 220.4–6 M. = 325 L.

PAUPERTAS generis feminini. neutri Caecilius Plocio:

ia[6]   ibo ad forum et pauperii tutelam geram.

pauperi *codd., corr. Ribbeck:* pauperio *Spengel:* pau-
perie *Bothe*

17 (185 R.[3]) Non., p. 513.1–9 M. = 825 L.

PUBLICITUS pro publice. . . . Caecilius Plocio:

ia[7]   (A) ibo domum. (B) ad plebem pergitur: publicitus
defendendum est.

ibo domum *codd.:* domum ibo *Gravert:* ibi demum
Bothe   pergitur *codd.:* peragetur *coni. in app. Ribbeck:* per-
agitur *vel* peragitor *L. Mueller:* pergitor *Spengel*

506

14 Nonius

auspicavi ["I have augured"; ante-classical] for *auspicatus sum* [classical form] . . . Caecilius in *The Necklace*:

An outrageous augury! Surely the actors' augury isn't altogether different from when the magistrates augur for the state, is it?[1]

[1] Leo ([2]1912, 192n2) thought this fragment came from the prologue. Warmington conjectured that it might even be Caecilius speaking *in propria persona*.

15 Nonius

rarenter ["rarely"; ante-classical] for *rare* [classical form]. Caecilius in *The Necklace*:

Surely you don't want a daughter-in-law you rarely see to be disagreeable to you?

16 Nonius

paupertas ["poverty"] is feminine in gender. A neuter form[1] in Caecilius' *The Necklace*:

I'll go to the forum and make a defense—of poverty.

[1] *pauperiei* or *pauperii* is genitive from *pauperies*, considered feminine in classical Latin.

17 Nonius

publicitus ["publicly"; ante-classical] for *publice* [classical form]. . . . Caecilius in *The Necklace*:

(A) I'll go home. (B) It's going to the people: it must be publicly defended.

18 (186–87 R.[3]) Non., p. 146.11–15 M. = 213 L.

OPULENTITAS pro opulentia. . . . Caecilius Plocio:

ia[6]   opulentitate nostra sibi iniuriam
factam

>   1 esse *post* sibi *add. Ribbeck*: sibi eam iniuriam *L. Mueller*:
> *alii alia*   2 factam *Mercier*: faciam *codd.*

19 (188 R.[3]) Non., p. 124.24–28 M. = 180 L.

INIBI pro sic et mox . . . Caecilius Plocio:

ia[6]   (A) liberne es?
(B) non sum liber, verum inibi est quasi.

>   non sum] nondum *dub. L. Mueller*   liber *cod.*: *om.*
> *rell.*   quasi *cod.*: *om. rell.*

20 (189 R.[3]) Non., p. 199.7–9 M. = 292 L.

CATELLAE diminutivum est catenarum; et dicuntur ge-
nere feminino. Caecilius Plocio:

?   catellae

18 Nonius

opulentitas ["wealth"; ante-classical] for *opulentia* [classical form]. . . . Caecilius in *The Necklace*:

> by means of our riches the crime against her[1]
> was committed

[1] Presumably the assault on the young woman in the play. Either the father or the mother of the young man could be speaking; Warmington thought the mother, indicating a change of heart near the end of the play.

19 Nonius

inibi for "thus" and "next" . . . Caecilius in *The Necklace*:

> (A) Are you a free man?
>   (B) No, not free, but it's that way—almost.

20 Nonius

catellae ["little chains"] is a diminutive from *catenae* ["chains"] and used with feminine gender. Caecilius in *The Necklace*:

> chainlets

POLUMENI (F 1)

Prior to Caecilius' Polumeni ("Men for Sale"), the only known Greek Πωλούμενοι (likewise "Men for Sale") is Menander's (F 315–20 K.-A.). Neither plot is reconstructible, although the title might suggest prisoners of war put up for sale. F Inc. 277 R.³ has been attributed to this play based on a similarity to Menander (F 317.2 K.-A.).[1]

1 (190 R.³) Non., p. 114.15–16 M. = 164 L.

FLOCES, faex vini. Caecilius:

ia⁸   at pol ego neque florem neque floces volo mihi:
       vinum volo.

Cf. Gell. *NA* 11.7.6.

PORTITOR (F 1)

Plautus uses the term portitor *("customs officer"), but otherwise no comparable title to Caecilius' Portitor ("The Customs Officer") is known.*[1]
    Bibl.: Schlüter 1884, 17; Cipriani 2010, 157–58.

POLUMENI (F 1)

Bibl.: Schlüter 1884, 17; Camilloni 1985, 219; Meini 2004; Livan 2005, 26–27.

[1] Seneca (*Tranq.* 10) attributes *aliquando et insanire iucundum est* to a Greek poet, and this seems to render Menander, *Poloumenoi*, F 317.2 K.-A. (καὶ συμμανῆ δ᾽ ἔνια δεῖ), but this might be Seneca's own translation rather than a quotation from Caecilius' version of the play.

1 Nonius

floces, dregs of wine. Caecilius:

> But, by Pollux, I want neither rosy dew[1] nor residue:
> wine's what I want.

[1] *flos* sometimes means the "bouquet" of wine, but it may also be a technical term for foam or lighter material floating on top of a liquid.

PORTITOR (F 1)

[1] Plautus, *Trin.* 794, and Non., p. 24.14–15 M. = 35 L.: POR-TITORES *dicuntur telonearii, qui portum obsidentes omnia sciscitantur, ut ex eo vectigal accipiant* ("Customs collectors are called *portitores*, stationed at the port, who examine everything in order to collect the excise due"). Later the noun can mean "porter" or "ferryman."

1 (191 R.^{3}) Non., p. 118.23–31 M. = 170 L.

GERRAE, nugae, ineptiae; et sunt gerrae fascini, qui sic in Naxo, insula Veneris, ab incolis appellantur. . . . congerro meus, ut conlusor meus, qui easdem exerceat nugas. Caecilius Portitore:

ia^6 cur depopulator? gerrae!

> depopulato *cod.*: fur depopulator gerro *Rost:* fur depopulator:: gerrae *Kiessling*

PROGAMOS (F 1–2)

Before Caecilius' Progamos ("Marrying Early"), Menander (F 311–12 K.-A.) and at least one other unknown comic poet wrote a Προγαμῶν, *a substantive participle meaning one who marries early, possibly a euphemism for rape or perhaps one living together with another before marriage.*

1 (192 R.^{3}) Non., p. 346.13–14 M. = 548 L.

MOLIRI, retinere, morari ac repigrare. Caecilius Progamo:

ia^8 ita quod laetitia me mobilitat, maeror molitur metu.

> laetitia *Palmer*: letiale *codd.*: letale *Gravert*

2 (*Progamos* F II R.^{3}) Non., p. 505.35–6.6 M. = 813 L.

AUDIBO pro audiam . . . Caecilius Nauclero [F 2] . . . Progamo:

audibo

1 Nonius

gerrae, "trifles, nonsense"; *gerrae* are also "charms,"[1] as they are so called by the inhabitants of Naxos, the island of Venus. . . . My *congerro* is my crony, one who makes the same kind of jokes. Caecilius in *The Customs Officer*:

> Why a marauder? Nonsense!

[1] Varro (*Ling.* 7.97) describes the custom of boys wearing phallic amulets (which he terms *turpicula res*) to ward off evil. In Horace (*Epod.* 8.18) *fascinum* is the speaker's penis, and in Petronius (*Sat.* 138) it is a leather dildo.

PROGAMOS (F 1–2)

Presumably Caecilius Latinized this term, but since it is attested only in the ablative, it is uncertain whether as nominative Progamon *or* Progamos; *the latter is conventional.*

Bibl.: Schlüter 1884, 17; Livan 2005, 67–69.

1 Nonius

moliri, "to hold back, delay, and make lazy." Caecilius in *Marrying Early*:

> Indeed, because gladness gets me going, sorrow sets
>   me slowing with fear.

2 Nonius

audibo ["I shall hear"; earlier future form] for *audiam* [classical future form] . . . Caecilius in *The Shipmaster* [F 2] . . . , in *Marrying Early*:

> I'll hear

PUGIL (F 1)

In Middle Comedy, Timotheus (t 1 K.-A.) and Timocles (F 31 K.-A.) both wrote a Πύκτης ("The Boxer"), but neither of these can be connected with any likelihood to Caecilius' Pugil ("The Pugilist"). The pancration, *a no-holds-barred form of boxing and wrestling, achieved considerable notoriety in antiquity, and plays entitled Παγκρατιαστής ("The Pancratiast") are known from Alexis (F 173 K.-A.),*

1 (193–94 R.[3]) Fest., pp. 182.30–84.3 L.

NICTARE et oculorum et aliorum membrorum nisu saepe aliquid conari, dictum est ab antiquis, ut . . . unde quidam nictationem; quidam nictum, ut Caecilius in Pugile:

ia[6]   tum inter laudandum hunc timidum tremulis
            palpebris
        percutere nictu; hic gaudere et mirarier.

1 laudandum] luctandum *Ribbeck*: ludendum *Fruterius*

Cf. Paul. *Fest.*, p. 183.12–14 L.

SYMBOLUM (F 1–2)

The original is unknown, and there is no comparable Greek title for Caecilius' Symbolum ("The Token") recorded. The title, however, strongly suggests some physical

PUGIL (F 1)

*Theophilus (F 8–9 K.-A.), and Philemon (F 56–57 K.-A.).
Ennius wrote a* Pancratiastes *(Com. F 2–4 FRL), whose
title may have been metaphorical for a comic slave of many
wiles. None of these helps in determining Caecilius' plot in
"The Pugilist." F 263 Inc. R.[3] has been attributed to this
play as well (or to Caecilius'* Triumphus*).
Bibl.: Schlüter 1884, 18.*

1 Festus

nictare ["to blink, twitch"] *is often to attempt something
by the exertion of both eyes and other body parts; it was
used by the ancients, for example . . . Hence some say*
nictatio ["blinking"], *some* nictus, *as Caecilius does in The
Pugilist*:

> then in the midst of all the praise he knocks down
>   this coward with the fluttering eyelids
> in the blink of an eye; he's delighted and amazed.

SYMBOLUM (F 1–2)

*sign used in the play to achieve a recognition (ἀναγνώρι-
σις).
Bibl.: Schlüter 1884, 18.*

1 (195 R.[3]) Non., p. 279.43–80.3 M. = 431 L.

DESTITUI rursum statui . . . Caecilius in Symbolo:

ia[6]   destituit omnes servos ad mensam ante se.

Symbolo *Mercier*: sembono *vel* embono *codd.*

2 (196 R.[3]) Non., p. 246.9–14 M. = 370 L.

AUSCULTARE est obsequi . . . Caecilius Symbolo:

tr[7]   audire, ignoti quod imperant,
soleo, non auscultare.

Symbolo *Mercier*: sembono *vel* embono *codd.*

SYNARISTOSAE (F 1)

Caecilius' Synaristosae ("Ladies Who Lunch") must have been adapted from Menander's Συναριστῶσαι ("Ladies Who Lunch"); Plautus used the same source material in composing his own Cistellaria. See F adesp. 479, 1074, and 1155 K.-A.; Menander, F 643; and Synaristosae, F 335–44 K.-A., with Arnott's translation and discussion in LCL 460, pp. 325–61. Normally Roman comic poets did not adapt Greek plays used as source material by previous Roman dramatists, but no other author of a Συναριστῶσαι

1 (197–98 R.[3]) Gell. *NA* 15.15.1–2

ab eo quod est pando "passum" veteres dixerunt, non "pansum," et cum "ex" praepositione "expassum," non "expansum." [2] Caecilius in Synaristosis:

516

1 Nonius

destitui is the same as *statui* ["set down"] . . . Caecilius in *The Token*:

> He sat down all the slaves at the table before himself.

2 Nonius

auscultare ["to listen"] is to obey . . . Caecilius in *The Token*:

> What unknown men give orders about,
> I tend to hear, not obey.

SYNARISTOSAE (F 1)

is known, so Caecilius here may be the exception. The sole fragment refers to a discovery that seems to point toward a wedding, though the plot of Plautus' Cistellaria *does not reach that far. Caecilius' adaptation may thus have included much that Plautus deemed expendable from Menander's plot.*

Bibl.: Schlüter 1884, 18–19; Fraenkel 1932; Suess 1935; Webster 1950, 91–97.

1 Gellius, *Attic Nights*

From the verb *pando* ["spread out"] older writers formed the participle *passum*, not *pansum*, and using the preposition *ex* they formed *expassum*, not *expansum*. [2] Caecilius in *Ladies Who Lunch*:

517

ia^6 heri vero prospexisse eum se ex tegulis,
haec nuntiasse et flammeum expassum domi

1 eum se *Gell.*: eum *Non.*: eumpse *Bergk*: se eum *L. Muel-
ler*   1–2 ex tegulis . . . flammeum *om. Non. (propter homoio-
teleuton)*   2 nuntiasse et *de Buxis*: nuntiasset *vel* nuntiasse
codd.: et nuntiasse *Bergk*   domi *codd.*: domini *cod.*

Cf. Non., p. 370.12–17 M. = 589 L.

SYNEPHEBI (F 1–4)

Menander wrote a Συνέφηβοι *("Fellow Recruits"), which
Cicero implies (T 7) was the source for Caecilius'* Syne-
phebi *("Fellow Recruits"). Euphron (F 9 K.-A.) and Apol-
lodorus (F 12 K.-A.) wrote plays of the same title, and a
Greek inscription (IG II² 2323, 127) records a* Συν]εφή-
βοις *at the City Dionysia by an unknown poet around 195
BC. Philemon wrote a* Συνέφηβος *("The Fellow Recruit,"
F 1 K.-A.).[1] Caecilius,* Imbrians *F 6 (= 97 R.³), may come
rather from* Fellow Recruits. *In an Athenian setting, the
title should imply not just young men but those engaged
in the ephebate, their first military training and service.
From Latin drama we know of a* Synephebi *by Pom-
ponius, an* Aequales *("Companions") by Afranius, and an*
Ephebus *("Recruit") by Laberius, while Varro wrote a
Menippean satire entitled* Synephebus *(περὶ ἐμμονῆς,
F 511–15 Astbury). Schlüter attributes to this play F 251–
55 Inc. R.³*

518

[that] yesterday in fact he spotted him from the roof
    tiles,
announced the news, and the bridal veil was spread
    out at home

Cf. Nonius: *passum*, "spread abroad, loose" . . . Caecilius in *Ladies
Who Lunch*: . . .

SYNEPHEBI (F 1–4)

*The plural title may well imply a double plot: two young
men with love affairs playing out very differently. In F 1,
one young man complains (ironically?) that it is much
more fun to be a son oppressed by a harsh father and
therefore needing to cheat the old man out of necessary
money, while his own father prevents any plots by being
so accommodating. Is it the same or another young man
who complains in F 3 about a hetaera who will not take
money from her lover? The dark joke about suicide in F 4
may concern this young man whose funds are rejected.*

Bibl.: Schlüter 1884, 19–20; Negro 1919, 38–39; Pascal
1926, 175–78; Argenio 1965, 266–69; Jacobson 1977; Gro-
ton 1990; Boscherini 1999, 103; Livan 2005, 70–71, 91–93;
Cipriani 2010, 140–46; Manuwald 2011, 235, 240; Hanses
2020, 147, 166n81.

[1] Guardì notes that Alexis, Diphilus, Demoxenus, and Posi-
dippus all wrote comedies entitled Σύντροφοι (*"Raised Together"*
or *"Foster Brothers"*), which might be similarly themed.

1 (199–209 R.[3]) Cic. *Nat. D.* 3.72

ille vero in Synephebis Academicorum more contra communem opinionem non dubitat pugnare ratione, qui . . . dicit:

ia^6 in amore suave est summo summaque inopia
         parentem habere avarum inlepidum, in liberos
         difficilem, qui te nec amet nec studeat tui.

atque huic incredibili sententiae ratiunculas suggerit:

ia^6 aut tu illum fructu fallas aut per litteras
5   advertas aliquod nomen aut per servolum
         percutias pavidum; postremo a parco patre
         quod sumas quanto dissipes libentius!

idemque facilem et liberalem patrem incommodum esse amanti filio disputat:

     quem neque quo pacto fallam nec quid inde auferam
     nec quem dolum ad eum aut machinam commoliar
10   scio quicquam; ita omnes meos dolos fallacias
     praestrigias praestrinxit commoditas patris.

quid ergo isti doli, quid machinae, quid fallaciae praestrigiaeque num sine ratione esse potuerunt?

1 *constituit Bothe*: in amore summo summaque inopia suave esse dicit parentem *Cicero*   3 sui *cod.*: sui tui (tui *del.*) *cod.*: vel tui *add. sup. cod.*   4 fructu] furto *coni. Buecheler, Ribbeck*
    6 pavidum] stupidum *aut* bardum *malit Ribbeck*
    7 dissipes *cod.*: dissipis *vel* dissipas *codd. rell.*
    8 nec quid inde *codd. dett., ed. Veneta 1471*: neque quid inde *cod.*: nequid inde *vel sim. rell.*   11 praestrigias *Buecheler*: praestigias *codd.*: praestringas *cod.*

1 Cicero, *On the Nature of the Gods*

The character in *Fellow Recruits* does not hesitate, in the style of the Academics, to fight received opinion with reason when . . . he says:

> It's so nice, in the depths of love and the depths of
>   poverty
> to have a stingy, graceless father, a trouble to his
> children, who neither loves you nor cares about your
>   situation.

And on top of this amazing dictum he piles some feeble reasons:

> You can either cheat him of income or forge
> some name in a letter or use a slave boy[1]   5
> to put him in a panic. In the end, how much more
>   happily
> you'll squander what you dug out of a tightfisted
>   father!

Moreover, he argues that an easygoing and generous father is a misfortune for a son in love:[2]

> I can't cheat him or make a withdrawal from there,
> I can't launch at him any scheme or contrivance
> that I know of; so all my schemes, deceptions,   10
> foils my father's forebearance has foiled.

How then have those schemes, contrivances, deceptions, and foils come to exist without reasoning?

[1] That is, one bearing a false report.   [2] Cicero's comment may not indicate a gap in the original text of Caecilius; Guardì takes the first seven lines as a continuous passage.

2a (210 R.[3]) Cic. *Sen.* 24

nemo enim est tam senex qui se annum non putet posse
vivere; sed idem in eis elaborant, quae sciunt nihil ad se
omnino pertinere:

cr[4]   serit
    arbores, quae alteri saeculo prosient

ut ait Statius noster in Synephebis. nec vero dubitat agri-
cola, quamvis sit senex, quaerenti cui serat respondere:
"dis immortalibus, qui me non accipere modo haec a
maioribus voluerunt, sed etiam posteris prodere."

2b Cic. *Tusc.* 1.31

"serit . . . prosint," ut ait ‹Statius› in Synephebis, quid
spectans nisi etiam postera saecula ad se pertinere?

2 saeculo *codd.*   saeclo *rell. Tusc. fere omnes*   pro-
sient *cod.*: prosint *rell.*   saeclo prosint alteri *Spengel, Rib-
beck*[3]: alteri saeclo prosint *Ribbeck*[2–3], *Havet*: saeclo alteri quae
prosient *Ramorino*: quae prosient saeclo alteri *Barriera*

3 (211–14 R.[3]) Cic. *Nat. D.* 1.13

quo quidem loco convocandi omnes videntur qui quae sit
earum vera iudicent . . . itaque mihi libet exclamare ut in
Synephebis:

tr[7]   pro deum popularium omnium, ‹omnium›
            adulescentium
        clamo postulo obsecro oro ploro atque inploro fidem

1 omnium ‹omnium› *Manutius*: omnium *codd.*

522

2a Cicero, *On Old Age*

No one is so old that he does not think he can live another year—yet these men work at projects which they know will bring them no return whatsoever:

> he plants
>   trees to benefit another age

as our [Caecilius] Statius says in *Fellow Recruits*. Nor in fact does a farmer hesitate, however old he may be, to answer if someone asks for whom he plants: "For the immortal gods, who wanted me not only to inherit these from my ancestors, but also to hand them on to posterity."

2b Cicero, *Tusculan Disputations*

"He plants . . . ," as Caecilius Statius says in *Fellow Recruits*, and with what in mind except thinking that even succeeding ages matter to him?

3 Cicero, *On the Nature of the Gods*

On this topic it seems that all should be called upon to judge which of these views is true . . . and so I feel like crying out, as in *Fellow Recruits*:

> to the gods, all the populace, all the youth
> I cry, demand, beg, plead, wail and bewail for belief

non levissima de re, ut queritur ille:

> . . . in civitate fiunt facinora capitalia,
> ⟨nam⟩ ab amico amante argentum accipere meretrix
>   noenu volt.

3 hac *vel* nunc *ante* in *add. Ribbeck*: in civitate fiunt *Bergk,
edd.*: in civitate fieri *Cicero*: fieri in civitate *Orelli*
   4 nam *add. Ribbeck*   noenu volt *Bergk, Ribbeck*[2–3]: non
vult *codd.*: nevolt *Wolf*: nunc nevolt *Ribbeck*[1]

4 (215 R.[3]) Non., p. 200.16–25 M. = 295 L.

COLLUS masculine . . . Caecilius Harpazomene (F 2) . . .
idem Synephebis:

ia[8]   (A) ad restim res redit. (B) immo collus, non res, nam
      ille argentum habet.

   ad restim *cod.*: Cadresum *vel* Cadretim *codd.*

SYRACUSII (F 1–3)

*Alexis wrote a Συρακόσιος ("The Syracusan," F 220 K.-A.),
but its one fragment reveals no connection to Caecilius'
Syracusii ("The Syracusans"). The Demea addressed in F 1
is likely to be an old man, perhaps the father (cf. Demea
in Terence's Adelphoe), and Davus in F 2 is a typical slave
name (though if the "sweetness" that affects him is love,*

1 (216 R.[3]) Non., pp. 176.29–77.1 M. = 260 L.

SIMILITAS, similitudo. Caecilius Syracusiis:

ia[6]   vide Demea, hominis quid fert morum similitas?

   homini *L. Mueller*   fert *edd.*: feret *codd.*

about a matter by no means trivial, as that character complains:

> . . . in this city capital crimes are being committed:
> a hetaera refuses to take cash from her smitten
>   sweetheart.

4 Nonius

collus, masculine gender . . . Caecilius in *The Ravished Woman* (F 2) . . . and the same in *Fellow Recruits*:

> (A) The matter comes back to a rope. (B) Rather a
>   neck, not the matter: he in fact has the money.

SYRACUSII (F 1–3)

that is more unusual for a slave). The unsympathetic view of love in F 3 likely comes from an older generation.
    Bibl.: Wase 1685, 8; Schlüter 1884, 20; Argenio 1965, 272; Camilloni 1985, 220; Arnott 1996, 623–24; Hanses 2020, 238 and n. 75.

1 Nonius

similitas ["similarity"], the same as *similitudo* ["similitude"], Caecilius in *The Syracusans*:

> Look, Demea, what does a man's similarity of
>   manners matter?

2 (217 R.[3]) Non., p. 96.27–31 M. = 137 L.

DULCITAS, DULCITUDO pro dulcedo. . . . Caecilius Syra-
cusiis:

ia[6]   tanta hinc invasit in cor Davi dulcitas.

     tanta *cod.*: tantam *rell.*: tantan *Mercerus*   huic *codd.*,
corr. Veltori   in cor Davi *Mercerus*: in corda in *codd.*: in cor
dandi *Buecheler*: in tua corda *vel* in cor, Dave *Ribbeck[1]*: in corol-
lam *Ribbeck[2–3]*   tanta invasit huic in corda indulcitas *War-
mington*

3 (218–19 R.[3]) Non., p. 391.28–31 M. = 627 L.

STARE iterum horrere significat. . . . Caecilius Syracusiis:

tr[7]   hic amet, familiae fame pereant, ager autem stet
       sentibus.

     familiae fame pereant *codd.*: fame familiae pereant *L. Muel-
ler*: familiae fame depereant *Beier*: fame aliei pereant *Bergk*:
familia ei fame perbitat *Bothe*: familiae fame perbitant *Ribbeck*

TITTHE (F 1–6)

*Prior to Caecilius' Titthe ("The Wet Nurse"), Menander
wrote a Τίτθη ("Wet Nurse," F 349–50 K.-A.), Alexis a
Τίτθη or Τίτθαι ("Wet Nurse" or "Wet Nurses," F 228–31
K.-A.), and Eubulus a Τίτθαι ("Wet Nurses," F 109–12
K.-A.). Menander is the likeliest source; one of its frag-
ments suggests a plot to conceal a baby. Caecilius' play has
a rape at a celebration of the Mysteries in the background*

526

2 Nonius

dulcitas and *dulcitudo* for *dulcedo* ["sweetness"]. . . . Cae-
cilius in *The Syracusans*:

> Hence so much sweetness has seized Davus' heart.

3 Nonius

stare ["to stand up"] moreover means to bristle. . . . Cae-
cilius in *The Syracusans*:

> Let him be in love, let his households starve to death,
> moreover, let his fields bristle with briars.

TITTHE (F 1–6)

*(F 2), and perhaps the title character helped conceal the
pregnancy and birth (F 4 and 5). F 6 suggests the setup for
an eavesdropping scene, which might have precipitated
the revelation of the birth.*

    *Bibl.: Schlüter 1884, 20; Frassinetti 1979, 86; Camilloni
1985, 220; Arnott 1996, 647–54; Boscherini 1999, 107.*

1 (221–22 R.[3]) Non., pp. 258.37–59.2 M. = 395 L.

CONTENDERE significat conparare. . . . Caecilius Titthe:

tr[7]
                        egon vitam meam
asticam contendam cum istac rusticana ‹tua›, Syra?

2 atticam *codd., corr. Bergk*   ista *codd.*   rusticina
cod.   tua *add. Bergk, Quicherat*: rustica dura *vel* vana *Spen-*
gel   oct. iamb. const. C. F. W. Mueller

2 (223 R.[3]) Non., p. 118.9–11 M. = 169 L.

GRAVIDAVIT, implevit. Caecilius Titthe:

ia[6]
                        per mysteria hic
inhoneste gravidavit probro.

2 inhonesto *Buecheler*: inhoneste honestam *Bothe in sept.*
troch., quem Ribbeck est secutus: inhoneste inceste *L. Mueller*:
inhoneste civem *Brakman*   probo *cod.*

3 (224–25 R.[3]) Non., p. 183.23–27 M. = 269 L.

UTRASQUE pro utrimque vel utrobique. . . . Caecilius
Titthe:

ia[6]
      atque hercle utrasque te, cum ad nos venis,
      subfarcinatam vidi.

1 te *Mercerus*: et *codd.*   2 subfraginatum *codd., corr.*
Mercerus   sept. iamb. atque hercle / utrasque . . . *praefe-*
runt Bothe, Spengel, Ribbeck, sen. L. Mueller

1 Nonius

contendere ["to strive"] means to compare. . . . Caecilius in *The Wet Nurse*:

> Shall I compare my
> city life with that rustic life of yours, Syra?[1]

[1] A slave name (if indeed vocative), borne by old slave women in Plautus' *Mercator* and *Truculentus* as well as Terence's *Hecyra*.

2 Nonius

gravidavit ["has loaded"], has filled / made pregnant. Caecilius in *The Wet Nurse*:

> During the Mysteries this man
> disgracefully impregnated her by rape.

3 Nonius

utrasque ["on both sides"] for *utrimque* or *utrobique*. . . . Caecilius in *The Wet Nurse*:

> And by Hercules, when you came to our house,
> I spotted that you were double-stuffed.[1]

[1] Possibly a reference to pregnancy with twins? Terence (*An.* 769–70) uses the same term when Davus suggests an older woman smuggled a baby in: *vidi Cantharam suffarcinatam* ("I saw Canthara with something stuffed under her clothes").

4 (220 R.^{3}) Non., p. 483.1–5 M. = 775 L.

LACTE nominativo casu ab eo quod est lac. . . . Caecilius
Titthe:

ia^6 praesertim quae non peperit lacte non habet

5 (226 R.^{3}) Non., p. 196.5–10 M. = 288 L.

COMPITA generis neutri. . . . masculino Varro de scaenicis
originibus lib. III: "ubi compitus erat aliquis." Caecilius
Titthe:

ia/tr   ubi adiacentem compitum

     ubi *ex Varronis loco inl. secl. Ribbeck*   adiacentem *Fru-
terius*: adicientem *codd.*   ubi? adicientem *vel* abi ad adi-
cientem *vel* ibi adjacentem *Bothe*: ubi adi ad adiacentem: *Spen-
gel*: abi in adiacentem *in app. Ribbeck*^{2}

6 (227 R.^{3}) Non., p. 270.5–10 M. = 413 L.

CONCEDERE, recedere vel cedere. . . . Caecilius Titthe:

ia/tr   hic dum abit, huc concessero.

TRIUMPHUS (F 1–2)

*Awarding a triumph to a victorious general is a character-
istically Roman custom, here in Caecilius'* Triumphus
*("The Triumph") certainly used metaphorically, perhaps
for the success of a character's scheme within the play, as
the military language of F 2 suggests. No further details
of the plot, let alone relation to any Greek source mate-*

4 Nonius

lacte ["milk"; solely ablative form in classical Latin] as a
nominative case, derived from *lac* [classical form of nom-
inative]. . . . Caecilius in *The Wet Nurse*:

> especially a woman who has not given birth does not
> have milk

5 Nonius

compita ["crossroads"] neuter gender. . . . Masculine in
Varro's *On Scenic Origins,* Book 3: "where there was some
crossroads." Caecilius in *The Wet Nurse*:

> where a nearby crossroads

6 Nonius

concedere ["to withdraw"], meaning to retire or depart.
. . . Caecilius in *The Wet Nurse*:

> While he leaves, I'll get out of the way over here.

TRIUMPHUS (F 1–2)

rial, are recoverable. *Afranius wrote a* Pompa *("Parade"),*
which might have had a similar theme.
  Bibl.: *Schlüter 1884, 21; Boscherini 1999, 102; Livan*
2005, 34–35.

1 (228 R.³) Gell. *NA* 6.7.9

"adprobus" tamen, quod significat "valde probus" non infi-
tias eo quin prima syllaba acui debeat. Caecilius in comoe-
dia quae inscribitur Triumphus vocabulo isto utitur:

*ia*⁶   Hierocles hospes est mi adulescens adprobus.

2a (229 R.³) Fest., p. 400.27–34 L.

SUCCENTURIARE est explendae centuriae gratia supplere,
subicere. . . . et Caecilius in Triumpho: "nunc . . . subcen-
turia."

2b Paul. *Fest.*, p. 401.7–9 L.

SUCCENTURIARE est explendae centuriae gratia supplere.
Caecilius: "nunc . . . succenturia."

*ia*⁶   nunc meae militiae astutia
    opus est. subcenturia!

1 militiae *Festus*: malitiae *Paulus*   astutiam *C. O. Muel-*
ler: astutiae *Kiessling*   2 subcenturia *Festus*: succenturia
Paulus: subcenturiare *C. O. Mueller*: subcenturiari *Bergk*: sub-
centuriata *Buecheler*: est succenturiata *Bothe*   sept. iamb.
posuit *Bergk*

VENATOR (F 1–2)

*Caecilius' Venator ("The Hunter") seems an unparalleled
title for a comoedia palliata,[1] but other examples of New
Comedy were set outside the city or included nonurban*

[1] Hence Spengel's suggestion to correct the manuscript at-
tribution in Nonius from "Hunter" (*Venator*) to the known title
"Moneylender" (*Faenerator*), followed by Ribbeck.

1 Gellius, *Attic Nights*

In fact, I don't deny that *adprobus* meaning "very *probus*" ["honest"] should be accented on the first syllable. Caecilius in his comedy entitled *The Triumph* uses this word:

My guest Hierocles is a very honest young man.

2a Festus

succenturiare means "supply" or "fill out" in the special sense of bringing a century up to strength. . . . And Caecilius in *The Triumph*: . . .

2b Paul the Deacon, *Epitome of Festus*

succenturiare means "supply" in the special sense of bringing a century up to strength. Caecilius: . . .

Now my warfare needs cleverness.
Draft her in!

VENATOR (F 1–2)

characters.[2] *The fragments do not suffice to tell us what group of people* (ordo, F 1) *was involved.*

[2] Terence in the prologue to *Phormio* (6–8) criticizes his rival Luscius Lanuvinus for a scene in one of his plays featuring a lovesick youth who apparently fantasized a hunting vignette in which hunting dogs pursued a hind in distress, but part of Terence's point may be that such material is inappropriate in comedy.

1 (129–30 R.[3]) Non., p. 483.18–35 M. = 776 L.

QUAESTI vel QUAESTUIS dictum pro quaestus. . . . Caecilius Venatore:

tr[7]   (A) satine huic ordini
etsi nihil ego egi, quaesti? (B) quaesti? (A) quia sunt
       aemuli.

> Venatore *codd.*: Faeneratore *Spengel*   1 huc *codd., corr. Bothe*   ordine *cod., Bothe*   2 ego *add. Ribbeck*[3]   egi] ego *codd.*: egisti *Ribbeck*[1–2]   quaesti quaesti *cod.*: quaesti *semel codd. rell.*   sunemuli *codd.*: *corr. Aldina*

2 (131 R.[3]) Non., p. 42.19–21 M. = 61 L.

VERNILITER pro adulatorie, a vernis quibus haec vivendi ars est. Caecilius Venatore:

ia/tr   credo, nimis tandem hoc fit verniliter.

> Venatore *codd.*: Faeneratore *Spengel*   hoc hercle fit *Ribbeck*[3]: tamen hoce fit *Ribbeck*[2]: tandem hoc quidem fit *Ribbeck*[1]: hocce *vel* tamen istuc fit *Bothe*: tandem hoc fiet *vel* fuit *Spengel*: hoc abs te fit *vel sim. Leo*

INCERTA (F 1–39)

Bibl.: Alfonsi 1955 (F 33); 1966 (F 7); Beare 1964, 79 (F 3); Argenio 1965, 270–76 (F 2–3, 5–9, 15, 18, 20, 33–34, 37); Camilloni 1985, 221–22 (F 3, 15, 18, 26, 28, 37, 38,

1 Nonius

quaesti or *quaestuis*, [genitives] used for *quaestus*
["profit"]. . . . Caecilius in *The Hunter*:

> (A) Did this group profit enough,
> even though I did nothing? (B) Profit? (A) Because
> they're rivals.

2 Nonius

verniliter ["slavishly"] for "in a flattering way," from *vernae*
["houseborn slaves"], since this is their way of living. Cae-
cilius in *The Hunter*:

> I think in the end this is happening too slavishly.

FRAGMENTS NOT ASSIGNED TO
ANY PLAY (F 1–39)

*43); Monda 1998 (F 2, 3); Livan 2005, 77–78 (F 8); Ci-
priani 2010, 146–59 (F 7, 13, 23, 33, 37); Manuwald 2011,
239–40 (F 3); Hanses 2020, 140–41 (F 3).*

1 (249 R.³) Varro, *Ling.*, 8.103

multa ab animalium vocibus tralata in homines, partim
quae sunt aperta, partim obscura; perspicua, ut . . .
⟨Cae⟩cilii:

ia⁶   tantam rem dibalare ut pro nilo habuerit

   tantum *codd., corr. Scaliger*

2 (230 R.³) Cic. *Cael.* 37

redeo nunc ad te, Caeli, vicissim ac mihi auctoritatem
patriam severitatemque suscipio. sed dubito quem patrem
potissimum sumam, Caeciliumne aliquem vehementem
atque durum:

tr⁸   nunc enim demum mi animus ardet, nunc meum cor
      cumulatur ira.

   enim *om. Cic. Fin.*   mi *Ribbeck*: mihi *codd. utroque loco*

Cf. Cic. *Fin.* 2.14: nunc demum mi animus ardet.

3 (231–42 R.³) Cic. *Cael.* 37

aut illum: "o infelix, o sceleste!" ferrei sunt isti patres:
"egone . . . velim" vix ferendi. diceret talis pater: "istam
. . . meae."

ia⁶   o infelix, o sceleste!

         *   *   *

   egone quid dicam? egon quid velim? quae tu omnia
   tuis foedis factis facis ut nequiquam velim.

         *   *   *

1 Varro, *On the Latin Language*

Many terms from animal cries have been used figuratively of humans, some obvious, some obscure. The clear terms include . . . from Caecilius:

> to bleat out so great a matter as being worth nothing

2 Cicero, *Pro Caelio*

Now I come back to you, Caelius, it's your turn, and I take up a father's authority and severity. But I hesitate as to which father would be best to choose—perhaps some furious and stern one, as in Caecilius:

> Now at last my mind's on fire, now my heart is
> heaped with wrath.

Cf. Cicero, *On Ends*: Now at last my mind's on fire.

3 Cicero, *Pro Caelio* (cont. from F 2)

or the following [father]: "Wretch! Scoundrel!" Those fathers are men of iron. "I . . . without effect!" They're almost unendurable! Such a father would say: "Why . . . my life."

> Wretch! Scoundrel!

* * *

> I, what should I say? What should I wish? I'd wish
> that all
> your dirty deeds done were without effect!

* * *

istam in vicinitatem te meretriciam
cur contulisti? cur illecebris cognitis
non . . . refugisti . . . .
. . . cur alienam ullam mulierem
nosti . . .
. . . . . . dide ac disiice
per me licebit . . .
. . . si egebis, tibi dolebit, mihi sat est,
qui aetatis quod reliquom est oblectem meae.

4a (F *Inc.* XXV R.[3]) Cic. *De or.* 2.40

et Crassus "nox te," inquit, "nobis, Antoni, expolivit, homi-
nemque reddidit: nam hesterno sermone, 'unius cuius-
dam operis,' ut ait Caecilius, 'remigem aliquem aut baiu-
lum,' nobis oratorem descripseras, inopem quemdam
humanitatis atque inurbanum."

4b Non., p. 80.9–10 M. = 112 L.: *baiolum*

?   unius cuiusdam operis remigem aliquem aut baiulum

   unius cuiusdam operis *codd.*: operis unius cuiusdam *War-
mington*   baiulum *cod.*: baiolum *cod. Non.*

Why did you take yourself to that sex trade district?
Once you learned about those allurements
why didn't . . . you flee . . . .
. . . why did you get to know any strange woman
in that way. . .
. . . . . . scatter and squander (your money)
it'll be fine as far as I'm concerned . . .
. . . if you end up poor, it'll be your problem. I'm all
    set,
I've got enough to entertain myself the rest of my
    life.[1]

---

[1] The arrangement of the text is not secure. Cicero quotes with intentional omissions in the interests of his defense speech.

4a Cicero, *On the Orator*

And Crassus said: "A night has smoothed you down, Antonius, and rendered you human again for us, since in yesterday's discussion you portrayed the orator, as Caecilius says, as 'some rower or porter with just one task,' some fellow without education or manners."

4b Nonius

some rower or porter with just one task

5 (245–46 R.[3]) Cic. *De or.* 2.257

saepe etiam versus facete interponitur, vel ut est vel pau-
lulum immutatus, aut aliqua pars versus; ut Stati a Scauro
stomachante[1]—ex quo sunt nonnulli, qui tuam legem de
civitate natam, Crasse, dicant—:

tr[7]   st, tacete, quid hoc clamoris? quibus nec mater nec
              pater
        tanta confidentia? auferte istam enim superbiam!

> [1] Bake emends the manuscript's *satius Scauro stomachanti* to
> this ablative of agent, in keeping with the notion that the patrician
> Scaurus would have used the quotation against those trying to
> claim citizenship, but it is difficult to see how the dative in the
> manuscript, implying someone else quoted the verses *to* Scaurus,
> would have arisen.

> 1 st *Stephanus*: si *codd.*: sed *rell.*   tacete *cod.*: facete *vel*
> facere *vel* tacere *vel* tacite *codd.*   quid *cod.*: qui *cod.*   nec[1]
> *codd.*: om. *rell.*   mater nec pater sit *cod.*: pater nec mater
> sit *cod.* (*post. transp.*) sit: *del. edd.*   2 confidentia *Schütz*:
> confidentia estis *codd.*   auferte *cod.*: aufert *cod.*   istam
> enim *cod.*: istanc enim *rell.*

6a (252 R.[3]) Cic. *Fin.* 2.13

nam et ille apud Trabeam "voluptatem animi nimiam" lae-
titiam dicit [*Com.* 6 R.[3]], eandem quam ille Caecilianus
quia "omnibus laetitiis laetum" esse se narrat.

5 Cicero, *On the Orator*

Often a verse is also cleverly introduced, either just as it is or slightly altered, or a part of a verse, like that one of [Caecilius] Statius quoted by an infuriated Scaurus[1]— from which, some say, your law on citizenship came about, Crassus[2]—:

> Shush, shut up, what's this uproar? Such impudence
>   in those
> with neither mother nor father? Away with that
>   arrogance of yours!

[1] M. Aemilius Scaurus (*RE* 140), a patrician allied to the Cae-cilii Metelli (cos. 115, censor 109 BC). He celebrated a triumph after a victory over the Ligurians and was appointed *princeps senatus* ("senior senator"), remaining in that position until his death. [2] L. Licinius Crassus (*RE* 55), an outstanding orator and the main speaker in Cicero's *De oratore*, cos. 95 BC with Q. Mucius Scaevola (*RE* 22). They passed the *Lex Licinia Mucia de redigundis civibus*, instituting a tribunal to investigate and re-move aliens who were illegally enrolled as citizens under the previous censors. Resentment of this move contributed to the outbreak of the Social War.

6a Cicero, *On Ends*

There's also the character in Trabea[1] who calls happiness "excessive delight of the mind" [*Com.* 6 R.[3]], the very same feeling meant by the character in Caecilius who reports that he was "happy with all happinesses."

[1] Writer of *palliatae*, from whom only two fragments survive, possibly earlier than Caecilius.

6b Cic. *Fam.* 2.9.2

repente vero "incessi omnibus laetitiis laetus."

tr[7]   omnibus laetitiis laetus incedo

versum ex utroque Ciceronis loco restituit Ribbeck

7 (266 R.[3]) Cic. *Tusc.* 3.56

hic Socrates commemoratur, hic Diogenes, hic Caecilia-
num illud:

tr[7]   saepe est etiam sub palliolo sordido sapientia.

8 (259–64 R.[3]) Cic. *Tusc.* 4.68

totus vero iste, qui volgo appellatur amor . . . tantae levi-
tatis est, ut nihil videam quod putem conferendum. quem
Caecilius:

ia[6]   deum qui non summum putet
aut stultum aut rerum esse imperitum existumem:
cuii in manu sit, quem esse dementem velit,
quem sapere, quem insanire, quem in morbum inici
    . . .
5   quem contra amari, quem expeti, quem arcessier.

1 ego vero Amorem *suppl. Bentley*: Cupidinem *suppl. Brak-
man*   2 rerum] venerum *coni. Meineke*   existumem
Ribbeck: existumat *cod., Pohlenz* (*qui Ciceroni tribuit*): existumet
cod.: existumo *Bentley*   3 cui *codd., corr. Ribbeck, Ciceroni
tribuit C. F. W. Mueller*: cuius *Ernesti*   demente *codd.*

4 insanire *codd.*: sanari *Manutius*: insanare *cod.*   post *v. 4
hunc fere versum excidisse statuit Bentley*: quem odio esse, quem
contemni, quem excludi foras   5 arcessier *Erasmus, Bent-
ley*: arcessiri *cod.*: arcesciri *cod.*

Cf. Eur. *Auge* F 269 Kannicht.

6b Cicero, *Letters to Friends* (to Caelius)

Suddenly in fact "I strode forth, happy with all happinesses":

> I stride forth, happy with all happinesses[1]

[1] Schlüter (1884, 14) suggests this fragment may belong to *Obolostates* ("*The Moneylender*"), but gives no grounds.

7 Cicero, *Tusculan Disputations*

Here Socrates is quoted, here Diogenes, here that line of Caecilius:

> There's often wisdom even under a dirty little cloak.

8 Cicero, *Tusculan Disputations*

In fact, all of that which is commonly called love . . . is so inconstant that I see nothing I could think comparable. As Caecilius puts it:

> Whoever thinks [love] is not the highest god
> I would consider either a fool or inexperienced in
>   life.
> Anyone under his power, he can make raving at will,
> or wise, or crazed, or afflict with disease
>   . . .
> or on the other hand make beloved, sought after, in   5
>   demand.

9a (*243–44* R.^{3}) Cic. *Amic.* 99

quid turpius quam inludi? quod ut ne accidat magis caven-
dum est:

ia^6 ut me hodie ante omnes comicos stultos senes
versaris atque ut lusseris lautissime.

1 ut me] tu me *Halm*   2 ut lusseris *Buecheler*: ut /// ius-
seris *cod.*: ut iusseris *rell.*: ut vixeris *cod.*: ut luseris concessive
cod.: illuseris *cod., Augustinus*: inlusseris *Baiter*: elusseris *Halm*:
emunxeris *Bentley*: lusseris *Langen*

9b Cic. *Sen.* 36

nam quos ait Caecilius "comicos stultos senes," hos signi-
ficat credulos obliviosos dissolutos, quae vitia sunt non
senectutis, sed inertis ignavae somniculosae senectutis.

10 (*258* R.^{3}) Cic. *Att.* 7.3.10

venio ad "Piraeea," in quo magis reprehendendus sum
quod homo Romanus "Piraeea" scripserim, non "Piraeum"
(sic enim omnes nostri locuti sunt), quam quod addiderim
<"in"> . . . nostrum quidem si est peccatum, in eo est quod
non ut de oppido locutus sum sed ut de loco, secutusque
sum non dico Caecilium:

ia^7 mane ut ex portu in Piraeum

(malus enim auctor Latinitatis est), sed Terentium (cuius
fabellae propter elegantiam sermonis putabantur a C.
Laelio scribi), "heri aliquot adulescentuli coiimus in Pi-
raeum" [*Eun.* 539].[1]

---

[1] Cicero seems to misquote, as our texts, confirmed by Dona-
tus, read *in Piraeo*. Schlüter (1884, 4) would ascribe this fragment
to the *Andria*, Ribbeck to the *Aethrio*.

9a Cicero, *On Friendship*

What's more disgraceful than being made a fool? So make very sure that it never happens:

> That you've twisted me round today and most
>   elegantly
> deluded me more than all the old fools in comedies.

9b Cicero, *On Old Age*

For when Caecilius speaks of "old fools in comedies," he means the credulous, forgetful, and negligent, which are not faults of old age generally, but of a sluggish, cowardly, half-asleep old age.

10 Cicero, *Letters to Atticus*

As for "Piraeea": as a native Roman I can be more blamed for writing "Piraeea" and not "Piraeus" (as all our fellow countrymen have said) than for adding the preposition "in" . . . If there's a mistake in my grammar, in speaking of it not as a town but a locality, I'm quoting—not Caecilius, who said:

> tomorrow as from the port into Piraeus

(for he is a bad authority on Latin style), but Terence (whose plays on account of the elegance of their diction were attributed to C. Laelius):[1] "Yesterday some of us boys gathered down in Piraeus" [*Eun.* 539].

[1] C. Laelius (ca. 235–ca. 160 BC; cos. 190 BC; *RE* 12), friend and protégé of P. Cornelius Scipio Africanus (*RE* 336).

11 (250 R.³) Paul. *Fest.*, p. 31.10–12 L.

BARDUS, stultus, a tarditate ingenii appellatur. Caecilius:

tr⁷/ia⁸   nimis audacem nimisque bardum barbarum

trahitur autem a Graeco, quod illi βραδύς dicunt.

12 (F *Inc.* 42 R.³) Fest., p. 256.22–24 L.

PROFESTI dies dic‹ti quod sint procul a religione numi-
nis› divini. Caecilius in . . . :

?   ‹ profe›sti tantundem

13 (251 R.³) Fest., p. 306.12–16 L.

QUISQUILIAE dici putantur, quidquid ex arboribus minutis
surculorum foliorumque cadit: velut *quicquidcadiae*. Cae-
cilius:

tr⁷   (A) quisquilias volantis, venti spolia memorant.
                                        (B) i modo!

memoras *Scaliger*

14 (275 R.³) Fest., pp. 494.33–96.3 L.

TAENIAS Graecam vocem sic interpretatur Verrius, ut di-

11 Paul the Deacon, *Epitome of Festus*

bardus ["bumbling"], "stupid," is derived from the slow-
ness of intelligence. Caecilius:

> an excessively bold, excessively bumbling barbarian

And it is borrowed from the Greek, as they say βραδύς
["slow"].

12 Festus

Days are called *profesti* ["nonfestival"] that are separated
from observance of divine power. . . . Caecilius in [name
lost] . . . :

> nonfestival days to the same degree

13 Festus

quisquiliae ["odds and ends"] is thought to describe what-
ever in the way of small twigs and leaves falls from tiny
trees; similarly, *quicquidcadiae* ["any kind of fallout"].
Caecilius:

> (A) Flying debris, spoils of the wind—that's what
> they're talking about.
>> (B) Get away now!

14 Festus

Verrius[1] explains *taeniae* as a Greek word meaning a wool

---

[1] M. Verrius Flaccus (ca. 55 BC?–ca. AD 20?; *RE* Verrius 2),
scholar and tutor to Augustus' grandsons, Gaius and Drusus; au-
thor of the lost *De verborum significatu*, epitomized by Festus.

cat ornamentum esse laneum capitis honorati, ut sit apud
Caecilium in Androgyno [F 7] . . . et alias:

ia^6 dum taeniam qui volnus vinciret petit.

hic versus C. O. Muellero Caecilii non esse videbatur, sed
tragoediae aptior

15 (270 R.^{3}) Paul. Fest., p. 504.21–22 L.

TRUO avis onocrotalus. Caecilius irridens magnitudinem
nasi:

ia^6 pro di inmortales! unde prorepsit truo?

16 (282 R.^{3}) Fronto, *Ad M. Caesarem et invicem libri, Ep.*
2.11.2 (p. 31.6–7 van den Hout)

igitur paene me Opicum animantem ad Graecam scriptu-
ram perpulerunt "homines," ut Caecilius ait, "incolumi
scientia."

?   homines . . . incolumi scientia

scientia *corr.* ex inscientia *van den Hout*: inscientia *edd., Rib-*
beck

17 (269 R.^{3}) Gell. *NA* 5.6.11–12

civica corona appellatur quam civis civi a quo in proelio
servatus est testem vitae salutisque perceptae dat. [12] ea
fit e fronde quernea, quoniam cibus victusque antiquissi-
mus quercus capi solitus; fit etiam ex ilice, quod genus
superiori proximum est, sicuti scriptum est in quadam
comoedia Caecilii:

548

adornment for the head to give honor, as found in Caecilius in *The Man/Woman* [F 7] . . . and elsewhere:[2]

> while he looks for a headband to bind the wound

[2] "Elsewhere" might mean another author rather than another play of Caecilius, possibly even tragedy. Warmington suggests the quotation might come from Naevius' comedy *Acontizomenos* (*Com.* F 1–3 *FRL*).

15 Paul the Deacon, *Epitome of Festus*

truo, a bird, the pelican or ὀνοκρόταλος. Caecilius mocking the size of someone's nose:

> By the immortal gods! Where did the pelican creep
> in from?

16 Fronto, *Correspondence*

[Marcus Aurelius to Fronto] Therefore almost like a living Oscan clown, I've been compelled to write in Greek, as Caecilius says, by:

> men . . . of unblemished intelligence

17 Gellius, *Attic Nights*

The so-called "civic" crown, given by one citizen to another who has saved the first in battle, testifies to whom he owes his life and safety. [12] It is made from leaves of the esculent oak, because esculent oak was the earliest source of food and sustenance; it was also made from the holm oak, the species most closely related to the former, as Caecilius wrote in one of his comedies:

ia^8/tr^7 † advehuntur cum ilignea corona et chlamyde: di
vostram fidem!

advehuntur *cod.*: advehitur *Bothe in oct. iamb.* iligna
Fleckeisen advehunt / Eum cum ilignea *C. F. W. Muel-*
ler *versum nondum sanatum cruce notavit Guardì*

18 (248 R.³) Apul. *Apol.* 5.3

sane quidem, si verum est quod Statium Caecilium in suis
poematibus scripsisse dicunt, innocentiam eloquentiam
esse . . .

ia^6 innocentia eloquentiast

verba ab Apuleio laudata in numeros redegit Ribbeck, qui
sic fere expleri versum iussit: saepe innocentia ipsast eloquen-
tia animi *praemisit Spengel*

19 (254–55 R.³) Non., p. 101.23–25 = 144 L.

DEINTEGRARE, deminuere. . . . Caecilius:

tr^7 nomen virginis, nisi mirum est, deintegravit

20 (268 R.³) Non., p. 119.14–15 = 171 L.

GRAMIAE, pituitae oculorum. Caecilius:

ia^6 grammonsis oculis ipsa atratis dentibus

gramiosis *Mercerus*: graminosis *Spengel* dentibus *cod.*:
gentibus *rell.*

550

† They're arriving clad in holm oak crown and
    military cloak: gods help us![1]

[1] Guardì suggests this verse might fit the theme of the *Tri-
umph*. The textual uncertainty involves both the first word and
the meter. The manuscripts report a plural verb ("they are arriv-
ing"), which does not scan easily; Bothe conjectured a singular
form ("he is arriving") in a regular iambic octonarius.

18 Apuleius, *Apology*

Indeed, if they say what Caecilius Statius wrote in his plays
is true, that innocence is eloquence . . .

    innocence is eloquence

19 Nonius

deintegrare, to lessen. . . . Caecilius:

    unless a miracle occurs, he's devalued the girl's name

20 Nonius

gramiae, rheum, mucus in the eyes. Caecilius:

    she's the one with rheumy eyes, blackened teeth

21 (267 R.[3]) Non., p. 197.28–32 = 290 L.

QUIS et generi feminino attribui posse veterum auctoritas
voluit. . . . Caecilius:

ia[6]   quaeso igitur, quisquis es mea mulier . . .

quaero *Onions*

22 (285 R.[3]) Non., p. 229.5–6 = 339 L.

TAPETE generis neutri. . . . et Caecilius:

?   glabrum tapete

et Caecilius *secl. L. Mueller*

23 (286 R.[3]) Charis., *GL* I, p. 104.1–2 = p. 132 B.

Leontion et Chrysion et Phanion ex neutris Graecis femi-
nina nostri fecere et Plautus [*Truc.* 323] quod dixit "haec
Phronesium," et Caecilius:

?   Leontium

nostri] neutra *cod*.   thrusion et paunion *cod.*: thyrsion
et faunion *cod., corr. Spengel*   haec Leontium *Fabricius*

24 (275 R.[3]) Charis., *GL* I, p. 122.11–12 = p. 156 B.

AMANTUM Caecilius . . .:

ia/tr   quantum amantum in Attica est

in Attica *Ribbeck*: in natica *cod.*: in riatica *ed. princ.*

21 Nonius

quis ["who"]. The authority of early writers allows this form to be used for the feminine gender [as well as masculine]. . . . Caecilius:

so I beg you, dear lady, whoever you are . . .

22 Nonius

tapete ["carpet"] as neuter gender. . . . and Caecilius:

a smooth carpet

23 Charisius

Our ancestors made Leontion and Chrysion and Phanion feminine nouns from neuter Greek forms, as did Plautus [*Truc.* 323] when he said "this [fem.] Phronesium," and Caecilius:

Leontium

24 Charisius

amantum ["of lovers"; rather than classical *amantium*, as the genitive plural] in Caecilius:

however big the amount of lovers in Attica is

25 (289 R.³) Charis., *GL* I, p. 130.4 = p. 165 B.

FACILIOREIS Caecilius, inquit Plinius [p. 27.5 B.]. idem et
SANCTIOREIS.

  ꟼ   facilioreis
         sanctioreis

26 (276–77 R.³) Charis., *GL* I, p. 201.10–14 = p. 261 B.

IN MUNDO pro palam et in expedito ac cito. Plautus . . .
Caecilius quoque, ut Annaeus Cornutus libro tabularum
castarum patris sui:

bacch⁴   profecto qui nobis in mundo futurum lectum

        profecto qui] profertoque *Ribbeck*

27 (278 R.³) Charis., *GL* I, p. 201.15 = p. 261 B.

item idem [cf. F 26]:

tr⁷ꟼ   namque malum in mundost, ere

28 (273–74 R.³) Diom., *GL* I, p. 345.4–12

HIARE et HIETARE veteres dixerunt . . . Caecilius:

tr⁸   (A) sequere me. (B) perii hercle! (A) tu, qui mi
        oscitans hietansque restas.

      peri hercle *codd.*: periercle *vel* pehercle *rell.*: perii hercle
Ribbeck: praei hercle *Putsch*   qui *om. cod.*: quid *Rib-
beck*   mi *Spengel*: mihi *codd.*   enim *vel* nam *Ribbeck*:
restans *cod.*   personas distinxit *Ribbeck*

25 Charisius

Caecilius uses *facilioreis* ["easier ones"; ante-classical accusative plural form] according to Pliny [p. 27.5 B.], and he also uses *sanctioreis* ["holier ones"].

> easier ones
> holier ones

26 Charisius

in mundo ["in order"; classical] for openly and at the ready as well as swiftly. Plautus . . . Caecilius as well, as Annaeus Cornutus[1] reports in the book of sacred tables of his father:

> who certainly [said] that a bed would be at the ready
>   for us

[1] An Annaeus Cornutus is otherwise unknown, as is the work cited, and there have been many attempts to emend Charisius' text, some of which delete any reference to Caecilius. I follow Guardì in retaining this and the next fragment, though with doubts.

27 Charisius

And the same author [Caecilius; cf. F 26] also:

> and in fact there's trouble at the ready, master

28 Diomedes

Early writers used both *hiare* and *hietare* [for "gaping"]. . . . Caecilius:

> (A) Follow me. (B) I'm done for, by Hercules! (A) You, you're just standing there, slouching and gaping.

29 (287 R.³) Diom., *GL* I, p. 383.18

GNOSCIT ait Caecilius:

?   gnoscit

     gnoscit *codd.*: ignoscit *cod.*

30 (279 R.³) Diom., *GL* I, p. 385.22–28

Attius QUITUS SUM ponit pro quivi . . . Caecilius praeterea:

ia⁶?   si non sarciri quitur

     sarcire *cod.*

31 (284 R.³) Donat. ad Ter. *Eun*. 815

DOMI et foci genetivi sunt. Caecilius:

?   decora domi

32 (271–72 R.³) Serv. Dan. ad Verg. *G*. 1.74

QUASSANTE, quae sonet cum quassatur. Caecilius:

ia⁷   si quassante capite tristes incedunt

     si] sic *in app. Ribbeck*

33 (265 R.³) Symm. *Ep*. 9.114

recte Caecilius comicus:

ia⁶   homo homini deus est si suum officium sciat.

29 Diomedes

Caecilius says *gnoscit*:

> [he] knows

30 Diomedes

Attius writes *quitus sum* for *quivi* ["I've been able"] . . .
Caecilius also [writes *quitur* for "can"]:

> if it can't be mended

31 Donatus, *Commentary on Terence, The Eunuch*

domi ["of the house"] and *foci* ["of the hearth"] are geni-
tives. Caecilius:

> beauties of the house

32 Servius Danielis, *Commentary on Virgil*

quassante, something that makes a noise when shaken.
Caecilius:

> if they sadly advance with rattling head

33 Symmachus, *Correspondence*

The comic poet Caecilius rightly says:

> A man is a god to his fellow man if he knows his duty.

34 (283 R.[3]) Macrob. *Sat*. 3.15.9

sed quis neget indomitam apud illos et, ut ait Caecilius,
vallatam gulam fuisse?

?   vallata gula

35 (280 R.[3]) Rufin. *Comm. in metra Terent.*, *GL* VI,
p. 556.7–13

Varro in septimo: clausulas quoque primum appellatas
dicunt, quod clauderent sententiam, ut apud Accium
[*Trag*. 665 R.[3]]: "an haec iam obliti sunt Phryges?" non
nunquam ab his initium fit, ut apud Caecilium:

cr?   di boni! quid hoc?

apud Terentium [*Ad*. 610]: "discrucior animi."

> di boni *Aldus*: dei boni *codd.*, *Ascensius*: de . . . *cod.*: dii
> boni *ed. princ.*   est *post* hoc *add. Traglia*

36 (290–91 R.[3]) Iul. Rufin., *RLM*, p. 43.29–30

ἀποφώνημα, sentention responsiva, ut apud Caecilium:

tr[7]   fac velis: perficies.

> caecilium *cod.*: caelium *cod.*

34 Macrobius, *Saturnalia*

But who would deny among those people the existence of an unrestrained and, as Caecilius says, well-fortified gluttony?

> well-fortified gluttony

35 Rufinus, *Commentary on the Meters of Terence*

Varro [says] in Book 7 [of *On the Latin Language*]:[1] "They say that *clausulae*[2] were first called that because they 'close' a thought, as in Accius [*Trag.* 665 R.[3]]: 'Have the Phrygians already forgotten these things?'" Sometimes a beginning is formed from these [*clausulae*], as for example in Caecilius:

> Great gods! What's this?

in Terence [*Ad.* 610]: "I'm tortured in mind."

[1] Not preserved in Varro (*Ling.* 7) at present, but our text there may be defective.   [2] Rhythmic patterns used to close a sentence or phrase.

36 Iulius Rufinianus

ἀποφώνημα, a saying containing a response, as in Caecilius:

> Strengthen your will: you'll succeed.

37 (247 R.³) Isid. *Orig.* 10.40

CONFIDENS, quod sit in cunctis fiducia plenus. unde et Caecilius:

ia⁶   si confidentiam adhibes, confide omnia.

si *om. codd.*   adhibes (adi-) *vel* adhibens (adi-) *vel* habes (ab-) *codd.*

38 (256–57 R.³) Isid. *Orig.* 19.4.5

SCAPHON funis in prora positus. de quo Caecilius:

ia⁶   Venerio cursu veni, prolato pede
         usque ad scaphonem.

1 cursum *codd.*: cursus *rell.*: cursu Venerio *dub. in app.* Warmington   prolatum *codd.*   pedes *codd.*: pedem *rell.*
2 scaphonem *Emeranus*: safonem *codd.*: saphonem *vel* favonem *vel* fabonem *vel* fabone *rell.*

39 (*Inc.* 37 R.³) Hor. *Ars P.* 237–39

    ut nihil intersit, Davusne loquatur et audax
    Pythias, emuncto lucrata Simone talentum,
    an custos famulusque dei Silenus alumni.

Ps.-Acro ad Hor. *Ars P.* 238: non dicit de Pythia Terentiana, sed quae apud Caecilium comoediographum[1] inducitur ancilla per astutias accipere argentum a domino; nam fefellit dominum et accepit ab eo argenti talentum. haec eadem meretricula rapax, ut Thais, quae lucrum facit.

Comm. Cruq. *ad loc.*: Pythias persona comica in comoedia Caecilii quae inducitur per astutias accipere argentum a Simone domino suo in dotem filiae.

[1] Caecilium comoediographum *Orelli*: Lucilium tragoediographum *cod.*

37 Isidore, *Origins*

confidens ["confident"], for one who is full of self-assurance in everything, for example in Caecilius:

> If you summon your confidence, be confident about everything.

38 Isidore, *Origins*

scaphon, a rope tied to the ship's prow. As in Caecilius:

> I came on Venus' route, with the sail sheet stretched all the way to the prow rope.

39 Horace, *The Art of Poetry*

> it doesn't matter whether Davus is speaking with the bold
> Pythias, who cheated Simo out of a talent,
> or Silenus, guard and servant of his divine nursling.

Ps.-Acro, *Commentary on Horace:* He does not speak of Terence's Pythia, but rather of the maid in the comic poet Caecilius who is brought in for a scheme to get money from the master. She cheats the master and receives a talent of silver from him. She was the same type of greedy little prostitute as Thais in making a profit.

"Commentator Cruquianus" on Horace: Pythias is a comic character in a play of Caecilius brought in for a scheme to receive money from her master Simo for the daughter's dowry.

DUBIA VEL SPURIA (F 40–43)

40 (281 R.^{3}) Sen. *Ep*. 113.26

haec disputamus attractis superciliis, fronte rugosa? non possum hoc loco dicere illud Caecilianum:

o tristes ineptias!

ridiculae sunt.

Caecilianum *vulgo edd. inde a Mureto*: caelianum *codd., edd. vett., Beltrami, Reynolds, Préchac*: cicilianum *cod.*

41 (292–93 R.^{3}) Non., p. 80.32–34 M. = 113 L.

BELLOSUM, bellicosum. Caecilius:

tr^7 tantum bellum suscitare conari adversarios
contra bellosum genus

Caecilius: caecilius *cod.*: caelius *rell.*: Caelio Antipatro referunt *edd.*

DOUBTFUL OR SPURIOUS
CITATIONS (F 40–43)

Textual attribution of three of the following fragments to Caecilius Statius is uncertain. The fourth may have been invented by an early modern scholar.

40 Seneca, *Epistles*

Are these the things we discuss with contracted eyebrows and furrowed forehead? Here I cannot quote the line of Caecilius:[1]

What sorry folly!

It's absurd.

[1] Earlier editions of Seneca gave the source as "Caelius," perhaps the politician defended by Cicero, and some doubt that Seneca would quote a Republican comic poet.

41 Nonius

bellosum ["warlike"], bellicose. Caecilius:

to try to rouse so great a war as combatants against a warlike race

42 (vacat R.[3]) Serv. Dan. ad Verg. *Aen.* 2.777

"sine numine divum," sine fati necessitate. ut enim Statius dicit:

tr[7]   fata sunt quae divi fantur

vel quae indubitanter eveniunt.

> 1–2 fata sunt quae dii fantur *codd.*: fata sunt quae dii fantur vel indubitanter eveniunt *cod.*: fata sunt quae indubitanter eveniunt vel fata sunt quae dii fantur *cod.*   1 divi *Bothe*

43 (vacat R.[3]) *Gloss. Terent. ap.* C. Barth, *Advers.* 38.14

aliquid monstri plus est quam aliquid monstrum . . . ut Caecilius:

ia/tr   quid hominis uxorem habes?

> uxoremne *Ribbeck*

ADDENDUM

44 (vacat R.[3]) Anon. Cuim., p. 112.308–12

sis . . . fit in historiis et pro confirmativo, ut Caecilius dicit:

ia/tr   cave sis, fortis vir

42 Servius Danielis, *Commentary on Virgil*

"without the will of the gods," without the necessity of fate. As indeed Statius[1] says:

> Destinies are what the gods destine

or things that eventuate without any doubt.

[1] Perhaps not Caecilius Statius, but Papinius Statius, or an otherwise unknown grammarian.

43 Gloss on Terence in Barth[1]

"Some specimen of monster" is more than "some monster" . . . as Caecilius says:

> What specimen of humanity do you have for a wife?

[1] Kaspar von Barth (German philologist, 1587–1658). Guardì (1974, 207) suggests that Barth invented this example in his *Glossarium Terentianum* based on Terence, *Hecyra* 643–44: *quid mulieris / uxorem habes* ("what kind of a women do you have for a wife?") and Donatus' comment thereon. Cf. Camilloni 1985, 222.

ADDENDUM

This undoubtedly genuine fragment, first published as such by Guardì 2001, is here numbered after the previously known incerta.

44 *Anonymus ad Cuimnanum*

sis [here, = *si vis*, "if you please"] . . . occurs also in discourse for confirmation, as Caecilius says:

> watch out, my fine fellow

CONCORDANCES

LIVIUS ANDRONICUS

TRAGEDIES

CONCORDANCE 1
FRL—Warmington—Ribbeck[3]—*TrRF*

FRL	Warmington	Ribbeck[3]	TrRF
Achilles			
1	1	1	1
Aegisthus			
2	12–13	13–14	2
3	11	12	3
4	9–10	10–11	4
5	14	7	5
6	7	8	7
7	8	9	8
8	5–6	5–6	6
9	2–4	2–4	9
Aias Mastigophorus			
10	15	15	10
11	16–17	16–17	11
Andromeda			
12	18	18	12

CONCORDANCES

FRL	Warmington	Ribbeck[3]	TrRF
Danae			
13	19	19	13
Equus Troianus			
14	20–22	20–22	14
Hermiona			
15	23	23	15
Tereus			
16	27–28	26–27	17
17	25–26	28–29	18
18	29	25	19
19	24	24	20
Tragica Incerta			
20	31	30	21
21	37	39	22
22	38	38	23
23	32	31	24
24	33–34	32–33	25
25	35	34	26
26	30	35	27
27	40	41	28
28	36	37	29
29	—	—	30
30	39	36	31
31	41	40	32
Tragicum Spurium: Ino			
32	41a–d	29[1-4]	16

CONCORDANCE 2
Warmington—*FRL*—Ribbeck[3]—*TrRF*

Warmington	*FRL*	Ribbeck[3]	*TrRF*
Achilles			
1	1	1	1
Aegisthus			
2–4	9	2–4	9
5–6	8	5–6	6
7	6	8	7
8	7	9	8
9–10	4	10–11	4
11	3	12	3
12–13	2	13–14	2
14	5	7	5
Aias Mastigophorus			
15	10	15	10
16–17	11	16–17	11
Andromeda			
18	12	18	12
Danae			
19	13	19	13
Equus Troianus			
20–22	14	20–22	14
Hermiona			
23	15	23	15

	Warmington	*FRL*	Ribbeck[3]	*TrRF*
Tereus				
	24	19	24	20
	27–28	16	26–27	17
	25–26	17	28–29	18
	29	18	25	19
Tragica Incerta				
	30	26	35	27
	31	20	30	21
	32	23	31	24
	33–34	24	32–33	25
	35	25	34	26
	36	28	37	29
	37	21	39	22
	38	22	38	23
	39	30	36	31
	40	27	41	28
	41	31	40	32
Tragicum Spurium: Ino				
	41a–d	32	29[1–4]	16

CONCORDANCE 3
Ribbeck[3]—*FRL*—Warmington—*TrRF*

Ribbeck[3]	*FRL*	Warmington	*TrRF*
Achilles			
1	1	1	1
Aegisthus			
2–4	9	2–4	9
5–6	8	5–6	6
7	5	14	5
8	6	7	7
9	7	8	8
10–11	4	9–10	4
12	3	11	3
13–14	2	12–13	2
Aias Mastigophorus			
15	10	15	10
16–17	11	16–17	11
Andromeda			
18	12	18	12
Danae			
19	13	19	13
Equus Troianus			
20–22	14	20–22	14
Hermiona			
23	15	23	15

CONCORDANCES

	Ribbeck[3]	*FRL*	Warmington	*TrRF*
Tereus				
	24	19	24	20
	25	18	29	19
	26–27	16	27–28	17
	28–29	17	25–26	18
Tragica Incerta				
	30	20	31	21
	31	23	32	24
	32–33	24	33–34	25
	34	25	35	26
	35	26	30	27
	36	30	39	31
	37	28	36	29
	38	22	38	23
	39	21	37	22
	40	31	41	32
	41	27	40	28
Tragicum Spurium: Ino				
	29[1–4]	32	41a–d	16

CONCORDANCE 4
TrRF—FRL—Warmington—Ribbeck[3]

TrRF	*FRL*	Warmington	Ribbeck[3]
Achilles			
1	1	1	1
Aegisthus			
2	2	12–13	13–14
3	3	11	12
4	4	9–10	10–11
5	5	14	7
6	8	5–6	5–6
7	6	7	8
8	7	8	9
9	9	2–4	2–4
Aias Mastigophorus			
10	10	15	15
11	11	16–17	16–17
Andromeda			
12	12	18	18
Danae			
13	13	19	19
Equus Troianus			
14	14	20–22	20–22
Hermiona			
15	15	23	23

CONCORDANCES

	TrRF	FRL	Warmington	Ribbeck[3]
Ino				
	16	32	41a–d	29[1-4]
Tereus				
	17	16	27–28	26–27
	18	17	25–26	28–29
	19	18	29	25
	20	19	24	24
Tragica Incerta				
	21	20	31	30
	22	21	37	39
	23	22	38	38
	24	23	32	31
	25	24	33–34	32–33
	26	25	35	34
	27	26	30	35
	28	27	40	41
	29	28	36	37
	30	29	—	—
	31	30	39	36
	32	31	41	40

LIVIUS ANDRONICUS

COMEDIES

FRL—Warmington—Ribbeck[3]

FRL	Warmington	Ribbeck[3]
Gladiolus		
1	1	1
Ludius		
2	2	2
Comica Incerta		
3	4	4–5
4	3	3
5	5	6–7
6	6	8

LIVIUS ANDRONICUS

ODYSSIA

CONCORDANCE 1
FRL—Warmington—Viredaz—Blänsdorf

FRL	Warmington	Viredaz	Blänsdorf
1	1	1	1
2	2	19	2
3	3–4	20	3
4	6	21	6
5	7	22	7
6	9	23	8
7	11	3	9
8	12	27	16
9	13	4	10
10	10	14	23
11	14	28	31
12	15	29	11
13	16	5	12
14	17	24	13
15	18	25	30
16	19	6	14
17	20–21	7	15
18	22	8	17

LIVIUS ANDRONICUS: ODYSSIA 1

FRL	Warmington	Viredaz	Blänsdorf
19	23–26	9	18
20	27	10	19
21	28–29	11	20
22	30	12	21
23	39	13	22
24	34	15	24
25	33	16	25
26	37	17	26
27	38	36	32
28	5	2	4
29	40	18	27
30	45	30	28
31	46	26	29
32	35–36	49	34
33	42	48	5

CONCORDANCE 2
Warmington—*FRL*—Viredaz—Blänsdorf

Warmington	*FRL*	Viredaz	Blänsdorf
1	1	1	1
2	2	19	2
3–4	3	20	3
5	28	2	4
6	4	21	6
7	5	22	7
8	Ps. Andr. 1	31	37
9	6	23	8
10	10	14	23
11	7	3	9
12	8	27	16
13	9	4	10
14	11	28	31
15	12	29	11
16	13	5	12
17	14	24	13
18	15	25	30
19	16	6	14
20–21	17	7	15
22	18	8	17
23–26	19	9	18
27	20	10	19
28–29	21	11	20
30	22	12	21
31–32	Ps. Andr. 3	32	38
33	25	16	25
34	24	15	24

LIVIUS ANDRONICUS: ODYSSIA 2

Warmington	*FRL*	Viredaz	Blänsdorf
35–36	32	49	34
37	26	17	26
38	27	36	32
39	23	13	22
40	29	18	27
41	Ps. Andr. 4	33	39
42	33	48	5
43–44	Ps. Andr. 5	34	40
45	30	30	28
46	31	26	29

CONCORDANCE 3
Viredaz—*FRL*—Warmington—Blänsdorf

Viredaz	*FRL*	Warmington	Blänsdorf
1	1	1	1
2	28	5	4
3	7	11	9
4	9	13	10
5	13	16	12
6	16	19	14
7	17	20–21	15
8	18	22	17
9	19	23–26	18
10	20	27	19
11	21	28–29	20
12	22	30	21
13	23	39	22
14	10	10	23
15	24	34	24
16	25	33	25
17	26	37	26
18	29	40	27
19	2	2	2
20	3	3–4	3
21	4	6	6
22	5	7	7
23	6	9	8
24	14	17	13
25	15	18	30
26	31	46	29
27	8	12	16

Viredaz	*FRL*	Warmington	Blänsdorf
28	11	14	31
29	12	15	11
30	30	45	28
31	Ps. Andr. 1	8	37
32	Ps. Andr. 3	31–32	38
33	Ps. Andr. 4	41	39
34	Ps. Andr. 5	43–44	40
35	3	3–4	3
36	27	38	32
37	*Com. Inc.* 3	*Com. Inc.* 4	—
38	*Com. Inc.* 5	*Com. Inc.* 5	36a
39	*Trag. Inc.* 24	*Trag. Inc.* 33–34	—
40	*Trag. Inc.* 31	*Trag. Inc.* 41	—
41	*Op. Inc.* 6	—	—
42	*Trag. Inc.* 21	*Trag. Inc.* 37	33
43	*Op. Inc.* 1	p. 596	—
44	*Op. Inc.* 7	35	—
45	—	—	—
46	Ps. Andr. 2	p. 42	—
47	—	—	—
48	33	42	5
49	32	35–36	34

CONCORDANCE 4
Blänsdorf—*FRL*—Warmington—Viredaz

Blänsdorf	*FRL*	Warmington	Viredaz
1	1	1	1
2	2	2	19
3	3	3–4	20
4	28	5	2
5	33	42	48
6	4	6	21
7	5	7	22
8	6	9	23
9	7	11	3
10	9	13	4
11	12	15	29
12	13	16	5
14	16	19	6
15	17	20–21	7
16	8	12	27
17	18	22	8
18	19	23–26	9
19	20	27	10
20	21	28–29	11
21	22	30	12
22	23	39	13
23	10	10	14
24	24	34	15
25	25	33	16
26	26	37	17
27	29	40	18
28	30	45	30

Blänsdorf	*FRL*	Warmington	Viredaz
29	31	46	26
30	15	18	25
31	11	14	28
32	27	38	36
33	*Trag. Inc.* 21	*Trag. Inc.* 37	42
34	32	35–36	49
35	*Op. Inc.* 7	—	44
36	*Op. Inc.* 1	p. 596	43
37	Ps. Andr. 1	8	31
38	Ps. Andr. 3	31–32	32
39	Ps. Andr. 4	41	33
40	Ps. Andr. 5	43–44	34

PSEUDO-ANDRONICUS

ODYSSIA

FRL	Warmington	Viredaz	Blänsdorf
1	8	31	37
2	p. 42	46	—
3	31–32	32	38
4	41	33	39
5	43–44	34	40

LIVIUS ANDRONICUS

UNIDENTIFIED WORKS

FRL	Warmington	Viredaz	Blänsdorf
1	p. 596	43	—
2	p. 596	—	—
3	p. 596	—	—
4	p. 596	—	—
5	p. 596	—	—
6	—	—	—
7	—	44	35

NAEVIUS

COMEDIES

CONCORDANCE 1
FRL—Warmington—Ribbeck[3]

FRL	Warmington	Ribbeck[3]
Acontizomenos		
1	2–3	2–3
2	4	4
3	1	1
Agitatoria		
4	9	8
5	8	13
6	5–6	9–10
7	7	14
8	10–12	5–7
9	13–14	11–12
Agrypnuntes		
10	16–17	15–16
11	15	17
Appella		
12	18–19	19
13	20	18

CONCORDANCES

	FRL	Warmington	Ribbeck[3]
Ariolus			
	14	21	20
	15	22–26	21–24
Carbonaria			
	16	27	26
Clamidaria			
	17	28	26[1]
Colax			
	18	32	30–31
	19	36	35
	20	33–35	32–34
	21	29–31	27–29
Corollaria			
	22	p. 597	48[1]
	23	p. 597	48[2]
	24	40–41	39–40
	25	37–39	36–38
	26	47	43
	27	46	45
	28	48	44
	29	p. 597	48[3]
	30	42–43	41–42
	31	44–45	46–47
	32	49	48
	33	—	—
Dementes			
	34	50	49

	FRL	Warmington	Ribbeck[3]
Demetrius			
	35	p. 88	49[1]
Diobolaria			
	36	—	—
Dolus			
	37	51	49[2]
Figulus			
	38	52	49[3]
Glaucoma			
	39	53	50–51
Gymnasticus			
	40	55	57
	41	58–59	53–54
	42	56	56
	43	57	60
	44	54	52
	45	61	59
	46	60	55
	47	62–63	58
Lampadio			
	48	p. 92	60[1]
Nagido			
	49	p. 579	60[2]
Nautae			
	50	p. 596	60[3]

	FRL	Warmington	Ribbeck[3]
Paelex			
	51	64	66
Philemporos			
	52	—	—
Proiectus			
	53	65	67
	54	66	68
Quadrigemini			
	55	67	69
Stalagmus			
	56	68	70
Stigmatias			
	57	p. 96	71
Tarentilla			
	58	p. 597	93[3]
	59	82	86
	60	p. 597	93[1]
	61	92	80
	62	88–89	90–91
	63	90–91	92–93
	64	80–81	83–84
	65	69–71	72–74
	66	86–87	88–89
	67	73	85
	68	72	81
	69	p. 579	93[2]
	70	83	87

FRL	Warmington	Ribbeck[3]
71	84–85	82
72	74–79	75–79

Technicus

73	p. 104	93[4]

Testicularia

74	93	94

Triphallus

75	94–96	96–98

Tunicularia

76	101	103–4
77	102	105
78	97–100	99–102

Comica Incerta

79	106	*Praet.* 7
80	107	*Praet.* 8
81	*Inc.* 28–29	107
82	*Inc.* 22	120
83	p. 597	35[2]
84	*Inc.* 11–12	129
85	*Inc.* 6	136
86	*Inc.* 25–26	111–12
87	*Inc.* 1–3	108–10
88	*Inc.* 19	117
89	*Inc.* 20	118
90	*Inc.* 31	124
91	*Inc.* 30[a–c]	121–21[1–2]
92	*Inc.* 27	113
93	*Inc.* 24	122

FRL	Warmington	Ribbeck[3]
94	*Inc.* 18	116
95	*Inc.* 7–8	126–27
96	*Inc.* 10	128
97	*Inc.* 23	123
98	*Inc.* 13–14	130–31
99	*Inc.* 15	114
100	104	65
101	103	25
102	*Inc.* 16	115
103	*Inc.* 32	135
104	105	95
105	*Inc.* 4–5	137–38
106	*Inc.* 9	125
107	*Inc.* 17	134
108	*Inc.* 21	119

CONCORDANCE 2
Warmington—*FRL*— Ribbeck[3]

Warmington	*FRL*	Ribbeck[3]
Acontizomenos		
1	3	1
2–3	1	2–3
4	2	4
Agitatoria		
5–6	6	9–10
7	7	14
8	5	13
9	4	8
10–12	8	5–7
13–14	9	11–12
Agrypnuntes		
15	11	17
16–17	10	15–16
Appella		
18–19	12	19
20	13	18
Ariolus		
21	14	20
22–26	15	21–24
Carbonaria		
27	16	26
Clamidaria		
28	17	26[1]

CONCORDANCES

	Warmington	*FRL*	Ribbeck[3]
Colax			
	29–31	21	27–29
	32	18	30–31
	33–35	20	32–34
	36	19	35
Corollaria			
	37–39	25	36–38
	40–41	24	39–40
	42–43	30	41–42
	44–45	31	46–47
	46	27	45
	47	26	43
	48	28	44
	49	32	48
Dementes			
	50	34	49
Dolus			
	51	37	49[2]
Figulus			
	52	38	49[3]
Glaucoma			
	53	39	50–51
Gymnasticus			
	54	44	52
	55	40	57
	56	42	56

	Warmington	*FRL*	Ribbeck[3]
	57	43	60
	58–59	41	53–54
	60	46	55
	61	45	59
	62–63	47	58
Paelex			
	64	51	66
Proiectus			
	65	53	67
	66	54	68
Quadrigemini			
	67	55	69
Stalagmus			
	68	56	70
Tarentilla			
	69–71	65	72–74
	72	68	81
	73	67	85
	74–79	72	75–79
	80–81	64	83–84
	82	59	86
	83	70	87
	84–85	71	82
	86–87	66	88–89
	88–89	62	90–91
	90–91	63	92–93
	92	61	80

CONCORDANCES

Warmington	*FRL*	Ribbeck[3]
Testicularia		
93	74	94
Triphallus		
94–96	75	96–98
Tunicularia		
97–100	78	99–102
101	76	103–4
102	77	105
Comica ambigui tituli		
103	101	25
104	100	65
105	104	95
106	79	*Praet.* 7
107	80	*Praet.* 8
Comica Incerta		
1–3	87	108–10
4–5	105	137–38
6	85	136
7–8	95	126–27
9	106	125
10	96	128
11–12	84	129
13–14	98	130–31
15	99	114
16	102	115
17	107	134
18	94	116
19	88	117

Warmington	*FRL*	Ribbeck[3]
20	89	118
21	108	119
22	82	120
23	97	123
24	93	122
25–26	86	111–12
27	92	113
28–29	81	107
30[a–c]	91	121–21[1–2]
31	90	124
32	103	135

CONCORDANCE 3
Ribbeck[3]—*FRL*—Warmington

Ribbeck[3]	*FRL*	Warmington
Acontizomenos		
1	3	1
2–3	1	2–3
4	2	4
Agitatoria		
5–7	8	10–12
8	4	9
9–10	6	5–6
11–12	9	13–14
13	5	8
14	7	7
Agrypnuntes		
15–16	10	16–17
17	11	15
Appella		
18	13	20
19	12	18–19
Ariolus		
20	14	21
21–24	15	22–26
Astiologa		
25	101	103
Carbonaria		
26	16	27

Ribbeck[3]	*FRL*	Warmington
Clamidaria		
26[1]	17	28
Colax		
27–29	21	29–31
30–31	18	32
32–34	20	33–35
35	19	36
Corollaria		
36–38	25	37–39
39–40	24	40–41
41–42	30	42–43
43	26	47
44	28	48
45	27	46
46–47	31	44–45
48	32	49
48[1]	22	p. 597
48[2]	23	p. 597
48[3]	29	p. 597
Dementes		
49	34	50
Demetrius		
49[1]	35	p. 88
Dolus		
49[2]	37	51
Figulus		
49[3]	38	52

Ribbeck[3]	*FRL*	Warmington
Glaucoma		
50–51	39	53
Gymnasticus		
52	44	54
53–54	41	58–59
55	46	60
56	42	56
57	40	55
58	47	62–63
59	45	61
60	43	57
Lampadio		
60[1]	48	p. 92
Nagido		
60[2]	49	p. 579
Nautae		
60[3]	50	p. 596
Nervolaria		
65	*Inc.* 100	*Inc.* 104
Paelex		
66	51	64
Proiectus		
67	53	65
68	54	66
Quadrigemini		
69	55	67

Ribbeck[3]	*FRL*	Warmington
Stalagmus		
70	56	68
Stigmatias		
71	57	p. 96
Tarentilla		
72–74	65	69–71
75–79	72	74–79
80	61	92
81	68	72
82	71	84–85
83–84	64	80–81
85	67	73
86	59	82
87	70	83
90–91	62	88–89
92–93	63	90–91
93[1]	60	p. 597
93[2]	69	p. 579
93[3]	58	p. 597
Technicus		
93[4]	73	p. 104
Testicularia		
94	74	93
Tribacelus		
95	104	105
Triphallus		
96–98	75	94–96

Ribbeck[3]	FRL	Warmington
Tunicularia		
99–102	78	97–100
103–4	76	101
105	77	102
Comica Incerta		
106	*Trag. Inc.* 51	*Trag. Inc.* 37
107	81	*Inc.* 28–29
108–10	87	*Inc.* 1–3
111–12	86	*Inc.* 25–26
113	92	*Inc.* 27
114	99	*Inc.* 15
115	102	*Inc.* 16
116	94	*Inc.* 18
117	88	*Inc.* 19
118	89	*Inc.* 20
119	108	*Inc.* 21
120	82	*Inc.* 22
121–21[1–2]	91	*Inc.* 30[a–c]
122	93	*Inc.* 24
123	97	*Inc.* 23
124	90	*Inc.* 31
125	106	*Inc.* 9
126–27	95	*Inc.* 7–8
128	96	*Inc.* 10
129	84	*Inc.* 11–12
130–31	98	*Inc.* 13–14
132	—	—
133	—	—

Ribbeck[3]	*FRL*	Warmington
134	107	*Inc.* 17
135	103	*Inc.* 32
136	85	*Inc.* 6
137–38	105	*Inc.* 4–5

NAEVIUS

TRAGEDIES

CONCORDANCE 1
FRL—Warmington—Ribbeck[3]— *TrRF*

FRL	Warmington	Ribbeck[3]	*TrRF*
Andromacha			
1	1–2	Novius *Atell.* 4[a–b]	1
Danae			
2	8	12	2
3	9	10	3
4	6–7	11	4
5	4	2	5
6	5	4	6
7	14	9	7
8	12	7	8
9	13	8	9
10	10–11	5	10
11	3	3	11
12	15	6	12
Equus Troianus			
13	16	13	13

FRL	Warmington	Ribbeck[3]	*TrRF*
Hector Proficiscens			
14	17	15	14
15	18	14	15
Hesiona			
16	19	*Aesiona* 1	—
Iphigenia			
17	21	16	16
Lycurgus			
18	57	50	17
19	30–32	26–28	18
20	46–47	24–25	19
21	37–38	29–30	20
22	49	35	21
23	55–56	46–47	23
24	52–53	45	24
25	36	33	25
26	50–51	37–38	26
27	45	44	27
28	25	18	28
29	58	39	29
30	26	19	30
31	35	20	31
32	33–34	31–32	32
33	48	36	33
34	27–29	21–23	34
35	59	48	35
36	24	17	36
37	44	34	37
38	40	40	38

FRL	Warmington	Ribbeck[3]	TrRF
39	54	49	39
40	39	43	40
41	41–42	41–42	22

Tragica Incerta

42	*Iph.* 23	62	41
43	*Inc.* 33	61	42
44	*Lyc.* 43	54	43
45	*Inc.* 35	56	44
46	*Inc.* 41	58	45
47	*Inc.* 38	51	46
48	*Inc.* 34	60	47
49	*Iph.* 22	53	48
50	*Inc.* 36	57	49
51	*Inc.* 37	*Com.* 106	—
52	*Inc.* 39	52	50
53	*Iph.* 20	59	51
54	*Inc.* 40	55	52

CONCORDANCE 2
Warmington—*FRL*— Ribbeck[3]— *TrRF*

Warmington	*FRL*	Ribbeck[3]	*TrRF*
Andromacha			
1–2	1	Novius, *Atell.* 4[a–b]	1
Danae			
3	11	3	11
4	5	2	5
5	6	4	6
6–7	4	11	4
8	2	12	2
9	3	10	3
10–11	10	5	10
12	8	7	8
13	9	8	9
14	7	9	7
15	12	6	12
Equus Troianus			
16	16	13	13
Hector Proficiscens			
17	14	15	14
18	15	14	15
Hesiona			
19	16	*Aesiona* 1	—
Iphigenia			
20	53	59	51
21	17	16	16
22	49	53	48
23	42	62	41

609

Warmington	*FRL*	Ribbeck[3]	*TrRF*
Lycurgus			
24	36	17	36
25	28	18	28
26	30	19	30
27–29	34	21–23	34
30–32	19	26–28	18
33–34	32	31–32	32
35	31	20	31
36	25	33	25
37–38	21	29–30	20
39	40	43	40
40	38	40	38
41–42	41	41–42	22
43	44	54	43
44	37	34	37
45	27	44	27
46–47	20	24–25	19
48	33	36	33
49	22	35	21
50–51	26	37–38	26
52–53	24	45	24
54	39	49	39
55–56	23	46–47	23
57	18	50	17
58	29	39	29
59	35	48	35
Tragica Incerta			
Inc. 33	43	61	42
Inc. 34	48	60	47
Inc. 35	45	56	44

Warmington	*FRL*	Ribbeck[3]	*TrRF*
Inc. 36	50	57	49
Inc. 37	51	*Com.* 106	—
Inc. 38	47	51	46
Inc. 39	52	52	50
Inc. 40	54	55	52
Inc. 41	46	58	45

CONCORDANCE 3
Ribbeck[3]— *FRL*—Warmington— *TrRF*

Ribbeck[3]	*FRL*	Warmington	*TrRF*
Aesiona (Hesiona)			
1	16	19	—
Danae			
2	5	4	5
3	11	3	11
4	6	5	6
5	10	10–11	10
6	12	15	12
7	8	12	8
9	7	14	7
10	3	9	3
11	4	6–7	4
12	2	8	2
Equus Troianus			
13	13	16	13
Hector Proficiscens			
14	15	18	15
15	14	17	14
Iphigenia			
16	17	21	16
Lycurgus			
17	36	24	36
18	28	25	28
19	30	26	30

Ribbeck[3]	*FRL*	Warmington	*TrRF*
20	31	35	31
21–23	34	27–29	34
24–25	20	46–47	19
26–28	19	30–32	18
29–30	21	37–38	20
31–32	32	33–34	32
33	25	36	25
34	37	44	37
35	22	49	21
36	33	48	33
37–38	26	50–51	26
39	29	58	29
40	38	40	38
41–42	41	41–42	22
43	40	39	40
44	27	45	27
45	24	52–53	24
46–47	23	55–56	23
48	35	59	35
49	39	54	39
50	18	57	17
Tragica Incerta			
51	47	*Inc.* 38	46
52	52	*Inc.* 39	50
53	49	*Iph.* 22	48
54	44	*Lyc.* 43	43
55	54	*Inc.* 40	52
56	45	*Inc.* 35	44
57	50	*Inc.* 36	49

Ribbeck[3]	*FRL*	Warmington	*TrRF*
58	46	*Inc.* 41	45
59	53	*Iph.* 20	51
60	48	*Inc.* 34	47
61	43	*Inc.* 33	42
62	42	*Iph.* 23	41

CONCORDANCE 4
TrRF—*FRL*—Warmington—Ribbeck[2-3]

TrRF	FRL	Warmington	Ribbeck[2-3]
Andromacha			
1	1	1–2	Novius, *Atell.*4[a-b]
Danae			
2	2	8	12
3	3	9	10
4	4	6–7	11
5	5	4	2
6	6	5	4
7	7	14	9
8	8	12	7
9	9	13	8
10	10	10–11	5
11	11	3	3
12	12	15	6
Equus Troianus			
13	13	16	13
Hector Proficiscens			
14	14	17	15
15	15	18	14
Iphigenia			
16	17	21	16
Lycurgus			
17	18	57	50
18	19	30–32	26–28
19	20	46–47	24–25

TrRF	*FRL*	Warmington	Ribbeck[2–3]
20	21	37–38	29–30
21	22	49	35
22	41	41–42	41–42
23	23	55–56	46–47
24	24	52–53	45
25	25	36	33
26	26	50–51	37–38
27	27	45	44
28	28	25	18
29	29	58	39
30	30	26	19
31	31	35	20
32	32	33–34	31–32
33	33	48	36
34	34	27–29	21–23
35	35	59	48
36	36	24	17
37	37	44	34
38	38	40	40
39	39	54	49
40	40	39	43

Tragica Incerta

41	42	*Iph.* 23	62
42	43	*Inc.* 33	61
43	44	*Lyc.* 43	54
44	45	*Inc.* 35	56
45	46	*Inc.* 41	58
46	47	*Inc.* 38	51
47	48	*Inc.* 34	60

TrRF	FRL	Warmington	Ribbeck[2-3]
48	49	*Iph.* 22	53
49	50	*Inc.* 36	57
50	52	*Inc.* 39	52
51	53	*Iph.* 20	59
52	54	*Inc.* 40	55

NAEVIUS

PRAETEXTAE

FRL—Warmington—Ribbeck[3]

FRL	Warmington *Praet.*	Ribbeck[3] *Praet.*
Clastidium		
1	1 n. b	1
2	1	2
Romulus sive Lupus		
3	—	3
4	—	4
5	2–3	5–6

NAEVIUS

BELLUM PUNICUM

CONCORDANCE 1
FRL—Warmington—Viredaz—Blänsdorf

FRL	Warmington	Viredaz	Blänsdorf
1	29–30	1	3
2	8–10	3	6
3	18	8	10
4	44–46	9	8
5	54	46	18
6	47	10	21
7	19–20	12	20
8	25–26	14	24
9	24	13	22
10	21–22	16	26
11	2–4	15	25
12	28	26	38
13	31–32	22	37
14	36	24	40
15	33	25	41
16	34–35	23	39
17	37	28	43
18	40	31	45

FRL	Warmington	Viredaz	Blänsdorf
19	38	29	44
20	39	27	42
21	41–42	32	47
22	43	30	46
23	65–66	55	55
24	16	6	15
25	12	34	31
26	1	35	1
27	p. 596	36	30
28	p. 597	38	57
29	17	7	16
30	55	39	54
31	p. 596	57	58
32	59–60	40	50
33	61–62	41	51
34	27	42	35
35	63–64	33	56
36	50	58	60
37	23	18	32
38	56	43	59
39	57	44	52
40	5–7	2	5
41	—	63	62
42	48	45	49
43	58	47	23
44	p. 597	48	36
45	13–15	49	9
46	49	51	48
47	11	50	19

CONCORDANCE 2
Warmington—*FRL*—Viredaz—Blänsdorf

Warmington	*FRL*	Viredaz	Blänsdorf
1	26	35	1
2–4	11	15	25
5–7	40	2	5
8–10	2	3	6
11	47	50	19
12	25	34	31
13–15	45	49	9
16	24	6	15
17	29	7	16
18	3	8	10
19–20	7	12	20
21–22	10	16	26
23	37	18	32
24	9	13	22
25–26	8	14	24
27	34	42	35
28	12	26	38
29–30	1	1	3
31–32	13	22	37
33	15	25	41
34–35	16	23	39
36	14	24	40
37	17	28	43
38	19	29	44
39	20	27	42
40	18	31	45
41–42	21	32	47

CONCORDANCES

Warmington	*FRL*	Viredaz	Blänsdorf
43	22	30	46
44–46	4	9	8
47	6	10	21
48	42	45	49
49	46	51	48
50	36	58	60
51–52	—	54	64
53	—	69	66
54	5	46	18
55	30	39	14
56	38	43	59
57	39	44	52
58	43	47	23
59–60	32	40	50
61–62	33	41	51
63–64	35	33	56
65–66	23	55	55

CONCORDANCE 3
Viredaz—*FRL*—Warmington—Blänsdorf

Viredaz	FRL	Warmington	Blänsdorf
1	1	29–30	3
2	40	5–7	5
3	2	8–10	6
4	t 15	p. 54	12
5	t 16	p. 52	14
6	24	16	15
7	29	17	16
8	3	18	10
9	4	44–46	8
10	6	4	21
11	—	—	18a
12	7	19–20	20
13	9	24	22
14	8	25–26	24
15	11	2–4	25
16	10	21–22	26
17	t 9	p. 54	11
18	37	23	32
19	t 10	p. 50	7
20	t 11	p. 52	13
21	t 14	—	4
22	13	31–32	37
23	16	34–35	23
24	14	36	40
25	15	33	41
26	12	28	38
27	20	39	42

CONCORDANCES

Viredaz	FRL	Warmington	Blänsdorf
28	17	37	43
29	19	38	44
30	22	43	46
31	18	40	45
32	21	41–42	47
33	35	63–64	56
34	25	12	31
35	26	1	1
36	27	p. 596	30
37	T 11	p. 46	2
38	28	p. 597	57
39	30	55	54
40	32	59–60	50
41	33	61–62	51
42	34	42	35
43	38	56	59
44	39	57	52
45	42	48	49
46	5	54	18
47	43	58	23
48	44	p. 597	36
49	45	13–15	9
50	47	11	19
51	46	49	48
52	t 3	p. 56	29
53	t 4	p. 56	28
54	—	51–52	64
55	23	65–66	55
56	—	p. 597	53
57	31	p. 596	58

Viredaz	FRL	Warmington	Blänsdorf
58	36	50	60
59	T 5	—	69
60	—	—	60a
61	t 12	p. 56	27
62	t 13	—	17
63	41	—	62
64	—	—	63
65	—	—	67
66	—	—	33
67	—	—	34
68	—	—	65
69	—	53	66

CONCORDANCE 4
Blänsdorf— *FRL*—Warmington—Viredaz

Blänsdorf	*FRL*	Warmington	Viredaz
1	26	1	35
2	T 11	p. 46	37
3	1	29–30	1
4	t 14	—	21
5	40	5–7	2
6	2	8–10	3
7	t 10	p. 50	19
8	4	44–46	9
9	45	13–15	49
10	3	18	8
11	t 9	p. 54	17
12	t 15	p. 54	4
13	t 11	p. 52	20
14	t 16	p. 52	5
15	24	16	6
16	29	17	7
17	t 13	—	62
18	5	54	46
19	47	11	50
20	7	19–20	12
21	6	47	10
22	9	24	13
23	43	58	47
24	8	25–26	14
25	11	2–4	15
26	10	21–22	16
27	t 12	p. 56	61

Blänsdorf	*FRL*	Warmington	Viredaz
28	t 4	p. 56	53
29	t 3	p. 56	52
30	27	p. 596	36
31	25	12	34
32	37	23	18
33	—	—	66
34	—	—	67
35	34	27	42
36	44	p. 597	48
37	13	31–32	22
38	12	28	36
39	16	34–35	23
40	14	36	24
41	15	33	25
42	20	39	27
43	17	37	28
44	19	38	29
45	18	40	31
46	22	43	30
47	21	41–42	32
48	46	49	51
49	42	48	45
50	32	59–60	40
51	33	61–62	41
52	39	57	44
53	—	p. 597	56
54	30	55	39
55	23	65–66	55
56	35	63–64	33
57	28	p. 597	38

CONCORDANCES

Blänsdorf	*FRL*	Warmington	Viredaz
58	31	p. 596	57
59	38	56	43
60	36	50	58
60a	—	—	60
62	41	—	63
63	—	—	64
64	—	51–52	54
65	—	—	68
66	—	53	69
67	—	—	65

CAECILIUS STATIUS

COMEDIES

CONCORDANCE 1
FRL (Guardì)—Warmington

FRL	Warmington
Aethrio	
1 (= 1 R.[3])	2
2 (= 2 R.[3])	5
3 (= 3 R.[3])	1
4 (= 4 R.[3])	3
5 (= 5 R.[3])	4
Andria	
1 (= 6 R.[3])	6
Androgynos	
1 (= 7 R.[3])	7
2 (= 8 R.[3])	8
Asotus	
1 (= 9–10 R.[3])	9
2 (= 14 R.[3])	10
3 (= 13 R.[3])	11
4 (= 11–12 R.[3])	12–13

FRL	Warmington
5 (= 17 R.[3])	15
6 (= 15 R.[3])	16
7 (= 16 R.[3])	14
Carine	
1 (= 104–5 R.[3])	100–101
2 (= 106–7 R.[3])	102–3
Carine vel Cratinus	
3 (= 108–9 R.[3])	104–5
Chalcia	
1 (= 18–19 R.[3])	17
2 (= 20–21 R.[3])	18
Chrysion	
1 (= 22–24 R.[3])	19–21
Dardanus	
1 (= 25 R.[3])	22
Davus	
1 (= 26 R.[3])	23
Demandati	
1 (= 27 R.[3])	24
Ephesio	
1 (= 28–29 R.[3])	25–26
Epicleros	
1 (= 30–31 R.[3])	27–28
2 (= 32 R.[3])	29

FRL	Warmington
Epistathmos	
1 (= 33 R.[3])	30
Epistula	
1 (= 34–35 R.[3])	31–32
2 (= 37 R.[3])	33
Exhautuhestos	
1 (= 38–39 R.[3])	34–35
Exul	
1 (= 40 R.[3])	36
2 (= 41 R.[3])	37
Fallacia	
1 (= 42–43 R.[3])	40–41
2 (= 44–45 R.[3])	38–39
3 (= 46 R.[3])	42
4 (= 47–48 R.[3])	43–44
5 (= 51–52 R.[3])	45–46
6 (= 50 R.[3])	47
7 (= 49 R.[3])	48
Gamos	
1 (= 53 R.[3])	49
Harpazomene	
1 (= 54–55 R.[3])	50
2 (= 56 R.[3])	51
3 (= 57–58 R.[3])	52–53
4 (= 59–60 R.[3])	54–55
5 (= 61 R.[3])	56
6 (= 62–63 R.[3])	57–58

CONCORDANCES

FRL	Warmington
Hymnis	
1 (= 64–65 R.[3])	59–60
2 (= 66–67 R.[3])	62–63
3 (= 71 R.[3])	61
4 (= 70 R.[3])	64
5 (= 68–69 R.[3])	68–70
6 (= 72 R.[3])	65
7 (= 73 R.[3])	66
8 (= 74 R.[3])	67
9 (= 74[1] R.[3])	p. 564
Hypobolimaeus (Subditivos)	
1 (= 75 R.[3])	76
2 (= 76 R.[3])	73–74
3 (= 77 R.[3])	75
4 (= 78 R.[3])	78
5 (= 79–80 R.[3])	81–82
6 (= 81 R.[3])	85
7 (= 82 R.[3])	71
8 (= 84 R.[3])	86
Hypobolimaeus Aeschinus	
1 (= 92 R.[3])	88
Hypobolimaeus Chaerestratus	
1 (= 85 R.[3])	87
Hypobolimaeus Rastraria	
1 (= 86 R.[3])	72
2 (= 87 R.[3])	84
3 (= 88 R.[3])	83
4 (= 89 R.[3])	77

FRL	Warmington
5 (= 90 R.[3])	79
6 (= 91 R.[3])	80
Imbrii	
1 (= 93 R.[3])	89
2 (= 94–95 R.[3])	91–92
3 (= 99 R.[3])	90
4 (= 100 R.[3])	93
5 (= 96–97 R.[3])	94–96
6 (= 98 R.[3])	97
7 (= 101–2 R.[3])	98
8 (= 103 R.[3])	99
Meretrix	
1 (= 110 R.[3])	106
2 (= 111–12 R.[3])	107
Nauclerus	
1 (= 113 R.[3])	108
2 (= 114 R.[3])	109
3 (= 115 R.[3])	110
Nothus Nicasio	
1 (= 116 R.[3])	111
2 (= 117 R.[3])	112
3 (= 118 R.[3])	113
Obolostates vel Faenerator	
1 (= 119–20 R.[3])	114
2 (= 121 R.[3])	115–16
3 (= 122–23 R.[3])	120
4 (= 126–28 R.[3])	121–23

FRL	Warmington
5 (= 124–25 R.[3])	124–25
6 (= 132–33 R.[3])	117–18
7 (= 134 R.[3])	119

Pausimachus

1 (= 135 R.[3])	126
2 (= 136–37 R.[3])	128–29
3 (= 138 R.[3])	127
4 (= 139–40 R.[3])	130–31
5 (= 140[1] R.[3])	p. 564

Philumena

1 (= 141 R.[3])	132
2 (= 141[1] R.[3])	133

Plocium

1 (= 142–57 R.[3])	136–50
2 (= 158–62 R.[3])	151–55
3 (= 163 R.[3])	156
4 (= 164–65 R.[3])	157–58
5 (= 166 R.[3])	162
6 (= 167 R.[3])	161
7 (= 168 R.[3])	159–60
8 (= 169–72 R.[3])	163–66
9 (= 173–75 R.[3])	167–69
10 (= 176 R.[3])	170
11 (= 177 R.[3])	171
12 (= 178–79 R.[3])	172
13 (= 180 R.[3])	173
14 (= 181–82 R.[3])	134–35

FRL	Warmington
15 (= 183 R.[3])	174
16 (= 184 R.[3])	176
17 (= 185 R.[3])	175
18 (= 186–87 R.[3])	177–78
19 (= 188 R.[3])	179
20 (= 189 R.[3])	p. 564

Polumeni
1 (= 190 R.[3])	180

Portitor
1 (= 191 R.[3])	181

Progamos
1 (= 192 R.[3])	182
2 (= *Progamos* F II R.[3])	vacat

Pugil
1 (= 193–94 R.[3])	183–84

Symbolum
1 (= 195 R.[3])	185
2 (= 196 R.[3])	186

Synaristosae
1 (= 197–98 R.[3])	187–88

Synephebi
1 (= 199–209 R.[3])	189–99
2 (= 210 R.[3])	200
3 (= 211–14 R.[3])	201–4
4 (= 215 R.[3])	205

FRL	Warmington
Syracusii	
1 (= 216 R.[3])	206
2 (= 217 R.[3])	207
3 (= 218–19 R.[3])	208
Titthe	
1 (= 221–22 R.[3])	209–10
2 (= 223 R.[3])	214–15
3 (= 224–25 R.[3])	212–13
4 (= 220 R.[3])	216
5 (= 226 R.[3])	211
6 (= 227 R.[3])	217
Triumphus	
1 (= 228 R.[3])	218
2 (= 229 R.[3])	219–20
Venator	
1 (= 129–30 R.[3])	221–22
2 (= 131 R.[3])	223
Incerta	
1 (= 249 R.[3])	249
2 (= 230 R.[3])	224
3 (= 231–42 R.[3])	225–35
4 (= *Inc.* 25 R.[3])	270
5 (= 245–46 R.[3])	251–53
6 (= 252 R.[3])	254
7 (= 266 R.[3])	255
8 (= 259–64 R.[3])	238–42
9 (= 243–44 R.[3])	236–37
10 (= 258 R.[3])	261

FRL	Warmington
11 (= 250 R.[3])	267
12 (= *Inc.* XLII R.[3])	274
13 (= 251 R.[3])	260
14 (= 275 R.[3])	275
15 (= 270 R.[3])	249
16 (= 282 R.[3])	269
17 (= 269 R.[3])	250
18 (= 248 R.[3])	*ad* 255
19 (= 254–55 R.[3])	246
20 (= 268 R.[3])	248
21 (= 267 R.[3])	247
22 (= 285 R.[3])	272
23 (= 286 R.[3])	p. 564
24 (= 275 R.[3])	245
25 (= 288 R.[3])	p. 564
26 (= 276–77 R.[3])	262–63
27 (= 278 R.[3])	264
28 (= 273–74 R.[3])	265
29 (= 287 R.[3])	p. 564
30 (= 279 R.[3])	273
31 (= 284 R.[3])	271
32 (= 271–72 R.[3])	266
33 (= 265 R.[3])	257
34 (= 283 R.[3])	*ad* 269
35 (= 280 R.[3])	268
36 (= 290–91 R.[3])	258
37 (= 247 R.[3])	256
38 (= 256–57 R.[3])	243–44
39 (= *Inc.* XXXVII R.[3])	*ad* 267
40 (= 281 R.[3])	276

CONCORDANCES

FRL	Warmington
41 (= 292–93 R.[3])	277–78
42 (vacat R.[3])	279
43 (vacat R.[3])	280
44 (vacat R.[3])	vacat

CONCORDANCE 2
Warmington—*FRL* (Guardì)

Warmington	FRL
Aethrio	
1	3
2	1
3	4
4	5
5	2
Andria	
6	1
Androgynos	
7	1
8	2
Asotus	
9	1
10	2
11	3
12–13	4
14	7
15	5
16	6
Carine	
100–101	1
102–3	2
Carine vel Cratinus?	
104–5	3

CONCORDANCES

Warmington	*FRL*
Chalcia	
17	1
18	2
Chrysion	
19–21	1
Dardanus	
22	1
Davus	
23	1
Demandati	
24	1
Ephesio	
25–26	1
Epicleros	
27–28	1
29	2
Epistathmos	
30	1
Epistula	
31–32	1
33	2
Exhautuhestos	
34–35	1
Exul	
36	1
37	2

Warmington	*FRL*
Fallacia	
38–39	2
40–41	1
42	3
43–44	4
45–46	5
47	6
48	7
Gamos	
49	1
Harpazomene	
50	1
51	2
52–53	3
54–55	4
56	5
57–58	6
Hymnis	
59–60	1
61	3
62–63	2
64	4
65	6
66	7
67	8
68–70	5
p. 564	9

Warmington	*FRL*

Hypobolimaeus (Subditivos) vel Hypobolimaeus
Chaerestratus vel Hypobolimaeus Rastraria

71	7
72	1 *(Hypobolimaeus Rastraria)*
73–74	2
75	3
76	1
77	4 *(Hypobolimaeus Rastraria)*
78	4
79	5 *(Hypobolimaeus Rastraria)*
80	6 *(Hypobolimaeus Rastraria)*
81–82	5
83	3 *(Hypobolimaeus Rastraria)*
84	2 *(Hypobolimaeus Rastraria)*
85	6
86	8
87	1 *(Hypobolimaeus Chaerestratus)*

Hypobolimaeus Aeschinus

88	1

Imbrii

89	1
90	3

Warmington	*FRL*
91–92	2
93	4
94–96	5
97	6
98	7
99	8

Meretrix
106	1
107	2

Nauclerus
108	1
109	2
110	3

Nothus Nicasio
111	1
112	2
113	3

Obolastates vel Faenerator
114	1
115–16	2
117–18	6
119	7
120	3
121–23	4
124–25	5

Pausimachus
126	1
127	3

CONCORDANCES

Warmington	*FRL*
128–29	2
130–31	4
p. 564	5

Philumena

132	1
133	2

Plocium

134–35	14
136–50	1
151–55	2
156	3
157–58	4
159–60	7
161	6
162	5
163–66	8
167–69	9
170	10
171	11
172	12
173	13
174	15
175	17
176	16
177–78	18
179	19
p. 564	20

Polumeni

180	1

Warmington	*FRL*
Portitor	
181	1
Progamos	
182	1
Pugil	
183–84	1
Symbolum	
185	1
186	2
Synaristosae	
187–88	1
Synephebi	
189–99	1
200	2
201–4	3
205	4
Syracusii	
206	1
207	2
208	3
Titthe	
209–10	1
211	5
212–13	3
214–15	2
216	4
217	6

CONCORDANCES

Warmington	*FRL*
Triumphus	
218	1
219–20	2
Venator?	
221–22	1
223	2
Incerta	
224–35	2–3
236–37	9
238–42	8
243–44	38
245	24
246	19
247	21
248	20
249	15
250	17
251–53	5
254	6
255	7
ad 255	18
256	37
257	33
258	36
249	1
260	13
261	10
262–64	26–27
265	28

Warmington	*FRL*
266	32
267	11
ad 267	39
268	35
269	16
ad 269	34
270	4
271	31
272	22
273	30
274	12
p. 564	23, 25, 29

Spuria?

275	14
276	40
277–78	41
279	42
280	43

CONCORDANCE 3
Ribbeck[2–3]—*FRL* (Guardì)

Ribbeck[2–3]	*FRL*
Aethrio	
1	1
2	2
3	3
4	4
5	5
Andrea	
6	1
Androgynos	
7	1
8	2
Asotus	
9–10	1
11–12	4
13	3
14	2
15	6
16	7
17	5
Carine	
104–5	1
106–7	2
Carine vel Cratinus	
108–9	3

Ribbeck[2-3]	*FRL*
Chalcia	
18–19	1
20–21	2
Chrysion	
22–24	1
Dardanus	
25	1
Davus	
26	1
Demandati	
27	1
Ephesio	
28–29	1
Epicleros	
30–31	1
32	2
Epistathmos	
33	1
Epistula	
34–35	1
36	2 (*Hypobolimaeus Rastraria*)
37	2
Exhautuhestos	
38–39	1

CONCORDANCES

Ribbeck[2–3]	*FRL*
Exul	
40	1
41	2
Fallacia	
42–43	1
44–45	2
46	3
47–48	4
49	7
50	6
51–52	5
Gamos	
53	1
Harpazomene	
54–55	1
56	2
57–58	3
59–60	4
61	5
62–63	6
Hymnis	
64–65	1
66–67	2
68–69	5
70	4
71	3
72	6
73	7

Ribbeck[2-3]	FRL
74	8
74[1]	9

Hypobolimaeus

75	1
76	2
77	3
78	4
79–80	5
81	6
82	7
84	8

Hypobolimaeus Aeschinus

92	1

Hypobolimaeus Chaerestratus

85	1

Hypobolimaeus Rastraria

86	1
87	2
88	3
89	4
90	5
91	6

Imbrii

93	1
94–95	2
96–97	5
98	6
99	3

CONCORDANCES

Ribbeck[2-3]	FRL
100	4
101–2	7
103	8
Meretrix	
110	1
111–12	2
Nauclerus	
113	1
114	2
115	3
Nothus Nicasio	
116	1
117	2
118	3
Obolostates	
119–20	1
121	2
122–23	3
124–25	5
126–28	4
129–30	1 (*Venator*)
131	2 (*Venator*)
132–33	6
134	7
Pausimachus	
135	1
136–37	2
138	3

Ribbeck[2–3]	FRL
139–40	4
140[1]	5
Philumena	
141	1
141[1]	2
Plocium	
142–57	1
158–62	2
163	3
164–65	4
166	5
167	6
168	7
169–72	8
173–75	9
176	10
177	11
178–79	12
180	13
181–82	14
183	15
184	16
185	17
186–87	18
188	19
189	20
Polumeni	
190	1

Ribbeck[2–3]	*FRL*
Portitor	
191	1
Progamos	
192	1
F II	2
Pugil	
193–94	1
Symbolum	
195	1
196	2
Synaristosae	
197–98	1
Synephebi	
199–209	1
210	2
211–14	3
215	4
Syracusii	
216	1
217	2
218–19	3
Titthe	
220	4
221–22	1
223	2
224	3
225	5

Ribbeck[2-3]	*FRL*
226	6
227	7

Triumphus
228	1
229	2

Venator
(under *Obolostates*)

Incerta
230	2
231–42	3
243–44	9
245–46	5
247	37
248	18
249	1
250	11
251	13
252	6
253	24
254–55	19
256–57	38
258	10
259–64	8
265	33
266	7
267	21
268	20
269	17
270	15

Ribbeck[2-3]	*FRL*
271–72	32
273–74	28
275	4
276–77	26
278	27
279	30
280	35
281	40
282	16
283	34
284	31
285	22
286	23
287	29
288	25
290–91	36
292–93	41

Inc. fr. and unnumbered

XXXV	F *Inc.* 4
XXXVII	F *Inc.* 39
XLII	F *Inc.* 12
Progamos F II	2

LATIN INDEX

LATIN INDEX

SUBJECT INDEX

665

SUBJECT INDEX